THE UNVARNISHED NEW TESTAMENT

THE UNVARNISHED NEW TESTAMENT

TRANSLATED BY
ANDY GAUS

WITH AN INTRODUCTION BY
GEORGE WITTERSCHEIN

PHANES PRESS

98 97 96 95 94   5 4 3

Published by Phanes Press, PO Box 6114, Grand Rapids, MI 49516, USA.

Library of Congress Cataloging-in-Publication Data

Bible. N.T. English. Gaus. 1991.
    The unvarnished New Testament / translated from the Greek by Andy Gaus ; with an introduction by George Witterschein.
        p.   cm.
    ISBN 0-933999-98-4 (alk. paper) — ISBN 0-933999-99-2 (pbk. : alk. paper)
        I. Gaus, Andy, 1946–   II. Title.
    BS2095.G38   1991
    225.5'209—dc20   91–26924
                                                          CIP

This book is printed on alkaline paper which conforms to the permanent paper standard developed by the National Information Standards Organization.

Printed and bound in the United States

The Unvarnished New Testament is available to organizations and associations at special quantity discounts. For further information, contact the Special Sales Department at Phanes Press.

Contents

CONTENTS

Acknowledgments

This edition of the New Testament germinated when my friend Judith Gibian of Allston, Massachusetts, presented me with a Greek New Testament she had spotted in a used bookstore. As I began to read the Gospels, I was struck by the simple and conversational tone and the mostly non-ecclesiastical vocabulary—qualities I would never have guessed at from any translation I'd seen. I approached Kabir and Camille Helminski of Threshold Books with the idea of a translation of the Gospels that would reflect their actual style as well as their substance, and the result was *The Unvarnished Gospels* (Brattleboro, VT: Threshold Books, 1988). The Helminskis also put me in touch with the present publishing company, Phanes Press, and David Fideler and Cynthia Weber-Brownell of Phanes Press, when they could not put out the entire New Testament. By arrangement, this Phanes Press edition contains the text of *The Unvarnished Gospels* with slight revisions, along with a new translation of the remaining books of the New Testament. My thanks to all of the abovementioned risktakers, and my particular thanks to George Witterschein of Union City, New Jersey, who combed through this translation meticulously, fine-tuning its accuracy while he polished its good judgment.

Encountered in their original Greek, the various New Testament books are definitely less imposing, at least as literary compositions, than in the stately measures of the King James version: Mark is rough and basic, John is chatty and windy, and Paul leaves sentences dangling and mixes metaphors (as when he says in Second Corinthians, at the beginning of chapter 5, that we long to put on God's house so that we won't be naked). As for Revelation, it *is* a literary masterpiece, but one that is written in very strange and ungrammatical Greek by someone whose native language can scarcely have been Greek. Indeed, New Testament Greek itself as a language is less "literary" than the Greek of Aeschylus and Sophocles: less concise—with longer compounds and more imported words and expressions from Hebrew and Latin.

Yet what makes the New Testament less imposing ultimately makes it more impressive: the Gospel accounts, particularly the miracles, must be taken more seriously because they *don't* look like legends of Hercules or fables of Aesop, and the history of the early church as revealed in Acts and the Epistles is more impassioned and more obviously relevant to today because it clearly doesn't take place in a statuary garden.

I have tried to reproduce this simplicity and humanity in English, but all translating is like a cabinet with a sliding door: you can slide it left to reveal the right side or slide it right to reveal the left, but the whole cabinet never stands open to view. For example, if you translate Matthew 8:10 as "having heard these things, Jesus marveled," you correctly mirror the original grammar but you incorrectly convey the impression that something very strange was said. If you translate the same words as "Jesus was amazed to hear that," you correctly convey the fact that normal Greek was used, but you are now farther away from the words of the original. This translation mostly takes the second tack; re-creating the original readers' experience, rather than re-creating the original author's words, has been the aim throughout. Along the way, the most useful guideline has been that the word is less important than the sentence, and the sentence is less important than the paragraph. Probably more than most translators, I have attached much importance to word order, since Greek word order is very free and represents a conscious choice of what to emphasize. Rather than keeping the grammatical construction of a sentence and changing "only" the word order, I have often changed the grammatical construction but kept the principal sentence elements in the original order. This tactic often makes it possible to recover a sentence's force as well as its meaning, and often allows the argument of a whole paragraph to flow more smoothly along its original course.

The result, I hope, is readable, but this is not a popularization or simplified version. It doesn't have to be. The Gospels, certainly, need no simplifying—you only have to let them be simple. Acts and Revelation are compelling stories. Even the "dusty old" Epistles are surprisingly impassioned, real letters from real human beings, typically in response to real trouble. Among them, only Romans and Hebrews are really difficult (perhaps a reason for reading them last).

To further smooth the reader's path, this edition features clear type, clean single-column pages and a minimum of footnotes. Verse numbers are useful for reference, but they make all normal reading impossible, so they have been dropped. And many other fine things an edition like this could contain—maps and charts and cross-references and tables of weights and measures—have been left aside to make an edition that purposely travels light. This way, you don't have to tackle the New Testament; as I hope you will agree, you can simply pick it up and read it.

—ANDY GAUS
BOSTON, MA

Introduction

Some years ago, I developed the habit of reading the Gospel of St. John, in the Greek, at Easter time. My routine evolved into the following: on Good Friday, after hearing the sermon on the Seven Last Words in my nearby Catholic church, I would return home in the afternoon and start: *En arche en ho logos*, "In the beginning was the word. . ." I'd read about halfway through, then stop until Holy Saturday, when I'd all but finish. The ending, those last few pages that deal with the Resurrection and the final days Jesus spent on earth with his followers, I'd save for Easter Sunday itself.

What an exercise that is! How beautiful and simple, John's Greek sentences, and how affecting, in the way that only simple, heartfelt language can be! Each year, I find myself burning to share this Greek Gospel with my family and friends, indeed with everybody. I daydream that, all over the world, people will drop what they are doing, march off to the local traditional liberal arts college, and enroll in the Classics Department for *Introduction to the Greek of the New Testament*.

Which is not such a bad daydream. Anyone who did well at high school French can learn to read New Testament Greek in two semesters. But, of course, in our age of leisure, almost no one has that kind of free time. Those who are not flying off to Los Angeles for business meetings are flying off to Chicago for business meetings. Those who are not caring for children are caring for an elderly parent, or both.

Andy Gaus, our translator, has gone a long way toward making my wish come true: without having to learn another language, the reader can now get a remarkable new perspective on the New Testament books, a "feel" for them that is very like the experience I enjoy at Easter time.

What Gaus has done is to translate the Greek as if the nearly two thousand years of Christian history had not occurred. He has translated the Greek into modern American English, period. (Of course I speak relatively here. It is not possible to get those two thousand years—the

11

"Christian era"—entirely out of one's mind. But the attempt is invaluable!)

At first, this idea may not sound so astonishing. After all, hasn't every translator tried to do the same—to carry the ancient language over into a contemporary tongue? Well, yes and no.

The versions of the New Testament we are familiar with all accept, to an overwhelming extent, a set of *interpretations* which arose some time after the books were written. The important Church Councils, the work of great Christian translators (St. Jerome, Martin Luther, the King James scholars), the comments of theologians from St. Augustine to Karl Rahner, all turn on a "Christianized" view of the text.

But the text precedes that Christianized view, both in historical and religious-cultural time. The New Testament, written in clear, and for the most part straightforward, Greek, said what it said and meant what it meant *before* a Christianized interpretation of it came to be. In fact, most of the books apparently antedate "Christianity" itself. (Early Christians used "The Way," an Essene expression, as one of the names of their community. The word "Christian" first occurs in the Acts of the Apostles, and may have been a term of derision coined by outsiders.)

Modern scholarship, as many readers are aware, has shown us that the first followers of Jesus did not consider themselves to be members of a new religion called Christianity. They considered themselves to be Jews. To be sure, they felt something new and revolutionary had happened: the Anointed One, the Messiah, had come to fulfill the Jewish religion, establish the rule of the One God on earth, refute polytheistic paganism once and for all, and get rid of the Roman Empire. And to transform human life through love.

This Anointed One was called Jesus, and was a Jew, and nowhere in the Gospels did he say, "What I am doing is founding a new religion, called Christianity." That conscious, extra-Hebraic founding was to happen later, as more and more non-Jews joined the movement and eventually dominated it to the point where it broke conclusively with Judaism. (The Jewish "Jesusites" lingered for a few centuries, then died out, leaving us with traditional Jews on the one hand and gentile Christians on the other. Was that development something different from the original intent?)

As I see it, the early sequence went something like this: first, there was the life of Jesus and the beginning of the community of his followers, during which time some people probably made written notes about those events; then, after his departure, the community lived for a time with his memory, with a fresh oral tradition, and with their written notes, as their point of unity, all the while sending letters (epistles) to each other as communities developed around the Mediterranean basin; then the community used the written notes to help in the creation of the gospels, perhaps because the fresh tradition was fading and a written record could help compensate for the loss. These events occurred before, and then just at, the time when an organized church, calling itself "Christian," began to emerge.

Later on, beset with heresies, splinter groups, dissidents, Gnostics, pagan intellectual critics, Imperial Roman hostility, and the sheer weight of growing organizational momentum, Christianity took a look at itself and over time defined its tenets. Jesus is Christ; he is wholly God and wholly human; he is one of three members of the Trinity, that is, one of the three persons of God; he founded a church through his disciple Peter, and this church passes Peter's authority down through time to the bishops.

In short, Christianity took a while to come to be. Perhaps, now that I think of it, it is still coming to be.

But in any event the writings were there earlier. The words are on the pages; Andy Gaus has sought to revive them, in a modern language, for our sake; as I see it, he has tried to translate the Greek, period.

To say the least, the effect of this is refreshing. Anyone fortunate enough to read the gospels in Greek is struck by the elementary power and simplicity of the vocabularly, and by the all-too-frequent loss of these qualities in the usual translations. "Sin," for example, connotes a deep separation between human will and God's will, a kind of flaw in our makeup that results in our acting wrongly. But the Greek word *hamartia* is startlingly different: it is a term from archery, and means "missing the mark"!

The very word itself implies a much more optimistic view of human volition than "sin" does. With *hamartia* we are talking about something essentially correct in human nature, a part of us that wants to do what is good and right, but misses the bull's eye. Our goal is the right one; but somehow we miss it. (Gaus rightly prefers to render *hamartia* as "mistake" or "doing wrong.")

Modern Greeks are fortunate in that their language has not changed so much that all this is lost. *Hamartia* is still the word. So is *pneuma*, "breath," for what we have seen translated as "spirit." Greeks (and the gospel writers) talk about the Holy Breath, not the "Holy Spirit," and this is infinitely richer and more immediate. Breath is essential and intimate, one of the fundamental things of life, something we "do" constantly, an activity that contains elements of the voluntary and the involuntary, of the conscious and the unconscious, at one and the same time. "Spirit" is a remote and vaporous word in comparison. While derived from the Latin for "breath," "spirit" has lost its force and immediacy in English; "the Holy Spirit" sounds like something diaphanous wafting through lace curtains under moonlight. Breath, on the other hand, is moving in and out of me right now.

At many points in the text, our translator has chosen to leave *pneuma* as "breath." And he points out in his glossary that while he uses "breath" and "spirit" interchangeably, they are one in the Greek.

Let's examine the difference this approach can make. *The New Jerusalem Bible* is certainly one of the great modern translations. It is a renowned work of academic scholarship, and it also succeeds to a large extent in capturing "the vitality and immediacy that the Bible had for the first Christians," as the Doubleday Reader's Edition claims.

In *The New Jerusalem Bible* John the Baptist speaks as follows (John 1:32–34) after seeing Jesus coming towards him:

> John also declared, "I saw the Spirit coming down on him from heaven like a dove and resting on him. I did not know him myself, but he who sent me to baptize with water had said to me, 'The man on whom you see the Spirit come down and rest is the one who is going to baptize with the Holy Spirit.' Yes, I have seen and I am the witness that he is the Chosen One of God."

Compare this with Gaus:

> And John has testified, saying, "I saw the breath descending like a dove from the sky, how it alighted upon him. And I didn't know him, but it was the one who sent me to bathe in water who said, 'Whoever you see the breath descending and alighting upon, that's the one who will bathe them in the sacred breath.' And I have seen and certified that this is the son of God."

Not only do we have "breath" and "sacred breath" instead of "Spirit" and "Holy Spirit," we also have:

—a much clearer image, at once palpable and mysterious: we watch breath, a movement of air, descend from the sky (not from "heaven"!) to mark the son of God.

—"to bathe in water" instead of "to baptize." *Baptizein* in Greek means "to bathe in water." A perfect example of Gaus letting the Greek, rather than Christian tradition, do the talking. To "bathe them in the sacred breath" is something we can feel on our very skins; that is not true of "to baptize with the Holy Spirit."

—"the son of God" instead of "the Chosen One of God." The Greek says *huios tou theou*, "son of God." Rather than interpret, Gaus leaves things as they are.

—a bit of superb English, ". . .like a dove from the sky, how it alighted upon him." That is every bit as noble, graceful, and evocative as the Greek. (I'll talk more about Andy Gaus' literary talents later on; for now let me say he has turned out some of the best-reading translations I've ever seen.)

Clearly, *The New Jerusalem Bible* rests on Christian interpetations of the vocabulary, which is exactly what Gaus' translation seeks to avoid. For all its accomplishments and excellence, the *NJB* is a derived, interpreted document. (Christians would prefer to say "a document informed by tradition," which description is also accurate.)

To my eye the most startling difference between Gaus' version and all the others I know occurs in the famous Prologue to John's gospel. Everyone has heard it: "In the beginning was the Word, and the Word was with God, and the Word was God."

Now, one of the first things I noticed upon reading this passage in Greek was that it *doesn't say* "the Word was with God." It says: ". . .and the Word was towards God" or ". . .was going towards God."

Which is another matter altogether. If the Word was in motion towards God, instead of being literally and plainly identical with God, then St. John is introducing the notion of development (or process, or progression) within the divine nature, as the explanation for the origin of the created universe!

"Movement toward" implies a separation that is in process of being overcome. The movement of the Word towards God can then be seen as history: the history of the created universe, going back to its very beginning, is one of overcoming a separation from God, a process of reunification.

Meditating on this "movement towards," we can even use the word *erotic* to describe a yearning for unity to overcome separation. In fact, to digress just slightly, that was how I first had it described to me, by Father Raymond York, the legendary Greek teacher at the Jesuit high school I attended. As Father York related it, the truth of the correct translation of the Prologue hit him like a thunderbolt one afternoon in the mid-1960s while he was in his room at the Jesuit Residence on Grand Street in Jersey City. (It is very possible that I was only a few hundred feet away from Father York at the time, attempting to parse Virgil or solving equations.)

Father York spent the brief remainder of his life meditating on this understanding of the Prologue. He felt that Christianity had made a grave error—had "missed the mark," perhaps—in failing to understand this "movement towards." The key to it all, he said, was the attraction between man and woman, which parallels (has the same source as) the attraction between the Word and God, and between the created universe and its origin in the separation between the Word and God.

This failure to understand John's Prologue, according to Ray York, accounts for the growing division between men and women, for our terrifying divorce and family break-up statistics, among many other things. (But not to worry: the good father believed it is America's function in world history to heal this rift, and that the hour of setting things right is at hand.)

I make this point in defense of Andy Gaus' translation. Certainly, I do not claim, in these paragraphs, to have explained the Prologue to the Gospel of St. John, one of the deepest, and in the best sense of the word, most mysterious passages in religious literature. But the fullness and depth, the richness, the possibilities, of the Prologue, are terribly reduced by saying "the Word was with God" instead of the much more suggestive and more mysterious "the Word was towards God."

And until now, you had to read Greek to get this distinction.

The example also illustrates the beauty of the basic premise of Gaus' translation. All the usual versions, relying as they do on developed Christian interpetation, have translated the Greek *pros ton theon* as "with God" instead of "[going] towards God." This is despite the fact that *pros* with the accusative case (*theon*) after the verb "to be" almost always means "to go towards." (As Father York pointed out, this construction occurs scores of times in the New Testament, and typically means "to go towards.") Any high school Greek student could state as much. Why then the "with" translation? My own suspicion is that doctrinal Christianity *had* to so translate the Greek for two reasons, both of them a function of the long polemic the early church waged against Gnostics and other heretics. First, the notion of movement/separation/progress within God as the origin of the universe sounded too much like Gnostic creation myths. (There are many different ones, but an element they seem to have in common is the idea that the universe is the result of a cataclysm, division, or separation within the divine nature.) Second, if the Word was something other than God, or not quite identical with God, or was in some real sense separated from God, then several important points of doctrine were in apparent danger: the full, unmitigated divinity of Jesus Christ as the Second Person of the Trinity; and by extension the doctrine of the Trinity itself.

As is so often the case, defensiveness leads to impoverishment. It is Andy Gaus' good fortune—and the reader's—that he is not defending a body of doctrine. He is just translating as faithfully as he can, like the good German-American Midwesterner he was raised to be.

To shift from theology to literature: as I mentioned earlier, Andy Gaus is one of the finest English translators I have ever run across. I have long been a lover of Rilke's poetry; I love to read it in the German, and I love to pore over the many translations of his lyrics that have appeared in English. Some of my favorite poets (Robert Lowell, John Hall Wheelock) have tried their hand at Rilke, but the best results I know of are Andy Gaus'. (See *Requiem for a Woman and Selected Lyric Poems of Rainer Maria Rilke*, translated by Andy Gaus; published by Threshold Books). He even manages to preserve Rilke's rhythms, line lengths, and rhyme schemes—the devil!

Andy Gaus succeeds at translating because he is hard-working, passionate, and scrupulous; and because he knows, somehow, the trick of making the English *sound* and *feel* like the original. The latter gift I cannot explain; but I accept its existence with gratitude.

And I believe the readers of this New Testament will also be grateful to the translator for his effort. And wonder, with me: Why didn't somebody do it sooner?

—GEORGE WITTERSCHEIN

The Gospels

The Good Word According to
Matthew

1

The book of the birth of Jesus the Anointed, son of David, son of Abraham: Abraham had Isaac, Isaac had Jacob, Jacob had Juda and his brothers, Juda had Phares and Zara by Thamar, Phares had Esram, Esram had Aram, Aram had Aminadab, Aminadab had Naasson, Naasson had Salmon, Salmon had Boaz by Rachab, Boaz had Jobed by Ruth, Jobed had Jesse, and Jesse had David the king.

David had Solomon by Urius's wife, Solomon had Roboam, Roboam had Abia, Abia had Asaph, Asaph had Josaphat, Josaphat had Joram, Joram had Oziah, Oziah had Joatham, Joatham had Achaz, Achaz had Hezekiah, Hezekiah had Manasses, Manasses had Amos, Amos had Josiah, and Josiah had Jechoniah and his brothers at the time of the Babylonian migration.

After the Babylonian migration, Jechoniah had Salathiel, Salathiel had Zorobabel, Zorobabel had Abiud, Abiud had Eliachim, Eliachim had Azor, Azor had Zadok, Zadok had Achim, Achim had Eliud, Eliud had Eleazar, Eleazar had Matthan, Matthan had Jacob, and Jacob had Joseph, the husband of Mary, from whom was born Jesus, known as the Anointed One, or "Christ." So the generations from Abraham to David made fourteen generations, and from David to the Babylonian migration fourteen generations, and from the Babylonian migration to Christ fourteen generations.

The birth of Jesus the Anointed was like this: When Mary his mother was engaged to Joseph, before they got together, she was found to be carrying a child in her belly by means of holy spirit. Joseph, her husband, being decent and not wishing to make an example of her, decided to break off with her discreetly. He had that on his mind when one night a messenger of the Lord appeared in a dream and said to him: "Joseph son of David, don't be afraid to take Mary for your wife. What has been conceived in her is of holy spirit. She will have a son, and you will call his name Jesus [which means "The Lord is salvation"], because he is the one who will save the people from their own errors."

All this happened to fulfill what was said by the Lord, speaking through the prophet: "Look! the virgin shall carry a child and bear a son, and they will call his name Emmanuel" (which is translated "God-with-us"). Getting up from sleep, Joseph did as the messenger of the Lord commanded and took her for his wife, but he had no relations with her till she bore a son, and he called his name Jesus.

2

When Jesus was born in Bethlehem, Judea, in the days of King Herod [the Great], one day wise men from the East showed up in Jerusalem, saying, "Where is the newborn king of the Jews? We saw his star in the East and came to adore him."

Hearing that, King Herod was disturbed and all of Jerusalem with him. And assembling all the high priests and canon-lawyers of the people he inquired of them, "Where has the Anointed One been born?"

They said to him, "In Bethlehem, Judea, because that's how it is written by the prophet:

And you, Bethlehem, land of Juda,
Are by no means the least of Juda's leaders,
Since from you shall come the leader
Who herds my people Israel."

Then Herod, secretly calling the wise men, ascertained from them the time of the appearing star, and sent them to Bethlehem, saying, "When you get there find out in detail about the child, and when you find him, report to me, so that I can go and adore him too." They, having heard the king, went on their way, and look! the star they'd seen in the East was guiding them, till it came and stood over where the child was. Seeing the star, they were delighted with a great delight indeed. And going into the house they saw the child with Mary his mother; and they fell down and adored him, and they opened up their treasure-chests and offered gifts to him: gold and incense and Arabian ointment. And being warned in a dream not to return to Herod, they went back to their country by another road.

When they had gone back, one night a messenger of the Lord appears* in a dream to Joseph and says, "Get up, take the child and his mother with you and flee to Egypt, and stay there until I tell you, because Herod is going to look for the child to kill him." So he got up and took the child and his mother by night and went on into Egypt and was there until Herod's end, fulfilling what was said by the Lord speaking through His prophet: "Out of Egypt I called my son." Then Herod, seeing he had been tricked by the wise men, was utterly enraged, and he sent out and disposed of all the children in Bethlehem and its environs two years old or younger, according to the time he had ascertained from the wise men. Then was fulfilled what had been said by Jeremiah the prophet:

A voice was heard in Rama,
Weeping and wailing aplenty:
Rachel crying for her children,
And she would not be consoled,
Because she has none.

When Herod died, a messenger of the Lord appears in a dream to Joseph in Egypt saying, "Get up and take the child and his mother with you and proceed to Israel, for those who wanted the life of the child are dead." So he got up and took the child and his mother and went on into Israel.

But when he heard that Archelaus was king of Judea instead of his father Herod [the Great]** he was afraid to go there; and being advised by a dream he proceeded to the regions of Galilee. And he went and settled in a town called Nazareth, to fulfill what was said by the prophets: "He shall be called a Nazarene."

---

* Yes, "appears" and "says" in the middle of an otherwise past-tense narrative. This mixing of present and past tenses is not illegal, as an occasional device, in either Classical Greek or the Greek of the New Testament period; but the constant use that Matthew, Mark, and John make of it, sometimes changing tenses in mid-sentence, would have to be rough in any language—and the best proof is that Luke is much more careful, keeping his past tenses past with few exceptions.

** Herod the Great was king of all Israel—subject to the Roman emperor, of course. He died in 4 B.C., and his kingdom was split up into four governorships. Herod's son Archelaus is now governor of Judea, his other son Herod Antipas is governor of Galilee.

3

In those days John the Baptist appeared, preaching in the desert of Judea and saying, "Repent, for the kingdom of the skies is approaching." He is the one described by Isaiah the prophet:

> *The voice of a crier in the desert:*
> *"Prepare the road of the Lord,*
> *Straighten his paths."*

This same John had a robe of camel hair and a leather belt around his waist, and his food was locusts and wild honey. At that time all Jerusalem and all Judea and all the surrounding country of the Jordan was going out to see him, and they were being bathed by him in the Jordan River and admitting their mistakes.

Seeing many of the Pharisees and Sadducees coming for his bathing he said to them: "Children of the snake, who tipped you off to run from the coming fury? Bear the fruit proper to a change of heart and do not think you can say amongst yourselves, 'We have Abraham for our father!' I tell you, God can raise up children for Abraham out of these stones here. Already the ax is poised at the root of the trees. And so any tree not bearing good fruit gets cut down and thrown into the fire.

"Now I bathe you in water to change hearts, but the one coming after me is stronger than me: I'm not big enough to carry his shoes. He will bathe you in holy breath and fire. Winnowing-fan in hand, he will clean up his threshing floor, and collect the grain to be put in the silo and the husks to be burned in unquenchable fire."

Then Jesus showed up from Galilee on the banks of the Jordan where John was, to be bathed by him. But John stopped him: "I have need of being bathed by you, and you come to me?"

Jesus answered and said to him, "Go ahead: it's right that we should fulfill all the law." So John let him do it.

After being bathed, Jesus came straight out of the water. And all of a sudden the skies opened and he saw the breath of God descending like a dove and coming toward him. And just then there was a voice from the skies saying, "This is my son, my beloved son in whom I am delighted."

4

Then Jesus was led into the desert by the spirit, to be tested by the devil. And after fasting forty days and forty nights, he was utterly starving. And drawing near, the Examiner said, "If you're the son of God, tell these rocks to turn into bread."

He answered: "It is written: 'Humanity shall not just live on bread, but on every word that comes from the mouth of God.' "

Then the devil takes him along into the holy city and sets him atop one wing of the temple and says to him, "If you're the son of God, throw yourself down, for it is written: 'His messengers have been instructed about you, and they will take you in their hands, so you don't stub your foot against a stone.' "

Jesus said to him, "It also says, 'You are not to experiment with the Lord your God.' "

Next the devil takes him along to a mountain way up high and shows him all the kingdoms of the world and their glory, and says to him, "I'll give these all to you if you fall down and adore me."

Then Jesus said to him, "Get out of here, Satan! It says, 'The Lord your God is whom you shall adore, and you shall serve only Him'!"

Then the devil left him alone, and just then holy messengers came and waited on him.

But when he heard that John had been handed over to the authorities, he moved on into Galilee. And leaving Nazareth, he went and settled in Capharnaum by the sea, in the regions of Zabulon and Nephthali, to fulfill what was said by the prophet Isaiah:

> *Earth of Zabulon and earth of Nephthali,*
> *On the way to the sea, beyond the Jordan,*
> *Galilee of the nationalities,*
> *The people lying in darkness saw a great light,*
> *And to those in that land lying in death's shadow,*
> *A light rose in the sky.*

After that Jesus began to proclaim and say, "Repent, for the kingdom of the skies is approaching!"

Walking by the sea of Galilee, he saw two brothers, Simon, known as Simon Rock ["Peter"], and Andrew his brother, casting their net into the sea, since they were fishermen. And he said to them, "Come along after me and I'll make you fishers of humanity." And they put their nets right down and followed him. And going on a ways he saw two more brothers, James, Zebedee's son, and John his brother, in the boat with their father Zebedee fixing their nets; and he called to them. And right away they left the boat and their father behind and followed him.

And he started traveling round all of Galilee teaching in their synagogues and proclaiming the good word of the kingdom and curing every disease and every infirmity among the people.

And word of him spread throughout all Syria. And they brought him everyone in bad health with all kinds of diseases, and people living with torments, and the possessed, and the insane, and the paralyzed; and he cured them. And giant crowds followed him from Galilee, the Decapolis, Jerusalem, Judea, and across the Jordan.

5

Seeing the crowds, he went up the mountain, and as he sat there his students came to him, and he opened his mouth and taught them, saying:

"The poor in spirit are in luck: the kingdom of the skies is theirs.

"The mourners are in luck: they will be consoled.

"The gentle are in luck: they will inherit the earth.

"Those hungering and thirsting for justice are in luck: they will get their fill.

"The merciful are in luck: they will be treated mercifully.

"The clean-hearted are in luck: they will see God.

"The peacemakers are in luck: they will be called God's sons and daughters.

"Those persecuted for the sake of justice are in luck: the kingdom of the skies is theirs.

"You are in luck—when they blame you and persecute you and tell all kinds of filthy lies about you, because of me. Be happy and delighted, because you will be well paid in the skies. After all, they persecuted the prophets before us the same way.

"You are the salt of the earth, but if the salt goes tasteless, what do you salt it with? It's good for nothing any more but to be thrown out and stepped on by everybody.

"You are the light of the world. A city can't be hidden lying on a mountaintop. Nor do people light a candle and cover it with a big basket; they put it up on a tall candlestick where it can shine for everyone in the house. That's how your light must shine in front of the world, so that people see your good deeds and give credit to your Father in the skies.

"Don't think I came to dissolve the law or the prophets: I didn't come to dissolve them, I came to fulfill them. I assure you, till the sky and the earth go away, not one letter or punctuation mark of the law will ever go away until everything has come to pass. So anyone who dissolves even one of the smallest commands and teaches others the same way, will be known as the lowest in the kingdom of the skies; whereas anyone who keeps the commands and teaches them too, will be known as someone great in the kingdom of the skies.

"I'm telling you, if you don't brim over with justice more than the canon-lawyers and Pharisees, you will not get into the kingdom of the skies.

"You've heard how your ancestors were told: 'You are not to murder. Whoever murders is liable to be brought to justice.' But I say everyone who gets angry at his brother will be subject to justice, and if he calls his brother 'swine,' it will go before the high court, and if he calls him 'idiot,' he's liable to be thrown into the fire of Gehenna.

"So if you're just about to put your offering upon the temple altar and then you remember that your brother has something against you, leave your gift on the floor and get out of there: first make up with your brother, and then go make your offering. Get friendly with your adversary fast, while you're still on the road with him, so your adversary doesn't hand you over to the judge, and the judge to the jailer, and you get thrown in jail; I assure you, you won't get out of there till you've paid off every last penny.

"You've heard how it was said, 'You are not to commit adultery.' But I say any man who looks at a woman and really wants her has already slept with her in his heart. If it's your right eye that gets in your way, pull it out and throw it off: you're better off losing one of your members than having your whole body thrown into the Gehenna fire. And if it's your right hand that gets in your way, cut it off and throw it aside: you're better off losing one of your members than if your whole body goes into the Gehenna fire.

"It was said, 'Whoever separates from his wife must present her with a divorce decree.' But I say anyone who divorces his wife for any reason but whoring is setting her up for adultery, and anyone who marries a divorced woman is living in adultery.

"You've also heard how your ancestors were told, 'You are not to break oaths, you give your oaths to the Lord.' But I say don't swear at all: don't swear by heaven, it's the throne of God. Don't swear by the earth, it's the footrest under His feet. Don't swear by Jerusalem, it's the city of the great King. Don't swear by your own head, you can't make a single hair white or black. Let your way of talking be 'yes' and 'no'; anything more than that comes from the Evil One.

"You've heard it said, 'An eye for an eye and a tooth for a tooth.' But I say don't stand up to the villain: if somebody raps you on the right side of your jaw, give him the other side, and if somebody sues you for your shirt, give him your coat too. And if somebody drags you a mile out of your way, go two miles with him. Give to those who ask you, and don't turn the person away who wants to borrow from you.

"You've heard it said, 'You are to love those close to you and hate your enemies.' But I say love your enemies and pray for your persecutors if you want to be children of your Father in the skies, because He shines his sun on villains and saints and rains on the innocent and the guilty.

"If you love those who love you, what pay do you get? Don't the tax-collectors do that much? And if you only say hello to your brothers, what are you doing special? Don't pagans do that much? So be perfect the way your heavenly Father is perfect.

6

"Be careful not to put your virtue in front of people to be noted by them. If you do, you will get no pay from your Father in the skies. So when you contribute to charity, don't have a trumpet-player go before you, like the fakes do in temples and down alleyways, so people will glorify them; believe me, they have already been paid their wages. But when *you* give to charity, your left hand shouldn't know what your right hand is doing, so that your charity is on the sly; and your Father, watching on the sly, will pay you back.

"And when you pray, don't be like the fakes who love to pray standing in the temples and on streetcorners so as to show off for everybody. Believe me, they have already been paid their wages. When *you* pray, duck into the store-room and lock the door and pray to your Father on the sly. And your Father, watching on the sly, will pay you back.

"When you pray, don't babble on like pagans who think they can make themselves heard with a great glut of words. Don't act like them, because your Father knows what you need before you ask Him.

"So pray like this:

> Our Father in the skies,
> Let Your name be sanctified.
> Let Your kingdom come,
> May Your will be seen
> On the earth, just as in the sky.
> Give us day by day the next day's bread,
> And forgive our debts
> The same as we forgave the debts that others owed us.
> And do not put us to the test,
> But snatch us from the Evil One's clutches, let it be so.

"If you forgive people for stepping out of line, your heavenly Father will forgive you too. But if you don't forgive other people, your Father also won't forgive you for stepping out of line.

"When you fast, don't be like the grim-looking fakes who disguise their faces so they'll look to people like they're fasting. Believe me, they have already been paid their wages. When you fast, put on a fragrance and wash your face, so you *don't* look to people like you're fasting, except to your Father on the sly. And your Father, watching on the sly, will pay you back.

"Don't save up your treasures on the earth, where moths and rust eat away at them and thieves tunnel in and steal them. Save up your treasures in the sky, where no moth and no rust eats away and thieves don't tunnel in and steal. Because where your treasure is, your heart will be too.

"The lamp of the body is the eye. So if your eye is in one piece, your whole body is lighted; whereas if your eye is bad, your whole body is in darkness. So if the light inside you is dark . . . what a lot of darkness!

"No one can serve two masters: either he'll hate one and love the other, or he'll put up with the one and despise the other. You can't serve God *and* the Almighty Dollar.*

"That's why I tell you, don't trouble your heart about what you will eat and drink or clothe your body with. Isn't the soul more important than food, and the body more important than clothing? Look at the birds in the sky: they don't plant, don't harvest, and don't fill silos, and your heavenly Father still feeds them. Don't you make more difference to Him than they do? Can any of you, by being vastly concerned, add a foot to your height? And why do you worry about clothing? Study how the lilies of the field grow: they don't work, and they don't spin cloth. But I am telling you that not even Solomon in all his glory was ever dressed like one of them. If that's how God clothes the wild grass of the field, there today and thrown into the furnace tomorrow, won't He do much more for you, unbelievers?

"So don't worry, saying, 'What will we drink? What will we wear?' The pagans ask for all these things, but your heavenly Father knows that you need all these things. Ask first for the kingdom of God and His justice, and these other things will be delivered to you. So don't worry about tomorrow, because tomorrow can worry about itself. Each day's evil is enough for the day.

7

"Don't judge, so that you won't be judged; you will be sentenced to the same sentence that you sentence others, and by whatever standard you measure you will be measured. Why do you look at the splinter in your brother's eye but don't notice the log in your own eye? And how can you say to your brother, 'Let me get that splinter out of your eye,' with that log there in your own eye? You fake, first get the log out of your own eye, and then you can see about getting the splinter out of your brother's eye!

"Don't give the holy of holies to dogs, and don't throw your pearls at the feet of pigs, or else they'll trample them with their hooves and then swing round and knock you down.

"Ask and you will receive, look and you will find, knock and you will

---

* "Mammon"—the Syrian god of riches, a word the Jews used in describing the paganistic worship of money. The use Jesus makes of the word here crystallizes a recurrent theme of his teaching: not money, but the deification of money, turns a person away from God.

be admitted. For the asker always gets, the seeker finds, and whoever knocks is admitted. Is there any person among you who, being asked by his son for bread, would give him a stone, or being asked for a fish, would give him a snake? If you, villains that you are, know enough to give good things to your children, how much more will your Father in the skies give good things to those asking Him!

"So everything you want people to do for you, you do the same for them, because that's the law and the prophets.

"Go in the narrow door; because the door is wide and the road is broad leading off to destruction, and many people are going that way. Whereas how narrow the door and how constricted the road leading off to Life, and how few people find it!

"Be careful of pseudoprophets who come to you in the clothing of lambs and are rapacious wolves inside. You'll know them by the fruit they bear: you don't get grapes from a thorn-tree or figs from a thistle-bush, do you? Likewise, every good tree bears good fruit, while the rotten tree bears bad fruit. A good tree can't bear bad fruit, and a rotten tree can't bear good fruit either. Any tree not bearing good fruit gets cut down and thrown into the fire. So definitely you'll know them by the fruit they bear.

"Not everyone saying 'Lord, Lord' to me will get into the kingdom of the skies, but only those who do the will of my Father in the skies. Many will say to me on that day, 'Lord, Lord, didn't we prophesy in your name and exorcise demons in your name and work many wonders in your name?'

"And I will say to them, 'I must confess I never met you; go away from me, workers of lawlessness.'

"So anyone who hears these words from me and does them, will become like a sensible man who built his house on bedrock, and the rain came down and the floods came and the winds hurled themselves at the house, and it didn't fall because it was grounded on the rock. And anyone who hears these words from me and doesn't do them, will become like a stupid man who built his house on sand, and the rain came down and the floods came and the winds beat at the house, and it fell, and its downfall was tremendous."

And it happened that when Jesus finished these words, the crowds were dumbfounded at his teaching, because he was teaching them as if on his own authority, not like their canon-lawyers.

8

Coming down from the mountain he was followed by giant crowds. And suddenly a leper came forward and bowed before him, saying, "Lord, if you want to, you can heal me."

And he reached out and touched him saying, "I do want to; be healed." And immediately his leprosy was washed away. And Jesus said to him, "Careful, don't talk to anyone, just go show yourself to the priest and bring the offering specified by Moses, as a testimony for them."

As he was going into Capharnaum, a captain, the leader of a hundred soldiers, came up to him, pleading with him and saying, "Lord, my child back home has been left paralyzed, suffering horribly."

And he said to him, "I'll come cure him."

And the captain answered, "Lord, I'm not important enough for you to come under my roof; just say it in words, and my child will be cured. After all, I'm a man under authority too, with soldiers under me, and if I tell one of them Go, he goes, and if I tell another Come, he comes, and if I tell my slave Do this, he does it."

Jesus was amazed to hear that and said to the onlookers, "Believe me, I never found that kind of trust in anyone in Israel. I tell you, many will come in from east and west and sit down to eat with Abraham, Isaac and Jacob in the kingdom of the skies, while the heirs of the kingdom will be thrown out into the darkness beyond, where the wailing and gnashing of teeth will be." And Jesus said to the captain, "Go home, and let it be for you as you have trusted." And the child was cured at that hour.

And going into Peter's home Jesus saw Peter's mother-in-law struck down with a fever; and he touched her hand, and the fever left her, and she got up and was at his service.

As it got late, they brought him many people with demons; and he threw the spirits out with his words and cured everyone in bad health, fulfilling what was said by Isaiah the prophet:

> *He himself took on our weaknesses*
> *And bore our diseases.*

Seeing the crowd around him Jesus gave orders to shove off for the other shore. And a clerk came up and said to him: "Master, I'll follow you wherever you go."

And Jesus said to him, "Foxes have holes, and the birds of the sky have places to camp, but the son of humanity doesn't have anywhere to lay his head."

Another of his students said to him, "Lord, let me go bury my father first."

Jesus said to him, "Follow me and let the dead bury their own dead."

And as he got on board the boat, his students followed him. Next thing you know there was such a great shaking in the sea that the boat was hidden under the waves—but he was sleeping. And they went over and roused him, saying "Lord! Help! We'll be killed!"

And he says to them, "What cowards you are, unbelievers." Then he got up and yelled at the winds and the sea, and there was a great calm.

The people were amazed and said, "Where did this guy come from who can make the winds and the sea listen to him?"

And when he got across to the country of the Gadarenes, he was met by two possessed men coming from the graveyard, extremely dangerous men, so much so that no one could go by that way. And just then they started shouting, "What have we done to you, son of God? Did you come to start torturing us ahead of time?"

Now off a ways from them there was a big herd of pigs grazing. So the demons started pleading with him, saying, "If you throw us out, send us into the herd of pigs."

And he told them, "Go ahead." And they came out and went into the pigs. And all of a sudden the whole herd of them rushed off the cliff into the sea and were killed in the waves. As for the herders, they ran away, and when they got into town they reported all about the possessed men. And look, the whole town came out to meet Jesus, and when they saw him they begged him to go away from their neighborhood.

9

And he got on the boat and went back across and returned to his own town. And next thing they were bringing him a paralyzed man lying on a stretcher, and Jesus, seeing their faith, said to the paralytic, "Take heart, son, you are forgiven your errors."

And at that, some of the canon-lawyers said to each other, "That's blasphemy!"

And Jesus, seeing their mood, said, "Why are you brooding evil in your hearts? Which is easier to say: 'You're forgiven your errors,' or 'Get up and walk away'? Well then, so you'll know that the son of humanity has authority to forgive errors on earth—" at that point he said to the paralytic, "get up and take your stretcher and go home." And he got up and went back to his house. Seeing that, the crowds were terrified and praised God for giving that kind of power to mortal beings.

And passing through there, Jesus saw a person sitting at the toll-station, name of Matthew, and says to him, "Follow me." And he stood up and followed him.

And it happened that as he was seated at table in his house this crowd of tax-collectors and godless people came in and sat down with Jesus and his students. And the Pharisees, seeing that, said to his students, "Why does your teacher eat with tax-collectors and godless people?"

He heard that and said, "It's not the healthy who need a doctor, but the sick. Go find out what 'I want mercy and not sacrifice' means. I came here, not to call the saints, but to call the godless people."

Then John's students came up to him and said, "Why is it that we and the Pharisees fast a lot, while your students don't fast?"

And Jesus said to them, "The wedding party can't be in mourning while the groom is with them, can they? There will come days when the groom will be taken away from them, and then they can fast. No one patches an old cloak with a scrap of brand-new cloth. It takes away the cloak's completeness, and a worse split results. Nor do they put new wine in old wineskins, because if they do, the skins break and the wine pours out and the skins are ruined; instead, they put new wine in new skins, and both are preserved."

As he was saying these things to them, next a high official came and bowed before him, saying, "My daughter has just died, but go and put your hand on her, and she'll live." And Jesus got up and followed him, and so did his students.

And then this woman who had been bleeding excessively for twelve years came up from behind and touched the bottom of his cloak, saying to herself, "If I just touch his cloak, I'll be saved."

Jesus, turning and seeing her, said, "Courage, daughter, your trust has saved you." And the woman was all right from that time on.

And Jesus, going into the official's house and seeing the flute-players and the noisy crowd, said, "Be on your way: the girl didn't die, she's sleeping." And they were laughing at him. But when the crowd was thrown out he went in and took her hand, and the girl woke up. And that story went out across the country.

And as he passed through there Jesus was followed by two blind men shouting, "Have mercy on us, son of David."

When he got back to his house the blind men came up to him and Jesus says to them, "You believe I can do this?"

"Yes, Lord," they say to him.

Then he touched their eyes, saying, "Let it be for you according to your trust." And their eyes were opened. And Jesus thundered at them, saying, "Make sure no one finds out!" But they went and publicized him throughout the country.

Then as they were going out, now look, they brought him a mute person with a demon. And with the demon thrown out, the mute man talked, and the crowds were amazed saying, "Nothing like this was ever seen in Israel!"

But the Pharisees said, "He throws out demons by the power of the demon king."

And Jesus made the rounds of all the towns and villages, teaching in their synagogues and proclaiming the good word of the kingdom and curing every disease and every infirmity.

Seeing the crowds, he felt sorry for them, because they were lying scattered and torn like sheep without a shepherd. Then he says to his students, "An ample harvest, and few workers. So ask the harvestmaster to send workers out into his fields."

10

Then, calling his twelve students together, he gave them authority over unclean spirits, to throw them out and cure every disease and every infirmity.

The twelve apostles' names are as follows: first Simon, the one known as Simon Peter, and his brother Andrew; James son of Zebedee and his brother John; Philip; Bartholomew; Thomas; Matthew the tax-collector; James son of Alpheus; Thaddeus; Simon of Canaan; and Judas Iscariot, his betrayer.

Jesus sent out these twelve after first giving them orders saying, "Don't go off on the road to the pagans and don't go to the Samaritan city. Instead go after the lost sheep of the Israel family. Go and announce that the kingdom of the skies is approaching. Cure the sick, raise the dead, wash lepers, throw out demons. Accept free gifts, and give for free. Don't have gold, silver, or brass in your belts. Don't take a knapsack on the road, or a second tunic, or shoes, or a cane. For the worker is worth his feed. When you get to a city or town, find out who there is appropriate, and stay there until you move on. Salute the house as you go into it, and if it's worthy, your peace will come over it; if it's not worthy, your peace will come back to you. And whoever doesn't receive you and doesn't listen to your words, when you get out of that house or that city shake its dust off your feet. I assure you, Sodom and Gomorrah will be in better shape on Judgment Day than that town.

"Here I am sending you out like sheep amid wolves, so be smart as snakes and innocent as doves.

"Be careful of the world, because they'll hand you over to the judges and flog you in their synagogues. You'll be haled before governors and kings because of me, as a testimony to them and the pagans. But when they hand you over, don't worry how you'll talk or what you'll say: you will be given something to say at that time, because it isn't you talking, it's the breath of the Father talking through you.

"Brothers will hand each other over to be executed, and fathers their children; children will rise up against their parents and kill them. And you will be hated by everybody because of my name. Whoever endures to the end, that's who will be saved.

"If they hound you in one city, escape to the next: believe me, you won't exhaust the cities in Israel before the son of humanity comes.

"No student is better than his teacher and no slave better than his master. It's enough for the student to become like his teacher and the slave like his master. If they called the head of the house Beelzebub, what will they call the servants there?

"So don't be afraid of them; because there's nothing covered that won't be opened up and nothing hidden that won't be found out. What I tell you in the darkness, say in the light; what I whisper in your ear, announce on the rooftops.

"And don't be afraid of those who kill the body but can't kill the soul. Instead, fear Him who can annihilate both soul and body in Gehenna-fire. Aren't sparrows sold two for a quarter? Not one of them falls on the ground without your Father, and every hair on your head is accounted for. So don't be afraid: you matter more than a heap of sparrows.

"So everybody who speaks up for me in front of the world, I'll speak up for them in front of my Father in the skies; and everybody who says they don't know me in front of the world, I'll say I don't know them in front of my Father in the skies.

"Don't think I came to cast peace across the land. I didn't come to cast peace, I came to wield a sword, because I came to divide a man against his father and a daughter against her mother and a bride against her mother-in-law, and to make a man's servants his enemies.

"Whoever prefers father or mother over me is not worthy of me; and whoever prefers son or daughter over me is not worthy of me; and whoever does not take his cross and follow after me is not worthy of me. Whoever found his life will lose it, and the one who lost his life because of me will find it.

"Whoever receives you receives me, and whoever receives me, receives my Sender. Whoever receives a prophet by the name of a prophet will receive a prophet's wages; whoever receives a just man by the name of a just man will receive a just man's wages. And whoever gives one of these lowly people even just a glass of cold water by their name as one of my students, I promise you, he will not forfeit his pay."

11

And as it happened, when Jesus finished giving orders to his twelve students, he moved on from there to teach and spread the word in their towns.

Now John, hearing in jail of the works of the Anointed, sent word to him through his students, saying to him, "Are you the one who's coming, or shall we expect another one?"

And Jesus said in answer to them: "Go back and report to John what you hear and see: blind people see and lame people walk, lepers are washed clean and deaf people hear; corpses rise; and the poor are given the good news. And lucky are those who have no trouble accepting me."

As they were leaving, Jesus started telling the crowds about John: "What did you go out in the desert to see? A reed shaken by the wind? Come on, what did you go out to see? A person dressed in nice soft clothes? Look, the people wearing the soft clothes are in the houses of kings. Come on, what did you go out to see? A prophet? Yes, I tell you, a prophet and more: He's the one about whom it is written:

Look, I'm sending my messenger before your face,
To prepare your road ahead of you.

"I assure you, among all those born of women no one has arisen greater than John the Baptist—but the lowest person in the kingdom of the skies is greater than him. Ever since the days of John the Baptist, right up to now, the kingdom of the skies has been suffering violence and violent people are laying hands on it. For the prophets and the law prophesied as far as John, and if you wish to receive him, he is the Elijah to come. Those with ears to hear, hear!

"What can I compare this generation to? They're like children sitting around the marketplace hollering at the others:

We-played-the-flute-and-you-wouldn't-dance,
We-beat-our-breasts-and-you-wouldn't-mourn!

"After all, John came along not eating or drinking, and they say, 'He's possessed.' The son of humanity came along eating and drinking, and they say, 'Look at this wine-drinking gourmand who's friendly with tax-collectors and godless people.' But wisdom always was vindicated by its works."

Then he began to complain that in the towns where his greatest wonders were worked, they didn't come round. "The worse for you, Chorazin! The worse for you, Bethesda! Because if the wonders had occurred in Tyre and Sidon that have occurred in you, they would long since have come round in sackcloth and ashes. Except I'm telling you, Tyre and Sidon will be better off on Judgment Day than you! And you, Capharnaum, won't *you* be exalted to the heavens? You'll sink into hell! Because if the wonders had occurred in Sodom that have occurred in you, it would still be there today. But I'm telling you, the Land of Sodom will be better off on Judgment Day than you."

At that point Jesus reacted by saying: "I praise you, Father, lord of the sky and the earth, that You hid these things from scholars and wits and opened them up to babies—yes, Father, because that's how Your divine pleasure could be manifested before You.

"Everything was handed to me by my Father, and no one knows the son but the Father, and no one knows the Father but the son and those he decides to reveal himself to.

"Come here to me, all you drudges and overburdened ones, and I will give you a rest. Put my yoke on and learn from me: I am gentle and humble of heart, and you will find rest for your souls, because my yoke is kindly and my load is light."

12

During that time Jesus once traveled through the grain fields on the Sabbath. And his students got hungry and started picking ears of grain and eating them. The Pharisees, seeing that, said to him, "Look, your students are doing what isn't allowed on the Sabbath."

And he said to them, "Haven't you ever read what David did when he and those with him began to starve, how he went into the house of God and they ate the sacramental loaves which he himself wasn't allowed to eat, nor those with him, but only the priests? Or didn't you ever read in the law how on the Sabbath the priests in the temple break the rules of the Sabbath but aren't guilty? And I'm telling you, there's something greater than the temple here. If you'd found out what 'I want mercy and not sacrifice' means, you wouldn't have charged those who aren't guilty. After all, the son of humanity is superior to the Sabbath."

And moving on from there he went into their synagogue, and there was this fellow with a withered hand. And they questioned him, saying, "Is it all right to cure people on the Sabbath?" so that they would be able to charge him.

And he said to them, "Which of you, if you had one sheep and it fell into a ditch, would not take hold and haul it out again because it was the Sabbath? So how much more important is a person than a sheep? Enough that it's all right to do good on the Sabbath." Then he says to the fellow, "Reach out your hand." And he reached it out, and it was restored to health like the other one.

But the Pharisees went out and had a meeting about him and how to get rid of him.

Jesus, learning of that, withdrew from those parts, and giant crowds followed him, and he cured all of them and strictly warned them not to make him famous, fulfilling what was spoken by Isaiah the prophet:

Here is the child of mine, whom I chose,
My beloved child, in whom my soul has delighted.

I will put my breath upon him,
And he will announce a verdict to the nations.
He will not squabble, he will not shout,
Nor will they hear his voice in the streets.
He will not snap a reed that's bruised
Nor douse a wick that's smoking,
Till he pronounces the decision for victory
And nations set their hopes on his name.

Then a man with a demon was brought to him, blind and mute, and he cured him, so the mute man could talk and see. And the crowds were all thunderstruck and said, "Is this the son of David?"

But the Pharisees heard, and said, "This guy only throws out demons through the power of Beelzebub, the demon king."

Sensing their feelings, he said to them: "Any country split in opposition to itself gets wiped out and any city or house split in opposition to itself won't stand up. And if Satan throws out Satan, that splits him in opposition to himself, so how will his country stand up? And if I'm throwing out demons by Beelzebub's power, whose power are *your* sons throwing them out by, and won't they condemn you on that account? But if I'm throwing out demons by the breath of God, then the kingdom of God has caught up with you. How can a person go into a strong man's house and steal his stuff without first tying up the strong man? *Then* he can rob his house. Whoever isn't with me is against me, and whoever doesn't go herding with me scatters the herd.

"For that reason I tell you, every wrong and every curse will be forgiven people, but cursing the spirit won't be forgiven people. If someone says something against the son of humanity, he will be forgiven; but if he speaks against the breath of the holy, he will not be forgiven in this century or the coming one.

"Either you have a good tree with its good fruit, or you have a rotten tree with its rotten fruit; because the tree is known by its fruit. Children of the snake, how can you say good things if you are bad? since the mouth speaks out what the heart is brimming over with. The good person dispenses good from his good treasury, and the bad person dispenses bad from his bad treasury. I tell you, every idle word that people say, they will have to account for on Judgment Day, because by your words you will be acquitted, and by your words you will be condemned."

Then some of the canon-lawyers and Pharisees answered him saying, "Master, we want to see a sign from you."

But he answered them: "This low and adulterous breed demands a sign, and they will be given no sign but the sign of Jonah the prophet. Because just as Jonah was in the hollow of the whale for three days and three nights, so the son of humanity will be in the heart of the earth for three days and three nights. Men of Nineveh will stand up on Judgment Day alongside this breed and condemn them, saying *their* minds were changed by the preaching of Jonah, and there's more than Jonah right here. The Queen from the South will rise in the middle of the judgment alongside this breed and condemn them, because *she* came from the ends of the earth to hear the wisdom of Solomon, and there's more than Solomon right here.

"When the unclean spirit goes out of a person it passes through arid regions, looking for a place to rest and not finding it. Then it says, 'I'll go back home where I came from,' and when it gets there it finds the place vacant, all swept and tidied up. Then it goes and brings along with it seven other spirits nastier than itself and goes in and settles down there, and the person ends up worse off than before. And that's what will happen to this vile race."

While he was still speaking to the crowds, there was his mother and his brothers and sisters standing on the outskirts, wanting to talk with him. And someone told him, "Your mother and your brothers and sisters are standing out there and they want to talk with you."

And he said to the person speaking, "Who is my mother, and who are my brothers and sisters?" And gesturing toward his students, he said, "Here's my mother and my brothers and sisters: whoever does the will of my Father in the skies, that's who my brother and my sister and my mother is."

13

That same day Jesus went out of his house and sat by the sea. And such great crowds were drawn to him that he got in a boat and sat down, while the crowd all stood along the shore.

And he talked to them a lot in metaphors, saying: "Once there was a man who went out sowing his seed. And in the course of his sowing some fell by the roadside, and the birds came and ate it up. Some fell on the rocky ground where there wasn't much soil, and it sprang right up, there being no depth to the soil; but when the sun came up it got scorched and dried out for lack of roots. Some fell on thorns, and the thorns came up and choked it off. And some fell on good soil and bore fruit, a hundred here, sixty there, thirty there. Those with ears, hear!"

And his students came up to him and said, "Why do you speak to them in metaphors?"

He answered, "To you it is given to know the mysteries of the kingdom of the skies; to them it isn't given. Because whoever has shall be given more and more, while whoever has nothing, even what he has will be taken away from him. That's why I talk to them in metaphors, so that when they see they don't see, and when they hear they don't hear or understand." (So the prophesy of Isaiah was fulfilled for them, the one saying:

> *With your ear you hear and never understand,*
> *And when you look, you look but never see.*
> *Because the heart of this people was weighted down,*
> *And with their ears they heard sluggishly,*
> *And their eyes were kept closed,*
> *Lest they see with their eyes,*
> *And hear with their ears,*
> *And understand with their heart,*
> *And come back and I heal them.*)

"How lucky your eyes are to see and your ears are to hear! Because believe me, many prophets and upright people longed to see what you are seeing and never saw it, and longed to hear what you are hearing and never heard it.

"So you heard the metaphor of the sower. If anyone hears the word of the kingdom and doesn't understand, the Evil One comes and robs what was sown in their heart: that's the seed sown by the roadside. The seed sown on rocky ground, that's the person who hears the word and joyfully seizes it at once. But it has no root in them, it's only temporary; and if there's pressure or persecution because of the word, that immediately trips them up. The seed sown among thorns, that's the person who hears the word, and then the worries of the times and the strategy of moneymaking strangle the word and it becomes unable to bear fruit.

The seed sown on good soil, that's the person who hears the word and understands it, and who really does bear fruit, a hundred here, sixty there, and thirty there."

He put another metaphor before them, saying: "The kingdom of the skies was once compared to a man who sowed good seed in his field. But while everybody was sleeping his enemy came and sowed weeds in the middle of the wheat and went away. But as the grain sprouted and bore fruit, then the weeds appeared too.

"So the landlord's servants came and said to him: 'Sir, didn't you sow good seed in your field? So where does it get these weeds from?'

"And he said to them, 'Some enemy did this.'

"And the servants said to him, 'Do you want us to go pull them out?'

"He said, 'No, because in pulling out the weeds you might uproot the wheat along with them. Let both grow together till the harvest, and at harvest-time I'll tell the harvesters, *First pull up the weeds and tie them in bundles to be burned, then collect the wheat and put it in my silo.*' "

He put another metaphor before them, saying: "The kingdom of the skies is like a seed of the mustard-plant that a man took and planted in his garden. Though it's the smallest of all seeds, when it grows it's bigger than the vegetables and turns into a tree, till the birds of the sky come and camp in its branches."

Another metaphor he spoke to them: "The kingdom of the skies is like yeast which a woman took and mixed in with three sacks of flour till it all rose." Jesus said all these things to the crowds in metaphors, and said nothing to them without metaphors, so as to fulfill what was spoken through the prophet saying,

> *I will open my mouth in metaphors,*
> *I will spew out things hidden since the founding of the world.*

Then he dismissed the crowds and went home, and his students came up to him saying, "Clarify the metaphor of the weeds in the field for us."

He replied, "The sower of good seed is the son of humanity. The field is the world, the good seed is the sons of the kingdom, the weeds are the sons of the Evil One. The enemy who sowed them is the devil. The harvest is the culmination of time, and the harvesters are messengers. So just as the weeds are collected and burned in the fire, that's how it will be in the culmination of time. The son of humanity will send his messengers and round up all the obstacles in his kingdom and all the workers of lawlessness and throw them into the furnace of fire, where the wailing and gnashing of teeth will be. Then the innocent will shine like the sun in the kingdom of their Father. Those with ears to hear, hear!

"The kingdom of the skies is like a treasure hidden in the field, which a person finds and re-hides, and in his joy goes off and sells all he has and buys that field.

"Again, the kingdom of the skies is like a businessman looking for high-quality pearls. Finding one costly pearl he went off and sold all he had and bought it.

"Once again, the kingdom of the skies is like a large net thrown in the sea, collecting some of every species, which, when it was full, they dragged onto dry ground, and sat down and sorted the good fish into their creels and threw the bad ones out. That's how it will be in the culmination of time. The messengers will ride out and separate the evil from the just and throw them into the furnace of fire, where the wailing and gnashing of teeth will be.

"Do you understand all that?"

They told him, "Yes."

And he said to them, "Because of this, any scholar versed in the kingdom of the skies is like the head of a household who brings out of his treasury new things and old."

And as it happened, when Jesus finished these metaphors, he moved on from there. And he went back to his home town and taught them in their synagogue, till they were stunned and said, "Where does he get this wisdom and these powers? Isn't this the carpenter's son? Isn't his mother named Mary and aren't his brothers named James, Joseph, Simon and Jude? And aren't his sisters all with us? So where does he get all this?" And they were offended by him.

But Jesus said to them: "A prophet is never dishonored if not in his home town and in his own house." And he didn't work many wonders there because of their lack of faith.

14

At that time Herod [Antipas] the governor heard of Jesus' reputation and said to his boys, "It's John the Baptist! He came back from the dead, and that's why these powers work in him!"

(You see, Herod had seized John, tied him up, and put him in jail on account of Herodias, his brother Philip's wife; because John had said to him, "You aren't allowed to have her." And though he wanted to kill him he was afraid of the masses, because they considered him a prophet. But when it was Herod's birthday, Herodias's daughter danced in front of everybody; and Herod liked her so much he swore under oath to give her whatever she asked. She—urged on by her mother—said, "Give me the head of John the Baptist on a tray." And the unhappy king, because of his oath and the other guests there, ordered it to be given to her, and sent out and had John beheaded in jail. And the head was brought to her on a tray and given to the girl, and she brought it to her mother. And his students came and took the body away and buried it and went and reported that to Jesus.)

Jesus, hearing that, headed out of there in a boat for a deserted place by himself. And the crowds, when they heard, followed him on foot out of the cities. And he came out and saw a great crowd and felt sorry for them and cured those of them that were sick.

When it got late, his students came up to him and said, "This place is in the middle of nowhere and it's already late. Send the crowds off so they can go into the villages and buy food for themselves."

But Jesus said to them, "They don't have to go away; give them something to eat yourselves."

They said to him, "We don't have anything here but five loaves of bread and two fish."

He said, "Bring them here to me." And after telling the crowds to sit down on the grass, he took the five loaves and two fish, looked up to the sky and blessed them, then broke the loaves and gave them to his students, and his students gave them to the crowds. And they all ate and had their fill. And they cleared away twelve basketfuls of leftover scraps. And those eating were about five thousand men, exclusive of women and children.

And right after that he made his students get in the boat and bring him to the other side until he could disband the crowds. And after disbanding the crowds he went up the mountain by himself to pray. When it got late he was there alone. But the boat was already several hundred yards offshore and being buffeted by the waves, since the wind was against them. Then during the fourth watch of the night he came toward them walking on the sea. His students, seeing him walking on the sea, were disturbed and said "It's a ghost!" and cried out in fear.

But Jesus spoke right up and said to them, "Courage, it's me, don't be afraid."

And Peter answered him, saying, "Lord, if it's you, command me to come toward you on the waters."

And he said, "Come on." And getting down out of the boat Peter walked on the waters and went toward Jesus. But seeing the strong wind he got scared, and cried out as he started to sink, saying, "Lord, save me!"

And Jesus stretched his hand right out and took hold of him and says to him, "Unbeliever, what did you hesitate for?" And when they climbed back into the boat the wind cut down.

And those in the boat bowed before him, saying, "You really are God's son."

And after crossing over they went on land to Gennesareth. And when they recognized him, the men of that place sent word into all the surrounding countryside, and they brought him everyone in bad health. And they asked him if they could just touch the edge of his cloak, and those who touched it were healed.

15

Then Pharisees and canon-lawyers from Jerusalem come up to Jesus saying, "Why do your students overstep the tradition of the elders? Why, they don't wash their hands when they eat bread."

He answered, "Why do you overstep the command of God on account of your tradition? After all, God said, 'Do right by your father and your mother,' and 'Whoever denounces father or mother, let them end in death.'

"But you say, 'Whoever says to his father or mother, *I'm giving to religion whatever you might have gotten from me*, doesn't have to worry about his father or his mother.' And you invalidate the word of God on the basis of your tradition. You fakes, Isaiah prophesied very well about you when he said,

> *These people honor me with their lips*
> *But their heart is far away from me.*
> *Pointlessly they worship me,*
> *Teaching as their doctrine the commandments of the world.*"

And calling the crowd closer he said to them, "Hear and understand: it isn't what goes into your mouth that pollutes a person, it's what comes out of your mouth—that's what pollutes a person."

Then his students come up and say to him: "You know the Pharisees were offended to hear those words?"

But he answered, "Every plant not planted by my heavenly father will be uprooted. Let them go. They are blind guides for the blind. But if one blind person guides the other around, both fall into the ditch."

Peter answered him saying: "Tell us about this metaphor."

He said: "Even *you* still don't understand? Don't you see that everything that goes into the mouth passes into the belly and is thrown out into the toilet? But what comes out of the mouth comes from the heart, and those things pollute the person. For out of the heart come evil designs, murders, adulteries, whoring, thefts, perjuries, blasphemies. . . those things pollute a person, but eating with unwashed hands doesn't pollute a person."

And going out of there Jesus proceeded into the parts of Tyre and Sidon. And this Canaanite woman from those regions came out and cried, "Pity me, Lord, son of David! My daughter is terribly possessed."

But he didn't answer her. And his students came up to him and asked him, "Set her free, she's screaming after us."

He answered, "I was only sent to the lost sheep of the Israel family."

And she came and bowed before him, saying, "Lord, help me."

He answered, "It isn't right to take the children's bread and throw it to the dogs."

But she said, "Yes it is, Lord! Even the dogs get to eat the scraps falling from their master's table."

Then Jesus answered her, "Madam, your faith is tremendous. Let it be for you as you wish." And her daughter was cured from that hour on.

And moving on from there Jesus went down by the sea of Galilee, and he went up the mountain and sat down there. And giant crowds came to him, bringing with them people who were lame, blind, deformed, mute, and all kinds of things, and threw them at his feet, and he cured them, so that the crowd was astonished to see mute people talking, deformed people sound, lame people walking, and blind people seeing. And they glorified the God of Israel.

But Jesus, calling his students to him, said, "I feel sorry for the crowd, because they've been following me around for three days and they don't have anything to eat. And I don't want to send them off still hungry because they might drop on the way."

And his students said to him, "Where in the middle of nowhere do we get enough bread to satisfy a crowd this size?"

And Jesus says to them, "How much bread do you have?"

They said, "Seven loaves, plus a few small fish." And after telling the crowd to sit down on the ground he took the seven loaves and the fish, gave thanks, broke them, and gave them to his students, who gave them to the crowds. And they all ate their fill, and they cleared away seven basketfuls of leftover scraps. (Those eating were four thousand men, exclusive of women and children.)

And after sending the crowds away he got in the boat and went to the regions of Magadan.

16

And the Pharisees and Sadducees came up to him and, testing him out, asked him to show them a sign from the sky. He answered them, "When it gets late you say, 'Nice day tomorrow, the sky's red,' and in the morning, 'A storm today, the sky's red and gloomy.' You know how to make out the face of the sky, but you can't make out the signs of the times? This low and adulterous breed demands a sign, and they won't be given any sign except the sign of Jonah." And he left them behind and went away.

And in crossing to the other bank his students forgot to bring bread. And Jesus said to them: "Watch and guard against the yeast of the Pharisees and Sadducees."

And they discussed that with each other saying, "We didn't *bring* any bread!"

Jesus, knowing that, said: "Why are you talking amongst yourselves, unbelievers, about how you didn't bring any bread? You don't know any more, you don't remember any more about the five loaves that fed five thousand and how many basketfuls you cleared away, or the seven loaves that fed four thousand and how many basketfuls you cleared away? How can you not see that I'm not talking to you about bread? But be careful of the yeast of the Pharisees and Sadducees." Then they understood that he hadn't said to guard against the yeast of their bread, but to guard against the teaching of the Pharisees and Sadducees.

After Jesus went into the regions of Philip Caesarea he asked his students, "Who do people say the son of humanity is?"

They said, "Some say John the Baptist, others say Elijah, the rest say Jeremiah or one of the prophets."

He said, "And you, who do you say I am?"

Simon Rock [that is, Peter] answered, "You are the Anointed, the son of the living God."

Jesus answered him, "You are in luck, Simon Johnson: flesh and blood didn't reveal this to you, but my Father in the skies. And I say to you that you *are* a Rock, and on this rock I will build my assembly, and the gates of the underworld will not overpower it. I will give you the keys to the kingdom of the skies, and what you bind on earth will be bound in the skies, and what you release on earth will be released in the skies." Then he ordered his students to tell nobody that he himself was the Anointed.

After that Jesus began to show his students how he had to go off to Jerusalem, and have many things done to him by the elders and chief priests and canon-lawyers, and be killed, and rise up on the third day. And Peter, taking him aside, began to remonstrate with him, saying, "Mercy on you, Lord! This won't happen to *you!*"

But he turned and said to Peter, "Out of my sight, you devil! You are an obstacle to me, because you're thinking about human concerns, not God's concerns." Then Jesus said to his students, "If anyone wishes to walk in my footsteps, let them repudiate themselves and pick up their cross and follow me, because whoever tries to save their life will lose it, whereas whoever loses their life because of me will find it. After all, what will a person gain if he wins the whole world and loses his life? Or what shall a person give in exchange for his life? Remember, the son of humanity is going to come with his messengers in the glory of his Father, and then he will pay back each person according to their deeds. I assure you, there are some among those standing here who will never taste death before they see the son of humanity coming in his monarchy."

17

And six days later Jesus takes Peter, James, and James's brother John with him and takes them up a high mountain off by themselves. And he was transformed before their eyes, and his face shone like the sun, and his clothes became as white as light. And suddenly there appeared to them

Moses and Elijah talking with him. Peter reacted by saying to Jesus, "Lord, it's good for us to be here. If you want, I will put up three tabernacles here, one for you, one for Moses, and one for Elijah." Even as he spoke, a cloud of light enveloped them, and suddenly there was a voice from the cloud saying, "This is my son, my beloved son, in whom I am delighted: listen to him!" And hearing that, his students fell on their faces and panicked completely. And Jesus came over to them and touched them, saying, "Get up and don't be afraid." Lifting their eyes they saw no one but Jesus alone.

And as they went down the mountain Jesus commanded them, "Don't tell this vision to anyone till the son of humanity has come back from the dead."

And his students asked him, "So why do the scribes say, 'First Elijah must come'?"

He answered, "Elijah is coming and will restore everything. Yet I'm telling you that Elijah came already, and they didn't recognize him; instead, they did with him as they pleased. And the son of humanity will be treated the same way by them." Then his students understood that he was talking to them about John the Baptist.

And as they went toward the crowd a fellow came their way who fell on his knees and said, "Lord, have mercy on my son; he is insane and suffering horribly. He falls into the fire repeatedly and into the water repeatedly. And I brought him to your students, but they couldn't cure him."

And Jesus answered, "You unbelieving and perverse-minded crew! How long will I be with you? How long will I put *up* with you? Bring him here to me." And Jesus yelled at him and the demon came out of him, and the child was cured from that time on.

Then his students came up to Jesus privately and said, "Why couldn't *we* throw it out?"

He said to them, "Because of your lack of faith. I assure you, if you have a mustard-seed's worth of faith, you'll tell this mountain to move from here to there and it will move; nothing will be impossible for you."

As they were making the rounds of Galilee Jesus told them, "The son of humanity will be betrayed into the hands of the world, and they will kill him, and on the third day he will rise up." And they were deeply saddened.

MATTHEW   51

As they were going into Capharnaum those who collected the fifty-cent toll came to Peter and said, "Your teacher doesn't pay his fifty cents?"

And he said, "That's right!"

And when he got home Jesus was there ahead of him, saying, "What do you think, Simon? On whom do the kings of the earth impose their taxes and their tolls? On their own children or on other people's?" And when he said "Other people's," Jesus said to him, "Then their own children go free. But so as not to get in these people's way, go down to the sea and throw in a hook and take the first fish that comes up, and you'll find a silver dollar in its mouth. Take it and give it to them for you and me."

18

At that hour Jesus' students came to him saying, "Tell us, who is the greatest in the kingdom of the skies?"

And he called to a child and put the child in front of them and said, "I assure you, if you don't turn round and become like children, you'll never get into the kingdom of the skies. So whoever brings himself down to the level of this child, that's who the greatest in the kingdom of the skies is. And whoever receives any child like this one in my name, receives me.

"Whereas whoever trips up one of these little ones who believe in me, would be better off to have a giant millstone hung around his neck and sink in the vastness of the sea.

"Woe to the world for stumbling-blocks! Because stumbling-blocks must come along, but woe to the person through whom they come! If your hand or your foot gets in your way, cut it off and throw it away. You're lucky if you enter deformed and crippled into Life, and aren't thrown with both hands and both feet into the everlasting fire. And if your eye gets in your way, pluck it out and throw it off. You're lucky if you enter with one eye into Life, and aren't thrown with both eyes into the fire of Gehenna.

"Watch out and don't be contemptuous of these little ones, because I tell you that their messengers at all times see the face of my Father in the skies.

"What do you think? If a fellow has a hundred sheep and one of them wanders off, isn't he going to leave the ninety-nine on the hillside and go look for the lost one? And if he manages to find it, I can tell you for sure that he will be happier about that one than about the ninety-nine that never wandered. In the same way, there is no desire on the part of your Father in the skies that the least important of these people should be lost.

"If your brother wrongs you, go have it out with him, just you and him. If he listens to you, you've gained your brother back. If he doesn't listen, bring one or two along with you, so that everything said stands on the word of two or three witnesses. If he won't listen to them, speak up at meeting. If he won't listen to the assembly, let him be the same to you as the foreigner and the tax-collector.

"I assure you, whatever you bind on the earth will be bound in the sky, and whatever you release on the earth will be released in the sky.

"Again, I tell you truly that if two of you on the earth agree about anything they ask for, it will come to them from my Father in the skies, because where two or three are assembled in my name, there I am in their midst."

Then Peter came up to him and said, "Lord, how many times shall my brother wrong me and I forgive him? Up to seven times?"

Jesus says to him, "I'm not telling you up to seven times, I'm telling you up to seventy-seven times.

"In this connection, the kingdom of the skies could be compared to a certain king who wanted to settle accounts with his slaves. As he started the settlement, they brought before him one who was indebted for ten million dollars. Since he didn't have it to pay back, the master ordered him and his wife and his children and everything he had to be sold in repayment. So the slave fell down and bowed before him, saying, 'Have patience with me, and I will pay it all back to you.' And the master, feeling sorry for that slave, let him go and forgave him the loan.

"Then that slave went out and found one of his fellow slaves who owed him a hundred dollars, and seized him and started choking him, saying, 'If you owe it to me, pay up!'

"So his fellow slave fell down and pleaded with him, saying, 'Have patience with me, and I will pay you back.' But he wouldn't hear it, and instead went off and threw him in jail till he should pay the debt.

"So his fellow slaves, seeing these events, were most unhappy, and went and informed their master about everything that had happened.

Then the master, calling him before him, said to him, 'Wretched slave, I let you off from your entire debt, because you pleaded with me. Shouldn't you also have pitied your fellow-slave, as I pitied you?' And in a rage the master handed him over to the torturers till he should pay back everything he owed. And that's what my heavenly Father will do to you, if each of you does not forgive your brother from your hearts."

19

And as it happened, when Jesus finished these words, he headed out of Galilee and went into the regions of Judea across the Jordan. And giant crowds followed him, and he cured them there.

And the Pharisees came up to him testing him out and saying, "Is a man allowed to divorce his wife for whatever cause?"

He answered, "Didn't you ever read that the Creator made them male and female from the beginning, and that he said, 'Because of this a man is to leave his father and his mother behind and stick with his wife, and the two are to become one living thing, so that they aren't two anymore, they're one living thing?' So what God joined together, let no man divide."

They said to him, "Why did Moses say to present her with a divorce decree and divorce her?"

He said to them, "Moses, in view of the hardness of your hearts, allowed you to divorce your wives, but it wasn't like that from the beginning. I tell you that whoever divorces his wife for anything but whoring and marries another is living in adultery."

His students said to him: "If the guilt of a man with a woman is so great, it doesn't pay to get married."

And he said to them, "Not all have room for this idea, it has to be given to you: but some eunuchs were born that way from their mothers' bellies, and some eunuchs were made that way by others, and some make themselves that way for the kingdom of the skies. Whoever can encompass it, let them do so."

Then some children were brought to him so he could put his hands on them and pray for them, but his students yelled at them. But Jesus said, "Leave the children alone and don't keep them back from coming toward me; the kingdom of the skies belongs to such as them." And after laying his hands on them he traveled on from there.

And someone came up to him and said: "Teacher, what good shall I do in order to have everlasting life?"

He said to him, "Why do you ask me about good? You only have one good Person. But if you wish to enter into that life, keep the commandments."

He says to him, "Which?"

Jesus said, " 'You are not to murder,' 'You are not to commit adultery,' 'You are not to steal,' 'You are not to perjure,' 'Do right by your father and your mother,' and 'You are to love those close to you as you love yourself.' "

The young man says to him, "I have kept all those. What do I still need?"

Jesus said to him, "If you want to be perfect, go sell what you have and give it to the poor, and you will have a treasure in the skies, and come here and follow me." Hearing those words the young man went away in mourning, because he was the owner of many possessions.

Jesus said to his students, "Believe me, a rich person won't find it easy to get into the kingdom of the skies. On the contrary, I tell you, it's easier for a camel to squeeze through the eye of a needle than for a rich person to get into the kingdom of God."

Hearing that, his students were completely stunned and said, "Then who *can* be saved?"

Looking straight at them, Jesus said, "For human beings it's impossible, but for God everything is possible."

Then Peter answered him, "Look at us: we left everything and followed you; so what will be ours?"

Jesus said to them, "I assure you that you who have followed me, in the time of rebirth when the son of humanity sits upon the throne of his glory, you too will sit on twelve thrones judging the twelve tribes of Israel. And everyone who left behind houses or brothers or sisters or father or mother or children or lands because of my name will get it back a hundred times over and inherit everlasting life. And many of the first will be last and many of the last will be first.

20

"You see, the kingdom of the skies is like a certain landowner who went out with the dawn to hire workers for his vineyard. After agreeing with the workers on a drachma a day he sent them off to his vineyard. And going out around nine o'clock he saw others standing around the marketplace idle and said to them: 'You go off to my vineyard too, and I will pay you what is reasonable,' and they went. Going out around noon and three he did the same.

"Around five o'clock he went out and found others standing and says to them, 'Why are you standing here all day with nothing to do?'

"They say to him: 'Nobody hired us.'

"He says to them, 'You go off to my vineyard too.'

"So when it got late the owner of the vineyard says to his foreman: 'Call the workers and pay them their wages going from last to first.' And the ones from five o'clock came forward and received a drachma apiece. And when the first ones came forward, they thought they'd get more, but they got a drachma apiece too.

"On receiving it they started grumbling at the landowner saying, 'These last ones worked one hour, and you make them equal to us who bore the burden and the heat of the day!'

"But he answered one of them, saying, 'I'm not cheating you, pal. Didn't you agree with me on a drachma? Take what's yours and go your way. I wish to give this latecomer the same as you; can't I do what I want with my own possessions? Must you cast an evil eye upon my being kind?' That's how the last will be first and the first will be last."

And going up to Jerusalem Jesus took his twelve students aside and said to them on the way: "Here we go up to Jerusalem, and the son of humanity will be handed over to the high priests and canon-lawyers, and they will condemn him to death and hand him over to the pagans to be made fun of, and whipped, and crucified; and on the third day he will rise again."

Then the mother of the sons of Zebedee came up to him with her sons, bowing before him as if asking him for something. He said to her, "What do you want?"

She says to him, "Say that these two sons of mine may sit one on your right and one on your left in your kingdom."

Jesus answered, "You don't know what you're asking. Can you drink the cup that I'm going to drink?"

They say to him, "We can."

He says to them, "Then you will drink my cup, but sitting at my right
and left is not mine to give, it's for whoever my Father has prepared it
for."

And the other ten were outraged at the two brothers. So Jesus called
them together and said, "You know how the rulers of nations lord it over
them and big men use their power. Among us it's not going to be like
that: on the contrary, if you want to be big, be everybody's servant, and
if you want to be number one, be everybody's slave—just as the son of
humanity didn't come to be served, but to serve and to give his life as a
ransom for many."

And as they traveled out from Jericho a large crowd followed him. And
these two blind men sitting by the road, hearing that Jesus was going by,
shouted, "Have mercy on us, son of David!" The crowd yelled at them
to be quiet, but they shouted all the louder, "Have mercy on us, Lord,
son of David!"

And Jesus stopped and called out to them, "What do you want me to
do for you?"

They say to him, "Make our eyes open, Lord." And Jesus was moved,
and touched their eyes, and immediately they could see, and they
followed him.

21

And when they got close to Jerusalem and came to Bethphage on Mount
Olive, at that point Jesus sent off two of his students, saying to them, "Go
on into the village ahead of you, and right away you'll come upon a
donkey tied up and her foal with her. Untie them and bring them to me.
And if anyone says anything to you, you'll say, 'The master needs these,'
and they'll send them right back with you." * This happened so as to
fulfill what was spoken by the prophet:

> *Tell your daughter Zion,*
> *Here comes your king,*
> *Gently, mounted on donkey-back,*
> *And on its foal, the beast of burden's son.*

---

* These instructions and similar ones given in advance of the Last Supper in Matthew, Mark,
and Luke, have been interpreted at least three ways: 1) Jesus can say "go into town and you'll

The students, going on their way and doing as Jesus ordered, brought back the donkey and the foal and spread their cloaks on them, and he sat down on top of them. And a very large crowd spread their cloaks in the roadway, while others cut branches from trees and strewed them in the road. And the crowds going ahead of him and the crowds following shouted, "Hooray for the son of David! Bless him who comes in the name of the Lord! Hooray to the highest heavens!"

And as he came into Jerusalem the whole city was shaken up, saying, "Who is this?"

And the crowds said, "This is the prophet Jesus, from Nazareth, Galilee."

And Jesus went into the temple, and threw out all those buying and selling in the temple, and overturned the tables of the moneychangers and the chairs of the pigeon-sellers. And he says to them, "It is written, 'My house will be known as a house of prayer,' whereas you make it a den of thieves."

And blind and lame people came up to him in the temple and he cured them. But the high priests and the canon-lawyers, seeing the wonders he had worked and the children shouting "Hooray for the son of David!" in the temple, were outraged and said to him, "Do you hear what these ones are saying?"

And Jesus says to them, "Yes. Didn't you ever read where it says, 'I will round out my praise in the mouths of babies and toddlers?'" And he left them behind and went out of town to Bethany and camped there.

The next morning, going back into town, he got hungry. And seeing a fig tree on the way he went toward it and found nothing but leaves on it, and said to it, "Let no fruit come from you ever again," and it dried up in a flash.

And his students were amazed to see that and said, "How could the fig tree dry up in a flash?"

Jesus answered, "Believe me, if you have faith and don't hesitate, not only will you do this business with the fig tree, but if you tell this mountain here, 'Get up and throw yourself into the sea,' it will happen; and everything you ask for in your prayers, if you believe, you will get it."

see this and that" by prophetic power; 2) Jesus can rely on the customs of Middle Eastern hospitality; 3) Jesus has arranged something like a spy rendezvous with a well-to-do secret sympathizer. The third explanation explains the most, including "go into town and see So-and-so" and "you'll see a fellow with a water jug" (usually women and not men carried water).

And after he'd gone into the temple, the high priests and the elders of the people come up to him as he was teaching and said, "What authority do you have to do this? Who gave you any such authority?"

Jesus answered, "I also want to ask you something, and if you tell me that I'll also tell you what authority I have to do this: Where did the washing of John come from? From heaven or from the world?"

They discussed that among themselves saying, "If we say from heaven, he'll say to us, 'Then why didn't you believe in him?' But if we say from the world, we have the crowd to be afraid of, since they all consider John a prophet." And they answered Jesus, "We don't know."

And he in his turn said to them, "I won't tell you what authority I have to do this either.

"What do you say? A fellow had two children: and he went to the first one and said, 'Son, go work in my vineyard today,' and he answered, 'I don't want to,' but later he thought better of it and went. And he went to the other one the same way, and he answered, 'Yessir,' and didn't go. Which of the two did the will of his father?"

They said, "The first."

And Jesus says to them, "Believe me, the whores and the tax-collectors will get into the kingdom of God before you, because John came toward you on the path of justice, and you didn't believe, while the whores and the tax-collectors *did* believe him. And you, even after seeing him, didn't convert to believing in him afterwards.

"Listen to another comparison. Once there was a certain landowner who planted a vineyard and put a fence around it and dug out a wine cellar in it and built a tower and contracted it out to some farmers and left the country. So when the harvest time got close, he sent his slaves to the farmers to get his produce. And the farmers, seizing the slaves, flogged one, killed another, and threw stones at a third.

"Again he sent some more slaves, more numerous than the first, and they did the same thing to them. Finally he sent his son to them, saying, 'They will respect my son.'

"But when the farmers saw his son they said to each other, 'This guy is the heir. Here, let's kill him and get his inheritance,' and they seized him and took him outside the vineyard and killed him. So when the owner of the vineyard comes, what will he do to those farmers?"

They say to him, "He'll get rid of those evil people by evil means and give the vineyard out to other farmers who will deliver the produce to him in good season."

Jesus says to them, "Haven't you ever read in the Scriptures:

A stone that the builders rejected,
That one ended up the corner-stone:
That was made by the Lord
And is the admiration of our eyes?

"Because of that, I tell you that the kingdom of God will be taken away from you and given to a nation that bears its fruits. And whoever falls on that stone will be crushed, and whoever it falls upon, it will scatter in pieces."

And when the high priests and Pharisees heard his comparisons they realized he was talking about them. And though they wanted to seize him they were afraid of the masses, since they regarded him as a prophet.

22

And Jesus again continued speaking to them in metaphors, saying, "The kingdom of the skies was once compared to a certain king who arranged a wedding for his son. And he sent his servants to call the guests to the wedding, and they wouldn't come. Again he sent some more servants, saying, "Tell the guests, 'Look, I've prepared the dinner, the steers and fat calves have been slaughtered, and everything's ready: come to the wedding.' But they ignored him and went away, one to his fields, another about his business; and others seized the servants, did violence to them, and killed them. So the king flew in a rage and sent out his army and got rid of those murderers and burned their city down. Then he says to his servants, 'The wedding is ready, but the guests didn't deserve it. So travel around the exits of the highways and invite whoever you find to the wedding.' And those servants went out into the streets and brought back whoever they found, bad and good alike, and the wedding was filled with guests. But when the king came in to look the guests over he saw a fellow there not dressed for a wedding, and said to him, 'Pal, how did you come here without wedding clothes?' But the man kept his mouth shut. Then the king said to his servants, 'Tie him hand and foot and throw him out into the darkness beyond, where the wailing and gnashing of teeth will be, because many are called, but few are chosen.'"

Then the Pharisees went out and had a meeting about how to trap him in his words. And they sent out their students to him with Herod's men, saying, "Teacher, we know that you're truthful and that you teach the word of God truthfully without being concerned about anybody, because you don't look to the face of the world. So tell us what you think: Is it all right to pay taxes to Caesar or not?"

Jesus, sensing the evil in them, said, "What are you testing me for, you fakes? Show me the coin paid in taxes." And they brought him a drachma. And he says to them, "Whose picture and inscription is this?"

They say to him, "Caesar's."

Then he says to them, "So give Caesar's things to Caesar, and God's things to God." And they were amazed to hear that, and left him alone and went away.

That same day Sadducees, who said there was no resurrection, came up to him and asked, "Teacher, Moses said, 'If someone dies without children, let his brother take his widow to wife and continue his brother's seed.' So in our town there were seven brothers: the first one married and died, and having no children, he left his wife to his brother. The second brother did the same, and the third, and so on for all seven, and the woman died last of all. So in the resurrection, which of the seven's wife will she be? After all, they all had her."

Jesus answered, "You're wandering in circles, knowing nothing of the scriptures or the power of God, because in the resurrection there are no brides and no grooms; instead, they're like the messengers in the sky. As for the resurrection of the dead, didn't you ever read what was spoken by God: 'I am the God of Abraham and the God of Isaac and the God of Jacob'? There is no god of the dead, only of the living." And the crowds were stunned to hear his teaching.

So then the Pharisees, hearing that he'd shut the Sadducees up, all got together in the same place. And one of them versed in law asked him as a test, "Teacher, which commandment in the law is important?"

He said to them, "You are to love your lord God with all your heart and all your spirit and all your mind. That is the important and first commandment. The second one is similar: You are to love those close to you as you love yourself. All the law and all the prophets hang from these two commands."

With the Pharisees assembled, Jesus asked them this question: "What

do you think about the Anointed One? Whose son is he?"
They told him, "David's."
He says to them, "Then how does David in the spirit call him Lord,
saying,

> *A lord said to my lord,*
> *Sit at my right,*
> *While I pin your enemies underneath your feet?*

So if David calls him Lord, how is he his son?"
And no one could give him an answer for that, nor did anybody dare
to ask him any more questions after that day.

23

Then Jesus talked to the crowds and his students, saying, "Where Moses
sat, the Pharisees and the canon-lawyers now sit. So do and keep what
they say to you, but don't go by what they do, because they say things and
then don't do them. They shackle us with unbearably heavy taxes and lay
that on people's shoulders, but they let no taxes come within arm's
length of *them*. Everything they do is done to be observed by the world:
their phylacteries with big broad strips, their cloaks with nice large
prayer-tassels. They love their seats at the head tables of banquets and
in the front pews of churches, and everyone saying hello to them
downtown, and having people call them 'Master.'

"Don't you be called 'Master': you only have one teacher, all of you are
brothers. And don't call your father on the earth your father, you only
have one heavenly Father. And don't be called leaders, because you only
have one leader, the Anointed. The highest person among you is to be
the servant of you all, so those who exalt themselves will be humbled and
those who humble themselves will be exalted.

"Woe to you canon-lawyers and Pharisees, you fakes, for shutting the
door to the kingdom of the skies in humanity's face: you don't go in
yourselves and you don't let anybody else go in either.

"Woe to you canon-lawyers and Pharisees, you fakes, for traversing
land and sea to make a convert, and then when one is made, turning him
into a son of Gehenna twice as bad as yourselves!

"Woe to you, blind pathfinders, when you say, 'If you swear *by the temple*, that's nothing, but if you swear *by all the gold in the temple*, that's swearing.' * Blockheads and blind men, which is more important, the gold, or the temple that sanctifies the gold?

"And you say, 'If you swear *by the temple altar*, that's nothing, but if you swear *by the offerings on the temple altar*, that's swearing.' Blind men, which is more important, the offering or the altar that sanctifies the offering?

"In other words, if you swear 'by the altar,' you're swearing by it *and* by everything on top of it, and if you swear 'by the temple,' you're swearing by it *and* by its inhabitant, and if you swear 'by heaven!', you're swearing by the throne of God and by its occupant.

"Woe to you canon-lawyers and Pharisees, you fakes, for singling out the mint, the dillweed, and the curry-powder of the law and leaving aside the hard parts, like judgment and mercy and faith! *Those* were the parts you should have done—and then the others shouldn't be omitted. Blind pathfinders, if there's a gnat in your soup, you strain it out; if there's a camel in your soup, you drink it down!

"Woe to you canon-lawyers and Pharisees, you fakes, for cleaning off the rim of your cup and saucer while on the inside you're bursting with greed and wild appetites. Blind Pharisee, wash out the inside of the cup and saucer first, if you want the outside to end up clean!

"Woe to you canon-lawyers and Pharisees, you fakes, for being like dusty monuments that look pretty on the outside but on the inside are full of the bones of corpses and all kinds of rot. You likewise from the outside appear to the world to be decent, but inside you're full of hypocrisy and ways around the law.

"Woe to you canon-lawyers and Pharisees, you fakes, for building monuments to the prophets and decorating the graves of the just, and saying, 'If we'd been around in our fathers' time, we'd have had no part in shedding the prophets' blood.' So you testify yourselves that you're the children of those who *did* murder the prophets. And you fully come up to the standard of your forefathers. Vipers, offspring of snakes, how

---

* *By the temple* doesn't count as a curse to the Pharisees because it's so short it can be said without thinking and has become so common that it has no force anymore; while *by all the gold in the temple* is considered more deliberate because it's longer, and more of a conscious choice because it's rarer.

will you run from the sentence of Gehenna?

"For this reason I hereby send you prophets, wise men and scholars. Some of them you'll kill, some of them you'll crucify, some of them you'll have flogged in the synagogue and hounded from town to town. So that there will come back upon you all the innocent blood poured out upon the earth from the blood of Abel the innocent to the blood of Zachariah the son of Barachiah, whom you murdered between the temple and the altar. I assure you, that will all come back upon this generation.

"Jerusalem, Jerusalem, killer of prophets, stoner of ambassadors to the city, how often I wanted to gather your children together the way a bird gathers her little birds under her wing—and you didn't want to. And now look, your house is left in ruins. I tell you, you won't see me again from now until you say

Bless him who comes in the name of the Lord!"

24

And Jesus went out of the temple and on his way, and his students came to him to show him the temple buildings. But he said to them, "You see all that? I assure you, not one stone will be left on top of another stone without being demolished."

As he sat on Mount Olive, his students came to him privately saying, "Tell us, when will that happen, and what will be the sign of your presence and of the culmination of time?"

And Jesus answered them, "Watch out, don't let anyone fool you, because there will be many people coming in my name and saying, 'I am the Anointed,' and they will fool a lot of people. You're going to hear wars, and reports of wars. Be careful, don't be afraid, because it has to happen, that's how it is at the end: race will rise up against race and country will rise up against country, and there will be famines, and places hit by earthquakes. All that is the beginning of the death-throes.

"Then they'll hand you over into torment and kill you off, and you'll be hated by people of every kind because of my name. And then many will be tripped up, and will betray each other and hate each other. And many pseudoprophets will come along and fool a lot of people. And on account of the full-scale lawlessness, the love in the hearts of the masses will be chilled. But whoever endures to the end, that's who will be saved. And this good word of the kingdom will be announced to all the inhabited earth as a testimony to all nations, and then comes the end.

"So when you see the monster of destruction, as spoken of by Daniel the prophet, standing in the holy place, when you recognize it, remember: those in Judea, evacuate into the mountains; those standing on housetops, don't go down to get anything from your house; those in the fields, don't go back to get your cloak. Woe to those with a child in their belly or nursing in those days!

"Pray that your flight doesn't happen in winter or on the Sabbath. For there will be trouble then like there has never been from the beginning of the world till now, and never will be again. And if those days were not cut short, no living thing would be left at all, but because of the chosen ones, those days will be cut short.

"If someone says to you then: Look here, it's the Anointed! or, Over here! don't believe them, because many pseudo-Christs and pseudo-prophets will come along and give such great signs and portents as to fool, if possible, even the chosen ones: I hereby warn you in advance. So if they say to you, 'There he is, out in the desert,' don't go out there; or if they say, 'There, in the secret chambers,' don't believe them. Like the lightning that comes shining from east to west, that's what the presence of the son of humanity will be like. Wherever the body is, the vultures gather.

"Then right after the troubles of those days, the sun will go dark, and the moon won't give her beams, and the stars will fall from the sky, and the powers of the skies will be shaken.

"And then the sign of the son of humanity will appear in the sky, and then all the tribes of the earth will weep, and they will see the son of humanity coming upon the clouds of the sky with power and great glory. And he will send out his messengers with a big trumpet, and they will collect the chosen ones out of the four corners of the earth, from peak to peak of heaven.

"Take a lesson from the fig tree: when the shoots are tender, and the leaves are out, you know the harvest is near. The same with you: when you see all these things happening, you'll know it's right at your doorstep. I assure you that this generation will not go by before all this happens. The sky and the earth will go by, but my words will not go by.

"As for the date and time, no one knows, not even the messengers of the sky, not even the son, only the Father alone.

"Just like the days of Noah, that's what the presence of the son of humanity will be like. Just as in those days before the cataclysm they were eating and drinking and taking husbands and wives, and didn't notice anything till the cataclysm came and took them all, that's what the presence of the son of humanity will be like. Then there will be two men working in the fields; one will be taken along and one will be left behind. Two women grinding at the mill: one will be taken along and one will be left behind.

"So keep awake, because you don't know what day your master is coming. This much you do know: if the owner of the house knew at what hour of the night the thief was coming, he'd stay awake and not let his house be tunneled into.

"Tell me, who is the faithful and prudent slave whom the master put in charge of his household to give them their food on time? Lucky for that slave if the master comes and finds him doing just that. I assure you, he will put him in charge of all his possessions. But if that lousy slave says to himself, 'My master is taking a while to get here,' and starts to beat up his fellow slaves and eat and drink with drunkards, that slave's master will show up on a day he wasn't expecting and at a time he didn't know, and will have him drawn and quartered and throw his portion to the hypocrites, where the wailing and gnashing of teeth will be.

25

"Then the kingdom of the skies will be like ten maidens who took their lanterns and went out to meet the bridegroom, but five of them were stupid and five were sensible. You see, the stupid ones took their lanterns without taking any oil with them, whereas the sensible ones took cans of oil with their lanterns. The bridegroom being delayed, they all got drowsy and lay down. Then at midnight the cry went up: 'Here comes the bridegroom, everybody out to meet him.' Then all those maidens got up and fixed their lanterns. But the stupid ones said to the sensible ones: 'Give us some of your oil, our lanterns are going out.'

"And the sensible ones answered, 'There may not be enough for us and you; you'd better go to those who sell it and buy yourselves some.' After they went off to buy oil, the bridegroom came, and those who were ready went in with him to the wedding, and the door was shut.

"Then later the other maidens came along saying, 'Master, master, open up for us.'

"But he answered, 'I swear I don't know you.' So stay awake, because you don't know the date or the time.

"You see, it's like a fellow who was going away and called his slaves and entrusted his goods to them: and he gave five bars of silver to one, two to another, and one to a third—to each according to his ability—and went away. The one who got the five bars went right out and did business with them and earned another five bars; likewise, the one who got the two bars earned another two. But the one who got the one bar went off and dug a hole and hid his master's silver.

"After a long time the master of those slaves comes back and settles accounts with them. And the one who got the five bars came forward and presented the other five bars, saying, 'Master, you entrusted me with five bars of silver; see, I earned another five bars.'

"And his master said to him, 'Well done, good and faithful slave! You were trustworthy in small things, I'll put you in charge of many things. Welcome to your master's joy.'

"And the one who got two bars also came forward and said, 'Master, you entrusted me with two bars of silver; see, I earned another two bars.'

"His master said to him, 'Well done, good and faithful slave! You were trustworthy in small things, I'll put you in charge of many things. Welcome to your master's joy.'

"Then the one who got the one bar also came forward and said, 'Master, knowing you to be a tough fellow, who reaps what he didn't sow and collects what he didn't scatter, I was afraid and went off and hid your bar of silver in the ground; here it is.'

"His master answered, 'Bad and cowardly slave, if you knew that I reap what I didn't sow and collect what I didn't scatter, then you should have put my silver in the bank, so I could have gone and gotten my money back with interest. Take the bar of silver away from him and give it to the one with ten bars: he who has everything shall be given more and more; whereas he who has nothing, even what he has shall be taken away from him. And throw the useless slave out into the darkness beyond, where the wailing and gnashing of teeth will be.'

"When the son of humanity comes in his glory and all his messengers with him, then he will sit upon a throne of his glory, and all the nations will be assembled before him, and he will separate them from each other, just as the herdsman separates the sheep from the goats, and he will put the sheep on his right and the goats on his left. Then the king will say to those on his right, 'Come here, you blessed of my father, inherit the kingdom prepared for you from the beginning of the world. After all, I was hungry and you gave me something to eat, I was thirsty and you gave me something to drink, I was wandering and you took me in, I was naked and you clothed me, I was sick and you looked after me, I was in jail and you came to see me.'

"Then the innocent will answer, 'Lord, when was it that we saw you starving and we fed you, or saw you thirsty and gave you something to drink? When did we see you wandering and take you in, or see you naked and clothe you? When were you sick or in jail and we came to see you?'

"And the king will answer, 'Let me assure you, however much you did it for any of the least important of these brothers and sisters of mine, you did it for me.' Then he will say to those on his left, 'Away from me, damned souls, into the everlasting fire prepared for the Devil and his messengers! Why, I was hungry and you wouldn't give me anything to eat, I was thirsty and you wouldn't give me anything to drink, I was wandering and you didn't take me in, I was naked and you didn't clothe me, I was sick and in jail and you didn't look after me.'

"Then they will also answer, 'Lord, when did we see you hungry or thirsty or wandering or naked or sick or in jail and we didn't take care of you?'

"Then he will answer, 'Let me assure you, however much you wouldn't do it for any of the least important of these people, you wouldn't do it for me either.' Then those ones will ride off to everlasting punishment, while the innocent ride off to everlasting life."

26

And it happened when Jesus finished all these words, he said to his students, "You know, in two days it will be Passover, and the son of humanity will be handed over to be crucified."

Then the high priests and elders of the people got together in the meeting-hall of the high priest named Caiaphas and exchanged ideas about some trick to lay hold of Jesus and kill him. But they said, "Not during the feast days, the people will make too much noise."

Jesus being in Bethany at the house of Simon Leper, a woman came to him with a bottle of expensive perfume and poured it over his head as he sat at dinner. His students were outraged to see that and said, "Why this waste? After all, this could have been sold for a lot and given to the poor."

Jesus, noticing this, said to them, "Why are you giving this woman grief? She did a fine thing for me. Remember, you always have the poor around, but you don't always have me around. Why, this woman who poured this perfume on my body made me ready for burial. I promise you, wherever this good word is proclaimed in all the world, what she did shall also be told in her memory."

Then off went one of the twelve, the one called Judas Iscariot, to the high priests and said, "What will you give me if I hand him over to you?" And they set thirty silverpieces on him. So from that time on he was looking for the right time to hand him over.

On the third day of the unleavened bread Jesus' students came to him and said, "Where do you want us to get things ready for you to eat the seder?"

He said, "Go into town and see So-and-So and tell him, 'The master says, *My time is near, I'm celebrating Passover with you, along with my students.*' " And his students did as Jesus ordered them and got the seder ready.

When it got late he sat down with the twelve. And while they were eating he said, "I tell you for sure, one of you is going to hand me over."

And they, deeply pained, started saying to him one by one, "*I* couldn't be the one, could I, Lord?"

He answered, "The one who dips his hand in the bowl with mine, that's the one who will hand me over. Yes, the son of humanity must go now, just as it was written about him, but woe to that person by whom the son of humanity is handed over. Better for him if he'd never been born."

Judas, his betrayer, answered, "*I* couldn't be the one, could I, master?" And he says, "You tell me."

Then as they were eating, Jesus took bread, said grace, and gave it to his students saying, "Take and eat this: this is my body." And taking a cup and giving thanks he gave it to them, saying, "Drink from this, all of you: this is my blood, the blood of the testament, poured out for many for the forgiveness of wrongs. I tell you, this is the last I will drink of this vintage from now till that day when I drink it new with you in the kingdom of my Father." And concluding with a hymn, they went out to Mount Olive.

Then Jesus says to them, "All of you will let me down tonight—just like the scripture says, 'I will strike at the shepherd, and the sheep in his herd will scatter.' But after rising up I will go on ahead of you into Galilee."

And Peter answered, "Even if everyone lets you down, I will never let you down."

Jesus said to him, "I promise you, in the night ahead, from now till cockcrow, you will say you don't know me three times."

Peter says to him, "Even if I had to die with you, I would never say I didn't know you," and all his students said the same.

Then Jesus goes with them to the place called Gethsemane and says to the students, "Sit here while I go over there and pray." And taking Peter and the two sons of Zebedee he began to grieve and mourn, then he says to them, "My soul is so full of grief that I could die; wait here and stay awake with me." Then he went off a little ways and fell on his face praying and said, "My Father, if it's possible, let this cup pass me by, but let Your will and not mine be done."

Then he comes over to his students and finds them asleep and says to Simon Peter, "You couldn't stay awake this one hour with me? Keep awake and pray that you don't get put to the test: the spirit may be eager, but the flesh is weak."

A second time he went off and prayed: "My Father, if this can't pass me by without my drinking it, let Your will be done." And again he came and found them sleeping, because their eyelids were so heavy.

And again he left them alone and went off and prayed saying the same words a third time. Then he comes back to his students and says to them: "Sleep and get your rest while you can, do you see how near the time is? And the son of humanity will be betrayed into the hands of the godless . . . up now! Come on! Here he comes, my betrayer!"

And even as he spoke, there was Judas, one of the twelve, and with him a large band of people with swords and clubs, sent by the high priests and elders of the people. The betrayer had given them the signal, "Whoever I kiss is the one, take him!" And going right over to Jesus he said, "Good evening, master," and kissed him.

Jesus said to him, "Buddy, what are you here for?" Then they all came up and laid hands on Jesus and took him away. And all of a sudden, one of those with Jesus reached for his sword and hit the high priest's servant, cutting off his ear. Then Jesus says to him, "Put your sword back where it belongs: those who fight swords with swords are lost. You think I can't call on my Father and have Him supply me even now with more than twelve legions of His messengers? But how will the scriptures be fulfilled that say this must happen?"

At that point Jesus said to the mob, "As if in pursuit of a robber you came out to get me with swords and clubs? I used to sit in the daytime in the temple when I was teaching and you didn't take me then. This has all happened to fulfill the prophets' writings." Then all his students left him behind and ran.

Next, those holding Jesus led him before Caiaphas the high priest, where the canon-lawyers and the elders had gathered. But Peter followed him from a distance as far as the courtyard of the high priest and went in and was sitting with the servants in order to see the outcome.

Now the high priests and the whole high court were looking for some false testimony against Jesus such that they could sentence him to death, but they weren't finding it, even with many false witnesses coming forward. Finally, two came forward saying, "This guy said, 'I can topple the temple of God and, in three days, build it again.' "

And the high priest, standing up, said to him, "Don't you have any answer as to why these people testify against you?" But Jesus kept silent. And the high priest said to him: "I command you by the living God to tell us if you are the Anointed, the son of God."

Jesus says to him, "That's what *you* say. But I do tell you this: next time you will see the son of humanity sitting at the right hand of power and coming on the clouds of the sky."

Then the high priest tore his cloak,* saying, "That's blasphemy! Why do we need any more witnesses? Didn't you hear that blasphemy just now? What do you say?"

They answered: "This is punishable by death."

Then they spat in his face and boxed his ears, while others hit him with a stick and said, "Prophesy for us, Mr. Anointed One: who just hit you?"

Meanwhile Peter was sitting out in the yard, and a girl came over to him and said, "You were with Jesus of Galilee too."

---

* By Jewish custom, ripping your garments expresses your horror at hearing blasphemy spoken.

But he denied it and said in front of everybody, "I don't know what you're talking about."

So he went into the outer hallway, where another girl saw him and said to the people there, "This guy was with Jesus of Nazareth."

And again he denied it with an oath, saying "I don't know the fellow."

A little while later those standing there came over and said to Peter, "*Of course* you're one of them; why, even your accent* makes you stand out!"

Then he started to curse and swear up and down, saying "I don't know the fellow," and just then a rooster crowed.

And Peter remembered the words in which Jesus had said, "Before the cock crows you'll say you don't know me three times." And he went outside and cried stinging tears.

27

When it was daylight, all the high priests and elders of the people had a meeting about Jesus and putting him to death. And after tying him up they led him away and gave him over to Pilate the governor.

Then Judas the betrayer, seeing that Jesus had been sentenced, had a change of heart and brought the thirty silverpieces back to the high priests and elders, saying, "I was wrong to betray innocent blood."

But they said, "What's that to us? That's your problem." And he hurled the silverpieces into the temple and stalked out and went off and hanged himself. And the high priests, picking up the silverpieces, said: "It isn't permissible to put this money in the temple coffers, because it's blood-money." So after talking it over they used the money to buy Potter's Field as a burial-place for strangers. (Which is why that field is known as Blood Field to this day. Thus the words of Jeremiah the prophet were fulfilled: "And they took the thirty silverpieces, the price of the prized one whom they had priced, from the sons of Israel, and gave it for the potter's field, as the Lord ordered me.")

Meanwhile Jesus stood in front of the governor, and the governor asked him: "So you're the king of the Jews?"

And Jesus said, "That's what *you* say." And he answered nothing to the

---

* Peter's Galilean accent is as conspicuous in Jerusalem as a Memphis accent would be in New York City.

denunciations by the high priests and elders.

Then Pilate says to him, "Don't you hear all the things they testify against you?" And he didn't answer him so much as a single word, which surprised the governor very much.

Now at festival time the governor was accustomed to release a prisoner to the crowd, whoever they wanted. At that time they were holding one well-known prisoner named Barabbas. So when they gathered, Pilate said to them, "Who do you want me to release to you: Barabbas? or Jesus, the so-called Anointed?" You see, he knew that they had betrayed him out of envy.

And as he sat on the podium his wife sent word to him saying, "Have nothing to do with that innocent man. I dreamt last night that I suffered horribly because of him."

Now the high priests and the elders had persuaded the crowds to ask for Barabbas and have Jesus be killed. So the governor said to them: "Which of the two do you want me to release to you?" and they said, "Barabbas." Pilate says to them, "Then what do I do with Jesus the so-called Anointed?"

They all said, "Crucify him."

And he said, "But what did he do wrong?"

But they shouted all the louder, "Crucify him."

Pilate, seeing that nothing helped and they only made more and more noise, took water and washed his hands in front of the crowd, saying, "I am innocent of this man's blood, see to it yourselves."

And the whole crowd answered, "Let his blood be on us and our children."

Then he released Barabbas to them, while Jesus he flogged and handed over to them to be crucified.

Then the governor's soldiers took Jesus into the governor's mansion and got the whole platoon together. And they took off his clothes and dressed him in a cloak of royal purple, and wove a crown of thorns and put it on his head, with a stick of cane in his right hand, and they had some fun with him, kneeling before him and saying, "Hail, king of the Jews!" and then spitting in his face and taking the cane and hitting him on the head with it. And when they'd had their fun with him, they took the cloak off and put his clothes back on and led him away to crucify him.

As they came out they found a Cyrenean man named Simon, whom they dragooned into carrying the cross.

And coming out to the place called Golgotha, that is, Skull Place, they gave him wine to drink mixed with wormwood, and after tasting it he wouldn't drink it. And after crucifying him they raffled off his clothes by rolling dice, and sat there keeping an eye on him. And up above his head they put the written charge against him: THIS IS JESUS, THE KING OF THE JEWS.

Then two thieves were to be crucified with him, one on his right and one on his left. And as they passed by they cursed him, nodding in his direction and saying, "Destroyer of the temple who rebuilds it in three days, save yourself if you're the son of God, come down off the cross."

Likewise, the high priests, with the canon-lawyers and elders, made fun of him, saying, "He saved others, he can't save himself. He's the king of Israel, so let's see him come down off the cross and we'll believe in him. He has placed his trust in God, let God pull him out of this if he wants him. After all, he did say, 'I'm God's son.' "

And the thieves crucified with him insulted him along the same line.

Starting at noon, darkness came over the whole earth till three o'clock, then around three o'clock Jesus cried out with a loud voice: "Eli, Eli, lema sabachthani?" that is, "My God, my God, why did you abandon me?" *

Some of those standing there heard that and said, "He's calling Elijah." And one of them ran right over and took a sponge and filled it with strong wine and put it on the end of a stick so he could drink from it.

The others said, "Let's see if Elijah comes to save him." But Jesus cried out again with a loud voice and breathed his last.

And in that instant the curtain of the temple's inner sanctum was sheared in two from top to bottom.** And the earth shook, and the rocks were split, and the graves were opened, and many bodies of the sleeping saints arose, and leaving their graves, after his resurrection, went into the holy city and appeared to many.

But the Roman captain and those with him who were watching Jesus, seeing the tremors and other events, were frightened out of their wits and said, "He really *was* the son of God!"

There were many women there observing from afar, some of whom

* The first words of the 22nd Psalm.
** The Temple of Jerusalem rips its garments in horror at the blasphemy of Christ's murder.

had followed Jesus from Galilee to serve him; among those, Mary Magdalen, Mary the mother of James and Joseph, and the mother of the sons of Zebedee.

But when it got late, a rich person from Arimathea named Joseph came along, who himself had studied under Jesus. This person went to Pilate and asked for the body of Jesus, at which point Pilate ordered it given to him. And taking the body, Joseph wrapped it in a clean sheet and put it in the tomb that had been newly cut for him in the rock, and rolled a big stone against the door of the tomb and went away, leaving Mary Magdalen and the other Mary sitting there opposite the tomb.

Next morning—that's after Friday night—the high priests and the Pharisees assembled at Pilate's door to say, "Your excellency, we can remember how that fraud said while alive, 'I will rise up after three days.' So order the grave to be guarded till the third day, so his students don't come and steal him and say to the people, 'He came back from the dead!' and the fraud ends up worse than before."

Pilate said to them, "You have custody. Go out and guard the grave until you know for sure."

So they went on their way and stationed a guard around the grave and marked the stone with their sign: IN CUSTODY.

28

Late Saturday night, as it was glimmering toward the first day of the week, came Mary Magdalen and the other Mary to watch the grave. And all of a sudden there was a giant rumbling: it was a messenger of the Lord coming down from the sky, stepping forward, and rolling away the stone, upon which he then sat down. His appearance was like lightning and his clothing white as snow. What with the fear, those watching were shaking all over and as good as dead. Reacting to that, the messenger said to the women: "Don't be afraid, I know you're looking for Jesus who was crucified. He isn't here, he came back just as he said. Look, here's the place where he was lying. So quick, go off and tell his students that he came back from the dead. And remember, he's going on ahead of you to Galilee, where you will see him. Remember I said that to you."

And going away from the tomb quickly, with great fear and great joy, they ran to tell his students. And next thing Jesus himself was there to meet them and said, "Hello!" And they went up and fell at his feet and bowed before him. Then Jesus says to them, "Don't be afraid: Go tell my brothers to go on to Galilee; they'll see me there."

When they had departed, the next thing was, the soldiers went into town and told the high priests everything that happened. And after getting together with the elders and having a meeting, they gave a hefty sum to the soldiers and said, "Say that his students came by night and stole him while you were sleeping. And if word of this reaches the governor, we'll talk to him and make sure you aren't punished." They took the money and did as they were instructed, and that story has been spread among the Jews even to this day.

But the eleven students went on to Galilee, to the mountain Jesus named, and saw him and bowed before him, though some were hesitant. And Jesus came forward and spoke to them, saying, "All authority in the sky and on the earth is given to me. So go out and teach all nations, bathing them in the name of the Father, the son, and the holy spirit, and teaching them to keep everything I commanded you. And do you see? I am with you, every day until the culmination of time."

The Good Word According to

Mark

1

Beginning of the good word of Jesus the Anointed, Son of God. As is written in Isaiah the prophet—

> *Look, I am sending my messenger before your face,*
> *Who will prepare your road,*
> *The voice of a crier in the desert:*
> *"Make the Lord's road ready,*
> *Straighten his paths"*—

so John came along, bathing others in the wilderness and announcing the washing of a changed heart for the forgiveness of wrongs. And all the country of Judea was coming out to see him, and all the people of Jerusalem too, and were being bathed by him in the Jordan River, admitting their mistakes. And John was dressed in camel hair and a leather belt about his waist, and eating locusts and wild honey.

And he was proclaiming, "After me comes someone so much stronger than me, I am not great enough to bend over and untie the thongs of his sandals. I bathed you in water, but he will bathe you in holy breath."

And it happened in those days that Jesus came from Nazareth, Galilee, and was bathed in the Jordan by John. And coming straight out of the water he saw the skies split apart and the breath like a dove coming down upon him. And a voice came out of the skies: "You are my son, my beloved son in whom I am delighted."

And directly the spirit drove him out into the wilderness. And he was in the wilderness for forty days being tested by Satan, and he was there among the wild beasts, and heavenly messengers were taking care of him.

But after John was handed over to the authorities, Jesus went to Galilee, proclaiming the good word of God and saying, "The time has come and the kingdom of God is approaching. Repent and trust in the good word."

And going along by the sea of Galilee he saw Simon and Simon's brother Andrew casting their nets into the sea, since they were fishermen. And Jesus said to them, "Come along behind me and I'll make you fishers of humanity." And they put their nets right down and followed him. And going on a little ways he saw James the son of Zebedee and John his brother, both of them in the boat mending their nets. And right away he called to them, and they left their father Zebedee in the boat with the hired hands and followed after him.

And they travel on to Capharnaum. And on the very next Sabbath he went into the synagogue and started teaching. And they were amazed at his teaching, because he was teaching them as if on his own authority, not like their canon-lawyers.

And right there in the synagogue was a fellow with an unclean spirit, and he started shouting, "What have we done to you, Jesus of Nazareth? Did you come to wipe us out? I know who you are, holy man of God!"

And Jesus yelled at him, saying, "Shut up and come out of him." And the unclean spirit, after convulsing him and crying with a loud voice, came out of him.

And everyone was so amazed that they started saying to each other: "What's this? New teaching on his own authority, and then he gives orders to unclean spirits and they obey him!" And word of him immediately went out everywhere, across the whole countryside of Galilee.

And as soon as they came out of the synagogue they went to Simon and Andrew's house with James and John. Now Simon's mother-in-law was in bed with a fever, and they immediately told him about her. And he went in and got her up, taking her by the hand, and the fever left her, and she was at their service.

When it got late and the sun was down they brought him all the people in bad health, and those with demons, and the whole town was gathered by the door. And he healed many people in bad health with various diseases, and threw out many demons, and didn't let the demons talk, because they knew who he was.

And getting up in the early hours of darkness he went outside and went off to a deserted place and prayed there. And Simon and those with him tracked him down and found him. And they say to him, "They're all looking for you."

And he says to them, "Let's go on to another place, into the next villages, so I can proclaim there too, because that's what I came for."

And he came through all of Galilee, proclaiming in their synagogues and throwing out demons. And a leper comes to him, pleading with him and begging on his knees, saying, "If you want to, you can heal me."

And feeling sorry for him, he reached out his hand and touched him and said to him, "I do want to: be healed." And the leprosy went right out of him and he was healed. And Jesus sent him right off, thundering at him and saying, "Careful, say nothing to anyone, just go show yourself to the priest and bring the offering specified by Moses for a purification, as a testimony to them." But he went out and began to proclaim it up and down and spread the word, to the point where he couldn't go openly into town anymore. Instead he stayed out in deserted places, and they came to him from everywhere.

2

And going back to Capharnaum, for days the word went round that he was in that house. And so many gathered together that they couldn't get close to the door, and he was speaking the word to them. And they came bringing him a paralyzed man, carried by four men. And when they couldn't bring him closer to him because of the crowd, they took off the roof over where he was and reached through and let down the cot on which the paralyzed man was lying. And Jesus, seeing their faith, says to the paralyzed man, "Son, your wrongdoing is forgiven."

Now some of the canon-lawyers were sitting there, thinking in their hearts, "Why does this guy talk like that? That's blasphemy! Who can forgive wrongs but God alone?"

And Jesus, immediately sensing in his spirit that they were thinking that way among themselves, says to them, "Why are you thinking those thoughts in your hearts? Which is easier: to say to the paralyzed man, 'Your wrongdoing is forgiven,' or to say, 'Get up and take your cot and walk away'? But so you may see that the son of humanity has authority to forgive wrongs on earth"—he says to the paralyzed man, "I tell you, get up and take your cot and go home."

And he got up and took his cot and went away, in front of everyone, so that everyone was beside themselves and praised God, saying, "We never saw anything like that!"

And he went out by the sea again, and all the crowd was coming toward him, and he was teaching them. And going on he saw Levi the son of Alpheus, sitting at the toll-station, and he says to him, "Follow me," and he stood up and followed him.

And he happened to be sitting down to dinner in his house, and a lot of tax-collectors and godless people were sitting with Jesus and his students—since there were many such that followed him—and the canon-lawyers of the Pharisees, seeing that he ate with godless people and tax-collectors, said to his students, "Tax-collectors and godless people, that's who he eats with?"

And Jesus, hearing that, says to them, "It's not the healthy who need a doctor, it's the sick. I didn't come to call the saints, I came to call the godless people."

And the students of John and the Pharisees were always fasting, and they come and say to him, "Why is it the students of John and the students of the Pharisees fast, but the students you have don't fast?"

And Jesus said to them, "The wedding party can't be fasting while the bridegroom is with them, can they? No, as long as they have the bridegroom with them, they cannot fast. There will come days when the bridegroom will be taken away from them, and then they can fast on that day.

"No one puts a patch of brand-new cloth on an old cloak, because if they do, the new takes away the completeness of the old, and a worse split results. And no one puts new wine into old wineskins, because if they do, the wine bursts the skins, and both wine and skins are lost. Instead, they put new wine in new skins."

And it happened one Sabbath that he was traveling through the grain fields, and his students started making a path for him by breaking off ears of corn. And the Pharisees said to him: "Look at that: why are they doing what isn't allowed on the Sabbath?"

And he says to them, "Didn't you ever read what David did when he was in need and starving, himself and those with him, how he went into the house of God under the high priest Abiathar and ate the sacrificial loaves, which no one was allowed to eat but the priests, and gave them to those with him?" And he said to them, "The Sabbath was made for humanity, not humanity for the Sabbath, so that the son of humanity is superior to the Sabbath."

3

And he went into the synagogue another time, and there was a fellow there with a withered hand. And they were watching him to see if he was going to heal on the Sabbath, so they could charge him with something. And he says to the fellow with the withered hand, "Come in the middle here." And he says to them, "Which is allowed on the Sabbath: doing good, or doing evil? Saving lives, or killing?" They were silent. And looking round at them in a fury, griefstricken at the stoniness of their hearts, he says to the fellow, "Reach out your hand." And he reached out, and his hand was restored. And the Pharisees, with Herod's men, went right out and had a meeting about him and how to get rid of him.

And Jesus retreated with his students toward the sea, and a great crowd followed from Galilee; and from Judea, Jerusalem, and beyond the Jordan, and round about Tyre and Sidon, a great crowd came toward him, hearing the things he'd done.

And he told his students to have a boat ready for him so they wouldn't crush him. Indeed, he cured many, to the point where everyone who suffered from some scourge was mobbing him, trying to touch him. And the unclean spirits, when they sighted him, fell down before him and cried out loud, "You're the son of God!" And over and over he warned them not to make him famous.

And he goes up the mountain and calls the ones he wanted to him, and they went to him. And he settled on twelve of them to be with him, and to be sent out by him to spread the word, and to have authority to throw out demons. And he gave Simon the name "Rock" ["Peter"]; and he gave James the son of Zebedee and his brother John the name Boanerges, which means "the Thunder Brothers"; plus Andrew, Philip, Bartholomew, Matthew, Thomas, James son of Alpheus, Thaddeus, Simon the Canaanite, and Judas Iscariot, who betrayed him.

And he comes back home, and the crowd gathers again, to the point where they couldn't even eat a meal. Hearing of that, his folks came out [from Nazareth] intending to take him away, saying, "He's gone mad!"

And the canon-lawyers came down from Jerusalem and said, "He serves Beelzebub and has the authority of the demon king to throw out demons."

And calling them together, he spoke to them in metaphors: "How can

Satan throw out Satan? If a country is split in opposition to itself, that country can't stand up; and if a house is split in opposition to itself, that house won't be able to stand up. And if Satan rebels against himself and becomes divided, he can't stand up, that's the end of him. But then, no one can go into a strong man's house and grab his things without first tying up the strong man; only then can he plunder his house.

"I assure you, the sons of humanity will be forgiven for many misdeeds and whatever blasphemies they may have blasphemed. But whoever blasphemes against the sacred breath will find no forgiveness in all eternity; no, he's guilty of eternal sin."

That was because they said, "He has an unclean spirit."

And his mother comes, and his brothers and sisters, and, standing outside, they sent word to him, calling for him. And a crowd was seated around him, and they say to him: "You know, your mother and your brothers and sisters are outside looking for you."

And he answered, "Who *is* my mother and my sisters and my brothers?" And looking round at those sitting in a circle around him, he says, "Look, here's my mother and my brothers and sisters: whoever does the will of God, that's who my brother and sister and mother is."

4

And again he started teaching by the sea. And such a gigantic crowd comes toward him that he had to get into a boat and sit on the waters, with all the crowd by the sea along the shore. And he started teaching them many things in metaphors and said to them in the course of his teaching:

"Listen: once there was a sower who went out sowing. And it happened in the course of his sowing that some of it fell by the roadside, and the birds came and ate it up. And some fell on the rocky ground where there wasn't much soil, and it sprang right up, there being no depth to the soil. And when the sun came up it got scorched and dried out, not having any roots. And some fell into the thorns, and the thorns came up and choked it off, and it bore no fruit. And some fell on good soil and sprang up and grew and bore fruit, here thirty, there sixty, and there a hundred." And he said, "Those with ears to hear, hear!"

And when they were by themselves, those around him, along with the twelve, asked him about the metaphors. And he said to them, "To you the mystery of the kingdom of God is given, but to those people outside it is all done in metaphors,

> *so that when they look, they look, but do not see;*
> *and when they hear, they hear but do not understand;*
> *lest they should come back, and it should be forgiven them."*

And he says to them, "If you don't get this metaphor, how will you get any of them? The sower sows the word. And some of these people are the ones by the wayside: where the word is sown, as soon as they hear it, Satan comes, and takes away the word that was sown. And some of them are the ones sown on the rocky ground: when they hear the word, right away they joyfully seize it, and yet it has no root in them, it's only temporary, so that if there's pressure or persecution because of the word, they fall right down. And others are the ones sown into the thorns: they hear the word, and then the worries of the day and the strategy of moneymaking and the concerns of the future come in and choke off the word, and it becomes unable to bear fruit. And still others are the ones sown on good soil, who hear the word and take it in and bear fruit, here thirty, there sixty, and there a hundred."

And he said to them, "The candle isn't there to be covered with a big basket or put under the bed, is it? Isn't it there to be put up on a tall candlestick? After all, things are hidden only to be revealed, and made secret only to be brought to light. If any have ears to hear, let them hear!" And he said to them, "Watch and listen: by the same measure that you have measured, things will be measured out and put before you. In fact, he who has will be given more, while he who has nothing, even what he has will be taken away from him."

And he said, "The kingdom of God is like a person throwing seeds on the ground, and going to sleep and getting up, by night and by day, while the seed germinates and grows without his knowing it. The earth bears fruit by itself: the first shoots, then the ear, then the grain in the ear. But when it gives ripened grain, he sends the thresher right out, because it's harvest-time."

And he said, "How shall we describe the kingdom of God, or what shall we compare it to? Perhaps to a seed of the mustard plant, which, when it's scattered upon the earth, is the smallest of all the seeds in the world; and yet when it's sown, it comes up and grows bigger than all the vegetables and puts out branches big enough for the birds of the air to be able to camp in its shadow."

And he kept speaking the word to them in metaphors, according as they could hear, and he said nothing to them without metaphors, but privately to his own students he always gave the key.

And he says to them on that day, with evening falling, "Let's go on across." And leaving the crowd behind, they take him along; so that he was in the boat and other boats were with him. And a giant windstorm comes up, and it was hurling the waves into the boat, till the boat was already filling up. And he was in the stern sleeping on a seat-cushion, and they wake him up, saying, "Teacher, you don't care if we get killed?"

And standing up tall he yelled at the wind and told the sea, "Quiet, hush your mouth," and the wind cut down and there was a great calm. And he said to them, "Why are you such cowards? Don't you have any faith?"

And they were as scared as scared could be and said to each other: "Who *is* this guy, that even the wind and the sea obey him?"

5

And they went across the sea to the land of the Gerasenes. And as soon as he got out of the boat he was accosted by a fellow with an unclean spirit, coming from the graveyard, who lived among the gravestones, and no one yet had been able to restrain him, even with chains, because every time he was chained and shackled hand and foot, he burst the chains and wore away the shackles, so no one was strong enough to control him. And all the time, night and day, he was there among the gravestones or in the hills, screaming and pounding himself with rocks.

And seeing Jesus from a distance he ran and bowed before him, shouting loudly, "What have I done to you, Jesus son of God the highest? For the love of God, don't torture me"—because he was about to say, "Unclean spirit, go out of this person."

And he asked him, "What is your name?"

And he answered, "My name is Legion: there's many of us." And he pleaded with him over and over not to send them out of the country.

Now there by the mountain there was a big herd of pigs grazing. And they pleaded with him, saying, "Send us to the pigs, let us go into them." And he let them, and the unclean spirits came out and went into the pigs, and the herd of them rushed over the edge of the cliff and into the sea, some two thousand of them, and drowned in the waters.

And their keepers fled and spread the news in town and from field to field, and they came to see what the matter was, and as they come toward Jesus they find the possessed man fully clothed and in his right mind, the one who had the Legion, and they were frightened. And those who saw it explained what happened to the possessed man, and about the pigs. And they started begging him to go away from their neighborhood.

And when he got in the boat, the formerly possessed man begged to go along with him. But he wouldn't allow it, saying instead, "Go home to your own and report to them what the Lord did for you and what mercy he had on you." And he went off and started proclaiming in the Decapolis what Jesus had done for him, and all were amazed.

And when Jesus crossed to the other side again in the boat, a giant crowd gathered toward him, there by the sea. And one of the chief priests of the synagogue, Jairus by name, comes along and when he sees Jesus falls at his feet and begs him over and over, saying, "My daughter's on her deathbed, come and put your hands on her so that she'll be healed and live." And he went with him, and a great crowd followed, pressing him hard.

And a woman who had been hemorrhaging twelve years and who had been treated all sorts of ways by various doctors, spending all she had and getting no relief, indeed, always getting worse, hearing about Jesus, came from behind him through the crowd and touched his cloak, saying to herself, "If I just touch his cloak, I'm saved." And her hemorrhaging dried right up at the source, and she could feel in her body that she was healed from the scourge.

And Jesus, immediately sensing the force being drawn out of him, turned to the crowd and said, "Who touched my cloak?"

And his students said to him, "You see this crowd pressing in from every side? And you say, 'Who touched me'?" And he looked round to see who did it.

So the woman, scared and trembling, knowing what had happened to her, came and fell down in front of him and told him the whole truth. And he said to her, "Daughter, your trust has saved you. Go in peace and be healed of your scourge."

Even as he spoke, they come from the chief priest's house and say, "Your daughter's dead, why are you still bothering the Master?"

But Jesus, overhearing the words spoken, says to the chief priest: "Don't be afraid, just believe." And he allowed no one to follow him but Peter and James and John, James's brother.

And they come into the chief priest's house, and he sees a great pandemonium of weeping and wailing, and comes in and says to them, "Why are you crying and making noise? The child didn't die, she's sleeping." And they were laughing at him. But he, after throwing everybody out, takes along the child's father and mother and those with him and proceeds to the place where the child was. And he takes her hand and says to her, "Talitha kum," which translates as, "Young girl, I tell you, get up." And the girl stood right up and started walking around; after all, she was twelve years old. And they were seized by a great ecstasy. And he commanded them repeatedly that no one should know of this, and said to give her something to eat.

6

And he went away from there; and he comes back to his home town, and his students follow him. And when the Sabbath came round he started teaching in the synagogue, and many people hearing him were stunned and said, "Where does he get all this? What is this wisdom given to him, how can wonders like these be worked through his hands? Isn't this the carpenter, Mary's son and the brother of James, Joseth, Jude, and Simon? And aren't his sisters all here with us?" And they were offended by him.

And Jesus said to them, "A prophet is never dishonored if not in his home town, among his relatives, and in his own house." And he couldn't work any wonders there, except for a few sick people whom he cured by laying his hands on them. And he was amazed at their lack of faith. And he journeyed on, teaching in the villages all around.

And he called the twelve together and started sending them out two by two and giving them authority over the unclean spirits, and he ordered them to take nothing on the road but a walking-stick: "no bread, no knapsack, no coins under your belt, just with sandals under your feet, and don't put on two tunics." And he said to them, "Whatever house you go into, stay there till you leave that place. And whatever place doesn't receive you or listen to you, when you go away from there, shake the dust from underneath your shoes as a testimony to them." And they went out and called on the people to have a change of heart, and threw out many demons and anointed many sick people with oil and cured them.

And King Herod [Antipas] heard of him, since his name became known, and they said John the Baptist had risen from the dead and that's why these powers work in him. Others said, "It's Elijah"; others, that he was a prophet like one of the prophets. Herod, after listening to them, said, "The one I beheaded, John, that's who has come back from the dead."

(You see, Herod himself had sent his men out and seized John and confined him in jail on account of Herodias his brother Philip's wife, whom he married, because John had told Herod, "You aren't allowed to have your brother's wife." So Herodias had it in for him and wanted to kill him, but couldn't: Herod, it seems, was afraid of John, knowing him to be an innocent and holy man, and so he kept him there, and was often perplexed hearing the many things he said, but liked listening to him.

So when the opportune day came round, when Herod, for his birthday, gave a dinner for his princes and tribunes and the most important men of Galilee, and the daughter of Herodias came in and pleased Herod and the guests with her dancing, the king said to the girl, "Ask me whatever you want, and I'll give it to you." And he swore up and down, "Whatever you ask I'll give you, even half my kingdom."

So she went out and said to her mother, "What shall I ask for?"

And she said, "The head of John the Baptist!"

And she came right back in and hastened to the king and asked, "I want you to give me the head of John the Baptist on a tray right now." And the king, most unhappy, didn't want to refuse her because of his oaths and the guests there. So the king sent his guard right out and ordered him to bring the head. And he went off and beheaded him in jail and brought his head on a tray and gave it to the girl, and the girl gave it to her mother. And when his students heard about it they came and took his body away and put it in a tomb.)

And the apostles got together with Jesus, and they reported to him all they'd done and what they had been teaching. And he says to them, "Come along by yourselves to some deserted place and rest a little," because there were many people coming and going, and they couldn't even find time to eat.

And they went off in a boat to a deserted place by themselves. But people saw them going, and many people figured it out and ran there on foot, coming from all different towns, and got there ahead of them.

And as he got out he saw a great crowd, and he felt sorry for them, because they were like sheep that had no shepherd, and he began to teach them many things.

And when many hours had already passed, his students came up to him and said, "This place is in the middle of nowhere and the hour is already late. Let them go, so they can go into the fields and villages around here and buy themselves something to eat."

He answered, "Give them something to eat yourselves."

And they say to him, "You want us to go buy two hundred drachmas' worth of bread and give it to them to eat?"

And he said to them, "How much bread do you have? Go see."

And having found out, they say, "Five loaves, plus two fish." And he told them to sit down, group by group, on the green grass. And they sat down, plot by plot, by hundreds and by fifties. And taking the five loaves and the two fish and looking up to the sky, he blessed and broke the loaves and gave them to his students to hand out to them, and he divided the two fish among them all. And they all ate and had their fill, and they cleared away twelve basketfuls of breadscraps and fish. And those eating were five thousand men.

And next he made his students get in the boat and go on across to Bethesda, until he dismissed the crowd. And after taking leave of them he went up the mountain to pray. And when it got late the boat was in the middle of the sea, and he was alone on land. And seeing that they were having a rough time crossing, because the wind was against them, around the fourth watch of the night he comes toward them walking on the sea and was going to join them. But when they saw him walking on the sea they thought it was a ghost and screamed, because they all saw him and were in consternation. And he spoke right up and said to them: "Courage, it's me, don't be afraid." And he got into the boat with them, and the wind cut down. And they were completely beside themselves, because they didn't understand about the loaves, their hearts were too stony.

And crossing over to the shore they came to Gennesareth and cast anchor. And as soon as they got out of the boat the people, recognizing him, went out all around that country and started bringing sick people on stretchers to the place where they heard he was. And wherever he was traveling into the villages or towns or fields, they set the sick down in the marketplace and begged him to let them touch even just the edge of his cloak, and those who touched it were healed.

7

And the Pharisees and some of the canon-lawyers come from Jerusalem and assemble in his presence. And seeing some of his students and how they ate their bread with dirty (that is, unwashed) hands—you see, the Pharisees and all the Jews, preserving the tradition of the elders, never eat without washing their hands up to the elbow and never eat what they got at market without washing up; and there is much more that has been handed down to them to keep about washing glasses and pots and copper pans and beds—so the Pharisees and canon-lawyers asked him, "How come your students don't walk according to the tradition of the elders, but rather eat their bread with dirty hands?"

He said to them, "Isaiah prophesied very well about you fakes. As it says,

> *These people honor me with their lips,*
> *But their heart is far away from me.*
> *Pointlessly they worship me,*
> *Teaching as their doctrine the commandments of the world.*

"Leaving aside the commandment of God, you keep the tradition of the world." And he said to them, "You're very good at setting aside the commandment of God to establish your own tradition. After all, Moses said, 'Do right by your father and your mother' and 'Let whoever denounces father or mother end in death.'

"But *you* say, if a person says to his father or mother, 'I'm making a gift (that is, a religious contribution) of whatever you might have gotten from me,' you won't let him do anything further for his father or his mother—thus nullifying the word of God in favor of the tradition you have handed down. And you do lots of things like that."

And calling the crowd toward him again he said to them, "All of you, hear me and understand: there is nothing outside a person that can befoul him going in; it's what comes *out* of a person that befouls him."

And when he had gone home, away from the crowd, his students asked him about that comparison. And he says, "Can you, even, be so uncomprehending? Don't you see that everything coming into a person from outside cannot befoul him because it doesn't go into his heart, but into his belly, and goes out from there into the toilet, purging all that is eaten? Whereas," he said, "what comes out of a person, *that* befouls that person; because from inside the heart come evil designs, whoring, thieving, murdering, adultery, greed, meanness, trickery, brutality, the evil eye, blasphemy, haughtiness, and foolishness. All those evils come from the inside out and befoul a person."

He arose from there and went into the area of Tyre. And going into a house, he didn't want to know anybody but couldn't escape notice. In fact, a woman who had heard about him, whose little daughter had an unclean spirit, came right in and fell at his feet. Now the woman was Greek, Syrophoenician by race, and she asked him to throw out the demon from her daughter. And he said to her, "First let the children eat their fill, because it isn't good to take the children's bread and throw it to the dogs."

But she answered, "Lord, even the dogs underneath the table get to eat of the children's scraps."

And he said to her, "In that case, go: the demon has gone out of your daughter." And when she went home she found her daughter lying in bed and the demon gone.

And going back out of the area of Tyre, he went through Sidon toward the sea of Galilee, down the middle of the Decapolis area. And they bring him a deaf mute and plead with him to put his hands on him. And taking him aside from the crowd, off by himself, he put his fingers in the other's ears, and spitting, took hold of his tongue, and looking up to heaven groaned and said to him, "Effatha," that is, "Open!" And his ears opened right up, and the restriction of his tongue was released and he could talk correctly.

And he commanded them to tell no one, but however much he commanded them, they only proclaimed it more and more. And they were amazed beyond measure and said, "How well he has done everything: he makes the deaf hear and the speechless speak!"

8

During those days, when again there was a great crowd without anything to eat, he calls his students to him and says to them, "I feel sorry for the crowd, because they've been staying with me for three days already and don't have anything to eat. And if I send them home hungry, they'll drop on the road, and some of them have come from far away."

And his students answered, "Where can anyone get bread to satisfy them here in the wilderness?"

And he asked them, "How many loaves do you have?"

They said, "Seven." And he ordered the crowd to sit down on the ground. And taking the seven loaves he gave thanks and broke them and gave them to his students to hand out, and they handed them out to the crowd. And they had a few small fish. And after blessing them he said to hand those out too. And they ate and had their fill, and they cleared away seven basketfuls of leftover scraps. (There were some four thousand people there.) Then he sent them off.

And getting right in the boat with his students he came to the area of Dalmanatha.

And the Pharisees came out and started arguing with him, asking him for a sign from the sky to test him out. And groaning in his spirit he says, "Why do these sorts ask me for a sign? I can tell you for sure whether a sign will be given to these sorts!" And leaving them behind he got in again and crossed to the other shore.

And they forgot to bring bread, and they didn't have even one loaf with them on the boat. And he commanded them, "Watch out, guard against the yeast of the Pharisees and the yeast of Herod." And they remarked to each other that they didn't *have* any bread. And knowing that, he says to them, "Why are you remarking that you have no bread? Do you still not see or understand? Do you have such stony hearts? Though you have eyes, you do not see, and though you have ears, you do not hear? And you don't remember, when I broke the five loaves for the five thousand, how many basketfuls of scraps you cleared away?"

They say to him, "Twelve."

"And when I broke the seven loaves for the four thousand, how many basketfuls of scraps you cleared away?"

And they say, "Seven."

And he said to them, "And you still don't understand?"

And they come to Bethesda. And they bring him a blind man and beg him to touch him. And taking the blind man's hand he brought him outside the village, and after spitting on his eyes and putting his hands on him he asked him, "Do you see anything?"

And looking up he said, "I see people . . . they look to me like trees walking around."

Again he put his hands on the man's eyes, and he looked again and was restored and saw everything perfectly clearly. And he sent him home, saying, "Don't go back into the village."

And Jesus and his students went out to the villages of Philip Caesarea. And on the way he asked his students, "Who do people say I am?"

And they said to him, "John the Baptist, or some say Elijah, or others say one of the prophets."

And he asked them, "And who do *you* say I am?"

Peter answered, "You are the Anointed." And he commanded them to tell no one about him.

And he began to instruct them that the son of humanity would have to undergo many things and be rejected by the elders and high priests and canon-lawyers, and be killed, and rise again after three days. And he said these words in front of everybody, but Peter, taking him aside, began to reproach him. So he, turning round and seeing his students, reproached Peter, saying, "Out of my sight, you Satan, because you're not thinking of God's concerns, you're thinking of human concerns."

And calling the crowd to him, together with his students, he said to them, "If anyone wants to follow after me, let him repudiate himself and pick up his cross and follow me, because whoever tries to save his life will lose it, and whoever loses his life for me and the good word will save it. After all, what does it help a person to gain the whole world and pay for it with his life? What could a person give in exchange for his life? Remember, whoever among this adulterous and sinful race is ashamed of me and my words, the son of humanity will be ashamed of them when he comes in the glory of his Father with his holy messengers."

9

And he said to them, "I tell you for sure, there are some among those standing here who will never taste death before they see the kingdom of God coming with all its power."

And six days later Jesus takes along Peter and James and John and brings them up a high mountain, alone by themselves, and he was transformed in front of them. And his clothes started shining whiter than white, in a way that no woolspinner on earth could ever whiten them.

And Elijah appeared to them with Moses, and they were talking with Jesus. And Peter reacted, saying to Jesus, "Master, it's good that we are here. Let us set up three tabernacles, one for you and one for Moses and one for Elijah." (In fact, he didn't know how to react, they were all so afraid.) And a cloud came up and overshadowed them, and there was a voice from the cloud: "This is my son, my beloved son: listen to him." And suddenly, looking round they no longer saw anyone, but only Jesus there with them.

And as they came down the mountain he commanded them not to relate what they saw to anyone until the son of humanity should arise from the dead. And they seized upon those words among themselves, debating what "arising from the dead" was.

And they asked him, "Why do the canon-lawyers say, 'First Elijah must come?' "

He said to them, "First Elijah is coming to restore everything. And what does it say about the son of humanity? That he must undergo many things and be treated like nothing. In fact, I tell you, Elijah has arrived, and they did with him whatever they liked, just as the scripture says concerning him."

And going to rejoin the other students they saw a great crowd around them, with canon-lawyers arguing with them. And right away the whole crowd, seeing him, was overwhelmed and ran up to greet him. And he asked them, "What are you arguing about with each other?"

And a voice from the crowd answered him, "Teacher, I brought my son to see you, stricken mute by a spirit: whenever it takes hold of him, it tears him apart, and he foams at the mouth and gnashes his teeth and becomes dehydrated. And I told your students to throw it out, but they couldn't."

He answered, "You unbelieving race, how long will I be with you? How long will I *put up* with you! Bring him here to me." And they brought him to him. And seeing him the spirit immediately convulsed him, and he fell and rolled on the ground, foaming at the mouth. And he asked his father, "How long has this been happening to him?"

He said, "Since childhood. And it keeps throwing him into the fire and into the water to destroy him. But if you can do something, have mercy on us and help us."

Jesus said to him, "As for whether I 'can do something,' everything is possible for the believer."

And right away the father of the child shouted, "I believe; help me in my lack of faith." Jesus, seeing that the crowd was rapidly surging toward him, yelled at the unclean spirit, "Spirit of muteness and deafness, I command you, go out of him and don't ever go into him again." And with a shout and many convulsions it came out of him. And he became like a corpse, and many people said, He's dead! But Jesus took his hand and pulled him up, and he stood up.

And as he was going home his students asked him privately, "Why couldn't we throw it out?"

And he said to them, "That kind of spirit can't be thrown out by any means but prayer."

And going on from there, they were traveling through Galilee, but he didn't want anyone to know, because he was teaching his students and telling them that the son of humanity would be betrayed into the hands of the world, and they would kill him, and he would rise again three days after being killed. But they didn't get what he was saying and were afraid to ask him.

And they came to Capharnaum. And when he got indoors he asked them, "What were you discussing on the way?" They were silent, because on the way they had been talking among themselves about who was bigger than who. And he sat down and called the twelve and said to them, "If anyone wants to be number one, be the lowest of all and everybody's servant." And taking a child he stood him in their midst and embraced him and said to them, "Whoever receives one of these children in my name receives me, and whoever receives me, receives not me but the one who sent me."

John said to him, "Teacher, we saw someone throwing out demons in your name and told him not to, because he wasn't one of our followers."

But Jesus said, "Don't tell him not to, because no one who works a wonder in my name can speak evil of me soon after: who isn't against us is for us.

"Remember, whoever gives you a glass of water on the grounds that you belong to the Anointed, I assure you that they will not forfeit their reward.

"And whoever trips up one of these little ones who believe in me, better for them to have a giant millstone hung around their neck and be thrown into the sea. And if your hand gets in your way, cut it off; you're lucky if you enter maimed into Life and aren't thrown with both hands into Gehenna, the inextinguishable fire.

"And if your foot gets in your way, cut it off; you're lucky if you enter crippled into Life and aren't thrown with both feet into Gehenna.

"And if your eye gets in your way, pull it out; you're lucky if you enter one-eyed into the kingdom of God and aren't thrown with two eyes into Gehenna, where the worm never dies and the fire is never put out.

"Everything is seasoned by fire, and seasoning is good. But if the seasoning loses its seasoning, what can you cook it in? So have your seasoning within you and make peace with each other."

10

And arising from there he goes into the area of Judea across the Jordan, and again the crowds assemble before him, and as usual he was teaching them again.

And some Pharisees came up and asked him if a man was allowed to break off with his wife, testing him out. He answered, "What did Moses command you?"

They said, "Moses permitted writing a divorce decree and untying the knot."

Jesus said, "Moses wrote that command in view of the hardness of your hearts. But from the beginning of creation, *male and female he made them, for which reason a man shall leave his father and his mother behind and stick to his wife. And the two shall become one living thing,* so that they aren't two any more, but one living thing. So what God joined, let no person divide."

Back at the house his students asked him about that. And he says to them, "Anyone who breaks off with his wife and marries another is committing adultery against her, and if she divorces her husband and marries another, she's living in adultery."

And they brought him some children so that he could touch them, but his students yelled at them. Jesus was outraged to see that and said to them, "Let the children come to me, don't prevent them, because the kingdom of God belongs to such as these. I assure you, anyone who doesn't receive the kingdom of God like a little child, will never get into it." And he hugged them and blessed them, putting his hands on them.

And as he went on his way someone ran up to him and knelt before him and asked him, "Good teacher, what shall I do to inherit everlasting life?"

Jesus said to him, "Why do you call me good? No one is good, only God. You know the commandments: *You are not to murder, you are not to commit adultery, you are not to steal, you are not to perjure yourself, you are not to defraud, do right by your father and your mother.*"

And he said to him, "Teacher, I have kept all those things since infancy."

Jesus, looking at him, felt love for him and said, "One thing is holding you back: go, sell what you have and give it to the poor, and you will have a treasure in the sky, and come here and follow me." At those words his face fell and he went off in mourning, because he was the owner of many possessions.

And looking around, Jesus says to his students, "How hard it will be for those with money to enter the kingdom of God!" His students were amazed at those words. And Jesus continued, saying again to them, "Children, how hard it is to enter the kingdom of God: it's easier for a camel to squeeze through the eye of a needle than for a rich man to enter the kingdom of God."

They were even more stunned and said to each other, "And who *can* be saved?"

Looking straight at them, Jesus says, "For human beings it's impossible, but not for God: everything is possible for God."

And Peter began speaking to him: "Look at us, we have left everything and followed you."

Said Jesus, "I assure you, no one who has left house or brothers or sisters or mother or father or children or land behind for me and the good word will fail to get back a hundredfold in this time now his houses and brothers and sisters and mothers and children and land, with persecution, and everlasting life in the time to come.* And many of the first will be last and many of the last will be first."

---

* This is one of very few passages in the Gospels that imply that Christians will prosper in this life as well as the next, and even these words are too obscure and contradictory to be interpreted decisively in that direction or any other. What does it mean to get your mother back a hundredfold? If it means joining the family of Christians, then couldn't getting your house back mean something equally figurative, such as amassing spiritual riches? And would it be a blessing anyway to get your house back "with persecution"? Could that even mean "persecution by the houseful"?

They were now on the road going up to Jerusalem, and Jesus was leading them on; and they were overwhelmed, and those following were frightened, and taking the twelve aside again he started telling them what was going to happen to him: "Here we go up to Jerusalem, and the son of humanity will be handed over to the high priests and canon-lawyers, and they will condemn him to death and hand him over to the people, and they will make fun of him and spit at him and whip him and kill him, and after three days he will rise again."

And James and John the sons of Zebedee come up to him saying, "Teacher, we want you to do for us what we ask of you."

He said to them, "What do you want me to do for you?"

They said to him, "Grant us that we may sit one on your right and one on your left in your glory."

Jesus said to them, "You don't know what you're asking. Can you drink the cup I drink, or bathe in the bath I am bathed in?"

They said, "We can."

And Jesus said to them, "You will drink the cup I drink and bathe in the bath I am bathed in, but as for sitting on my right or my left, that's not mine to give, it's for whom it has been prepared for."

And when the other ten heard, they were outraged about James and John. And calling them together Jesus says to them, "You know how those who are esteemed the rulers of nations lord it over them, and how big men use their power. Among you it isn't going to be like that: whoever wants to be great among you is to be your servant, and anyone who wants to be number one is to be everyone's slave; because the son of humanity also did not come to be served, but to serve and give his life as a ransom for many."

And they come to Jericho. And as he went out of Jericho with his students and a considerable crowd, Bartimeus the son of Timeus, a blind beggar, was sitting by the roadside. And hearing that Jesus of Nazareth was there he started shouting, "Jesus son of David, have mercy on me." And a lot of people were yelling at him to be quiet, but he only shouted all the more, "Son of David, have mercy on me."

And Jesus stopped and said, "Call him."

So they call to the blind man, saying, "Courage, get up, he's calling you!"

And he, throwing off his cloak, sprang to his feet and went toward Jesus. And Jesus said in answer to him, "What do you want me to do for you?"

The blind man said to him, "Master, let me see again."

And Jesus said to him, "Go, your faith has saved you." And immediately he could see again and followed him on the road.

11

And as they approach Jerusalem, Bethphage, and Bethany by Mount Olive, he sends two of his students off, saying to them: "Go into the village across from you, and as soon as you get there you'll find a young donkey tied up, on which no person has ever sat; untie it and bring it. And if anyone says to you, 'Why are you doing that?' say, 'The master needs it,' and they'll send it right back here with you."

And they went and found a young donkey tied outside a door at the intersection, and they untie it. And some of the people standing there said to them, "What are you doing untying the donkey?" But they said what Jesus told them to, and they let them alone. And they bring the donkey to Jesus and throw their cloaks upon it, and he sat down upon it. And many people spread their cloaks on the road, and others cut branches from the fields, and those leading and those following shouted:

> *Hooray! Bless him who comes in the name of the Lord.*
> *Bless the coming kingdom of our father David!*
> *Hooray to the highest heavens!*

And he entered Jerusalem as far as the temple and looking round at everything—the hour being already late—he went out to Bethany with the twelve.

And the next day as they came out of Bethany he got hungry. And spotting a leafy fig tree from a distance, he came to see if in fact he could find anything on it, but when he got to it he found nothing but leaves, because it wasn't fig season. And in response he said to it, "Never again shall anyone eat your fruit," and his students were listening to him.

And they come into Jerusalem. And he went into the temple and started throwing out the sellers and buyers in the temple, and he upended the tables of the money-changers and the chairs of the pigeon-sellers. And he wouldn't let anyone transport goods through the temple. And he started teaching, saying to them, "Doesn't it say,

My house shall be called a house of prayer for all nations?

You have made it a den of robbers."

And the chief priests and canon-lawyers heard that and were looking for a way to get rid of him. The thing was, they were afraid of him, because all the crowd was amazed at his teaching.

And when it got late, they traveled back outside the city.

And in the morning, traveling along they saw the fig tree withered to its roots. And Peter, remembering, says to him, "Master, look, the fig tree you cursed has withered away."

And Jesus answered them, "Have faith in God. I assure you that whoever says to this mountain, 'Get up and throw yourself in the sea,' and doesn't waver in his heart but believes that what he says will happen, it will come true for him. Therefore I tell you, everything you pray for and ask for, believe that you'll get it, and it will come true for you. And when you stand praying, forgive anything you may have against anyone so that your Father in the skies may also forgive your transgressions."

And they come back into Jerusalem, and as he was walking around in the temple the high priests and canon-lawyers and elders come toward him and said to him, "What authority do you have to do this? Who gave you any authority to do this?"

Jesus said to them, "I'm going to ask you one question, and when you answer me I'll also tell you what authority I have to do this: Did the washing of John come from heaven or from the world? Answer me."

And they discussed that among themselves, saying, "If we say from heaven, he'll say, 'Then why didn't you believe him?' But if we say from the world"—they were afraid of the crowd, because everyone considered that John was truly a prophet. And they answered Jesus saying, "We don't know."

And Jesus says to them, "I'm not telling you what authority I have to do this either."

12

And he started talking to them in metaphors: "Once there was a fellow who planted a vineyard and put a fence around it and dug a wine-cellar and built a tower and let it out to some tenant-farmers and left the country. And in due season he sent a servant to collect part of the produce of the vineyard from the farmers. And they seized him and whipped him soundly and sent him off emptyhanded. And again he sent another servant to them, and they beat him over the head and mistreated him. And he sent another, whom they killed, and many more, some of whom they flayed and some of whom they killed. He still had one beloved son. He sent him to them last of all, saying, 'They will respect my son.'

"But those farmers said to each other, 'It's the heir! Come on, let's kill him, and the inheritance is ours!' And they seized him and killed him and threw him outside the vineyard. So what will the master of the vineyard do? He will come and wipe those farmers out and give the vineyard to others. Didn't you ever read this passage in the scripture:

> *A stone that the builders rejected,*
> *That one ended up the cornerstone*
> *That was made by the Lord*
> *And is the admiration of our eyes?"*

And they were looking to seize him but feared the crowd, because they realized he was making this comparison about them. And they left him behind and went away.

And they send some of the Pharisees and Herod's men to him to trap him in his words. And they come and say to him, "Teacher, we know that you are truthful and no respecter of persons, because you do not look to the face of the world, but teach the way of God based on the truth. Are we allowed to pay taxes to Caesar or not? Should we pay or shouldn't we?"

Seeing through their performance, he said to them, "Why are you testing me? Bring me a drachma and let me see it." And they brought it, and he says to them, "Whose picture and inscription is this?"

They said to him, "Caesar's."

Jesus said to them, "Give Caesar's things to Caesar and God's things to God." And they were astonished by him.

And some Sadducees come to him (who say there is no resurrection) and asked him, "Teacher, Moses wrote, 'If someone's brother dies and leaves a wife behind but leaves no child, his brother should take her to wife and produce offspring for his brother.' Once there were seven brothers, and the first took a wife and left no offspring when he died. And the second took her and also died leaving no offspring. And the third did likewise. And all seven left no offspring, and the wife died last of all. In the resurrection, whose wife will she be when they rise again? After all, all seven had her for a wife."

Said Jesus, "Surely you aren't led astray by that, ignorant of the scriptures and the power of God? Because when they arise from the dead there are no brides and no grooms: they are just like God's messengers in the skies. About the fact that the dead are raised up again, didn't you ever read in the book of Moses and the burning bush how God said to him, 'I am the God of Abraham and the God of Isaac and the God of Jacob'? There is no God of the dead but only of the living. You're wandering far afield."

And one of the canon-lawyers who came up and heard them arguing, seeing how well he had answered them, asked him, "Which commandment is first of all?"

Answered Jesus, "The first is, 'Listen, Israel, the Lord your God is one Lord, and you are to love the Lord your God with all your heart and all your soul and all your thoughts and all your strength.' The second is this: 'You are to love your neighbor as you love yourself.' There is no other commandment greater than these."

And the lawyer said to him, "Teacher, you say well and truly that 'he is one and there is no other besides him,' and that 'loving him with all your heart and all your understanding and all your strength' and 'loving your neighbor as yourself' is greater than all burnt offerings and sacrifices."

And Jesus, seeing with what presence of mind he answered, said to him, "You are not far from the kingdom of God." And after that no one dared to ask him any more questions.

And Jesus continued teaching in the temple, saying, "How can the canon-lawyers say that the Anointed is the son of David? David himself said in the holy spirit,

> *Said a lord to my lord,*
> *'Sit on my right*
> *While I put your enemies underneath your feet.'*

David himself calls him Lord, so how is he his son?"

And a great crowd stood listening to him with delight.

And in the course of his teaching he said, "Watch out for clerics who love walking around in their robes and everyone saying hello to them downtown, and their seats in the front of churches and at the head tables of banquets, who wolf down the houses of widows and make a show of praying at great length. They will receive an extra condemnation."

And as he sat across from the collection-box he saw all the crowd throwing money into the box, and many rich people threw in a lot. And a poor widow came and threw in two small coins, like pennies. And calling his students to him he said to them, "I assure you that this widow put in more than all the other people who put something in the box, because all the others threw in what they had left over, while she threw in the last of all she had to live on."

13

And as he was going out of the temple one of his students said to him, "Teacher, look how many stones and how many buildings there are!"

And Jesus said to him, "You see all these great buildings? There isn't one stone upon another here that won't be destroyed."

And as he was sitting on Mount Olive, across from the temple, Peter and James and John and Andrew asked him privately, "Tell us, when will these things be, and what will be the sign when all these things are about to end at once?"

And Jesus started telling them, "Watch out lest anyone delude you: many people will come in my name, saying they are me, and they will fool many people. And when you hear wars, and reports of wars, don't be afraid: it has to happen, but it won't be the end yet. Race will rise up against race, and country against country; there will be earthquakes in places, and famines. These things are the beginning of the death-throes.

"Look to yourselves. They will hand you over to the courts, and you will be whipped in the synagogues and stand before governors and kings on account of me, as a testimony to them. And first the good word must be proclaimed to all peoples. And when they take you away to betray you, don't worry what you will say, because what is given to you in that hour is what you will say: it won't be you talking, but the sacred breath. And brother will hand over brother to his death, and fathers their children, and children will rise up against their parents and kill them. And you will be hated by everyone because of my name. But whoever endures to the end, that's who will be saved.

"So when you see the monster of destruction standing where it shouldn't be, let whoever reads [the Book of Daniel] remember: those in Judea, flee into the mountains. Those on the rooftop, don't come down or go in to get anything out of your house. Those in the fields, don't turn back to get your cloak. Woe to those with a child in their bellies, or who are nursing, in those days!

"Pray that it may not happen in winter, because those will be days of oppression such as there has never been from the beginning of creation till now nor ever will be. And if the Lord had not limited those days, no living thing would be saved. But for the sake of those chosen ones whom he has chosen, he has set a limit to those days.

"And then if someone says to you, 'Look here, it's the Anointed,' or 'Look there,' don't believe them, because pseudo-Christs and pseudo-prophets will come along and give signs and wonders to the point of fooling, if possible, even the chosen ones. But *you* be on your guard: I have told you everything in advance.

"But in those days, after that oppression,

> *The sun will darken,*
> *And the moon won't give her beams,*
> *And the stars will be falling out of the sky,*
> *And the powers in the skies will be shaken.*

"And then they will see the son of humanity coming on the clouds with great power and glory. And then he will send out his messengers and round up his chosen ones from the four winds, from the top of the earth to the top of the sky.

"Learn from the fig-tree by comparison: when its shoots grow tender and it puts out leaves, you know the harvest-time is near. The same for you: when you see these things happening, you know that he is close by the door.

"I assure you that this generation will not pass away till all these things happen. The sky and the earth will pass away, but my words will never pass away.

"As for the date and the hour, no one knows, not even the messengers in the sky, not even the son, but only the Father.

"Watch out, don't fall asleep, because you don't know when the time is. It's like a fellow going out of the country, who left his house behind, and gave to each of his servants authority to do their job, and commanded the doorkeeper to keep watch. So stay awake, because you don't know when the master of the house is coming, whether evening or midnight or cockcrow or morning; when he comes unexpectedly, don't let him find you sleeping."

14

Now the Passover and the unleavened bread was two days off, and the high priests and canon-lawyers were looking for a way to seize him by some trick and kill him. They were saying, "Not during the feastdays, there'll be an uproar among the people."

And when he was in Bethany, in the house of Simon Leper, as he was sitting there, a woman with a jar of costly ointment of genuine spikenard broke the jar and poured it over his head. Some of the people there were outraged and said to each other: "What is this waste of perfume for? Why, she could have sold that perfume for three hundred drachmas and given it to the poor." And they were yelling at her.

But Jesus said, "Leave her alone. Why are you giving her grief? She did a fine thing for me. You always have the poor around, and whenever you want you can do them good, but me you do not always have. What she could do, she did: she started in advance to perfume my body for burial. I assure you, wherever the good word is proclaimed in all the world, what she did will also be told in memory of her."

And Judas Iscariot, one of the twelve, went off to the high priests to betray him to them. They were delighted to hear that and promised to give him money. And he was looking for a way to hand him over when the time was right.

And on the first day of unleavened bread, when they were sacrificing for Passover, his students say to him, "Where do you want us to go get ready for you to eat the seder?"

And he sends off two of his students, saying to them, "Go into town, and you'll be met by a fellow carrying a water jug: you're going to follow him, and wherever he goes in, say to the master of the house, 'Our teacher says, *Where is my banquet hall where I can eat the seder with my students?*' And he himself will show you a big upstairs room spread out and ready, where you can make preparations for yourselves."

And the students went out and went into town, and found it as he had told them and got the seder ready.

And when it gets late he comes with the twelve. And as they were sitting and eating Jesus said, "I tell you for sure, one of you is going to hand me over, one of you here eating with me."

And they started agonizing and saying to him one by one: "It couldn't be me, could it?"

He said to them, "One of the twelve, dipping his bread in the gravy-boat with me. Yes, the son of humanity is going just as it is written about him, but woe to that person by whom the son of humanity is betrayed. Better for that person if he'd never been born."

And as they were eating he took bread, blessed it and broke it and gave it to them saying, "Take this, this is my body." And taking a cup and giving thanks he gave it to them, and they all drank of it. And he said to them, "This is my blood, the blood of the covenant, poured out for many. I tell you for sure, I will drink no more of the produce of the vineyard till that day when I drink it new in the kingdom of God."

And concluding with a hymn they went out to Mount Olive. And Jesus says to them, "All of you will let me down. After all, what does it say?

I will strike the shepherd, and the sheep will scatter.

"But after arising I will go ahead of you to Galilee."

Peter said to him, "Even if everyone lets you down, I still won't."

Says Jesus, "I'm telling you the truth: this very night, before the cock crows twice, three times you'll say you don't know me."

But he kept saying over and over, "Even if I have to die with you, I'll never say I don't know you." And they all said the same.

And they come to the place whose name is Gethsemane, and he says to his students, "Sit here till I've finished praying." And he takes Peter and James and John with him and he started wailing and mourning and said to them, "My soul is so sick with grief that I could die. Wait here and stay awake." And going a little ways off he fell on the ground and prayed that, if possible, his hour might pass him by, and said, "Papa, Father, everything is possible for You. Take this cup away from me. But not what *I* want, what You want." And he comes and finds them sleeping and says to Peter: "Simon, are you sleeping? You couldn't stay awake one hour? Stay awake, and pray that you don't get put to the test: the spirit may be eager, but the flesh is weak." And he went off and prayed again, saying the same words. And he came again and found them sleeping—their eyes were just so heavy, they didn't know what to say. And he comes a third time and says to them: "From here on you can sleep and take your rest, that's all right, the hour has come: watch the son of humanity being betrayed into the hands of criminals. Get up, come on! See there? My betrayer has arrived!"

And even as he spoke, Judas, one of the twelve, shows up, and with him a crowd with swords and clubs, sent by the high priests and canon-lawyers and elders. His betrayer had given them the signal, "Whoever I kiss, that's the one, make sure to seize him and drag him away." And when he came he went right over to him and called him "Master" and kissed him. And they laid hands on him and seized him. One of those standing there drew his sword and struck the high priest's slave and took off his ear.

And Jesus answered them: "As if you were going after a robber, you came out here with swords and clubs to arrest me? During the day I was there among you in the temple teaching and you didn't take me then—but let the scriptures be fulfilled."

And they all left him behind and turned and ran. And one guy, a teenager, was following him, wrapped in a sheet and nothing else. And they seized him, but he jumped out of the sheet and ran off naked.

And they took Jesus away and brought him to the high priest, and all the high priests and canon-lawyers and elders assembled. And Peter was following from a distance as far as the high priest's courtyard and was sitting there with the servants, warming up by the fire.

Now the high priests and the whole high court were looking for evidence against Jesus on the basis of which they could execute him, and they weren't finding it, because there were many people perjuring themselves against him, but their stories were never the same. And some stood up and started lying about him under oath, saying, "We heard him say, 'I will destroy this man-made temple and in three days build another one not made by man,' " but even so the story didn't come out the same.

And the high priest stood up in front of everyone and asked Jesus, "Don't you have any answer as to why these people testify this way against you?" But he was silent and made no answer. Again the high priest asked him: "Are you the Anointed, the Son of the Most Blessed?"

Jesus said, "Yes I am, and you will see the son of humanity sitting on the right hand of power and trailing the clouds of the sky."

Tearing his garments, the high priest says, "What do we need witnesses for any more? You heard that blasphemy! How does it look to you?" They all judged that it was punishable by death.

And some of them started spitting at him, and covering his face, and punching him and saying, "Prophesy!" and the servants hit him blows with canes.

And Peter being down in the courtyard, one of the high priest's girls comes and sees Peter warming himself and looks at him and says: "You were with the Nazarene too—you know: Jesus."

But he denied it, saying, "I don't know or understand what you're talking about." And he went out on the porch, and a cock crowed.

And the girl, seeing him again, started telling the people who were standing there, "This guy is one of them." And he denied it again.

And a little later the people who were standing around started saying to Peter, "Of course you're one of them: after all, you *are* a Galilean."

And he started cursing and swearing, "I don't know this fellow you're talking about." Just then the rooster crowed for the second time. And Peter remembered the words Jesus had spoken to him about how "Before the cock crows twice, three times you'll say you don't know me," and he rushed out and started crying.

15

And as soon as it was daylight the high priests, after calling a meeting with the elders and canon-lawyers and the whole high court, tied Jesus up and led him away and gave him over to Pilate.

And Pilate asked him, "You're the king of the Jews?"

He answers, "That's what *you* say."

And the high priests charged him with all sorts of things, and again Pilate asked him, "Don't you have anything to answer? See all these things they're charging you with?" But Jesus still answered nothing at all, much to Pilate's amazement.

Now at festival time he always released to them one prisoner that they asked for. So there was one called Barabbas, chained among the rebels who had committed murder in the recent uprisings. And the crowd surged toward him and started asking what he would do for them. And Pilate answered, "Do you want me to let the king of the Jews go?" You see, he knew the high priests had delivered him up out of envy.

But the high priests stirred up the crowd to say, "No, let Barabbas go instead."

And Pilate answered again, "What do you want me to do with the so-called king of the Jews?"

And they shouted back, "Crucify him."

And Pilate said to them, "But what has he done wrong?"

But they just kept shouting over and over, "Crucify him."

So Pilate, wishing to do as much as possible for the masses, let Barabbas go for them, and handed over Jesus—whipping him soundly first—to be crucified.

The soldiers took him away to the hall, that is, the courthouse, and they call together the whole platoon. And they put him in a robe of royal purple and put a crown on him that they wove out of thorns. And they started paying him homage and saying, "Good day your majesty, king of the Jews," and hitting him on the head with a cane and spitting on him, and they were on their knees bowing down in front of him.

And after they'd had their fun with him, they took the royal purple off him and put his own clothes back on.

And they're leading him out to crucify him, and there's a certain Simon Cyrenean, Alexander and Rufus's father, passing by on his way from the country, and they dragoon him into carrying the cross.

And they bring him up to the place Golgotha, which translates to Skull Place. And they tried giving him myrrh-laden wine, which he wouldn't take.

And they put him on the cross, and they're dividing up his clothes and rolling dice to see who'd get them. It was about nine o'clock, they crucified him then. And the name of his crime was written overhead: THE KING OF THE JEWS. And along with him they crucify two robbers, one on his right and one on his left.

And the people passing by yelled curses at him, shaking their heads and saying, "Bah! Destroyer of the temple and rebuilder in three days, save yourself by coming down off the cross."

Along the same line the high priests were joking with each other and the canon-lawyers, saying, "He saved others, but he can't save himself. Hey, Anointed King of Israel, come down now off the cross, so we can see and believe!" And even the others crucified with him were insulting him.

And when it got to be noon, darkness came over the whole land, from then till three o'clock. And at three o'clock, Jesus cried out in a loud voice, "Eloi, Eloi, lema sabachthani," which translates to "My God, my God, why did you desert me?"

And some of the people standing there heard him and said, "Look at that, he's calling on Elijah." And somebody ran and filled a sponge with the sour wine and put it on the end of a cane for him to drink out of, saying, "Let's see if Elijah comes to get him down." But Jesus let out a loud cry and breathed his last.

And the curtain of the temple's inner sanctum was sheared in two from top to bottom. When the Roman captain who had been standing in front of him saw the way he had died, he said, "This person really was the son of God!"

There were also some women watching from a distance, among them Mary Magdalen and Mary mother of James and Joseth, and Salome, who had followed him and served him when he was in Galilee, and many others who had come up to Jerusalem with him.

And since it was already getting late and it was Friday, meaning the day before the Sabbath, Joseph of Arimathea, an upstanding member of the high court who himself lived in expectation of the kingdom of God, went boldly to Pilate and asked for the body of Jesus. Pilate was amazed that he was dead already and called the captain over and asked him if he just died, and when he found out from the captain, he made Joseph a present of the body. And first he bought a sheet, and then took him down and wrapped him in the sheet and put him in a tomb that had been cut out of the rockface, and rolled a stone up against the doorway of the tomb. Mary Magdalen and Mary, Joseth's mother, saw where they put him.

16

And when the Sabbath was over, Mary Magdalen and Mary, James's mother, and Salome brought perfumes so they could go embalm him. And going at the crack of dawn on the first day of the week, they get to the tomb just after sunrise. And they were saying to each other, "Who's going to roll the stone away from the doorway of the tomb for us?" And then they look again and see that the stone *is* rolled away—and it was a very big stone indeed.

And going into the tomb they saw a young man sitting on their right in a white robe, and they were dumbfounded. And he said to them,

"Don't be astonished. You're looking for Jesus of Nazareth, the one who was crucified. He rose up, he isn't here. See? There's the place where they laid him. Now go tell his students and Peter that he's going on ahead of you to Galilee, where you will see him, just as he told you."

And they ran out of the tomb in the grip of terror and ecstasy and said nothing to anybody, they were so afraid.*

After he arose early on the first day of the week, he appeared first of all to Mary Magdalen, from whom he had thrown out seven demons. She went and told those who had been with him as they were mourning and wailing. And when they heard he was alive and had been seen by her, they didn't believe it.

After that he appeared in another form to two of them walking, as they were going to the fields, and they also went and reported to the others, and they didn't believe them either.

Finally, as the eleven were sitting at a meal, he appeared and castigated them for their lack of faith and hardness of heart in not believing those who had seen him risen. And he said to them, "Travel through the whole world and spread the good word to all creation. Whoever has faith and is washed will be saved, and whoever has no faith will be condemned. The faithful will be attended by the following signs: in my name they will throw out demons; they will speak new languages; they will take snakes in their hands, and even if they drink the poison it won't hurt them; and they'll put their hands on sick people, and they'll be well again."

And so then, Lord Jesus, after talking to them, was taken up into the sky and sits at the right hand of God. But they went out and spread the word everywhere, while the Lord worked with them, underscoring their words with accompanying miracles.

* The earliest manuscripts of Mark stop right here, and what follows is generally conceded to be a later addition. We don't know whether the evangelist really meant to end so abruptly or whether a final page or two was lost or deliberately removed.

The Good Word According to

Luke

1

Most honorable Theophilus,

Since indeed many people have tried to draw up an account of the things fulfilled in our midst as transmitted to us by those who were eyewitnesses from the beginning and became servants of the word, I thought that I also, having followed it all from the first, would write it down for you correctly in order so that you may know the solid truth about the things that have reached your ears.

There was, in the days of Herod king of the Jews, a priest named Zachariah, from the line of Abijah, and he had a wife, one of the daughters of Aaron, and her name was Elizabeth. They were both innocent in the sight of God, walking in the ways of all the commands and judgments of the Lord, without a fault. But they had no child, seeing as how Elizabeth was sterile and both of them were advanced in years.

Now it happened that in the course of his priestly duties before God in the order of the day, according to the custom of the priesthood he drew the assignment of going in and incensing the temple of the Lord, while all the multitude of the people were outside praying during the hour of incensation. And a messenger of the Lord appeared to him, to the right of the incensing altar. And Zachariah was disturbed by the sight, and fear came over him. But the messenger said to him:

> "Don't be afraid, Zachariah;
> Because your prayer has been heard,
> And your wife Elizabeth will have a son,
> And you will call his name John.
> And he will be a joy and a delight to you,
> And many will rejoice in his birth,
> Because he will be great in the sight of God
> And will drink no wine and no liquor,

And will already be full of the sacred breath
In his mother's womb.
And he will bring many of Jerusalem's sons
Back to the Lord their God.
And he will go before God's face in the breath and power
    of Elijah,
To bring the hearts of fathers back to their children,
And reestablish unbelievers in the consciousness of the just,
And prepare for the Lord a reformed race."

And Zachariah said to the messenger, "How am I to understand this? Remember, I'm an old man, and my wife is getting on in years."

And the messenger answered, "I am Gabriel, who stands before the face of God, and I was sent to talk with you and give you this good news. But now look, you will be silent and unable to talk from now till the day when all this happens, on account of your not believing my words, words that will be fulfilled in their time."

And the people were waiting for Zachariah and were surprised he was taking so long in the temple. Then when he came out, he couldn't talk to them, and they could tell he'd seen a vision in the temple, and he just kept nodding at them and remained mute. And as it happened, when his days on duty were finished, he went home. After those days, his wife Elizabeth conceived, and she kept out of sight five months, saying, "This is what the Lord has done for me on the day when He saw fit to lift my shame from before the world."

During her sixth month, Gabriel the messenger was sent from God to a town in Galilee named Nazareth to see a girl engaged to a man named Joseph, from the family of David; and the girl's name was Mary. And he came in saying, "Hello, favorite of God, the Lord is with you!" She was confused at those words and wondered what kind of greeting that was. And the messenger said to her:

"Don't be afraid, Mary: you found favor with God.
Watch: you're about to conceive in your belly and bear a son,
    and you will call his name Jesus.
He will be great and called son of the Most High.
And the Lord your God will give him the throne of David
    your father,

And he will be king of the family of Jacob for all time,
And his reign will have no end."

Said Mary to the messenger, "How will this happen if I haven't been
with a man?"
And the messenger answered,

"The sacred breath will come over you,
And the power of the Most High will overshadow you.

"Because of his being sacredly born, he will be called God's son. And
look: your relative Elizabeth? She's conceived a child, at her age, and that
child is six months along, after they called her sterile. Because nothing
you can name is impossible for God."
Said Mary, "Here I am, the slave of the Lord: let it happen to me the
way that you have said." And the messenger went away.
One day soon after, Mary hastened into the highlands to the town of
Juda and stopped at Zachariah's house and said hello to Elizabeth. And
what happened was, that when Elizabeth heard Mary's "Hello," the baby
gave a jump inside of her, and Elizabeth, filling up with the sacred breath,
raised her voice in a great shout and said,

"Blessings upon you of all women,
And blessings on the fruit of your womb.

"And how do I come to have the mother of my Lord coming to see me?
Did you see? As the sound of your greeting reached my ears, the baby
inside of me jumped for joy. And good luck to the woman who believes
that there will be a fulfillment for these words of the Lord to her."
Said Mary,

"My soul magnifies the Lord,
And the breath within me has been delighted by God my savior,
That He should look down upon the lowness of His slave.
Why, look! from now on, all races will call me the lucky one,
Because the All-Powerful did great things with me.
His name is holy, and His mercy is for generations and
    generations toward those who fear Him.

He summoned strength to His arm,
He scattered the proud with the thoughts in their heart;
He pulled dynasties off thrones
And put peasants on high.
He loaded starving people with goods
And sent rich people away emptyhanded.
Israel has claimed its child
As a reminder of mercy,
As He said to our fathers, to Abraham and his seed forever."

Mary stayed with her some three days and returned home.

Then Elizabeth's time to give birth came round, and she bore a son. And her neighbors and relatives heard that the Lord had lavished his mercy on her, and they were happy with her. And as it happened, they went a week later to circumcise the baby, and they were going to call him by his father's name, Zachariah. And his mother answered, "No, he's supposed to be called John." And they said to her, "But there's no one in your family by that name."

Then they signaled his father as to what he wanted him called. And motioning for a tablet, he wrote, "John is his name," which astonished everybody. And instantly his mouth and tongue were reopened, and he started talking, praising God.

And fear came over all those who lived in the area, and in all the highlands of Judea these words were spoken and respoken. And all who heard them took them to heart saying, "Who will *this* child be? Because the Lord's hand was certainly with him."

And Zachariah his father was filled with the sacred breath and prophesied, saying,

"Blessed is the Lord God of Israel,
That He should look down and pay the ransom on His people,
And extend to us the brimming horn of salvation,
Here in the house of David His child.
As He spoke through the mouth of the holy prophets of
    ages ago:
About safety from our enemies, from the hands of everyone who
    hates us,
About being merciful with our fathers

And remembering the holy covenant,
The oath He swore to Abraham our father,
To grant that we, fearlessly snatched from the enemy's
    clutches,
Might serve Him in holiness and innocence,
There before Him, all the days of our lives.
And you, child, you will be called prophet of the Most High,
Because you will walk in front of the Lord to clear his path,
So as to give the knowledge of salvation to his people
For the forgiveness of their wrongs
Through the merciful senses of our God,
Which will make Him look down on us as a sunrise from on
    high,
To shine for those in darkness and sitting in the shadow of
    death,
To correct our steps back to the road of peace."

So the baby grew and got stronger in spirit, and he was out in the
wilderness until the day of his presentation to Israel.

2

It happened during those days that a decree went out from Caesar
Augustus to register the whole world. This first census happened when
Syrias Cyrenius was governor. So everyone was going to get registered,
each to their own home town. And Joseph came up from Galilee, from
the town of Nazareth, into Judea, to a city of David which is called
Bethlehem—he being of the family and descent of David—to be
registered with Mary his fiancee, who was pregnant. As it happened,
during their stay there her days of childbirth came round, and she bore
her son, her firstborn, and wrapped him up and made his bed in a grain-
crib, because there was no room for them in the living-quarters.

Now shepherds were in that area, staying up late and taking turns
through the night watching out for their sheep. And a messenger of the
Lord stood in front of them, and the Lord's glory surrounded them, and
they felt the fear of fears. And the messenger said to them, "Don't be
afraid, I hereby give you the good news of a great joy which will be for
all the people, namely that a savior was born for you today who is an

anointed lord in a city of David. And this is your sign: you'll find the baby wrapped up and lying in a grain-crib."

And all of a sudden beside that messenger there was a mass of the heavenly army praising God and saying,

> "Glory in the highest to God,
> And on earth, peace among people in his good favor."

And it happened, as off into the sky went the messengers, that the shepherds were saying to each other, "Now let's get on to Bethlehem and see this word fulfilled that the Lord revealed to us." And they went off as fast as they could and came upon Mary and Joseph and the baby lying in the grain-crib. When they saw that, they understood what had been told them concerning this child. And everyone was amazed to hear what the shepherds said to them, but Mary preserved all these things that were said, turning them over in her heart. And the shepherds returned, glorifying and praising God to all who heard and saw how they were being spoken to.

And when a week was up, the time to circumcise him, his name was indeed called Jesus, the name he was called by the messenger of God before he was conceived inside his mother.

And when the purification days came round according to the law of Moses, they brought him up to Jerusalem to present him to the Lord (as it says in the law of the Lord: "Every male child that comes first out of the womb shall be called sacred to the Lord") and also to give sacrifice as it says in the law of the Lord: "A brace of turtledoves, and two fledgling pigeons."

And there was this man in Jerusalem named Simeon, and this fellow lived innocently and correctly while he waited for the consolation of Israel, and the sacred breath was upon him. And he had been promised by the sacred breath not to see death without first seeing the Anointed of the Lord.

And in this spirit he went to the temple. And while the parents of Jesus were bringing him in so they could do the usual with him according to the law, this same Simeon was there to greet him, and took him in his arms and blessed God and said,

> "Here You are letting Your slave go, Master,

In peace, according to Your promise,
Now that my eyes saw the salvation
You prepared with all races watching,
A light for the revealing of nations
And a glory to his people Israel."

And his father and his mother stood wondering at the things said about him. And Simeon blessed them and said to Mary his mother, "Here he lies, the fall and rising up again of many in Israel, and the sign, much disputed—yes, the sword will run your heart right through—by which the thoughts of many hearts will be revealed."

And there was a prophet, Anna, Thanuel's daughter from the line of Aser, she being very advanced in years, having lived with a husband for seven years after her girlhood and by herself as a widow up to her eighty-fourth year; she never left the temple, devoting herself night and day to fasting and prayer. And coming on the scene at the same time, she started thanking God in advance and talking about him to all who waited for the rescue of Israel.

And when they'd done everything according to the law of the Lord, they went back to their own town, Nazareth; the child grew and gained strength as he filled with wisdom, and God's grace was upon him.

And his parents used to make an annual trip to Jerusalem for the feast of Passover. And when he was twelve, after they came up as usual for the festival and finished out the day, as the rest of them were going back, the boy Jesus stayed behind in Jerusalem, and his parents didn't know that. Thinking he was somewhere in the caravan they went several days' journey and kept looking for him among their relatives and family friends, and after they didn't find him they came back to Jerusalem to look for him. And it turned out that after three days they found him in the temple, sitting among the scholars and listening to them and asking questions. All those who heard him were overwhelmed by his under-standing and his answers. And when they saw him they were amazed, and his mother said to him: "Son, why did you do this to us? See how your father and I have been looking for you in agony?"

And he said to them, "For me? Why were you looking for me? Didn't you know I have to be immersed in the things of my Father?" And they didn't understand the words he was saying to them. And he left the city with them and went back to Nazareth and was obedient to them. And his mother preserved all these words in her heart. And Jesus kept forging ahead in wisdom, maturity, and favor with God and the world.

3

In the fifteenth year of Tiberius Caesar's rule, with Pontius Pilate governing Judea; and Herod being governor of Galilee, Philip his brother governor of the countries Ituria and Trachonitis, and Lysanius governor of Abilena; during the high priesthood of Annas and Caiaphas the words of God came to John, Zachariah's son, there in the wilds.

And he went through all the country round the Jordan, announcing the washing of a changed heart for the forgiveness of wrongs. As is written in the book of the words of Isaiah the prophet,

> *The voice of a crier in the desert,*
> *Get the Lord's road ready,*
> *Straighten his paths.*
> *Every gully will be filled in,*
> *And every mountain and hill worn down,*
> *And the twists will come out straight,*
> *And rough will be on its way to smooth,*
> *And every living thing will see the savior of God—*

so he said to the crowds traveling out to be washed by him, "Children of vipers, who tipped you off to run from the coming fury? Bear fruit worthy of a changed heart and don't start saying to each other, '*We* have Abraham for our father!' because I'm telling you, God can raise children for Abraham out of these stones. The ax is already poised at the root of the trees, so any tree not bearing good fruit gets cut down and thrown into the fire."

And the crowds were asking him, "So what do we do?"

He answered, "Whoever has two robes, share with someone who has none; whoever has food, do likewise."

And some tax collectors came to be washed and said to him, "Teacher, what do we do?"

And he said to them, "Don't do anything beyond what you're assigned to."

And some Army men asked him, "What about us, what do we do?"

And he said to them, "No harassing anybody, no backbiting, and be content with your wages."

Since the nation was waiting, and since in their hearts all were considering about John, whether *he* might not be the Anointed, John answered, saying to everybody, "I'm washing you in water, but someone is coming who is so much stronger than me, I'm not great enough to untie the thongs of his sandals: *he* will wash you in holy breath and fire, whose winnowing-fan is in his hand to clean up his threshing-floor, collecting the wheat into his silo, while he burns the chaff in a never-extinguished fire."

With many and various exhortations he brought the good word to the people. But Herod the governor, when he got told off by him on account of Herodias, his brother's wife—and all the bad things Herod had done—putting that on top of all the other offenses, he clapped John in jail.

In the course of the whole country being washed, when Jesus had also been washed and was praying, the sky happened to open, and the holy breath to alight in the physical form of a dove upon him, and a voice to come from the sky: "You are my son, my beloved son, in you I am delighted."

And Jesus himself was getting to be some thirty years old, the son, so he was considered, of Joseph son of Eli son of Matthat son of Levi son of Melchi son of Jannae son of Joseph son of Mattathias son of Amos son of Nahum son of Esli son of Naggae son of Maath son of Mattathias son of Semein son of Josech son of Joda son of Johanan son of Resa son of Zorobabel son of Salathiel son of Neri son of Melchi son of Addi son of Kosam son of Elmadam son of Er son of Jesu son of Eliezer son of Jorim son of Matthat son of Levi son of Symeon son of Juda son of Joseph son of Jonam son of Eliakim son of Melea son of Menna son of Mattatha son of Nathan son of David son of Jesse son of Jobed son of Boaz son of Salmon son of Naasson son of Aminadab son of Admin son of Arni son of Esrom son of Phares son of Juda son of Jacob son of Isaac son of Abraham son of Thara son of Nachor son of Serouch son of Ragau son of Phalek son of Eber son of Sala son of Cainan son of Arphaxad son of Shem son of Noah son of Lamech son of Methuselah son of Enoch son of Jared son of Maleleel son of Cainan son of Enos son of Seth son of Adam son of God.

4

Now Jesus returned from the Jordan full of holy spirit and was led in that spirit into the wilds for forty days, being tested by the devil. And he didn't eat a thing during those days, and at the end of them he was starving. So the devil said to him, "If you're God's son, tell this stone to become bread."

And Jesus answered him, "It is written, 'A person is not to live only on bread.' "

And taking him up high, he showed him—in an instant of time—all the kingdoms of the world. And the devil said to him, "I will give you every bit of that power, and the glory of them all; it's been given to me, and I can give it to whomever I like. Just bow down in front of me, and it will all be yours."

And Jesus answered, "It says, 'The Lord your God is whom you shall adore, and you shall serve only Him.' "

So he took him into Jerusalem and set him up on top one wing of the temple and said to him, "If you're God's son, throw yourself down from there. After all, it says,

His messengers have been instructed about you, to guard you,

and

They will take you in their hands,
So you don't stub your foot against a stone."

And Jesus answered, "It says, 'You are not to experiment with the Lord your God.' "

And after exhausting all his tests the devil retired from him awaiting a better time.

And Jesus returned in the power of the spirit to Galilee, and the word went out across the whole neighborhood about him. And he was teaching in their synagogues, acclaimed by all.

And he came to Nazareth, where he had grown up, and, as his custom was, went to the synagogue on the day of the Sabbath and stood up to read. And he was given a book of the prophet Isaiah, and opening the book up he found the place where it says,

A spirit of the Lord is upon me,
The one for which he anointed me
To bring the good word to the poor.
He has sent me out
To proclaim release for prisoners
And sight for the blind,
To send the bone-crushed away with a cure
And proclaim the official Year of the Lord.

And closing the book he gave it to the acolyte and sat down. And all eyes in the synagogue were staring at him, as he began saying to them, "Today this scripture is fulfilled in your ears."

And they all witnessed him and were amazed at the words of grace coming out of his mouth and said, "Isn't this Joseph's son?" And he said to them, "From all sides you're going to use the expression, 'Physician, heal thyself: what we heard of, happening in Capharnaum, do that here in your own home town.'

"But," said he, "I tell you for sure, no prophet is accepted in his home town. I assure you, there were plenty of widows in Israel in the days of Elijah, when the sky was sealed for three years and six months so that there was a great famine over all the earth, but Elijah wasn't sent to any of them, but rather to Sarepta, in Sidonia, to see a widowed woman there. And there were plenty of lepers in Israel in the time of Eliseus the prophet, but none of them were cleansed, only Naman the Syrian." And it filled everybody with anger to hear him say those things in the synagogue, and they got up and threw him out of town and took him right up to the edge of the cliff on which the town was built, to throw him down. But he slipped through their midst and went his way.

And he went down to Capharnaum, a town in Galilee. And he was teaching them on the Sabbath. And they were stunned at his teaching, because his words were on his own authority.

And in the synagogue there was a fellow with the spirit of an unclean demon, and it raised its voice in a loud cry: "Stop, what have we done to you, Jesus of Nazareth? Did you come to wipe us out? I know who you are, holy one of God."

And Jesus yelled at it, saying, "Shut up and come out of him." And after throwing him down in the middle of the floor, the demon came out without injuring him in the least.

And awe came over everyone, and they said to each other, "What words does he use so that by his own power and authority he commands unclean spirits and they come out?" And the clamor about him traveled out to every place in the surrounding countryside.

But after getting up and leaving the synagogue, he went to Simon's house. Now Simon's mother-in-law was suffering from a great fever, and they asked him about her. And he stood over her and yelled at the fever, and it left her. Standing suddenly upright, she was at their service.

As the sun was setting, everyone who had someone sick with various diseases brought them to him, and he put his hands on every one of them and cured them. And demons came out of many people shouting, "You're the son of God!"

And he yelled at them and forbade them to speak; *they* knew he was the Anointed.

When it was daylight, he went out traveling to a deserted place. And the crowds were looking for him and came to him and hindered him from leaving them. But he said, "I have to spread the good word of the kingdom of God in the other cities too, that's what I was sent for." And he was spreading the word in the synagogues of Judea.

5

As it happened, while the crowd was hanging on him and hearing the words of God, he was standing by Lake Gennesareth. And he saw two boats sitting by the lake. The fishermen had gotten out of them and were washing their nets. So getting into one of the boats, which was Simon's, he asked him to shove off from shore a ways, and sitting in the boat, he was teaching the crowds.

Then when he finished talking, he said to Simon, "Head out for deep water and lower your nets for the catch." And Simon answered, "Chief, we didn't catch anything, sweating away all night long, but on your word I'll let the nets down." And when they did, they closed their nets on a great mass of many fish, their nets were bursting with them. And they signaled their mates in the other ship to come help them take hold of it. And they came and filled both boats till they were riding low in the water. Seeing that, Simon Peter fell at the knees of Jesus and said, "Get away from me, I'm an evil man, Lord"; astonishment overwhelmed him and all who had joined him in pursuit of the fish they'd caught, including

James and John the sons of Zebedee, who were associates of Simon's. And Jesus said to Simon, "Don't be afraid: from now on you will be fishers of humanity." And after bringing their boats in to shore they left everything and followed him.

And it happened while he was in one of the towns, there was this man with full-blown leprosy. Seeing Jesus, he fell on his face and begged him, "Lord, if you want to, you can heal me."

And he reached out his hand and touched him, saying, "I *do* want to. Be healed." And the leprosy went right out of him. And he instructed him to say nothing to anybody: "Just go show yourself to the priest and contribute what Moses commanded in thanks for your purification, as a testimony to them." More and more the word got out about him, and great crowds assembled to listen and be healed from their illnesses, but he was retreating to the wilds and praying.

And it happened on one of those days that he was teaching, and there were Pharisees and teachers of the law sitting there who had come from every village in Galilee and Judea, and from Jerusalem. And the power of the Lord was on him to heal. And these men came bringing a man on a bed who was paralyzed, and they were looking for a way to bring him inside and put him in front of him. And finding no way to bring him in, what with the crowd, they climbed up on the roof and let him down, with his cot, between the shingles onto the floor in front of Jesus. And seeing their faith, he said, "Fellow, your wrongs are forgiven you."

And the canon-lawyers and Pharisees started mulling that over and saying, "Who is this guy who speaks such blasphemies? Who can forgive wrongs but God alone?"

But Jesus, observing their thoughts, answered them, "Why are you muttering in your hearts? Which is easier: to say, 'Your wrongs are forgiven,' or to say, 'Get up and walk'? But so you see that the son of humanity has authority to forgive wrongs on earth"—he said to the paralyzed man—"I tell you, get up, pick up your cot, and go on home."

And he stood up suddenly in front of them, picked up the cot he'd been lying on, and went home praising God. And everyone was gripped by an ecstasy and praised God, and they filled with fear, saying, "We saw the impossible today."

And after that he came out and spotted a tax-collector named Levi sitting at the toll-station and said to him, "Follow me." And he left everything behind and stood up and followed him. And Levi gave him a grand reception at his house, and there was a big crowd of tax-collectors and other people who were sitting with them. And the Pharisees and their canon-lawyers started grumbling at his students, saying, "What do you eat with tax-collectors and godless people for?"

And Jesus answered them, "It's not the healthy who need a doctor, it's the sick. I am not here to call the virtuous to a change of heart, I'm here to call the godless people."

Then they said to him, "John's students fast heavily and make petitions to God, and so do those of the Pharisees, but yours eat and drink away."

Jesus said to them, "You can't make the wedding party fast while the bridegroom is with them, can you? There will come days when the bridegroom will be taken away from them; then they will fast, on those days."

Then he made them a comparison about how no one cuts a patch from a new garment and patches an old garment with it, because if they do, it cuts the new garment up, besides which the patch from the new garment doesn't match the old. And no one pours new wine into old skins, because if they do, the new wine bursts the skins, and it itself pours out, while the skins are destroyed. Instead, new wine should be poured into new skins. And no one drinking old wine wants new wine instead; they say, "The old stuff is nice."

6

Once on the Sabbath he happened to be traveling through the grain fields, and his students were picking the ears of grain and eating them, cleaning them by hand. Some of the Pharisees said, "Why are you doing what isn't allowed on the Sabbath?"

In answer to them Jesus said, "Haven't you even read what David did when he and those with him were starving: how he went into the house of God and took and ate the sacramental loaves and gave them to those with him, bread which no one was allowed to eat except the priests?" And he said to them, "The son of humanity is superior to the Sabbath."

On another Sabbath he happened to go into the synagogue and teach, and there was a fellow there, and his right hand was withered. Now the canon-lawyers and Pharisees were watching him to see if he would heal on the Sabbath, so they could find something to charge him with. But he knew their thoughts, so he said to the man with the withered hand,

"Get up and stand here in the middle." And he got up and stood there. Jesus said to them, "I ask you, which is permissible on the Sabbath: doing good, or doing evil—saving a life or destroying it?" And looking round at them all he said to him, "Reach out your hand." He did, and his hand was restored. But they were filled with mindlessness and started talking with each other about what they were going to do to Jesus.

It happened in those days that he went up the mountain to pray and was spending the night in prayer to God. And when the day came, he called his students to him, and picking twelve of them, named them emissaries ["apostles"]: Simon, whom he named the Rock ["Peter"], and Andrew his brother, and James and John and Philip and Bartholomew and Matthew and Thomas and James Alpheus and Simon "the Revolutionary" and Judas Jacobson and Judas Iscariot, who turned traitor.

And after coming down with them he stood on level ground, and with him a great crowd of his students, and a giant mass of the people from all Judea and Jerusalem and the shores of Tyre and Sidon, who came to hear him and be healed from their diseases; and those afflicted by unclean spirits were healed, and all the crowd were trying to touch him, because a force was coming out of him and healing everybody.

And raising his eyes toward his students, he said,

"You the poor are in luck, because the kingdom of God is yours.
You who are starving now are in luck,
Because you will have your fill.
You who are crying now are in luck,
Because you will laugh.

"You are in luck when the world hates you and excludes you and defames you and casts your name out like something evil, because of the son of humanity. Be happy on that day and jump for joy; because look, your reward will be great in the sky. After all, that's the same way their forefathers treated the prophets.

"But woe to you the rich,
Because you have had your consolation.
Woe to you who are satisfied now,
Because you will starve.
Woe to those who are laughing now,

Because you will grieve and mourn.
Woe to you when all the world speaks well of you:
After all, that's the same way their forefathers treated
    the pseudoprophets.

"But I speak to you who are listening: love your enemies, treat well those who hate you, bless those who curse you, pray for those who rail against you. If someone slaps you on one side of your jaw, give him the other side, and if someone takes your coat, don't begrudge him your shirt either. To all those who ask of you, give; and from those who take what is yours, don't ask to have it back.

"And just as you want people to treat you, treat them the same: if you love those who love you, what grace do you get? After all, even the evildoers love those who love them. And if you do good to those who do good to you, what grace do you get? Even wrongdoers do the same. And if you lend to those from whom you hope to get something, what grace do you get? Even wrongdoers lend to wrongdoers in order to receive in kind. But rather love your enemies, and do good and make loans expecting nothing back, and your reward will be great, and you will be sons and daughters of the Most High, because He too is kind to the ungrateful and the evil.

"Be merciful just as your Father is merciful. And don't judge, and you won't be judged. And don't condemn, and you won't be condemned. Let others off, and you'll be let off. Give, and you'll be given to—they'll put it in your pocket in good measure, shaken and pushed down and overflowing the top, because by the same measure you use, things will be measured for you."

And he made this comparison for them: "A blind man can't lead a blind man around, can he? Won't they both fall into the ditch? No pupil is above his teacher; when perfected, in every case he will be like his teacher.

"Why do you look at the splinter in your brother's eye, but don't notice the log in your own eye? How can you say to your brother, 'Brother, let me get that splinter out of your eye,' not seeing the log in your own eye? You fake, first get the log out of your eye, and then you can see about getting the splinter out of your brother's eye.

"You see, there is no good tree that gives rotten fruit, nor, on the other hand, any rotten tree that gives good fruit. Indeed, each tree is known by its own fruit. After all, they don't gather figs from thorn-trees, nor do they dry out grapes gotten from a bramble-bush. The good person brings forth good from his heart's good treasury, and the bad person, from his bad treasury, brings forth bad, because his mouth speaks out what his heart is brimming over with.

"Why do you call me 'Lord, Lord,' and don't do what I tell you? Everyone who comes to me and hears my words and does them, I'll give you a glimpse of what he's like: he's like a person building a house who dug a hole and made it deep and set a foundation on the rock. So when there was a flood, the river came up to that house and couldn't shake it because of its being well grounded. But whoever hears, and doesn't act, he's like a person building a house on the ground with no foundation, which, when the river came up to it, fell right down, and the smashing-up of that house was tremendous."

7

When he had filled the ears of the people with all his words, he went to Capharnaum.

Now a certain Roman captain's slave was sick and going to die, one who was dear to him. So when he heard about Jesus, he sent some of the elders of Judea to him to ask him to come save his slave. When they got to where Jesus was, they begged him earnestly, saying, "He deserves that you should do him this service: he loves our people and built our synagogue for us." So Jesus went along with them.

But when he was already not far from the house, the captain sent friends to him saying, "Lord, don't trouble yourself, because I'm not important enough for you to come under my roof, which is why I also didn't consider myself worthy to come see you; just say the word, and let my child be healed. After all, I'm a person placed under authority, with soldiers under me, and I tell this guy 'Go,' and he goes, and another guy 'Come,' and he comes, and I tell my slave 'Do this,' and he does it."

Hearing that, Jesus was amazed by him and turned to the crowd following him and said, "Even in Israel I never found so much trust." And the ones sent out returned to the house and found the slave healthy.

And it happened next that he traveled to a town called Nain, and his students and a great crowd were traveling with him. But as they got near the gate of the city, there was this dead man being carried out, his mother's only son, and she was a widow; and a sizable crowd from the town was with her. And seeing her, the Lord was sorry for her and said to her, "Don't cry." And he came up and touched the coffin, and the pallbearers stopped, and he said, "Young man, I tell you, get up!" And the dead man sat up and started talking, and he gave him back to his mother.

But fear gripped everyone, and they praised God, saying, "A great prophet has arisen among us," and "God looked down upon His people." And this story about him went out among all of Judea and all the country round.

And his students went and reported to John about all these things, and John, calling two of his students to him, sent them to the Lord, saying, "Are you the one who's coming, or should we look for another?" When they got to him, the men said, "John the Baptist sent us to you saying, 'Are you the one who's coming, or should we look for another?'"

In the same hour he cured many people of diseases and afflictions and evil spirits, and bestowed sight on many of the blind. And he answered them, "Go report to John what you see and hear: the blind see, the lame walk, lepers are cleansed, the deaf hear, the dead arise, the poor are given the good word, lucky are those who have no problem accepting me."

When John's messengers had left, he started speaking to the crowds about John: "What did you go out into the wilds to see? A reed shaken by the wind? No, what did you go out to see? A person dressed in nice soft clothes? See here, the people in splendid clothing and living in luxury are in the royal houses. Come on, what did you go out to see? A prophet? Yes, I tell you, a prophet and more: he is the one about whom it is written,

> *Look, I am sending my messenger before your face,*
> *To prepare your way before you.*

I'm telling you, among all those born of women there is no greater than John—but the lowest person in the kingdom of God is greater than him.

"And all the people who heard, and all the tax-collectors, did justice to God by being bathed in the bath of John. But the Pharisees and lawyers rejected God's will toward them when they were not bathed by him.

"What shall I compare the people of this generation to, and what are they like? They're like little kids sitting in the marketplace and hollering at the others, as they say,

We-played-the-flute-and-you-wouldn't-dance,
We-beat-our-breasts-and-you-wouldn't-mourn!

After all, John the Baptist has come along eating no bread and drinking no wine, and you say, 'He's possessed!' The son of humanity has come along eating and drinking, and you say, 'Look at this wine-drinking gourmand, the friend of tax-collectors and godless people.' But wisdom always was vindicated by all of its offspring."

Now one of the Pharisees asked him to eat with him, and he went into the house of the Pharisee and reclined at table. And the next thing was, a fallen woman who was in the town and who had found out that he was having dinner at the Pharisee's house brought in a vial of perfume and stood behind him crying, and started wetting his feet with her tears and drying them off with the hair of her head; and she was kissing his feet and applying the perfume to them. Seeing that, the Pharisee who had invited him said to himself, "If this guy was a prophet, he'd know what kind of woman was touching him, that she's a fallen woman."

And Jesus reacted, saying to him, "Simon, I have something to say to you."

"Speak, Master," he said.

"Once there was a lender who had two debtors: one owed five hundred drachmas and the other fifty. Since they had no way to pay him back he absolved them both. So which of them will love him more?"

Answered Simon, "I presume, the one who was absolved of more."

And he said to him, "You guessed right." And turning to the woman he said to Simon, "See this woman here? I came into your house and you didn't bring me water for my feet, but she watered my feet with her tears and dried them with her hair. You didn't give me a kiss, but she, since I came in here, hasn't stopped kissing my feet. You didn't anoint my head with olive oil, but she anointed my feet with perfume; by grace of which, I tell you, her wrongs shall be forgiven, many as they are, because she showed so much love. Who is forgiven less, loves less." Then he said to her, "Let your wrongs be forgiven."

And the others sitting there started saying to themselves, "Who is this guy who even forgives wrongdoing?"

But he said to the woman, "Your trust has saved you; go in peace."

8

And it happened afterwards that he himself journeyed through town and village, proclaiming and bringing the good word of the kingdom of God, with the twelve coming along, and also certain women who had been cured of evil spirits and sicknesses—Mary known as Magdalen, from whom seven demons had come out, and Joanna, wife of Chuza the trustee of Herod, and Susanna and many others—who took care of them with what possessions they had.

With a great crowd assembling and people of this town and that traveling out to see him, he said by way of comparison: "Once the sower went out to sow his seed. And in the course of his sowing, some fell by the roadside and was trampled, and the birds of the sky ate it up. And some fell upon stone, and when it came up it withered away from having no moisture. And some fell in the middle of thorns, and the thorns growing with it choked it off. And some fell on the good soil and came up and yielded fruit a hundredfold." Saying these things, he cried, "Whoever has ears to hear, let them hear."

But his students asked him what the comparison was about. He said, "To you it is given to know the mysteries of the kingdom of God, but to the rest of them it is only given in metaphors, so that 'seeing they may not see, and hearing they may not understand.'

"This is the comparison: the seed is the word of God. Those by the roadside are those who hear, but the devil comes and takes the word from their heart, so they won't believe and be saved. The ones upon stone are those who, when they hear the word, receive it with joy; but they have no roots, those who believe for a time but in trying times fall away. Those who fell into the thorns, those are the ones who hear, but as they travel on with their worries, and their wealth, and the pleasures of life, they get choked off and never yield anything. The seed on good soil, those are the ones who hear and preserve the word in a good and clean heart and bear fruit by perseverance.

"No one who lights a candle covers it with a pot or puts it under the bed; they put it up on a tall candlestick so those who come in can see the light. After all, there is no secret thing that won't be made public, nor anything hidden away that won't be made known and come to light.

"So watch how you listen, because he who has will be given more, and he who doesn't have, even what he thought he had will be taken away from him."

Then his mother showed up to see him, with his brothers and sisters, and they couldn't get at him because of the crowd. And he was given the message, "Your mother and your brothers and sisters are standing out there and want to see you."

And he answered them, "My mother and my brothers and my sisters are those who hear the word of God and do it."

It happened on one of those days also that he got into a boat along with his students and said to them, "Let's cross to the other side of the lake," and they sailed off.

As they were sailing, he dozed off; and a windstorm descended on the lake, and they were taking on water, and in danger. They went up to him and roused him, saying, "Chief, chief, we'll be killed!"

And he got up and yelled at the wind and the surging waters, and they stopped short, and it became calm. And he said to them, "Where is your faith?"

But they were frightened and amazed and said to each other, "Who *is* this guy that he even gives orders to the winds and the water and they obey him?"

And they landed at the country of the Gerasenes, which is on the shore opposite Galilee. As he got out on shore he was met by a certain man with a demon, who for quite some time had worn no clothes, nor lived in a house, but in the graveyard instead. Seeing Jesus, he gave a shout and fell down in front of him and said in a loud voice, "What have I done to you, Jesus son of God the highest? I beg you, don't torment me," because he was about to order the unclean spirit to go out of the fellow. It seems that for many seasons they had tried seizing him, and he had been bound with chains and kept shackled, but he always broke free of the bonds and was driven by the demon into the wilds. So Jesus asked him, "What is your name?"

He said, "Legion," because many demons had entered into him. And they pleaded with him not to order them into the abyss. Now there was a sizable herd of pigs grazing on the mountain. And they asked him to let them go into those, and he agreed. So the demons came out of the fellow and went into the pigs, and the herd rushed over the edge of the cliff into the lake and drowned.

When the herdsmen saw what happened they ran off and reported it in town and in the fields. They came out to see what had happened and came toward Jesus and saw the fellow that the demons had gone out of, sitting there fully dressed and in his right mind, by the feet of Jesus, and they were terrified. Those who had seen it explained to them how the possessed man had been saved. And they asked him, that whole crowd of people from the environs of the Gerasenes, to go away from them, because they were seized by a great fear. So he got in the boat and went back. And the man from whom the demons had come out asked to go with him. But Jesus left him, saying, "Go back home and tell the story of what God did for you." And he went all through town spreading the word of what Jesus had done for him.

Upon the return of Jesus, the crowd was glad to see him: they had all been expecting him. And along came a man named Jairus, and he was the chief of the synagogue, and falling at the feet of Jesus, he begged him to come to his house, because he had an only daughter, some twelve years old, and she was dying. And as he went off with him the crowds pressed him hard. And a woman who had been hemorrhaging for twelve years, who had spent her whole life's savings on doctors but couldn't be cured by any of them, came up to him from behind and touched the edge of his cloak, and suddenly her hemorrhaging stopped. And Jesus said, "Who was that touching me?"

When everyone denied it, Peter said, "Chief, the crowds are pressing in on you and rubbing against you."

But Jesus said, "Somebody touched me, because I felt the force going out of me." Seeing that she hadn't gotten away with it, the trembling woman came and fell before him* and explained in front of all the people the reason she had touched him and how all of a sudden she had been cured. And he said to her, "Daughter, your trust has saved you, go in peace."

Just as he says that, someone comes from the chief of the synagogue's house saying, "Your daughter's dead, don't bother the teacher any further."

But Jesus heard that and said to him, "Don't be afraid, just have faith, and she'll be saved."

---

* She isn't afraid because she stole a cure, but because her bloody sickness was considered unclean and she wasn't supposed to be touching anybody.

Going into the house, he wouldn't let anyone come in with him except Peter, James, John, and the father and mother of the child. Everyone was wailing and beating their breasts, but he said, "Don't cry: she didn't die, she's only sleeping." And they were laughing at him, because they knew she had died. But he, taking her hand, cried, "Child, get up!" And the breath came back into her, and she stood up suddenly, and he ordered that she be given something to eat. And her parents were ecstatic, but he commanded them not to tell anybody what happened.

9

Then calling the twelve together, he gave them power and authority over all demons and for the healing of diseases and sent them out to spread the word of the kingdom of God and cure the sick. And he said to them, "Take nothing on the road, no walking stick, no knapsack, no bread, no silver, nor two tunics on your back. And whatever house you go into, stay there till you leave that place. And wherever they don't receive you, when you leave that town shake the dust from your feet as a testimony to them." And they went out and started going through the villages, bringing the good word and curing people everywhere.

Now Governor Herod [Antipas] heard about all that had happened and was at a loss, because it was said by some that John had risen from the dead, by others that Elijah had appeared, and by still others that one of the ancient prophets had arisen. But Herod said, "John? I beheaded him. So who is this guy I keep hearing these things about?" And he was anxious to see him.

And the apostles came back and recounted to him what they had done. And taking them along he retreated privately to a town called Bethesda. But the crowds found out and followed him. And he, glad to see them, talked to them about the kingdom of God, and cured those who had need of a healing.

Now the sun was beginning to set, and the twelve came up to him and said, "Let the crowd go, so they can head for the villages and farms around here to find lodging and food, since we're here in the middle of nowhere."

He said to them, "Give them something to eat yourselves."

They said, "We have no more than five loaves of bread and two fish, unless we're supposed to go buy food for this whole population"—there were some five thousand men there.

But he said to his students, "Have them sit down in groups of fifty or so." And they did, and got them all seated. Then taking the five loaves and the two fish he looked up to the sky and blessed them and broke them and gave them to his students to put before the crowd. And they ate, and everybody ate their fill, and what they had left over was cleared away, twelve basketfuls of scraps.

And it happened while he was praying privately that his students were with him, and he asked them, "Who do the crowds say I am?"

They answered, "John the Baptist . . . others say Elijah, others say one of the ancient prophets risen again."

Then he said to them, "And you, who do you say I am?"

Peter answered, "The Anointed of God." But he strictly ordered them not to tell that to anyone, saying that the son of humanity would have to undergo many things and be rejected by the elders and high priests and canon-lawyers, and be killed, and rise up on the third day.

He said to them all, "If anyone wants to follow after me, let him repudiate himself and take up his cross day by day and follow me, because whoever wants to save his life will lose it, but whoever loses his life because of me, that's who will save it. After all, what does it help a person to gain the whole world if he loses himself or pays himself as the price? Because whoever is ashamed of me and my words, the son of humanity will be ashamed of him too when he comes in his glory and the glory of his Father and the holy messengers. I tell you truly, there are some of those standing right here who will never taste death before they see the kingdom of God."

It happened a week or so after he said these words that taking Peter and John and James along, he went up the mountain to pray. And in praying, his face took on a different appearance, and his clothing turned lightning white. And look, two men were talking with him: it was Moses and Elijah, appearing in glory, who were telling about the expedition he was going to make to Jerusalem. Peter and those who were with him were dragging with sleep, but they stayed awake and saw his glory and the two men standing there with him. And it happened while the others were taking leave of him that Peter said to Jesus, "Chief, it's good for us to be here, and let's make three tabernacles, one for you and one for Moses and one for Elijah"—he didn't know what he was saying. As he said that, a cloud came down and overshadowed them. They got scared, going into the cloud. And a voice came out of the cloud, saying, "This is my son, my chosen son: listen to him!" And as the voice came, Jesus was found alone. But they kept silent and told no one at the time of any of the things they'd seen.

It happened on the next day, as they were going down the mountain, that he was met by a great crowd. And this man came out of the crowd shouting, "Teacher, I beg you to have a look at my son, who is my only child, because one minute the spirit takes him and all of a sudden it screams, and it convulses him, with foaming at the mouth, and keeps wearing him down, hardly ever receding from him. And I asked your students to throw it out and they couldn't."

And Jesus answered, "Oh perverse and faithless crew, how long will I be with you and put up with you? Bring your son up here." Even as he came forward the demon made him break into convulsions, but Jesus yelled at the unclean spirit and healed the boy and gave him back to his father. And everyone was thunderstruck by the greatness of God.

As everyone was marveling at all the things he'd done, he said to his students, "Store these words in your ears: the son of humanity is going to be betrayed into the hands of the world." But they didn't know what he was saying, it was hidden from them so they wouldn't perceive it, and they were afraid to ask him about what he'd said.

And a dispute arose in their ranks about who was greater than who. And Jesus, knowing the thoughts in their hearts, went over to a little child and stood the child near him and said to them, "Whoever accepts this child in my name, accepts me. And whoever accepts me accepts the one who sent me. The lowest person among you, that's someone great."

At that, John said, "Chief, we saw someone throwing out demons in your name and stopped him, because he isn't one of our followers."

Jesus said to him, "Don't stop him: whoever isn't against us is for us."

It happened as the days of his exaltation were coming closer that he set his sights on journeying to Jerusalem. And he sent messengers before his face, and going their way they went into the village of the Samaritans so as to prepare things for him; and they wouldn't receive him, because his sights were set on journeying to Jerusalem. When his students saw that, James and John said, "Lord, do you want us to tell the fire to come down from the sky and burn them to ashes?" But he turned to them and told them off. And they traveled on to another village.

And with them traveling on the road, someone said to him, "I will follow you anywhere you go."

Said Jesus, "Foxes have dens, and the birds of the sky have places to camp, but the son of humanity has nowhere to lay his head."

He said to another, "Follow me."

And he said, "Let me first go bury my father."

But he said to him, "Let the dead bury their own dead, but you go off and tell about the kingdom of God."

Another one said, "I'll follow you, Lord, but first let me say goodbye to the people at home."

Jesus said to him, "No one who looks behind him when he puts his hand on the plow is cut out for the kingdom of God."

10

After that the Lord designated seventy-two others and sent them out by twos before his face to every town and place where he himself was going to come. And he said to them, "An ample harvest, and few workers! So ask the harvestmaster to send out workers to help with the harvesting. Go: I hereby send you out like lambs in the midst of wolves. Don't take a wallet or a knapsack or sandals, and don't pause to greet anyone along the way.

"Whatever house you go into, first say, 'Peace to this house.' And if a son of peace is there, your peace will alight on him; if not, it will turn round and come back to you. Stay in that place, eating and drinking with them, because the worker is worth his wages; don't move around from house to house. And whatever city you go into and they receive you, eat what's put before you, and cure the sick, and tell them, 'The kingdom of God is close upon you.' But whatever city you go into and they don't receive you, go out on the main streets and say, 'Even the dust of your town that clings to our feet we are wiping off in your face; but know this much, that the kingdom of God is approaching.' I'm telling you, Sodom will be better off than that city on that day.

"The worse for you, Chorazin! The worse for you, Bethesda! Because if the wonders had occurred in Tyre and Sidon that have occurred in you, *they* would long since have repented, sitting in sackcloth and ashes. But Tyre and Sidon will be better off on the judgment day than you. And you, Capharnaum, won't *you* be exalted to the skies? You'll sink into hell!

"Whoever listens to you, listens to me, and whoever rejects you, rejects me; but whoever rejects me, rejects the one who sent me."

The seventy-two came back saying joyfully, "Lord, even the demons are subject to us in your name."

And he said to them, "I saw Satan falling like lightning from the sky. Here, I have now given you authority to step on snakes and scorpions and all the power of the enemy, and none of it shall ever hurt you. But don't be glad that the spirits are subject to you, be glad that your names are inscribed in the skies."

In that hour he was delighted by the holy spirit and said, "I praise you, Father, lord of the sky and earth, that You hid these things from scholars and wits and opened them up to babies—yes, Father, because that's how Your good pleasure could be manifested before You. Everything was given me by my Father, and no one knows who the son is but the Father, and no one knows who the Father is but the son and those to whom the son chooses to reveal Him."

And turning privately to his students, he said, "How lucky your eyes are to see what you see, because I'm telling you, many prophets and kings wanted to see what you see and never saw it, and wanted to hear what you hear and never heard it."

And this lawyer stood up to test him saying, "Teacher, what do I do to inherit everlasting life?"

He said to him, "What does it say in the law? What do you read there?"

He answered, "You are to love the Lord your God with all your heart and all your soul and all your strength and all your thoughts, and love your neighbor as yourself."

He said to him, "You answered right. Do that and you'll live."

He, trying to defend himself, said to Jesus, "But who *is* my neighbor?"

By way of answer Jesus said, "Once there was a fellow coming back from Jerusalem to Jericho, and he fell among thieves, who stripped him, gave him a beating, and went off leaving him half dead. Now by chance a priest was coming down the same road, and seeing him, he walked the other way. Likewise a Levite who happened on the spot saw him and walked the other way. But a certain Samaritan who was on the road came upon him and felt sorry for him, and went up and bandaged his wounds, poured oil and wine on them, and seating him on his own mount, brought him to the inn and looked after him. The next day he pulled out two drachmas and gave them to the innkeeper saying, 'Look after him, and whatever you lay out I will repay you on my way back.' Which of these three would you say turned out to be the neighbor of the one who fell among thieves?"

He said, "The one who had mercy on him."

Said Jesus, "Go and do likewise."

In the course of their traveling he went into a certain village, and a woman named Martha received him. And she had a sister called Mary, who sat at the Lord's feet and listened to his words. Martha, meanwhile, was busy with all the work. So she got up and said, "Lord, you don't care that my sister left me here to work alone? Tell her to share the work with me."

But the Lord answered, "Martha, Martha, you're worrying and making noise about many things, when only one thing is needed. Mary chose the better half, and it won't be taken away from her."

11

And it happened when he was in a certain place praying, that when he stopped, one of his students said to him, "Lord, teach us to pray, the same as John taught his students."

And he said to them, "When you pray, say:

> Father,
> Let Your name be sanctified,
> May Your kingdom come.
> Give us day by day the next day's bread,
> And absolve us of our wrongs,
> For we too absolve all those indebted to us.
> And do not expose us to temptation."

And he said to them, "Which of you has a friend and if you went to him at midnight saying, 'Friend, lend me three loaves of bread, because a friend of mine just showed up from the road to see me and I have nothing to give him,' he would answer from within, 'Don't bother me! My door is locked already, my children are with me in bed, I can't get up and give you anything'? I'm telling you, if he doesn't get up and give it to you on account of your friendship, on account of your sheer effrontery he will get up and give you what you need. So I say to you, ask and you will be given to, look and you will find, knock and they will open for you.

Because every asker receives, every seeker finds, and whoever knocks is always admitted. Which of you, if your son asked you for a fish, would give him a snake instead of a fish? Or if he asked for an egg, you'd give him a scorpion? Well then, if you, villains that you are, know enough to give good gifts to your children, how much more will your Father send the sacred breath down from the sky to all who ask Him."

And he was throwing out a demon of muteness. And as it happened, when the demon was out, the mute man started talking, and the crowds were amazed. But some of them said, "By the power of Beelzebub, the demon ruler, he throws out demons." Others, testing him, asked him for a sign from the sky.

But he, knowing their thoughts, said to them: "Any kingdom split against itself gets wiped out, with one house falling on another. And if Satan is divided against himself, how will his kingdom stand up?—since you say I'm throwing out demons by Beelzebub's power. But if I'm throwing out demons in Beelzebub's name, by whose power are *your* children throwing them out, and won't they have reason to condemn you on that account? But if I throw out demons by the finger of God, truly the kingdom of God has caught up with you.

"When the strong man stands guarding his front yard in full armor, his possessions are at peace; but if someone stronger than him comes and overpowers him, he takes the armor in which the other had trusted and divides up the loot. Whoever isn't with me is against me, and whoever doesn't come herding with me scatters the herd.

"When the unclean spirit goes out of a person, it wanders through arid regions looking for a rest and not finding it. Then it says, 'I'll go back home where I came from.' And arriving it finds everything swept and tidied up. Then it goes and brings in seven spirits worse than itself, and they all go in and settle down there, and the person ends up worse off than before."

It happened as he was saying these things that a woman raised her voice from the crowd and said to him, "How lucky the womb that carried you and the breasts that nursed you!"

But he said, "More to the point, how lucky those who hear the word of God and keep it!"

As the crowds were collecting, he started talking: "This generation is an evil generation. It looks for a sign, and won't be given any sign but the sign of Jonah, because just as Jonah became a sign to the Ninevites, so will the son of humanity be a sign to this generation. The Queen of the South will stand up on judgment day among the men of this generation and will condemn them, because *she* came from the ends of the earth to hear the wisdom of Solomon, and here's more than Solomon right here. The men of Nineveh will stand up on judgment day among this generation and condemn it, because *they* had a change of heart in the face of Jonah's message, and here's more than Jonah right here.

"No one lights a candle and hides it away or puts it under a big basket; no, they put it up on a tall candlestick, so the people coming in can see the light.

"The candle of the body is the eye. If your eye is in one piece, your whole body is also lighted. If your eye goes bad, your body is likewise in darkness. So make sure the light within you isn't dark. If your whole body is lighted, with no part dark, everything will be as shining as when the candle illumines you in a flash."

As he was talking, a Pharisee asked him to have lunch with him, and he went in and sat down. The Pharisee was surprised to see that he didn't wash up first before lunch. But the Lord said to him, "Now as for you Pharisees, you clean off the outside of your cup and your platter, but the insides of you are full of greed and dishonesty. Fools, didn't the same maker who made the outside make the inside too? Instead, show concern for what is on the inside, and watch how everything comes clean for you.

"But woe to you Pharisees for getting your ten percent of the mint, parsley, and mixed vegetables and ignoring justice and the love of God: *those* are the things you should have done, and then the others shouldn't be omitted.

"Woe to you Pharisees for being in love with your seats in front of the church and the way everyone says hello to you downtown.

"Woe to you for being like obscure graves that people walk on without even knowing it."

Replied one of the lawyers, "Teacher, when you say that you're insulting us too."

And he said, "And woe to you lawyers for burdening the people with unbearable taxes, while you let no taxes come within arm's length of *you*.

"Woe to you for building monuments to the prophets, when it was your forefathers that killed them. You bear witness and give your approval to the deeds of your fathers: they killed them, you build the monuments. That's why the wisdom of God also said, 'I will send them prophets and emissaries, whom they will kill and persecute,' so that all the prophets' blood shed from the beginning of the world will be taken out on them, from the blood of Abel to the blood of Zachariah, who was killed between the altar and the temple proper. Yes, I tell you, that will all be taken out on this generation.

"Woe to you lawyers for holding the key to knowledge: you don't go in yourselves, and you stop the others from going in."

And by the time he left that place, the canon-lawyers and Pharisees had begun to be fiercely against him, and they started firing questions at him about various things, waiting in ambush for him to trap him with his own mouth.

12

Meanwhile with a crowd in the tens of thousands gathered, so many they were trampling each other, he started telling his students, "First of all, keep away from the yeast—that is, the hypocrisy—of the Pharisees.

"There is nothing hidden that won't be discovered, and no secret that will never be known; which means that what you said in the darkness will be heard in the light, and what you whispered in someone's ear inside a vault will be proclaimed from the housetops.

"But I tell you, my friends, don't be afraid of those who kill the body but after that have nothing more they can do. I'll tell you who to be afraid of: be afraid of Him who after your death has power to throw you into Gehenna. Yes, I tell you, fear Him! Aren't five sparrows sold for fifty cents? And not one of them is overlooked by the sight of God. No, even the hairs on your head are all accounted for. Don't be afraid. You matter more than a heap of sparrows.

"Let me tell you, everyone who stands behind me in front of the world, the son of humanity will stand behind them in front of the messengers of God. But whoever ignores me in front of the world will also be ignored in front of the messengers of God.

"And everyone who says something against the son of humanity, that will be forgiven them, but whoever speaks blasphemies against the sacred breath won't be forgiven.

"When they haul you into the synagogues and before the powers and authorities, don't worry about what defense you'll make or what you'll say. The sacred breath will tell you at the proper time what you must say."

Said someone from the crowd, "Teacher, tell my brother to share his inheritance with me."

But he said to him, "Fellow, who made me judge or executor between you?" Then he said to them all, "Watch and guard against having to have it all, because though you may be in the midst of plenty, real life doesn't come from possessions."

He made a comparison for them, saying: "Once there was a rich fellow whose land yielded a bumper crop. And he thought to himself, 'What shall I do? I don't have anywhere to store my crops.' And he said, 'This is what I'll do: I'll tear down my old silos and build bigger ones and store all my grain and goods there, and then I will say to my soul, *Soul, you have enough goods stored up for many years: relax; eat, drink, be merry.*'

"But God said to him, 'Fool, this very night you must give up your life. The things you got together, who are they for?' That's how it is with a person who stores up treasures for himself instead of being enriched in God."

And he said to his students, "That's why I tell you not to trouble your heart about what you'll eat or what you'll put on your back, because the breath of life is greater than food, and the body is greater than its clothing. Look at the crows: they don't sow, don't harvest, and don't have store-rooms or silos, and God still feeds them. And you matter so much more than birds. Which of you, by worrying about it, can add a foot to his height? Well then, if you can't do even the smallest things, why worry about the others? Look how the lilies grow: they don't toil and don't spin, but I'm telling you, not even Solomon in all his glory was ever dressed like one of them. And if that's how God clothes the wild grass in the field, there today and thrown into the furnace tomorrow, how much more will He clothe you, unbelievers. And don't wonder what you'll eat and what you'll drink, and avoid stargazing: all the nations of the world ask for these things, but your Father knows that you need these things. Just ask for His kingdom, and those other things will be put before you. Don't be afraid, little flock, because your Father saw fit to give you the kingdom.

"Sell your possessions and give to charity. Make yourselves wallets that don't wear through, an inexhaustible treasure in the skies, where no thief comes near and no moth eats away. After all, where your treasure is, that's where your heart will also be.

"Let your waist be belted and your lanterns lighted, and be like people waiting for their master when he breaks away from the wedding, so that when he comes and knocks they can open right up for him. Lucky for those slaves if the master comes and finds them awake. I tell you for sure, he will put on an apron and have them sit down and come serve them dinner. And if he comes in the second watch of the night, or the third, and finds them that way, lucky for them. You know this much: if the owner of the house knew what time the thief was coming, he would not let his house be tunneled into. And you be ready, because the son of humanity is coming at a time when you don't expect it."

Said Peter, "Are you making this comparison for our benefit or for everyone's?"

Said the Lord, "Who is the good and faithful steward whom the master appointed for his staff to give them their rations on schedule? Lucky for that slave if the master comes and finds him doing just that. I tell you truly, he will put him in charge of everything he owns. But if that slave says in his heart, 'My master is a long time coming' and starts beating up on the other serving-boys and -girls and eating and drinking and getting drunk, that slave's master will come on a day he isn't expecting and at a time he doesn't know, and will tear him apart and rank him among the infidels.

"That slave who knows the will of his master and doesn't get anything finished or do anything in line with his will, will receive many lashes, while the one who does something that deserves a beating without knowing it will receive few lashes: from the one to whom much was given, much will also be asked, and from the one to whom they entrusted much, they will ask even more.

"I came to set the earth on fire, and what do I wish? That it were already ablaze! I have a bath to be bathed, and how can I rest easy till that is carried out? Do you think I came to bring peace on earth? No, I tell you, I came to bring division: from now on there will be five in one house split three against two or two against three. Father will be turned against son and son against father, mother against daughter and daughter against mother, mother-in-law against daughter-in-law and daughter-in-law against mother-in-law."

Then he said to the crowds: "As soon as you see the clouds rising in the west, you say, 'It's going to be overcast'; and so it turns out. And when the south wind blows you say, 'It's going to be blazing hot,' and so it is. You fakes, you know how to read the face of the earth and sky, how come you don't know how to read the signs of these times?

"Why don't you discern, even by yourselves, what justice is? Because if you're going with your adversary before the governor, while you're on the road make an effort to settle with him, so he doesn't hale you before the judge, and the judge hands you over to the jailer, and the jailer throws you in jail. I'm telling you, you won't get out of there till you've paid off every last penny."

13

There were some people there at that time reporting to him about the Galileans whose blood Pilate had mixed with his sacrifices. And he answered them, "Do you think those Galileans were any greater criminals than all the other Galileans? I say no, but if you don't all have a change of heart you'll die the same way. Or how about those eighteen people on whom the tower fell at Siloam, killing them all: do you think they deserved to have that happen more than all the other people inhabiting Jerusalem? I say no, but if you don't all have a change of heart you'll die the same way."

Then he made this comparison: "Once there was someone who had a fig tree planted in his orchard and came looking for the fruit and found none. So he said to the gardener, 'This is three years now I've been coming to look for some fruit on this fig-tree and not finding any. Cut it down: why should it even take up space?'

"But he answered, 'Master, leave it alone this one year more, while I dig around the roots and give it manure, to see if it bears fruit in the future; if not, you can cut it down.' "

He was teaching in one of the synagogues on the Sabbath. And there was this woman who had had a spirit weakening her for eighteen years, and she was bent over and unable to lift her head all the way up. Jesus saw her and called to her, "Madam, you are delivered from your weakness," and he put his hands on her, and she suddenly straightened up and glorified God.

But the chief of the synagogue, outraged at Jesus for healing on the Sabbath, said to the crowd: "You have six days on which work is to be done, you can come on one of those days and heal, and not on the Sabbath-day."

But the Lord answered him, "You fakes, which of you, when it's the Sabbath, doesn't let his ox or his ass out of the stall and give it water? But this daughter of Abraham, whom Satan bound these eighteen years, wasn't supposed to be released from those chains because it was the Sabbath?" And when he said that all his opponents were put to shame, and all the crowd rejoiced at all the glorious things done by him.

So he said, "What is the kingdom of God like, and what shall I compare it to? It's like a seed of the mustard-plant which a person took and threw into their garden, and it grew and turned into a tree, and the birds of the sky settled among its branches."

And again he said, "What shall I compare the kingdom of God to? It's like yeast, which a woman took and mixed in with three sacks of flour till it all rose."

And he went on through towns and villages, teaching and making his way to Jerusalem.

Said someone to him once, "Lord, are only a few saved?"

And he said to them, "Struggle to get in through the narrow door, because many people, I'm telling you, try to get in and don't make it. And at the point when the master of the house gets up and bars the door, and you start standing outside and beating on the door, saying, 'Lord, let us in,' he will answer you, 'I don't know where you come from: away from me, all workers of iniquity!' That's where the wailing and gnashing of teeth will be, when you see Abraham, Isaac, Jacob, and all the prophets in the kingdom of God, and you thrown outside. And they will come in from east and west and from north and south and sit down to dinner in the kingdom of God. And watch how many of the last will be first and how many of the first will be last."

At that hour some Pharisees came up to him saying, "Go on your way and get out of here, because Herod's looking to kill you."

And he said to them, "Go tell the old fox, 'Look, I'm throwing out demons and completing cures today and tomorrow, and day after tomorrow I'll be done. But for today and tomorrow and the day after, I have to go free—because it's against the rules for a prophet to be killed anywhere outside Jerusalem.'

"Jerusalem, Jerusalem, killer of prophets, stoner of ambassadors to the city, how often I have wished to gather your children together the way a bird gathers her nestlings under her wing—and you didn't want to!

And now look, your house is taken away from you. But I tell you, you will see me no more until you say, 'Bless him who comes in the name of the Lord.' "

14

And it happened once when he came to the home of one of the leaders of the Pharisees to take bread on the Sabbath, that the others were also watching him.

And there was this fellow with dropsy there in front of him. And Jesus reacted by saying to the lawyers and Pharisees, "Is it all right to heal on the Sabbath or not?" They were silent. And taking hold of the man he cured him and sent him off. Then he said to them: "Which of you would let your son—or your cow—fall into a ditch and not immediately reach out your hand, because it was the Sabbath-day?" And they had no answer for that.

And he made this comparison for the guests, noticing how they picked out the choicest seats for themselves: "When you sit down to the banquet at someone's wedding, don't sit at the head table, in case some more honored guest than you has been invited, and the one who invited both him and you comes and says, 'Give this person your seat,' and then you have to get up red-faced and go to the very back. But when you're invited someplace, go sit down in the back, so that when your host comes he'll say to you, 'Dear friend! Please come up front!' That way it will be an honor for you in front of all your fellow-guests, because the one who exalts himself will be humbled and the one who humbles himself will be exalted."

Then he said to his host, "When you give a luncheon or dinner, don't invite your brothers and sisters or your relatives, or your rich neighbors, because then they'll return the invitation and you'll be paid back. But when you give a party, invite the poor, the sick, the crippled, the blind; and you'll be in luck, because they have nothing to pay you back with: you'll be paid back in the resurrection of the just."

One of the guests, on hearing that, said to him, "How lucky the person who eats bread in the kingdom of God!"

And he said to him, "Once there was a fellow who gave a big dinner party and invited a lot of people and sent his slave at dinner time to tell the guests, 'Come on, everything's all ready.'

"And they started begging off one after the other. The first one said, 'I just bought a field, and it's vital that I go out and see it.' And another said, 'I just bought five yokes of oxen and I'm going just now to look them over; please consider me excused.' And another said, 'I just got married, that's why I can't come.' And when the slave got back he told all that to his master.

"Then the master of the house said to his slave in a fury, 'Go through the main streets and side-alleys of the city and bring the poor here and the maimed and the blind and the lame.'

"And the slave said, 'Lord, what you ordered is done, and there's still room.'

"And the master said to the slave, 'Go out into the streets and yards and make them come, till my house is full, because I'm telling you, none of those men who were invited will ever taste my dinner.' "

Now giant crowds were gathering around him, and he turned and said to them, "If anyone comes to me and cares about his father or his mother or his wife or his children or his brother or his sisters or even his own life, he can't be my student. Whoever doesn't pick up the cross and walk behind me, can't be my student.

"After all, which of you planning to build a tower would not first sit down and weigh the expenses to see if there would be enough to finish it?—so you don't end up laying the foundation and then being unable to finish it off, and everyone who sees it starts making fun of you and saying, 'Look at this fellow who started building and couldn't finish!' And what king marching forth against another king to engage him in war does not first sit down and take stock as to whether with his ten thousand he can take on the one coming against him with twenty thousand? Because if not, before the other even gets close he will send his emissaries to ask terms of peace. Well, in the same way, anyone of you who doesn't say goodbye to all your possessions can't be my student.

"Salt is certainly a good thing, but if it goes tasteless, what will you spice it with? It's no good for the soil, nor even for the dung-heap, you just throw it out. Whoever has ears to hear, hear!"

15

Now all the tax-collectors and godless people were coming close to hear him. And the Pharisees and canon-lawyers were grumbling, "This guy gives godless people a warm welcome and eats with them."

But he made this comparison for them, saying, "What person among you who had a hundred sheep and lost one of them would not leave the ninety-nine there in the wilds and go look for the lost one till he finds it? And when he finds it won't he happily put it on his shoulders and go home and call his friends and neighbors in, saying, 'Be happy with me: I found my sheep that was lost'? Likewise, I tell you, there will be joy in the sky over one evildoer's change of heart more so than over ninety-nine of the just who have no need of a change of heart.

"Or what woman who has ten drachmas and loses one wouldn't light a lantern and sweep the house and carefully look till she finds it, and on finding it wouldn't call her friends and neighbors in, saying, 'Be happy with me, because I found the drachma I had lost'? Likewise, I tell you, there is joy among the messengers of God over one evildoer's change of heart."

And he said, "Once there was a fellow who had two sons. And the younger of them said to the father, 'Father, give me the part of your property coming to me.' So he divided his property between them. And not many days later, the younger son collected all his things and took off for a faraway country where he squandered his fortune with dissolute living. After he'd spent it all, an intense famine came over that country, and he started to run short. So he went and attached himself to one of the citizens of that country, who sent him into his fields to keep the pigs. And he was dying to eat some of the carob pods that the pigs were eating, but no one gave him any. And coming to himself he said, 'Think of all the hired hands in my father's house who have plenty of bread, and here I am dying of hunger. I'll get up and go to my father and say to him, *Father, I did wrong against heaven and in your eyes. I don't deserve to be called your son any more, treat me like one of your hired hands.*' And he got up and went to his father. While he was still at a distance, his father saw him and was moved, and ran and threw his arms around him and kissed him. The son said to him, 'Father, I did wrong against heaven and in your eyes. I don't deserve to be called your son any more.'

"But the father said to his slaves, 'Quick, bring the finest robe and put it on him, and put a ring on his finger and shoes on his feet. And bring the fattened steer and slaughter it, and let's eat and be happy, because this son of mine was dead and came to life again, he was lost and was found again.' And they started making merry.

"Now his older son was in the fields, and as he came near the house, he heard the music-making and singing, and he called one of the boys over and inquired what that was all about. He said to him, 'Your brother came back, and your father slaughtered the fattened steer, because he got him back safe and sound.' But he got mad and wouldn't go inside.

"So his father came out and pleaded with him, but he answered his father: 'How many years is this that I have slaved away for you and never sidestepped any command of yours? And you never let *me* have a goat so I could have a good time with my friends. But when this son of yours who frittered away your fortune on whores came back, for him you slaughtered the fattened steer!'

"But he said to him, 'Child, you're always with me, and everything that's mine is yours. But we had to make merry and rejoice, because this brother of yours was dead and came alive again, and was lost and was found again.' "

16

And he said to his students further: "Once there was a rich fellow who had an estate manager who was reported to him as squandering his goods. And calling him in he said to him, 'What's this I hear about you? Hand in the manager's books, you can't be my manager any more.'

"The manager said to himself, 'What will I do now that my master is taking my manager's job away from me? I'm not strong enough to dig and I'm ashamed to beg. I know what I'll do, so that when I move out of my manager's position I'll be welcome in their houses.'

"And calling each one of his master's creditors in he said to the first, 'How much do you owe my master?'

"And he said, 'A hundred tubs of olive oil.'

"He said to him, 'Here's your certificate, sit right down and make it fifty.'

"Then he said to another, 'And how much do you owe?'

"He said, 'Four hundred bushels of wheat.'

"He says to him, 'Here's your certificate, make it three hundred.'

"And the master commended the manager for the felony insofar as he had acted prudently: 'The children of the here and now are so much more prudent in dealing with their own kind than the children of the light!' And I say to you, use your ill-gotten wealth to make friends for yourselves, so that when it runs out you will always be welcome in their eternal lodgings.*

"Whoever is trustworthy in the smallest matter is also trustworthy in something larger, and whoever is dishonest in the smallest matter is also dishonest in something larger. So if you couldn't be trusted with ill-gotten gains, who will credit you with your legitimate earnings? And if you couldn't be trusted with other people's things, who will give you what is yours?

"No servant can serve two masters. Either he'll hate the one and love the other, or he'll put up with one and despise the other. You can't serve God *and* the Almighty Dollar." **

Some of the Pharisees who were moneygrubbers heard all that and started sneering at him. And he said to them, "You're the kind who justify yourselves in the eyes of the world. But God knows your hearts: what is sublime to the world is a horror in the eyes of God.

"The Law and the Prophets go up to John; from that point on the good word of the kingdom of God has been spread, while everyone does violence against it. But it is easier for the sky and the earth to go away than for a single comma to fall out of the law.

"Anyone who puts away his wife and marries another is living in adultery, and anyone who marries a divorced woman is living in adultery.

"Once there was a rich fellow, and he was dressed in royal purple and fine linen and spent every day feasting in splendor. And there was a beggar named Lazarus lying outside his gates, full of ulcers and dying to satisfy his hunger with the crumbs dropping from the rich man's table. But the dogs even came and licked his wounds. Finally the beggar died and was carried by God's messengers to the bosom of Abraham. The rich man died too and was buried.

"And lifting up his eyes in hell, where he was in torment, he sees Abraham from afar and Lazarus in his lap. And he called out, 'Father Abraham, have pity on me and send Lazarus to dip the tip of his finger in water and cool off my tongue, because I'm tormented by these flames.'

---

* On the whole this parable is understandable as an example of "being forgiven our debts as we forgave our debtors," but why will the debtors who were let off easy welcome the dishonest manager into their "eternal" lodgings? Perhaps because they will be his defenders on Judgment Day? Or is the word an exaggeration: "they will welcome you into their lodgings forever"?

** See the note on page 30.

"Said Abraham, 'Child, remember that during your life you had all the good things, and Lazarus likewise all the bad. But now here he is consoled, while you are tormented. And all through here there is fixed a great gulf, so that those who want to cross from here to you can't do so, nor can they cross from there toward us.'

"So he said, 'Then father, I beg you, send him to my father's house—you see, I have five brothers—so he can bear witness to them, so that they don't end up in this place of torment too.'

"Says Abraham, 'They have Moses and the prophets, let them listen to them.'

"But he said, 'No, father Abraham, but if one of the dead goes to them they will change their minds.'

"He said to him, 'If they won't listen to Moses and the prophets, even if someone arises from the dead they won't be persuaded.' "

17

He said to his students, "It's unavoidable that scandals should come along, but woe to him through whom they come. It would be a good thing for him to have a millstone tied around his neck and be thrown into the sea, rather than mislead one of these little ones: watch yourselves!

"If your brother does you wrong, have it out with him, and if he changes his mind, forgive him. And if seven times a day he does you wrong and seven times comes back and says, I'm sorry, you shall forgive him."

And the apostles said to the lord, "Give us more faith!"

Said the Lord, "If you have a mustard-seed's worth of faith, if you said to this mulberry tree, 'Pull up your roots and plant yourself in the sea,' it would obey you. Which of you who has a slave plowing or herding would say to him as he comes in from the fields, 'Go right on in and have dinner' instead of saying to him, 'Make dinner for me and serve me with your apron on till I've finished eating and drinking, and then you can eat and drink'? And do you feel obliged to the slave because he carried out your orders? No. The same goes for you, then: when you've carried out all the commandments, say, 'We're just good-for-nothing slaves who've done our job.' "

And it happened as he was journeying to Jerusalem that he passed through the middle of Samaria and Galilee.

And as he was entering a certain village he was met by ten men with leprosy, who stood at a distance and raised their voices, saying, "Master Jesus, have pity on us."

And seeing them he said, "Go show yourselves to the priests." And what happened was that as they went their way, they were cleansed. One of them, though, seeing he had been healed, came back glorifying God with a loud voice and fell on his face at his feet thanking him—he was a Samaritan. Jesus responded, "Weren't all ten cleansed? Where are the other nine? Was nobody seen returning to give glory to God but this one foreigner?" And he said to him, "Get up and go your way, your trust has saved you."

Asked by the Pharisees when the kingdom of God was coming he answered: "The kingdom of God doesn't come with watching like a hawk, and they won't say, Here it is, or There it is, because, you know what? the kingdom of God is inside you."

Then he said to his students, "There will come days when you will be dying to see one of the days of the son of humanity, but you won't see it. And they will say to you, Look there, or Look here, but don't go there and don't go hunting. Because as the lightning flashes from underside to underside of the sky, that's what the son of humanity will be like when his day comes. First, though, he must undergo many things and be rejected by this generation. And just as it happened in Noah's day, so will it be in the son of humanity's day: they were eating, drinking, and taking wives and husbands up to the day when Noah went into the ark and the cataclysm came and destroyed them all. Likewise, just as it happened in the days of Lot, they were eating, drinking, buying, selling, planting, building; then on the day Lot went out of Sodom, it rained fire and sulfur from the skies and destroyed them all. It will be along the same lines on the day the son of humanity is revealed. On that day whoever is up on the roof with their things down in the house, don't go down to get them, and whoever is in the fields, likewise, don't turn back: remember Lot's wife. Whoever tries to keep their life safe will lose it, whereas whoever loses their life will engender it. I'm telling you, that night there will be two in one bed: one will be taken along and the other left behind. Two women will be grinding corn together: one will be taken along and the other left behind."

And they said, "Where will that be, Lord?"

He said to them, "Where the body is, the vultures also gather."

18

He spoke to them making a comparison about how necessary it is always to pray and never to lose heart, saying, "There was a certain judge in a certain city who neither feared God nor respected humanity. Now there was a widow in that city, and she came to him saying, 'Take on my case against my adversary,' and for a long time he wouldn't.

"But finally he said to himself, 'Even if I don't fear God nor respect humanity, because of the grief this widow is giving me I'll take on her case, so that she doesn't end up giving me a black eye.' "

Said the Lord, "Hear what that dishonest judge says? Now won't God take the side of His chosen ones crying to Him night and day, and have patience with them? I tell you He will take their side at once. The real question is, will the son of humanity when he comes find any faith upon the earth?"

He spoke further to some people who were convinced of their own innocence and inclined to regard the others as nothing, making this comparison: "Once there were two fellows who went up to the temple to pray, one a Pharisee and the other a tax-collector. The Pharisee stood and prayed to himself as follows: 'God, I thank you that I'm not like the rest of the world—greedy, unjust, unchaste—nor indeed like this tax-collector here. I fast twice a week, I give ten percent of everything I own.'

"Whereas the tax collector stood way in the back, wouldn't even raise his eyes skyward, just beat his breast and said, 'God, be kind to a loser like me.' I'm telling you, he went home cleared of his guilt—more so than the other one, because all who exalt themselves will be humbled, and all who humble themselves will be exalted."

Now they were even bringing the little kids to him so he could put his hands on them; when they saw that, his students yelled at them. But Jesus called them to him, saying, "Let the kids come to me and don't hold them back: the kingdom of God belongs to such as these. I tell you for sure, anyone who does not accept the kingdom of God like a little child will never get into it."

And a certain prince asked him, "Good teacher, what shall I do to inherit everlasting life?"

Said Jesus, "Why do you call me good? No one is good but God alone. You know the commandments: 'You are not to commit adultery, you are not to murder, you are not to steal, you are not to perjure yourself, do right by your father and your mother.' "

He said, "I have kept all those since childhood."

Hearing that, Jesus said to him, "One thing is still missing in you: sell everything you have and give it out to the poor, and you will have a treasure in the skies, and come here and follow me." Hearing that, he was most unhappy, because he was very rich indeed.

Seeing how unhappy he had become, Jesus said, "How difficult it is for those with money to enter the kingdom of God. Indeed, it's easier for a camel to squeeze through the eye of a needle than for a rich man to get into the kingdom of God."

Those who heard him said, "Then who *can* be saved?"

He said, "What's impossible for human beings is possible for God."

Said Peter, "Look at us: we have left behind what was ours and followed you."

He said to them, "I assure you, no one who has left house or wife or brothers or parents or children for the kingdom of God will fail to get it back many times over in this life, along with everlasting life in the time to come."

Taking the twelve along he said to them: "Here we go up to Jerusalem, and all the writings of the prophets will be fulfilled for the son of humanity: he will be handed over to the people and made fun of and mistreated and spat upon, and after whipping him they will kill him, and on the third day he will rise again." And they didn't understand any of that; his words were hidden from them and they didn't know what he was saying.

It happened as he was nearing Jericho that a certain blind man was sitting by the road begging. Hearing the crowd passing through he inquired what was going on. They told him Jesus of Nazareth was passing by. And he cried out, "Jesus, son of David, have mercy on me." And the people in the front of the crowd yelled at him to be quiet, but he shouted all the more, "Son of David, have mercy on me."

Stopping in his tracks, Jesus ordered him to be brought to him. When he got closer, he asked him, "What do you want me to do for you?"

He said, "Lord, let me see again."

And Jesus said, "See again! Your trust has saved you." And suddenly he could see again and followed him, praising God. And all the people, seeing that, gave praise to God.

19

And after entering Jericho he passed on through. And there was this man, Zacchaeus by name, and he was the chief tax-collector and a very rich man. And he wanted to see who this Jesus was and couldn't because of the crowd, since he was too short. And running up front he climbed up a mulberry tree to see him, because he was about to pass by it.

And as he reached the spot, Jesus looked up and said to him, "Zacchaeus, come down as fast as you can, I'm going to stay at your house today." And he came down as fast as he could and joyfully received him.

And seeing that, everyone started grumbling, "He went to stay with that evil man."

But Zacchaeus, stopping in place, said to the Lord, "I hereby give half my possessions to the poor, and if I have strongarmed anybody out of anything, I'll give it back quadruple."

Jesus said to him, "Today salvation came to this house, which is indeed descended from Abraham; after all, the son of humanity came to look for and recover what was lost."

While they were listening to these things he made a further comparison having to do with his being near to Jerusalem and their belief that the kingdom of God would appear any second. He said, then: "Once there was a nobleman who went to a faraway land to take possession of a kingdom and return. Calling ten of his underlings he gave them a thousand drachmas and said to them, 'Do business while I'm gone.'

"But his subjects hated him and sent messengers after him, saying, 'We don't want this person ruling us.' And as it happened, upon his return after taking possession of the kingdom he also had these underlings called in to whom he had given the money, to find out how they'd handled it.

"The first came along saying, 'Master, your hundred drachmas brought in a thousand.'

"And he said to him, 'Well done, good servant! Since you proved trustworthy in the smallest matter, receive authority over ten cities.'

"And the second came and said, 'Your hundred drachmas, master, made five hundred.'

"And he said to him, 'So take over five cities.'

"And another came and said, 'Master, here's your hundred drachmas back which I kept hidden in a handkerchief. Thing is, I was afraid of you, you being the hard fellow that you are, who withdraws what he didn't deposit and reaps what he didn't sow.'

"He says to him, 'Your own mouth convicts you, you terrible servant! You knew I was a hard fellow, did you, withdrawing what I didn't deposit and reaping what I didn't sow? Then how come you didn't put my money in the bank, where I could have gone and gotten it back with interest?' And he said to those assembled, 'Take the hundred drachmas from him and give it to the one with a thousand.'

"And they said, "But master, he already *has* a thousand!'

" 'I'm telling you,' he said, 'he who has will be given more, from him who has nothing even what he has will be taken away. But as for those enemies of mine that didn't want me ruling over them, bring them here and slaughter them in front of me.' "

And after saying all that he journeyed onward, going up to Jerusalem.

And it happened as he got near to Bethphage and Bethany, by the mountain called Mount Olive, that he sent off two of his students saying, "Go into that village over there, where upon entering you'll find a young donkey tied up which no person has ever sat upon: untie it and bring it here. And if anyone asks you, 'What are you untying it for?' just say, 'Its master needs it.' "

The ones dispatched went off and found it as he had told them. As they were untying the donkey its keepers said to them, "What are you doing untying that donkey?"

So they said, "Its master needs it."

And they brought it to Jesus, and after throwing their cloaks over it they seated Jesus upon it. And as he rode on, they were throwing their cloaks along the road. By the time he was close to coming down Mount Olive the whole mass of his students had already started the jubilee, loudly praising God for all the wonders they had seen and saying, "Bless him who comes there, the king in the name of the Lord! Peace in the sky! Glory to the highest heavens!"

And some of the Pharisees came out of the crowd and said to him, "Teacher, restrain these students of yours."

And he answered, "I tell you, if they fell silent, the rocks would scream out."

And as they neared the city he saw it and wept for it saying, "If you only knew on this day which way leads to peace—but now it is hidden from your eyes; because there will come upon you days when your enemies corner you in a hollow and surround you and press in on you from every side, and hurl you and your children to the ground, and leave no stone upon another amongst you all, because you didn't know when the time of your inspection was."

And going into the temple he started throwing out the dealers, saying to them, "It says,

My house shall be a house of prayer,

but you've made it a den of thieves."

And he was teaching in the temple daily, and the high priests and canon-lawyers wanted to get rid of him and so did the leaders among the people, but they couldn't figure out what to do, because the people were all listening to him, hanging on his every word.

20

And it happened on one of the days when he was teaching the people in the temple and spreading the good word that the high priests and canon-lawyers, along with the elders, finally said to him, "Tell us what authority you have to do this. Who gave you any such authority?"

He answered them, "I also want to ask you a question: Tell me, did the washing of John come from heaven or from the world?"

They discussed that among themselves, saying, "If we say from heaven, he'll say, 'Then why didn't you believe him?' But if we say from the world, the entire mob will pelt us with rocks, they're so convinced that John was a prophet." So they answered, "We don't know where it came from."

And Jesus said to them, "I won't tell you what authority I have to do this either."

He began to make this comparison for the people: "Once there was a fellow who planted a vineyard and leased it to some tenant-farmers and left the country for quite a while. In time he sent his slave to the farmers to get the produce of the vineyard from them, but the farmers whipped him soundly and sent him off emptyhanded. He sent an additional slave, whom they also flayed and brutalized and sent off emptyhanded. And he went on sending a third, whom they wounded and threw out. Said the owner of the vineyard, 'What shall I do? I will send my beloved son: maybe they will respect *him*.'

"But when they saw him, the farmers said to each other, 'Look, it's the heir! Let's kill him, and the inheritance is ours.' And they dragged him outside the vineyard and killed him. So what will the owner of the vineyard do? He'll come and wipe those farmers out and give the vineyard to others."

When they heard that they said, "Let's hope it never happens."

Looking straight at them he said, "What does it say there:

> *A stone that the builders rejected,*
> *That one ended up the cornerstone?*

Anyone who falls on that stone will be smashed to bits. And anyone it falls upon will be crushed."

And the canon-lawyers and high priests wanted to put their hands on him at that point, except that they were afraid of the people; they knew he was making that comparison about *them*.

And as they looked on, their henchmen were sent forth, acting innocent, to get some word out of him such that they could hand him over to the government and the authority of the governor. And they asked him, "Teacher, we know you talk and teach straightforwardly and are no respecter of persons, but rather teach God's way based on truth: Is it all right to pay taxes to Caesar or not?"

Sensing their plot he said, "Show me a denarius. Whose picture and inscription does it have on it?"

They said, "Caesar's."

So he said to them, "Well, then, give Caesar's things to Caesar and God's things to God." And they weren't able to catch him in his words in front of the people and were dumbfounded at his answer.

Some Sadducees came forward, the ones who said there was no resurrection, and asked him this question: "Teacher, Moses prescribed for us that 'If someone's brother dies who had a wife, but was childless, let the brother take his wife and raise up offspring for his brother.' So: once there were seven brothers, and the first took a wife and died childless. And the second took her, and the third, and in this manner finally all seven died without leaving children; last of all the wife died. So, in the resurrection, whose wife will that woman be? After all, all seven had her for a wife."

And Jesus said to them, "The sons and daughters of the here and now take wives and husbands, but those who have proven worthy to receive that other Life and be resurrected from the dead take no wives and no husbands, because they can't die any more: they're equal to the angels and are sons and daughters of God, being sons and daughters of the resurrection. That the dead rise again was mentioned even by Moses before the burning bush, when he talks about 'the Lord, God of Abraham and the God of Isaac and the God of Jacob.' There is no God of the dead, only of the living: to him, everyone is alive."

Some of the canon-lawyers answered, "Teacher, you spoke well." After that they didn't dare ask him any more questions.

Then he said to them, "How can they say the Anointed is David's son? Why, David himself says in the book of Psalms,

A Lord said to my Lord,
Sit on my right
Till I've finished making your enemies
Into a footstool for your feet.

David, then, called him 'Lord,' so how can he be his son?"

Then with all the people listening he said to his students, "Watch out for clerics who want to walk around in fine robes and who like everybody saying hello to them downtown and their seats in the front of churches and at the head tables of banquets, who wolf down the houses of widows and make a show of praying at great length. They will receive an extra condemnation."

21

Then he looked round and saw the rich people throwing their contributions into the collection-box, and he saw a poor widow throwing in a couple of dimes. And he said, "I'm telling you the truth, that poor widow put in more than all the others. Because all the others put in what they had left over as their contributions while she in her extremity put in all she had to live on."

And as some were talking about the temple, what fine masonry and what fine artworks it was decorated with, he said, "As for what you see here, there will come days when not a stone of it will rest upon another without being toppled."

And they asked him, "Teacher, when will that be, and what will be the sign that it's going to happen?"

He said, "Watch out, don't be fooled, because many will come along in my name saying, 'Here I am,' and 'The time has come.' Don't follow after them. And when you hear of wars and revolutions, don't go into shock. Those things have to happen first, but that's not quite the end."

Then he said to them, "Nation will rise against nation, country against country. There will be giant earthquakes, famines and plagues in places, terrors and mighty signs from the sky.

"But before all that they will lay their hands upon you and persecute you, handing you over to synagogues and jails; you'll be haled before kings and governors because of my name. It will happen to you as a testimony. So put in your hearts that you're not going to worry about speaking in your defense: I will give you a mouth and wisdom such as all your adversaries together cannot withstand or gainsay. You will also be betrayed by parents, sisters, brothers, relatives, and friends; they will kill some of you, and you will be despised by everyone because of my name. And not a hair of your head will be lost; your perseverance will gain you your souls.

"When you see Jerusalem surrounded by armies, then you know its destruction is approaching. Then those in Judea, flee into the mountains, and those in the central region, get out, and those in the other countries, don't come in; because those will be days of settling scores, of fulfilling all the scriptures. Woe to those with a child in their belly or nursing in those days! There will be great need upon the earth and anger toward this people, and they will fall by the tooth of the sword and be enslaved to all the nations, and Jerusalem will be stamped on by pagans, till the pagans' time is up.

"And there will be signs in the sun and moon and stars, and on earth an anxious mass of people in confusion over the roar of the sea and the tides, with people dying of fear and apprehension about what's coming over the world. Yes, the powers of heaven will be shaken. And then they will see the son of humanity coming on a cloud with power and great glory. When these things start to happen, look up and raise your heads, because your redemption is approaching."

And he made a comparison for them: "You see the fig tree—indeed, all the trees? When they're already bearing fruit, you can tell from looking at them that the harvest time is already close. In the same way, when you see these things happening, you know the kingdom of God is close. I assure you that this generation will not pass away till it all happens. The sky and the earth will pass away, but these words of mine will never pass away.

"Watch yourselves now; don't let your hearts get sluggish with debauchery and drinking and the worries of life, and then all of a sudden that day comes upon you, because it will spring like a trap on all those who inhabit the face of all the earth.

"So stay awake, begging at all times that you will be able to escape from all these things that are going to happen and stand before the son of humanity."

He was teaching in the temple by day and going out by night and camping on the mountain called Mount Olive. And all the people were getting up early to go hear him in the temple.

22

The feast of the unleavened bread was getting close, the one called Passover. And the high priests and canon-lawyers were searching for the way to get rid of him, except that they were afraid of the people.

Then Satan entered Judas, known as Judas Iscariot, who was numbered among the twelve, and he went off and talked with the priests and generals about the way for him to hand him over to them. And they were delighted and promised to give him money. And he gave them his word and started looking for the right time to hand him over to them without a crowd around.

So came the day of the unleavened bread, when it was time to sacrifice for Passover. And he sent off Peter and John saying, "Go get the seder ready for us to eat."

They said to him, "Where do you want us to get it ready?"

He said to them, "Just as you're getting into town you'll be met by a fellow carrying a water jug. Follow him into the house he enters and say to the owner of the house, 'Our teacher says, *Where are the quarters where I can eat the seder with my students?*' And he'll show you a big furnished room on the second floor. That's where you'll get it ready." They went and found things as he had told them and got the seder ready.

And when the time came, he sat down, and the apostles with him. And he said to them: "I wanted with all my heart to eat the seder with you before my suffering begins, because I'm telling you, I'll never eat it again until it is fulfilled in the kingdom of God." And being handed a cup he gave thanks and said, "Take this and share it among you, because I'm telling you, I'll never drink again of the produce of the vineyard till the kingdom of God comes." And taking bread he gave thanks and broke it and gave it to them saying, "This is my body given for you: do this in my memory." And he did the same with the cup after dinner, saying, "This cup is the new contract, sealed in my blood poured out for you.

"But what's this? The hand of my betrayer is with me on the table! Yes, the son of humanity is going to meet his destiny, but woe to that person by whom he is betrayed." And they started arguing with each other about which of them it could possibly be who was going to do such a thing.

And finally rivalry broke out among them about who was greater than who. And he said to them, "The kings of nations lord it over them and those who throw their weight around are called patriots. But you're different: whoever is greatest among you, act like the youngest person there; whoever is the leader, act like the servant. After all, who is higher up: the guest or the servant? The guest, right? But here I am in your midst like a servant.

"You are the ones who have stayed with me through all my trials, and I am putting a kingdom in your hands as my Father put it in mine, that you may eat and drink at my table in my kingdom and sit upon your thrones judging the twelve tribes of Israel.

"Simon, Simon, look there! Satan asked for you to be given up, for him to winnow his wheat with. But I pleaded for you that your faith might not give out. And you will return the favor someday by shoring up your brothers."

And he said to him, "Lord, with you at my side I'm ready to go to jail or even to my death."

He said, "I'm telling you, Peter, the cock won't crow tomorrow morning before you have said three times that you don't know me."

And he said to them: "When I sent you off with no wallet or knapsack or shoes, you didn't run short of anything, did you?"

They said, "No, nothing."

He said to them: "But now, whoever has a wallet, take it along, and your knapsack likewise; and whoever doesn't have a sword, you'd better sell your cloak and buy one, because I'm telling you that the scriptures will be fulfilled through me, the part about 'And he was numbered among the outlaws'—in fact, its words about me are coming to fulfillment."

And they said, "Lord, we have two swords here."

And he said, "That's enough."

And going outside he walked as usual up Mount Olive, with his students also following him. Reaching the spot, he said to them, "Pray not to be put to the test." And he excused himself, going about a stone's throw away from them, and went down on his knees and prayed: "Father, if you can, take this cup away from me, but let your will be done, not mine." A messenger appeared to him from the sky to give him strength. And sinking into agony he prayed even harder, and his sweat came like drops of blood raining down on the ground. And when he stood up from praying and came back to his students he found them sleeping off their pain and said to them, "Why are you sleeping? Get up and pray that you may not be put to the test."

Even as he spoke, there was the crowd, and the one of the twelve called Judas was leading them, and he came close to Jesus to kiss him. And Jesus said to him, "Judas, are you going to betray the son of humanity with a kiss?"

Those around him, seeing what was coming, said "Master, shall we strike them with the sword?" And one of them struck the high priest's slave and took his right ear off.

But Jesus answered, "Let's stop short of that," and picked up the ear and restored it.

Said Jesus to the high priests and generals of the temple and elders who had come out after him, "As if to catch a robber you came out with swords and clubs? When I was there in the temple with you in broad daylight you didn't put your hands on me, but this is your hour and your authority is the authority of darkness."

Seizing him they led him away and brought him to the high priest's house.

Now Peter was following him from a distance. They'd made a fire in the middle of the courtyard and were sitting around it, and Peter sat down in their midst. One of the serving-girls, when she saw him sitting there by firelight, stared at him and said, "This guy was with him too."

But he denied it saying, "I don't know him, lady."

And after a while someone else saw him and said, "You're one of them too."

But Peter said, "No, man, I'm not."

And after the space of about an hour someone else said emphatically, "Of course this guy was with him too: after all, he *is* a Galilean."

But Peter said, "Fellow, I don't know what you're talking about." And suddenly, before he even finished speaking, a rooster crowed, and the Lord turned round and looked at Peter, and Peter was reminded of the words in which the Lord said to him: "Before the cock crows tomorrow morning you'll say three times that you don't know me." And going outside he cried stinging tears.

And the men holding him had some fun with him, beating him black and blue, blindfolding him and saying, "Prophesy for us—who just hit you?" And they made all sorts of blasphemous remarks about him.

And when day came, the elders of the people, the high priests, and the canon-lawyers met and haled him before their bench, saying, "Are you the Anointed? Tell us."

And he said to them, "If I tell you, you won't believe me. And if I ask you a question, you won't answer. From now on the son of humanity will be seated at the right hand of God's power."

And they all said, "So you're the Son of God!"

And he said to them, "You said it yourselves, that's what I am."

So they said, "What do we need witnesses for any more? We heard it from his own mouth."

23

And standing up en masse they led him off to Pilate.

They started accusing him, saying, "We caught this guy undermining our society and keeping people from paying taxes to Caesar and saying he had been anointed the king."

So Pilate asked him, "Are you the king of the Jews?"

He answered, "That's what *you* say."

Pilate said to the high priests and the crowds, "I don't see any charge against this person."

But they were carrying on and saying, "He's inciting the populace, teaching all through Judea, starting with Galilee and ending here."

When he heard that, Pilate asked if the fellow was a Galilean. And confirming that he was under Herod's jurisdiction, he sent him to Herod, who happened to be in Jerusalem at the time.

Herod was simply delighted to see Jesus. For quite a while now he'd wanted to see him because he'd heard so much about him and he was hoping to see some miracle performed. So he asked him questions at great length, but he didn't answer at all, while the high priests and canon-lawyers were standing there stridently denouncing him. After Herod and his armies had once again treated him with contempt and made a joke of him, he put a shining white robe* on him and sent him back to Pilate. From that day on Herod and Pilate became friends with each other; they had been at odds with each other before.

Then Pilate, calling together the high priests and rulers and the people, said to them: "You brought me this person on the grounds that he was undermining society, and you see how I examined him in front of you and found no charge against the fellow of the kind you accused him of.

"Nor could Herod. That's why he sent him back to us: he just hasn't done anything worthy of death. So we'll whip him to teach him a lesson and let him go."

But they shouted in chorus, "Keep him and release Barabbas"—who had been thrown in jail on account of some uprising in the city and charged with murder. Again Pilate called to them, trying to let Jesus go. But they were shouting out, "Crucify, crucify him!"

A third time he said to them, "But what did he do wrong? I couldn't find any capital charge against him. So I'll whip him soundly and let him go." But they persisted, loudly demanding that he be crucified, and their voices grew more and more insistent.

Finally Pilate decided to let their request be granted. He released the man thrown into jail for rioting and murder whom they had asked for and handed Jesus over to them to do as they wished with.

And as they led him away, picking out a certain Simon the Cyrenean who was coming from the country, they imposed on him to carry the cross behind Jesus.

Following behind him was a great crowd of the people, with many women too, beating their breasts and mourning him. Turning to them,

* A "royal" robe for "the king of the Jews": Herod has the same sense of humor as Pilate's soldiers.

Jesus said, "Daughters of Jerusalem, don't cry for me, cry for yourselves and your children, because watch, there will come days when they will say, 'Lucky for those who were sterile, for the wombs that never bore and the breasts that never nursed.' Then they will start saying to the mountains, 'Fall upon us,' and to the hills, 'Cover us up,' and if they do that when the wood is still green, what will they do by the time it dries?"

Now they were also bringing out two criminals to be executed with him.

And when they reached the spot they called The Skull, they crucified him there, and the criminals, too, one on his right and one on his left. And Jesus said, "Father, forgive them: they don't know what they're doing." And they rolled dice and divided up his clothes.

And the people were standing around watching, and the rulers were sneering at him, saying "He saved others, let him save himself, if he's the Anointed chosen by God."

Even the soldiers watching him were making fun of him, bringing him the sour wine and saying, "If you're the king of the Jews, save yourself." And there was a sign over his head: THIS IS THE KING OF THE JEWS.

One of the criminals hanging there started cursing him saying, "Aren't you the Anointed? Save yourself and us."

The other barked at him and said, "Do you have no fear of God, just because your sentence is the same? We're rightly getting what's coming to us for what we did, but he did nothing unlawful." Then he said, "Jesus, remember me when you get to your kingdom."

And he said to him, "I promise you, today you will be with me in Paradise."

And it was already about noon when darkness came over the whole land, from then till three o'clock, during which time there was no sun. And the curtain of the temple's inner sanctum was sheared down the middle. And after crying out in a loud voice, Jesus said, "Father, I put my spirit in your hands"; having said that, he breathed his last.

When the Roman captain saw what had happened, he praised God saying, "This person really was innocent." And all the crowds who had collected in front of the spectacle, when they saw what had happened, went home beating their breasts.

Everyone who saw him was standing at a distance, including the women who had followed him there from Galilee and were now watching all this.

And this man named Joseph, who was a member of the high court, a good and innocent man—he hadn't gone along with the high court and its actions—who came from Arimathea, a Judean city, and lived in expectation of the kingdom of God, this man went to Pilate and asked for the body of Jesus. And after taking it down he wrapped it up in a sheet and put it in a carved-out tomb where no one had ever lain. And the day was Friday, with the Sabbath dawning.

Following along, the women who had come with him from Galilee observed the tomb and how his body was laid to rest; then they went back and prepared spices and perfumes, and since it was the Sabbath, kept quiet according to the command.

24

On the first day of the week, at the crack of dawn, they came to the tomb bringing their prepared spices. But they found the stone rolled away from the tomb. Going inside, they couldn't find the body of Lord Jesus. And it happened, as they were looking around, all of a sudden these two men were standing in front of them in lightning-white clothing. As they fell into a panic and sank their faces down against the ground they said to them, "Why are you looking for the living among the dead? He isn't here, he rose up. Remember how he told you when he was still in Galilee that the son of humanity would have to be betrayed into the hands of evil people and be crucified and rise again on the third day?" And they remembered what he had said.

And returning from the tomb they reported all this to the eleven and all the rest. There was Mary Magdalen, and Joanna, and Mary, James's mother, and the others with them. They said these things to the apostles, but to them it seemed like delirium what they were saying, and they didn't believe them.

But Peter got up and ran to the tomb and bent down and saw the shroud and nothing more, and went back to his place amazed at what had happened.

And the next thing was, two of them were traveling that same day to a village by the name of Emmaus, seven or eight miles from Jerusalem, and they were conversing with each other. And it happened while they were conversing and arguing that Jesus himself approached and started walking on with them, but their eyes were overpowered so as not to recognize him. And he said to them, "What are these words you're trading as you walk along?" and they stood there looking grim.

Then one of them—his name was Cleopas—said to him, "You must be the only inhabitant of Jerusalem who doesn't know what has happened there in the last few days."

And he said to them, "Like what?"

They said, "All about Jesus of Nazareth, the man who had become a powerful prophet in word and action before God and all the people, and how our high priests and rulers handed him over to his death sentence and they crucified him. And we were hoping he was the one who would ransom Israel. But what with one thing and another it's going on the third day since it happened. Actually, some of our women gave us a shock, because they were at the grave at dawn and when they couldn't find his body they came back saying they'd seen a vision of holy messengers saying he was alive. And some of the people there with us went to the grave and found it as the women had said, but they didn't see him."

And he said to them, "Mindless and slow in your hearts to believe all the things that were said by the prophets! Didn't the Anointed have to die and enter into his glory?" And starting with Moses and all the prophets he interpreted for them all the passages in all the scriptures that were about him.

And they were getting close to the village where they were going, and he acted as if he was going to travel on. And they pressured him, saying, "Stay with us: it's getting toward evening, the daylight is already sinking away." And he went inside to stay with them. And it happened as he sat down with them to eat that he took bread and blessed it and broke it and gave it to them, and their eyes opened and they recognized him, and he vanished from their sight. And they said to each other, "Weren't our hearts blazing within us when he talked to us on the road and disclosed the scriptures to us!"

And at that point they got up and returned to Jerusalem and found the eleven gathered together and those who were with them, saying the Lord really did rise up, and appeared to Simon. And they explained what happened on the road and how he made himself known to them in the breaking of the bread.

As they were saying all this he himself stood in front of them and says to them, "Peace to you!" Electrified and panic-stricken, they thought they were seeing a ghost. And he said to them, "Why are you so confused and what are these questions rising in your hearts? You can see from my hands and feet that it's me in person. Feel me, and see that a ghost doesn't have flesh and bones, as you will observe I have." And saying that he showed them his hands and his feet. When they were still incredulous with joy and amazement he said to them, "Do you have anything to eat here?" and they gave him a piece of roast fish. And he took it and ate it in front of them.

And he said to them, "Those were the words I said to you when I was still among you, that everything written about me in the law of Moses and the prophets and the Psalms had to be fulfilled." And he disclosed to them the sense in which to understand the scriptures. And he said to them, "That's what it says, that the Anointed suffered and rose again from the dead on the third day, and to announce to all nations in his name a change of heart for the forgiveness of wrongs, starting from Jerusalem. You are witnesses of all this. I hereby devolve the mission of my Father upon you. But stay in the city till you are clothed in power from on high."

He led them out to Bethany, and lifting his hands he blessed them. And as it happened, during his blessing he moved away from them and was carried up into the sky.

And they, after bowing down before him, returned to Jerusalem with great joy, and were always in the temple blessing God.

The Good Word According to

John

1

In the beginning was the Word, and the Word was toward God, and God was what the Word was. It was with God in the beginning. All things happened through it, and not one thing that has happened, happened without it. Within it there was Life, and the Life was the light of the world. And in the darkness the light is shining, and the darkness never got hold of it.

There was a person sent from God, and he had the name John. He came as a witness to testify about the light, so that all would have faith through him. He wasn't the light himself, he was to testify about the light.

The light was the true light that comes into the world and shines for every human being. He was in the world, and the world was created by him, and the world didn't know him. He came to his own kind, and his own kind wouldn't accept him. But to those who did accept him he gave the right to become children of God if they had faith in his name, they who were born not of blood, nor the flesh's will, nor a man's will, but of God.

And the Word turned flesh and lodged among us, and we witnessed his glory, the kind of glory a father gives his only son, full of grace and truth. John testifies about him, and has been heard crying, "This is the one of whom I said that the one coming after me has come ahead of me, because he *is* ahead of me," because from his abundance we all received grace for grace; since the law was given through Moses, but grace and truth came through Jesus the Anointed. No one has seen God ever; God's only son who has been on his Father's lap, he himself explained that to us.

And such was the testimony of John when the Jews sent priests and Levites from Jerusalem to ask him, "Who are you?" And he admitted it and didn't try to deny it, he admitted, "I am not the Anointed."

And they asked him, "Are you Elijah?"

And he says, "No, I'm not."

"Are you the Prophet?"

And he answered, "No."

So they said to him, "Who *are* you? So we can give some kind of answer to the people who sent us. What do you have to say about yourself?"

He said, "I am

> *The voice of a crier in the wilderness:*
> *Make the Lord's way straight!*

as Isaiah the prophet said."

And the envoys were of the Pharisee party. And they questioned him, saying, "Why are you bathing these people if you aren't the Anointed, nor Elijah, nor the Prophet?"

John answered, "I bathe in water, but someone is standing in your midst whom you do not know, who is coming after me and whose sandals I am not worthy to untie." That happened in Bethany, beside the Jordan, where John was washing.

The next day he sees Jesus coming to him and says, "Look here, it's the lamb of God who takes upon himself the wrongdoing of the world. This is the one about whom I said, 'Behind me is a man who has come ahead of me, because he *is* ahead of me.' Even I didn't know him, but it was to proclaim him to Israel that I came along bathing in water." And John has testified, saying, "I saw the breath descending like a dove from the sky, how it alighted upon him. And I didn't know him, but it was the one who sent me to bathe in water who said, 'Whoever you see the breath descending and alighting upon, that's the one who will bathe them in the sacred breath.' And I have seen and certified that this is the son of God."

The next day John was standing there again with two of his students and, with his eyes on Jesus as he walked by, he says, "Look there, it's the lamb of God." And his two students heard him talking and followed Jesus.

Turning and noticing that they were following, Jesus says to them, "What do you want?"

They said to him, "Rabbi"—which would be translated as "Teacher"—"where are you staying?"

He says to them, "Come and see." So they came and saw where he was staying and stayed with him that day till it got to be about four o'clock.

Andrew the brother of Simon Rock ["Peter"] was one of the two who followed him after hearing of him from John.

He went first and found his brother Simon and said to him, "We have found the Messiah," which translates as "Anointed."

He brought him to Jesus. Jesus looked straight at him and said, "You are Simon, the son of John: you will be called Kephas"—which translates as "Rock."

The next day he decided to go out to Galilee. And he comes across Philip, and Jesus says to him, "Follow me."

Now Philip was from Bethesda, the same town as Andrew and Peter. Philip finds Nathaniel and says to him, "We have found the one written about by Moses in the Law and the Prophets: Jesus son of Joseph, from Nazareth."

Said Nathaniel, "Can anything from *Nazareth* be any good?"

Says Philip, "Come and see."

Jesus saw Nathaniel coming toward him and said about him, "Here is truly an Israelite without guile."

Nathaniel says to him, "Where do you know me from?"

Jesus answered him, "Before Philip called you, I saw you under the fig tree."

Nathaniel answered him, "Rabbi, you are the son of God, you are the king of Israel."

Jesus answered him, "Because I said I saw you underneath the fig tree, now you believe? You'll see more than that." And he says to him: "Truly, truly I tell you, you will see an opening in the sky and the messengers of God ascending from and alighting upon the son of humanity."

2

Two days after that there was a wedding in Cana, Galilee, and Jesus' mother was there. Also, Jesus and his students were invited to the wedding. And when the wine ran out, Jesus' mother said to him, "They don't have any wine."

Says Jesus, "What is that to you and me, madam? My time hasn't come."

Says his mother to the servants, "Whatever he tells you, do it."

Now there were six stone jars which were there for the Jewish purification, holding twenty or thirty gallons apiece. Jesus says to them, "Fill the jars with water," and they filled them up to the top. And he says to them, "Scoop it out and bring it to the headwaiter," and they did so.

But when the headwaiter tasted the water-turned-wine, not knowing where it came from—only the servants who had scooped the water out knew—the headwaiter called to the bridegroom and said to him, "Everyone else in the world puts out the fine wine first, and then the cheaper stuff when they're soused. But you've kept the fine wine till now."

Thus Jesus marked the beginning of his miracles in Cana, Galilee, and manifested his glory; and his students put their faith in him.

Afterwards he went down to Capharnaum, and so did his mother, his brothers and sisters, and his students, and they stayed there a few days.

And it was close to the Jewish Passover, so Jesus went up to Jerusalem.

And he found people in the temple selling cattle and sheep and doves, and the moneychangers sitting there; and he made a whip of ropes and threw them out of the temple—sheep, cows and all—and scattered the coins and upended the tables of the moneychangers. And to the pigeon-sellers he said, "Get that stuff out of here, don't make my father's house a house of merchandise." His students recalled how scripture says, "The zeal for your house consumes me."

So the Jews responded, saying to him, "What sign can you show us as to why you're doing this?"

Jesus answered them, "Destroy this temple, and in three days I will raise it up."

So the Jews said, "This temple was forty-six years in the building, and you'll raise it up in three days?" But he was talking about the temple of his body. So when he rose from the dead, his students remembered that he'd said that, and believed in the scripture and the words that Jesus said.

While he was in Jerusalem for the feast of Passover, many came to believe in his name after witnessing the wonders he performed. But Jesus didn't confide in them, because they all knew him, and because he didn't need anyone to give him evidence about people, he already knew what was inside people.

3

Now there was a fellow named Nicodemus, one of the Pharisees, a leader among the Jews. He came to him by night and said to him, "Master, we know you have come from God to be our teacher. After all, no one could work the wonders you work if God wasn't with him."

Jesus responded by saying to him, "Anyone who is not born again will never see the kingdom of God."

Says Nicodemus, "How can a person be born in old age? Can he climb into his mother's belly a second time and be born?"

Answered Jesus, "Truly, truly I tell you: anyone who isn't born of water and breath can never get into the kingdom of God. What's born of the flesh is flesh, and what's born of the breath is breath. Don't be amazed because I told you you have to be born again. The wind blows where it will and you hear the sound of it, but you don't know where it comes from or where it goes; it's the same with everyone born of the breath."

Nicodemus answered him, "How can all this happen?"

Jesus answered him, "You are the teacher of Israel and you don't know? Truly, truly I tell you that we are talking of what we know and testifying what we have seen and you don't accept our testimony. If I told you earthly things and you don't believe, how, when I tell you heavenly things, will you ever believe? And no one has ascended into the sky but the one who came down from the sky, the son of humanity. And as Moses held the serpent on high in the desert, so the son of humanity must be held on high, so that everyone who believes in him can have everlasting life. You see, God loved the world so much He gave His only son, so that everyone who believes in him would not be lost but instead have everlasting life. God didn't send His son into the world to condemn the world, but so the world could be saved by him. Whoever believes in him is not condemned, while the unbeliever is already condemned for not believing in the name of God's only son. This is the world's condemnation: that the light came into the world and the people liked the darkness better than the light, because their deeds were so foul. Naturally, anyone who's up to no good hates light and doesn't come near the light, so his doings won't be scrutinized. Somebody who is carrying out the truth comes toward the light, so that their deeds will be known as having been done in the spirit of God."

After that Jesus came with his students to the land of Judea and stayed there with them for some time and continued bathing people.

John was also bathing his followers in Enon, near Salem, where there was a lot of water, and people were showing up to be bathed. (At this point John hadn't been thrown in jail.)

So an argument arose between the students of John and a Jew about purification. And they came to John and said to him, "Master, the one who was with you on the other side of the Jordan, about whom you testified, guess what! he's bathing the people and they're all coming to him now."

John answered, "No one on earth can receive a single thing beyond what is given them from the sky. You yourselves are my witnesses that I said I was not the Anointed, but that I was sent on before him. The possessor of the bride is the bridegroom. The bridegroom's best man, who stands and listens, finding the joy of joys in the voice of the bridegroom—that pleasure, which has been my own, is done. He is to be augmented, I am to be diminished."

The one who comes from above is above everything. Whoever comes from the earth is of the earth and talks of the earth; he who comes from the sky is above everything. What he has seen and heard is what he testifies, yet no one accepts his testimony. But whoever accepts his testimony has signed his name to the reality of God. Because the one whom God sent tells what God said; there's no limit to the spirit he gives forth. The Father loves the son and has put everything in his hands. Whoever believes in the son has everlasting life, but whoever isn't convinced by the son will never see Life; no, the wrath of God rests upon him.

4

When Jesus found out that the Pharisees had heard that Jesus was gathering more students and bathing more people than John—though to be sure Jesus himself didn't bathe them, his students did—he left Judea and went back to Galilee.

Now he had to go through Samaria. So he went into a Samaritan town called Sicher near the spot that Jacob gave to Joseph his son. There was a "Well of Jacob" there. So Jesus, worn out from traveling, sat down there at the well—it was about noon. A Samaritan woman comes to draw water. Jesus says to her, "Give me a drink." (His students had gone into town to buy food.) So the Samaritan woman says to him, "How can you as a Jew ask for something to drink from a Samaritan woman like me?

Jews don't associate with Samaritans."

Jesus answered her, "If you knew what a gift from God this is and who is saying 'Give me a drink' to you, you would ask him for a live spring of water and he would give it to you."

Says the woman, "Sir, you don't have a bucket and the well is deep: where are you going to get a live spring of water? Are you greater than our father Jacob, who gave us the bucket and drank from it himself, as did his sons and daughters and their offspring?"

Jesus answered her, "Everyone who drinks that water will get thirsty again, but whoever drinks the water I give him will never thirst again for all eternity; no, the water I give him will become a spring of water rushing toward everlasting life."

Said the woman, "Sir, give me that water, so I'll never thirst again and won't have to keep coming down here to draw water."

He says, "Go call your husband and come back here."

The woman answered, "I don't have a husband."

He says to her, "That's a good way to put it: 'I don't have a husband'! You've had five husbands and the man you have now is not your husband, so you told the truth."

Says the woman, "Sir, I see you are a prophet. Our fathers worshipped on this mountain, but your people say Jerusalem is the place where one must worship."

Says Jesus, "Believe me, madam, the time is coming when you will worship the Father neither on this mountain nor in Jerusalem. You worship you know not what; we worship something we know, because salvation comes from the Jews. But the time is coming, indeed is here already, when the real worshipers will worship the Father in truth and spirit. And in fact that's the kind of worshipers the Father wants. God is spirit, and His worshipers must worship in spirit and truth." *

Says the woman, "I know the Messiah is coming, the so-called Anointed. When *he* comes, he'll tell us everything."

Jesus says to her, "That's who I am, here speaking to you."

And at that his students came back and were surprised to see him

---

* With these words, the idea of worshiping in a holy place is superseded by the idea of worshiping in a holy state—an enormous change when you consider how much the Jewish worship of the time was centered in, indeed confined to, the Temple of Jerusalem: imagine that Mass isn't supposed to be said in New Jersey; you're supposed to come into New York and hear it at Saint Patrick's Cathedral, where it can be said properly.

talking with a woman, but no one said, "What do you want with her?" or "Why are you talking with her?" So the woman put her pitcher down and went into town, where she said to the people, "Come see this fellow who told me everything I'd ever done. He couldn't be the Anointed, could he?" And they came from the town and went out to see him.

In the meantime his students were asking him, "Master, please eat."

But he said to them, "I have food to eat that you don't know about."

So his students said to each other, "Nobody brought him anything to eat, did they?"

Jesus says to them, "My food is to do the will of the one who sent me and complete His work.

"Don't you say yourselves, 'We're four months into the season, the harvest is coming'? Well, look now! raise your eyes and see how the lands are golden with the harvest. Already the reaper pockets his wage and gathers the produce in to eternal life, so that the sower can be just as happy as the reaper. I have sent you reaping what you didn't labor over: others labored over it and now you ride upon their labor."

In that town many of the Samaritans believed in him because of the words of the woman who testified, "He told me everything I'd ever done." So when the Samaritans came to see him, they asked him to stay with them, and he stayed there two days. And many others were convinced by his words and said to the woman, "We no longer believe because of what you said: we've heard him and know for ourselves that this is really the savior of the world."

After the two days he left that place for Galilee. Jesus himself testified, in fact, that a prophet in his home town goes without respect. So when he went to Galilee, the Galileans accepted him on the basis of having seen all the things he did during the festival at Jerusalem, since they'd been to the festival themselves.

So he came back to Cana, Galilee, where he'd made the water wine.

And there was a royal person whose son was sick in Capharnaum. Hearing that Jesus was coming from Judea to Galilee, he went to him and asked him to come down and cure his son, because he was about to die. So Jesus said to him, "If you don't see signs and wonders, you refuse to believe."

The royal person says, "Lord, come down with me before my child dies."

Jesus says, "Go your way, your son's going to live." The fellow believed the words Jesus said to him and went his way. As he started downhill his slaves were already there to meet him saying, "Your boy's going to live." So he asked them what time it was when he started having it easier. So they told him, "Yesterday afternoon at one o'clock the fever left him." Then the father knew that that was the hour when Jesus said to him, "Your son's going to live," and he was convinced and so was his wife and his whole household. This, then, was the second wonder that Jesus worked while coming out of Judea into Galilee.

5

After that there was a Jewish festival, and Jesus went up to Jerusalem.

Now in Jerusalem, at the Sheep Gate, there is a pool called, in Hebrew, Bethesda, with five porticos, in which a great mass of the sick, the blind, the lame, and those with withered limbs used to lie. Now there was one fellow there who had lived thirty-eight years with his sickness. When Jesus saw him lying there and realized he'd been there a long time already, he says to him, "Do you want to be well?"

"Sir," answered the sick man, "I don't have anyone to push me into the pool after the water's been stirred up. While I'm coming along, someone else steps in before me." *

Jesus says, "Get up, take your cot and walk away." And the fellow was suddenly well, and picked up his cot and walked away.

Now it was the Sabbath that day, so the Jews said to the cured man, "This is the Sabbath, you aren't allowed to carry your cot around."

And he answered them, "The person who made me well, he told me, 'Pick up your cot and walk away.' "

They asked him, "Who was the fellow who told you, 'Pick it up and walk'?"

But the cured man didn't know who it was, because Jesus had slipped off, there being a crowd of people in the place. Later Jesus comes across him in the temple, and he said to him, "See, now you're well again: do no more wrong, lest something worse should happen to you." The fellow went and reported to the Jews that Jesus was the one who made him well. And the Jews went after Jesus for that, because he did it on the Sabbath.

---

* To be cured, you have to be the first one in after the pool has been stirred up by an angel.

But Jesus answered them, "My Father has been working up to this point and now I am working." For that, the Jews wanted to kill him more than ever, because he didn't just break the Sabbath, he called God his own father, making himself equal to God.

So Jesus answered them, "Truly, truly I tell you, the son cannot do anything by himself, only what he sees his Father doing; whatever He does, the son does likewise. You see, the Father likes the son and shows him everything He does, and shows him how to do greater things than this, so that you will be amazed: because just as the Father raises the dead and makes them live, so the son gives life to whomever he wants. You see, the Father doesn't even judge anyone, He has left all judging to the son, so that all will honor the son as they honor the Father. Whoever doesn't honor the son, doesn't honor the Father who sent him.

"Truly, truly I tell you, whoever hears my words and believes in the one who sent me has everlasting life and doesn't come to judgment, but instead has turned away from death toward life. Truly, truly I tell you, that time is coming and indeed is here when the dead will hear the voice of the son of God and having heard will live. Because just as the Father has life within Him, so He has given it to the son to have life within him. And He gave him the authority to make judgments, because he is the son of humanity.

"Don't be surprised at that, because the time is coming when all those who are in their graves will hear his voice and come out: those who did good, to a resurrection of life; those who did no good, to a resurrection of punishment.

"I can do nothing by myself. As I hear, so I judge, and my judgment is just, because I don't seek my own way but the way of the one who sent me.

"If I testify about myself, my testimony isn't valid. There is someone else testifying about me, and I know the testimony is valid that he gives about me. You have sent to John, and he has testified to the truth. Now I'm not going on the word of a human witness myself, I'm saying these things for you, so you will be saved.

"He was the lantern, blazing and conspicuous, but you didn't want to rejoice in his light at the time.

"But I have a more important testimony than that of John: the deeds my Father gave me to complete, those deeds I do testify about me, saying that the Father has sent me. And the Father who sent me has also testified about me Himself. You've never heard His voice ever, nor have you seen His face. And you don't have His words lodged within you, either, because the one He sent to you, you won't believe. Pore over the scriptures, if you think that within them there's everlasting life to be had: they are the very witnesses about me. And *still* you don't want to come to me and receive true life!

"I don't look for glory from the human kind, but I have noticed about you that you have no love of God within you. I have come in the name of my Father, and you won't accept me. If someone else came in his own name, him you'd accept. How can you believe you're giving each other glory and want none of the glory that comes from the only God there is?

"Don't think that I will file charges against you with my Father. Your accuser is Moses, in whom you place your hopes; because if you believed in Moses, you'd believe in me—after all, he wrote about me. If you don't believe his written word, how will you believe my spoken word?"

6

After that Jesus went across the sea of Galilee, by Tiberias. He was followed by a great crowd, because they observed the wonders he worked with the sick. He went up the mountain and sat there with his students. It was near Passover, the festival of the Jews.

So Jesus, raising his eyes and noticing that a great crowd was coming toward him, says to Philip, "Where can we buy bread for them to eat?" (He said that to him as a test: he knew what he was going to do.)

Answered Philip, "Two hundred drachmas worth of bread wouldn't be enough for each of them to get a little piece."

One of his students, Andrew the brother of Simon Peter, says, "There's a kid here who has five loaves of barley-bread and two small fish, but what's that among all these people?"

Said Jesus, "Tell the people to sit down." There was a lot of grass in the place. So the men sat down, numbering about five thousand. So Jesus took the bread and gave thanks and gave them out to the seated crowd, and gave them the fish too, as much as they wanted. When they were full, he says to his students, "Collect the leftover scraps so nothing goes to waste"; they collected it all and filled twelve baskets with the scraps of the five loaves of barley-bread that were left over after they'd eaten.

So the people, seeing what a miracle he had performed, said, "This is truly the Prophet, coming into the world." Jesus, therefore, realizing that they were about to come and take him away and make him a king, slipped away again to the mountain, all by himself.

Then as evening came his students went down to the sea, boarded a boat, and went across the sea to Capharnaum. And it had already gotten dark and Jesus hadn't come to them yet. The sea was stirred up with a great wind blowing. So, after getting some three or four miles out they sighted Jesus walking on the sea and getting close to the boat, and they got scared. But he said to them, "It's me, don't be afraid." So they readily took him into the boat, and in no time the boat was on the shore where they were going.

The next day the crowd standing on the other shore saw that there was no other boat but just that one and that Jesus hadn't gotten into the boat with his students, his students had gone off by themselves.

But some boats came by from Tiberias near the spot where they ate the bread after the Lord gave thanks. So when the crowd saw that Jesus wasn't there, nor his students, they boarded the boats and went to Capharnaum looking for Jesus. And on finding him on the other side of the sea, they said to him, "Rabbi, when did you get here?"

Jesus answered them, "Truly, truly I tell you, don't look for me because you saw miracles, or because you ate the bread and were full. Provide yourself, not with perishable food, but with the food leading to everlasting life that the son of humanity will give you, because he bears the stamp of God the Father."

So they said to him, "What do we do to perform the works of God?"

Answered Jesus, "This is the work of God: to believe in the one He sent."

So they said to him: "Then what sign will you perform so we can see it and trust in you? What works will *you* perform? Our fathers ate the manna in the wilderness, just as it says: 'Bread from the sky he gave them to eat.' "

So Jesus said to them, "Truly, truly, I tell you, Moses didn't give you the bread from the sky, but my Father is giving you bread from the sky for real, because the bread of God is the one who descends from the sky and gives his life for the world."

So they said to him, "Lord, give us this bread for good."

Said Jesus to them, "I am the bread of life: whoever comes to me will never starve, and whoever trusts in me will never thirst again.

"But I told you that you've even seen me and you still don't believe. Everything my Father gives to me, comes to me, and whoever comes to me is never thrown out, because I have not come down from the sky to do my own will but the will of the one who sent me. And this is the will of the one who sent me: that I shouldn't lose any of all He has given me, but raise it all up on the last day. You see, it is the will of God that everyone who beholds the son and believes in him shall have everlasting life, and I will raise him up on the last day."

So the Jews were grumbling about him, because he said, "I am the bread come down from heaven," and they said, "Isn't this the son of Joseph, don't we know who his father and his mother are? So now how does he say, 'I have come down from heaven'?"

Answered Jesus, "Don't grumble among yourselves. No one can come to me unless the Father who sent me draws him, and I raise him up on the last day. It says in the books of the prophets, 'And they will all be pupils of God.' Whoever hears from the Father and learns, comes to me. Not that anyone has seen the Father except the one who is from God: *he* has seen the Father. Truly, truly I tell you, whoever believes has everlasting life.

"I am the bread of life. Your fathers ate the manna in the wilderness and they died. This is the bread that comes down from heaven so that a person can eat of it and *not* die. I am the living bread that has come down from heaven. If someone eats of this bread they will live forever, and the bread I will give is my flesh, given for the life of the world."

So the Jews started arguing with each other, saying, "How can this guy give us his flesh to eat?"

So Jesus said to them, "Truly, truly I tell you, if you don't eat the flesh of the son of humanity and drink his blood, you have no life within you. The one who eats my flesh and drinks of my blood has life everlasting, and I will raise him up on the last day. You see, my flesh is true food and my blood is true drink. The one who eats my flesh and drinks my blood remains in me and I in him. Just as the living Father sent me and I live through the Father, so the one who eats me also lives through me. This is the bread come down from the sky, not like your fathers ate and died: the one who eats this bread will live forever."

He said all that while teaching in a synagogue at Capharnaum. As a result, many of his students after listening said, "These are hard words! Who can listen to him?"

Jesus, though, knowing inside that his students were grumbling about that, said to them: "Does that throw you? Then what if you see the son of humanity ascending where he was before? Breath is the lifegiver, flesh serves for nothing. The words I have said to you are breath and life. But there are some of you who don't believe"—you see, Jesus knew from the beginning who the unbelievers were and who his future betrayer was. And he said, "That's why I have told you that no one can come to me unless that is given to him by the Father."

From that point on, many of his students went back where they came from and stopped traveling around with him. So Jesus said to the twelve, "You don't want to go too, do you?"

Answered Simon Peter, "Lord, who should we go to? You have words of everlasting life, and we are convinced and certain that you are the holy one of God."

Jesus answered them, "Didn't I pick you twelve? And yet one of you is a devil." (He meant Judas, son of Simon Iscariot, because he, one of the twelve, was going to betray him.)

7

And after that Jesus started walking around Galilee: he didn't want to walk around Judea, because the Judeans were looking to kill him.

It was close to Succoth, the Jewish "festival of the tents." So his brothers and sisters said to him: "Leave that place and come back to Judea so that even your students can witness the deeds you do. After all, no one does something in secret who himself wishes to be in the public eye. If you're doing these things, show yourself to the world"—even his own brothers and sisters didn't believe in him.

So Jesus says to them, "My time isn't here yet, whereas your time is always at hand. The world can't hate you; but it hates me because I testify about it, saying that its deeds are evil. You go on up to the festival, I'm not going up to the festival this time, because my time isn't fulfilled yet." Saying that, he remained in Galilee.

But when his brothers and sisters had gone up to the festival, then he went too, not openly but more or less incognito. So the Jews were looking for him at the festival and said, "Where is that guy?" And there was a lot of murmuring about him among the crowds, with some saying, "He's a good man," and others saying, "No, he misleads the masses." No one, however, talked publicly of him for fear of the Jews.

Then with the festival already in full swing, Jesus went up to the temple and started teaching. So the Jews were amazed and said, "How does this guy know how to read without ever going to school?"

So Jesus answered them, "My teaching isn't my own, but that of the one who sent me. If anyone desires to do His will, he will find out about this teaching as to whether it comes from God or whether I'm speaking for myself. Someone who speaks for himself seeks his own glory. But someone who seeks the glory of the one who sent him, that's an honest person, and there's nothing crooked about him.

"Didn't Moses give you the law? Yet none of you follows the law. Why are you looking to kill me?"

The crowd answered, "You're crazy, who's looking to kill you?"

Jesus answered them, "I did one deed and you're all amazed. This is what Moses gave you circumcision for—not that it comes from Moses, it comes from your forefathers—and yet you circumcise a man on the Sabbath. If a man can get circumcised on the Sabbath without the law of Moses being broken, why are you angry with me for making a whole man healthy on the Sabbath? Don't judge by appearance, render true judgment."

So some of the people of Jerusalem said: "Isn't this the one they're looking to kill? And look at that, he's talking in public and they aren't saying anything to him. You don't suppose the rulers actually found out that he's the Anointed? But no, we know where he's from. When the Anointed comes, no one knows where he's from."

So Jesus raised his voice while he taught, saying, "So you know me and know where I'm from. Yet I am not here on my own; no, the one who sent me is real, the one whom you don't know. I know Him because I am from Him and that is who sent me."

So they tried to seize him, but no one got their hands on him, because his time hadn't come yet.

But many in the crowd believed in him and said, "When the Anointed comes, could he ever work greater wonders than this man worked?"

The Pharisees heard the crowd murmuring these things, and the high priests and the Pharisees sent their assistants to seize him. So Jesus said, "I am with you for only a little while more, then I go to the one who sent me. You will look for me and not find me, and where I go you cannot follow."

So the Jews said to each other: "Where is this guy going to travel that we won't be able to find him? Could he be planning to go among the Jews of the Greek diaspora and bring his teaching to the Greeks? What are the words he said about that: 'You'll look for me and not find me,' and 'Where I go you cannot follow'?"

On the last big day of the festival Jesus was standing and shouting, "If any are thirsty let them come to me and drink. For the one who trusts in me, it is just as the scripture said: rivers of living water flow from his insides." He was talking about the spirit those who trusted in him would receive: the spirit wasn't there yet, because Jesus hadn't yet been glorified.

Some of those in the crowd who heard these words said, "He is truly the Prophet"; others said, "This is the Anointed." Others said, "Doesn't the Anointed come from Galilee? Didn't the scripture say that the Anointed comes from the seed of David and from Bethlehem, the village where David was?" So a split developed in the crowd over him. And some of them wanted to seize him, but no one put their hands on him.

So the assistants came back to the high priests and Pharisees, who said to them, "How come you didn't bring him with you?"

The assistants answered, "No one ever talked like that in all the world!"

So the Pharisees answered them, "Don't tell us you've been fooled too! None of the rulers or the Pharisees believed in him, did they? But this crowd that doesn't know the law, they're all under his spell!"

Nicodemus says to them—the one who went to him earlier—since he was one of their number: "Surely our law doesn't judge a person without first hearing from him and finding out what he's doing?"

And they answered him, "You aren't from Galilee too, are you? Look it up, see for yourself: no prophet ever arises out of Galilee." And each of them traveled back to their own home.

8

But Jesus traveled out to Mount Olive. Come the dawn, he showed up in the temple and all the people were coming to see him, and he sat there teaching them. Then the canon-lawyers and Pharisees bring in a woman caught in the act of adultery, and standing her up in front of everyone they say to him: "Teacher, this is a woman caught right in the act of her adultery. In the law Moses ordered us to stone women like her. So what do *you* say?" (They were saying this to test him, so they could have something to charge him with.)

Jesus bent down and started scratching with his finger in the soil. Then as they kept on asking him he raised his head and said to them, "Let whoever among you is guiltless be the first one to throw stones at her." And he bent back down and went on scratching in the soil.

On hearing that, they started going out one by one, starting with the eldest, till he and the woman standing in the middle were left alone. Looking back up, Jesus said to her, "Where are they, madam? Didn't anyone condemn you?"

She said, "No one, Lord."

Said Jesus, "I don't condemn you either. Go your way, and from now on stop doing wrong."

Then another time Jesus spoke to them saying: "I am the light of the world. The one who follows me will never walk in darkness, but instead will have the light of life."

So the Pharisees said to him, "You're testifying about yourself, so your testimony isn't valid!"

Answered Jesus, "Even if I am testifying about myself, my testimony is valid, because I know where I came from and where I'm going to, whereas you don't know where I came from *or* where I'm going to. You judge by the flesh; I don't judge anybody. And if I do judge, my judgment is valid, because I'm not alone, it's me and the Father who sent me. And it says in your law that the testimony of two people is valid. I'm one witness testifying about myself and then the Father who sent me testifies about me too."

So they said to him, "Where is your father?"

Answered Jesus, "You don't know either me or my Father. If you knew me, you'd know my Father too." He said these words standing near the collection-box while he was teaching in the temple. And no one seized him, because his time hadn't come.

Then he said to them another time: "I am going away, and you will look for me in vain and die in your errors. Where I go you cannot follow."

So the Jews said: "He isn't going to kill himself, is he? Is that why he says, 'Where I go you cannot follow'?"

And he said to them: "You are lower beings, I am a higher being. You come from this world, I don't come from this world. So I said that you'll die in your errors because if you don't believe that I am who I am, you *will* die in your errors."

So they said to him, "Who are you?"

Said Jesus: "Just what I tell you in the first place. I have many things to say and judge about you, but the one who sent me is true, and what I heard from Him is what I say to the world." (They didn't understand he was talking about the Father.) So Jesus said to them: "When you raise the son of humanity on high, then you will find out that I am who I am, and that I do nothing on my own, but as the Father taught me, so I speak. And the one who sent me is with me. He hasn't left me alone, because I do just what He likes at all times."

When he said these things, many believed in him. So Jesus said to the Jews who had placed their faith in him, "If you stay with my words, you are truly my students, and you will know the truth, and the truth will free you."

They answered him, "We are Abraham's seed and were never the slave of anyone. How can you say, 'You'll be freed'?"

Jesus answered, "Truly, truly I tell you that everyone who does wrong is the slave of wrongdoing. The slave doesn't remain in the household forever, the son remains forever. So if the son frees you, then you will really be free.

"I know you're Abraham's seed, but you're looking to kill me, because you have no room for my words. I am speaking what I have seen at my Father's side, so whatever you hear from the Father, do it."

They answered him, "Our father is Abraham."

Says Jesus, "If you were children of Abraham, you'd do Abraham's work; but here you are trying to kill me, the person who has told you the truth that I heard from God. That's not what Abraham did! You're doing your father's work, all right."

So they said to him, "We weren't born out of wedlock, and we have one father: God."

Said Jesus, "If God were your father you would love me, because I come from God, I am here from God. Nor did I come on my own, He sent me. Why is it you can't make sense of my speech? Because you can't stand to hear my words. You come from your father the devil and you wish to carry out your father's fervent desires: he always was a killer from the beginning and never did stand for the truth, because there is nothing true about him. When he tells lies, he tells something of himself, since he's a liar and his father before him. But when I speak the truth you don't believe me. Which of you accuses me of a crime? If I speak the truth, how come you don't believe me? The one who comes from God listens to what God says: the reason you don't listen is that you don't come from God."

The Jews answered, "Aren't we correct in saying that you're a Samaritan, and crazy?"

Answered Jesus, "I'm not crazy. I honor my Father and you dishonor me. I'm not seeking my own glory; there is someone who seeks and who judges. Truly, truly, I tell you, if someone keeps my word, they will not see death ever."

So the Jews said to him, "Now we *know* you're crazy. Abraham died, and so did the prophets, and you say, 'If someone keeps my word, they will not taste death ever.' Are you greater than our father Abraham who died? Even the prophets died. Who are you making yourself out to be?"

Jesus answered, "If I glorify myself, my glory is nothing. It is my Father who glorifies me, about whom you say, 'He is our God.' But you haven't come to know Him; *I* know Him. If I ever say I don't know Him, I'll be as much of a liar as you. But no, I do know Him and I keep His words. Abraham your father was delighted that he should ever see my day, and he saw it and rejoiced."

So the Jews said to him, "You're not yet fifty years old and you've seen Abraham?"

Jesus said to them, "Truly, truly I tell you: before Abraham was born, I have already been." So they picked up stones to throw at him, but Jesus ducked out of sight and got out of the temple.

9

And walking along he saw a fellow blind from birth, and his students asked him, "Rabbi, whose crime is it, his own or his parents', that caused him to be born blind?"

Jesus answered, "Neither his nor his parents': it was so the works of God could be manifested in him. We must do the work of the one who sent me while the day lasts: the night is coming when no one can work. As long as I am in the world, I am the light of the world."

Having said that much he spat on the ground and made mud with his spit and applied the mud to the man's eyes. And he said to him: "Go wash yourself in Siloam (which translates to 'Emissary') Pool." So he went off and washed himself and came away seeing.

So the neighbors and those who had previously observed that he was a beggar said, "Isn't this the guy who sits and begs?"

Some said, "Yes, it's him."

Others said, "No he just looks like him."

"It *is* me," he said.

So they said to him, "How did your eyes get opened up?"

He answered, "This fellow named Jesus made some mud and applied it to my eyes and told me, 'Go to Siloam Pond and wash.' So after going there and washing off, I could see."

And they said to him, "Where is that person?"

He says, "I don't know."

So they go to the Pharisees with the formerly blind man. Now it was the Sabbath on the day when Jesus made the mud and opened his eyes. So the Pharisees asked him again how come he could see now. And he said, "He put this mud on my eyes, and I washed myself, and now I can see."

So some of the Pharisees said, "That fellow can't be from God, because he doesn't keep the Sabbath."

Others said, "How could an evil man work such wonders?" So there was a split among them. So they said to the ex-blind man, "What do you say about him and the way he opened up your eyes?"

He said, "That he's a prophet."

So the Jews weren't convinced about him, how he was really blind and then became sighted, till they called on the parents of the newly seeing man and asked them, "This is your son, who you say was born blind? So how can he see all of a sudden?"

His parents answered, "We know that's our son and that he was born blind. How he comes to see now we don't know, and who opened up his eyes we also don't know. Ask him: he's an adult, he can tell you about himself." His parents said that because they were afraid of the Jews. You see, the Jews had already agreed among themselves that anybody acknowledging him as the Anointed would be barred from the synagogue. That's why his parents said, "He's an adult, you can ask him."

So they called the fellow in for a second time, the one who had been blind, and said to him, "Give glory to God! We know that this is a godless person."

Said the other, "Whether he's a godless person or not I don't know. One thing I do know: I was blind and now I can see."

So they said to him, "What did he do to you? How did he open up your eyes?"

He answered them, "I told you already and you didn't listen! Why do you want to hear it again? Do you want to become his students too?"

And they called him names and said, "You're one of his students yourself! We, on the other hand, are students of Moses. We know that Moses has been spoken to by God, but as for this guy, we don't know where he comes from."

The fellow answered them, "The amazing part about this is that you don't know where he comes from—but he opened up my eyes! We know God doesn't listen to the godless; instead, if somebody is God-fearing and does His will, that's who He listens to. In all history no one ever heard of anyone opening the eyes of a person blind from birth. If this person didn't come from God, he couldn't do anything."

They answered, "You were born in sin from head to foot and you're teaching us religion?" And they threw him out.

Hearing that they threw him out, Jesus found the man and said, "Do you believe in the son of humanity?"

Answered the other, "And who is it, sir, so I can believe in him?"

Said Jesus, "You have seen him: the person talking with you now is the one."

"I believe, sir," he said, and bowed before him.

And Jesus said, "I came into this world to bring it to judgment, that the blind might see and the seeing be blinded."

Some of the Pharisees who were with him heard that and said to him, "Then are we blind too?"

Said Jesus, "If you *were* blind, you wouldn't be at fault, but since you say, 'We can see,' the fault remains with you.

10

"Truly, truly I tell you, anyone who doesn't come into the sheep-pen by the gate but climbs over some other way, that person is a robber and a thief. The one who comes in by the gate is the shepherd of the sheep. The watchman opens up for him and the sheep respond to his voice, and he calls his own sheep by name and leads them out. When he's gotten all his sheep outside, he goes on his way at their head and the sheep follow him, because they know his voice. For a stranger they'll never follow along, they'll run away from him, because they don't know the voice of strangers." Jesus said this figure of speech to them, but they didn't know what those things were he was telling them.

So Jesus said again, "Truly, truly I tell you that I am the gate of the sheep-pen. All who came before me are robbers and thieves, but the sheep didn't listen to them. I am the door. Whoever enters through me will be saved and will go in and out and find grazing-land. The thief only comes to steal, slaughter, and destroy. I came so they would have life and more life.

"I am the good shepherd. The good shepherd puts his life down for his sheep. The hired hand is not the shepherd, and the sheep are not his own. He sees the wolf coming and leaves the sheep there and runs—and indeed the wolf attacks them and scatters them—because he's a hired hand and doesn't care about the sheep.

"I am the good shepherd, and I know my own, and my own know me, just as my Father knows me and I know my Father, and I put my life down for my sheep. I also have other sheep which are not from this fold; and I must bring them here, and they will respond to my voice, and then they will be one fold with one shepherd.

"That's why my Father loves me, because I lay down my life to get it back again. No one takes it from me, I lay it down myself. I have authority to lay it down, and authority to take it back again: I received just such orders from my Father."

Again a split developed among the Jews about those words. Many of them said, "He's possessed and he's stark raving mad. Why do you listen to him?"

Others said, "Those aren't the words of a possessed person. And a demon can't open the eyes of the blind, can he?"

Then it came to Hanukkah, the Feast of the Temple's Rededication, in Jerusalem during the winter, and Jesus was walking around in the temple in the porch of Solomon. So the Jews encircled him and started saying to him: "How long are you going to keep killing us? If you're the Anointed, say so outright."

Jesus answered them, "I told you, and you don't believe me. The deeds I do in the name of my Father testify for me. But you don't believe, because you aren't sheep of mine. My sheep respond to my voice; I know them and they follow me, and I give them everlasting life. And they will not perish ever, nor will anyone snatch them from my hands. What my Father has given me is greater than everything else, and no one can snatch anything from the hands of the Father. I and the Father are one."

Again the Jews picked up stones to throw at him. Jesus responded, "I showed you many fine deeds that came from the Father. Which one of those deeds will you stone me for?"

Answered the Jews, "We're not stoning you for fine deeds, we're stoning you for blasphemy, and for making a mortal like yourself into a god."

Answered Jesus, "Doesn't it say in your law, 'I have said you are gods?' If he called those people gods who were reached by the word of God—and the scripture can't be contraverted—how can you call it blasphemy if I, whom the Father sanctified and sent into the world, should say I am the son of God? If I don't do my Father's work, don't believe me. But if I do, and you still don't believe me, believe my deeds, so that you may know and understand that my Father is in me and I in my Father." So they tried to seize him again, but he slipped out of their hands.

And he went back across the Jordan to the place where John had first been bathing the people, and stayed there. And many came to see him and said, "John performed no miracles, but everything John said about him was true." And many came to believe in him there.

11

Now there was a person sick, Lazarus of Bethany, from the same village as Mary and Martha her sister. Mary was the one who anointed the Lord with perfume and dried his feet off with her hair; it was her brother Lazarus who was sick. So the sisters sent word to him, saying, "Lord, look, your friend is sick."

Hearing that, Jesus said, "This is not a sickness to death, it is for the glory of God, that the son of God may be glorified through it." Now Jesus loved Martha and her sister and Lazarus dearly. So when he heard he was sick, he stayed in the place where he was two more days, then after that he says to his students, "Let's go back to Judea."

His students say to him, "Rabbi, the Judeans were just trying to stone you, and you're going back there?"

Answered Jesus, "Aren't there twelve hours of daylight? If someone walks around by day, he doesn't bump into things, because he sees the light of this world; whereas if someone walks around by night, he bumps into things, because he has no light within him."

He said that much, and afterward he says to them, "My friend Lazarus is sleeping, but I'm going to go wake him up."

So his students said to him, "Lord, if he's sleeping, he's going to be all right." But Jesus was talking about his death, whereas they thought he was talking about going to bed and sleeping.

So then Jesus said to them outright, "Lazarus died, and I'm delighted with you for believing me, because I wasn't there; now let's go to him."

So Thomas, the one called the Twin, said to the other students, "Let us go too, and die with him."

Arriving, Jesus found he had spent four days in the tomb already. Now Bethany was near Jerusalem, about two miles away. So many of the Jews had come to see Martha and Mary and offer condolences to them about their brother. So when Martha heard that Jesus was coming she went out to meet him, while Mary stayed at home.

So Martha said to Jesus, "Lord, if you had been here, my brother wouldn't have died. But even now I know that anything you ask of God, he will give you."

Says Jesus, "Your brother will rise again."

Says Martha, "I know he will rise in the resurrection on the last day."

Said Jesus, "I am resurrection and life: whoever believes in me, even if he dies, will live, and everyone who lives and believes in me will never die ever. Do you believe that?"

She says to him, "Yes, Lord, I am convinced that you are the Anointed Son of God coming into the world."

And having said that she went and called Mary her sister aside, saying, "The teacher is here and calling for you." She, when she heard, got up quickly and came out to see him. Jesus hadn't gotten to the village yet, he was still at the spot where he had been met by Martha. So the Jews who were with her in the house and consoling her, seeing how Mary got up in haste and went out, followed her, thinking that she was going off to the tomb to mourn there.

So when Mary got to where Jesus was, seeing him she fell at his feet and said to him, "Lord, if you'd been here, my brother wouldn't have died."

Jesus, as he saw her crying, and all the Jews with her crying, went into an upheaval of the spirit and stirred himself up. And he said, "Where have you put him?"

They say to him, "Lord, come and see." Jesus wept.

So the Jews said, "See how much he meant to him." Some of them, though, said, "Couldn't the one who opened the eyes of the blind man also have kept the other from dying?"

So Jesus, still in an inner upheaval, comes to the tomb: it was a cave, and there was a stone blocking it. Says Jesus, "Take the stone away."

The sister of the deceased, Martha, says to him, "Lord, he'll be smelly by now: he's four days gone."

Says Jesus, "Didn't I tell you that if you believe you will see the glory of God?" So they took the stone away. Jesus then lifted up his eyes and said, "Father, I thank you for hearing me. I knew that you hear me at all times, but I said that for the benefit of the crowd around me, so that they might believe that you sent me." And after saying that, he shouted at the top of his voice: "Lazarus, come out here!" The dead man came out bound hand and feet with bandages and with his face covered by a cloth. Says Jesus, "Untie him and let him go."

So many of the Jews who had come to see Mary and then witnessed what he did believed in him. But some of them went to the Pharisees and told them what Jesus had done.

Then the high priests and Pharisees assembled in council, and they were saying, "What are we going to do about this fellow who works all these wonders? If we let him go on like this, they'll all believe in him, and the Romans will come in and take away both our land and our people."

One of them, Caiaphas, being the high priest for that year, said to them, "You don't know anything. Haven't you even considered that it's better for one person to die for the people than for the whole nation to die?"

He didn't say that on his own, but as high priest for that year he prophesied that Jesus was going to die for the nation—and not just for the nation, but to bring the scattered children of God together as one. So from that day on they were plotting to kill him.

So Jesus didn't walk around openly among the Jews, but went away to the country near the desert, to the town called Ephraim, and stayed there with his students.

Now it was close to the Jewish Passover, and many from that country were going up to Jerusalem before Passover to seek a blessing. So they were looking for Jesus and standing around in the temple saying to each other, "What do you say? He'll never show up for the festival, will he?" In fact, the high priests and Pharisees had given orders that anyone who knew where he was should alert them so they could seize him.

12

So six days before Passover, Jesus came to Bethany, where Lazarus was, whom Jesus had raised from the dead. So they gave a dinner for him there, and Martha was serving, and Lazarus was one of the guests with him.

So Mary, taking a pound of genuine spikenard, very expensive, anointed the feet of Jesus and used her hair to dry his feet. The house was filled with the smell of the perfume. Says Judas Iscariot, one of his students, the one who was going to betray him, "Why wasn't that perfume sold for three hundred drachmas and given to the poor?" He said that not because he cared about the poor, but because he was a thief and as purseholder was dipping into the common funds.

So Jesus said, "Leave her alone, let this preserve me for my day of burial. Remember, you always have the poor around, but me you do not always have."

So a great crowd of the Jews found out he was there and came, not just to see Jesus, but also to see Lazarus, whom he had raised from the dead. But the high priests were plotting to kill Lazarus too, since on account of him many of the Jews were going off and believing in Jesus.

The next day, the great crowd that was there for the festival, on hearing that Jesus was coming to Jerusalem, took branches of palm-trees and came out to meet him and shouted:

> "Hooray!
> Bless him who comes in the name of the Lord,
> The king of Israel!"

And Jesus found a donkey and sat down on it, just as it says:

> Have no fear, daughter Zion:

Look! your king is coming,
Seated on the foal of a donkey.

(His students didn't think of it at first, but when Jesus was glorified, then they remembered that that is what was written about him and that's also what they did for him.)

So the crowd of people was bearing witness, those who had been with him when he called Lazarus out of the tomb and raised him from the dead. That's why the crowd was there to meet him: they had heard about his performing that miracle. So the Pharisees said to each other: "See how nothing you do does any good? Look, there went the world, all trooping off behind him."

Now there were some Greeks among those who were going up to worship on the feast-day. So they came up to Philip of Bethesda, Galilee, and asked him, "Sir, we want to see Jesus." Philip comes and tells Andrew, Andrew and Philip come and tell Jesus.

Jesus answered, "The time has come for the son of humanity to be glorified. Truly, truly I tell you, if the grain of wheat never falls to the ground and dies, it remains the only one. But if it dies it produces a great crop. The one who loves his life, loses it; the one who doesn't care about his life in this world will keep it safe for life everlasting. If someone serves me, let them follow me, and wherever I am, my servant will also be. If anyone serves me they will be honored by my Father.

"Now my soul is in consternation, and what shall I say? 'Father, save me from this hour'? But that is what I came to this hour for. Father, glorify your own name."

So a voice came from the sky: "I glorified it before and will glorify it again." The crowd standing around, when they heard that, said there had been thunder, while others said, "A holy messenger has spoken to him."

Answered Jesus, "That voice wasn't for me, it was for you. Now it is judgment time for this world, now the ruler of this world will be thrown out the door. And I, if I am raised high above the earth, will draw all people toward me." (He said that to signify by what death he would die.)

So the crowd answered, "We heard in the Law that the Anointed remains forever. So how can you say that the son of humanity must be raised on high? Who is this son of humanity?"

So Jesus said to them, "For a little while longer the light is among you. Walk around while you have light, so the darkness doesn't overtake you; the person walking in darkness doesn't know where he's going. While you have the light, believe in the light, so that you may become sons and daughters of the light." So spoke Jesus, and went away and hid from them.

After he had performed all those miracles in front of them, they still didn't believe in him, which fulfilled the word of Isaiah the prophet when he said,

> *Lord, who believed our report?*
> *And to whom was the Lord's arm revealed?*

The reason they couldn't believe was because of what Isaiah said elsewhere:

> *He has blinded their eyes*
> *And petrified their heart*
> *Lest they see with their eyes*
> *And think with their heart,*
> *And come back, and I heal them.*

Isaiah said that because he saw his glory and spoke about him. However, though many of the ruling class came to believe in him, on account of the Pharisees they didn't admit it, so as not to be barred from the synagogue: they loved the glory of the world, it seems, even more than the glory of God.

Jesus cried out and said: "Whoever believes in me believes, not in me, but in the one who sent me. And whoever looks upon me looks upon the one who sent me. I the Light have come into the world so that anyone who believes in me will not remain in darkness. And if somebody hears what I say and doesn't keep it, I don't judge them, because I didn't come to judge the world, I came to save the world. The person who refuses me and won't accept what I say has his judge: the word I spoke will be his judge on the last day, because I didn't speak it on my own, the Father who sent me also gave me commands as to what to speak and what to say. And I know that His commandment means everlasting life. So as for the things I speak, it's just as my Father told me, that's how I speak."

13

Before the feast of Passover, knowing that the hour had come for him to pass out of this world and back to the Father, Jesus, who had loved those who were his own in this world, loved them to perfection.

And as a dinner was going on—at a time when the devil had already put it in Judas Simon Iscariot's heart to betray him—knowing that his Father had given everything into his hands and that he had come from God and was going back to God, he got up from the table and put his clothes on and took a linen towel and tied it around his waist. Then he poured water into the basin and started washing his students' feet and drying them with the towel around his waist. So he comes to Simon Peter, who says to him, "Lord are *you* going to wash *my* feet?"

Answered Jesus, "For now you don't know what I'm doing, later you will know."

Says Peter, "Never in the world are you going to wash my feet."

Answered Jesus, "If I don't wash you, you will have no part of me."

Says Simon Peter, "Lord, wash not only my feet, but also my hands and my head!"

Says Jesus, "The cleansed person needs no more than to wash his feet: he's clean all over. And all of you are clean—well, not all." (He knew who would betray him; that's why he said, "Not all of you are clean.")

So after he washed their feet and took his clothes and sat down again he said to them, "Do you understand what I have done for you? You call me Teacher and Lord, and rightly so: that I am. So if I washed your feet, the Lord and the Teacher, you should also wash each other's feet. I gave you an example so that just what I did for you, you will also do yourselves. Truly, truly I tell you, there is no slave greater than his master, nor any emissary greater than the one who sent him. If you know these things, lucky for you if you do these things.

"It is not about all of you that I say 'I know those I have chosen'; it is so that the scripture may be fulfilled: 'He who eats my bread raised his heel against me.' I'm telling you now before it happens, so that you will believe when it happens that I am who I am. Truly, truly I tell you, whoever accepts the one I send accepts me, and whoever accepts me accepts the one who sent me."

Having said that, Jesus was stirred up in his spirit and bore witness, saying, "Truly, truly I tell you that one of you will betray me." His students looked at each other, at a loss as to whom he could be talking about.

One of his students, whom Jesus loved, was lying in Jesus' lap. So Simon Peter signals him to ask who it might be that he was talking about. So as the other lay there with his head on Jesus' chest he says to him, "Lord, who is it?"

Answers Jesus, "Whoever I dunk this piece of bread and offer it to, that's the one." So he dunks a piece of bread and offers it to Judas Simon Iscariot. And after he took the piece of bread, it was then that Satan entered into him. So Jesus says to him, "Do what you're doing and be quick about it." No one at the table understood what he was speaking to him about. Some thought because Judas held the purse that Jesus was saying to him, "Go buy what we need for the feast days," or that he should go give something to the poor. So the other took the piece of bread and went right out. It was night already.

So when he had left, Jesus says, "Now the son of humanity has been glorified, and God has been glorified in him. And if God was glorified in him, God will also glorify him in Himself, and He will glorify him without delay. Children, I am with you for a little longer: you will look for me, and just as I told the Jews that where I go you cannot come, I am telling you now. I give you a new commandment: to love each other, just as I loved you so that you would also love each other.

"That's how all will know you are my students: if you have love amongst yourselves."

Says Simon Peter, "Lord, where are you going?"

Answered Jesus, "Where I am going, you cannot follow me now, you will follow later."

Says Peter, "Lord, why can't I follow you right now? I'll give my life for you."

Answers Jesus, "You'll give your life for me, will you? Truly, truly I tell you that the rooster will not crow before you have said you don't know me three times."

14

"Don't let your hearts be troubled: believe in God and believe in me. In my Father's house there are many dwellings. If there weren't, would I tell you that I am going to prepare a place for you? And if I go and prepare a place for you, I will come again and bring you along with me, so that where I am you may also be. And where I am going, you know the way there."

Says Thomas, "Lord, we don't know where you're going. How can we know the way?"

Says Jesus, "I am the way, and truth, and life. No one comes to the Father if not through me. If you know me, you will know my Father too. And from now on you know Him and have seen Him."

Says Philip, "Lord, show us the Father and we will be satisfied."

Says Jesus, "All this time I've been with you and you don't know me, Philip? Whoever has seen me has seen the Father. How can you say, 'Show us the Father'? Don't you believe that I am in the Father and the Father is in me? The things I tell you, I don't say on my own: the Father does His work, remaining in me. Believe me that I am in the Father, and the Father is in me. If you don't believe me, believe my deeds themselves.

"Truly, truly I tell you, if someone believes in me, the deeds I do he will also do—indeed, he will do greater things than those, because I am going to the Father. And what you ask in my name I will do, so that the Father may be glorified in the son.

"If you love me, keep my commands. And I will ask the Father, and He will give you another Comforter to be with you forever. The breath of truth, which the world cannot receive because it doesn't see it or even know about it, is known to you because it stays with you and will continue to be in you. I will not leave you orphaned, I am coming to you. A little while longer, and the world will see me no more, but you will see me, because I am alive and you will be alive. On that day you will know that I am in my Father, and you in me, and I in you. The one who holds on to my commandments and keeps them, that's who loves me. Whoever loves me will be loved by my Father, and I will love him and reveal myself to him."

Says Jude—not Judas Iscariot—"Lord, how has it happened that you will reveal yourself to us and not to the world?"

Answered Jesus: "If anyone loves me, he will keep my words, and my Father will love him, and we will come to him and make our home with him. The person who doesn't love me doesn't keep my words. And the words you hear are not mine but those of the Father who sent me.

"I have told you these things while still remaining with you. But the Comforter, the sacred breath, whom the Father will send in my name, he will teach you everything and remind you of everything I told you.

"Peace I leave you, my peace I give to you; not as the world gives do I give to you. Don't let your hearts be troubled or intimidated. You heard how I told you, 'I am going away and coming back to you.' If you loved me you would be delighted that I'm going to the Father, because the Father is greater than me. And I have told you now before it happens, so that when it does happen you will believe. I will not talk much more with you, because the ruler of the world is coming, and in me there is nothing but that the world should know that I love the Father and that what the Father commanded me is just what I do. Arise, let us go on from here.

15

"I am the true vine, and my Father is the farmer. Every branch of me that bears no fruit, He takes away, and every branch that does bear fruit He cleans so it will bear more fruit. Already you are clean because of the words I have said to you. Remain in me, as I in you. Just as the branch can't bear fruit by itself without staying on the vine, neither can you unless you remain in me. I am the vine, you are the branches. Whoever remains in me and I in him, bears fruit aplenty, because without me you can do nothing. If someone doesn't remain in me, he's already thrown out and withered like the branches which are collected and thrown into the fire and burned. If you remain in me and what I said remains in you, ask whatever you like and it will be done for you. My Father has made it His glory for you to bear fruit aplenty and become my students.

"Just as the Father loved me, I loved you; remain in my love. If you keep my commands you will remain in my love, as I have kept my Father's commands and remain in His love. I have told you all this so that my joy may be in you and your joy may be complete. This is my command: to love each other just the way I loved you. No one has greater love than this: to lay down his life for his friends. You are my friends if you do what I command you. I do not call you slaves any more, because the slave doesn't know what his master does; you I have named my friends, because everything I heard from my Father I made known to you. You didn't choose me, I chose you; and I ordained that you should go and bear fruit and that your fruits should remain, so that whatever you ask the Father in my name He will give you. This is what I command you: to love each other.

"If the world hates you, know that it has hated me before it hated you. If you were of the world, the world would be friendly toward its own. But since you are not of the world, rather I have picked you out of the world, the world hates you for that. Remember the words I told you, that there is no slave greater than his master. If they hounded me, they will hound you too. If they kept my words, they will keep yours too. But they will do all these things to you because they don't know who sent me. If I hadn't come and talked to them, they would not be at fault, but now they have no excuse for their faults. Whoever hates me hates my Father too. If I had not done deeds in their midst that no one else ever did, they would not be at fault. But now they have seen and hated both me and my Father. But that is to fulfill the words written in their law: 'They hated me for nothing.'

"When the Comforter comes whom I will send you from the Father, the breath of truth that travels out from the Father, he will testify about me. And you will testify about me too, since you have been with me from the beginning.

16

"I have told you all this so you won't be caught off guard. They will ostracize you from their synagogues; indeed, the hour is coming when everyone who kills you will think he is doing God a service. And they will do that because they didn't know either the Father or me. But I have told you these things so that when their time comes you will remember that I told you of them. I didn't tell you these things from the beginning, because I was still with you.

"Now I go to the one who sent me, and now none of you are asking, 'Where are you going?' But because I have told you all this your heart has filled with grief. But I tell you the truth, it's better for you that I should go, because if I don't go, the Comforter will not come to you, whereas if I go, I will send him to you. And he when he comes will show the world better about wrongdoing and justice and condemnation. About wrongdoing, because they don't believe in me. About justice, because I go to the Father and you see me no more; and about condemnation, because the ruler of this world has been condemned.

"I have much more to say to you, but you can't bear it just yet. But when the other comes, the breath of truth, he will guide you in the ways of all truth, because he will not speak on his own, but will speak what he hears and announce to you what's coming. He will glorify me, because he will take of what is mine and announce it to you. Everything the Father has is mine: that's why I said he will take of what is mine and announce it to you.

"A little while, and you see me no more, and again a little while, and you will see me."

So some of his students said to each other, "What is this that he's telling us—'A little while, and you don't see me, and again a little while, and you will see me,' and 'I'm going to the Father'?" So they said, "What is this 'little while' he speaks of? We don't know what he's talking about."

Jesus realized that they wanted to ask him that, and said, "Are you arguing with each other about the fact that I said, 'A little while and you don't see me; and again, a little while, and you will see me'? Truly, truly I tell you that you will weep and wail, while the world rejoices. You will be grieved, but your grief will turn to joy. The woman is grieved when she gives birth because her hour has come, but when she bears the child, she no longer remembers her suffering for her joy that a person has been brought into the world. So you also are grieved now, but I will see you again, and your heart will rejoice, and no one will take your joy away from you.

"And on that day you will have no questions to ask me. Truly, truly I tell you, if you ask the Father something in my name, He will give it to you. So far you haven't asked Him anything in my name. Ask and receive, so that your joy may be complete.

"I have told you these things in figures of speech. The time is coming when I will no longer talk to you in figures of speech, I will give you the word straight out about the Father. On that day you will ask the Father, and I won't even say that I'll ask the Father on your behalf: because the Father Himself is your friend, since you have been my friends and have believed that I came forth from God. I came forth from God and have come into the world; now I am leaving the world again and traveling back to the Father."

His students say, "There! Now you're talking straight out, with no figures of speech. Now we know that you know everything, and do not need for anyone to ask you anything. By that sign we believe that you came forth from God."

Answered Jesus, "Now you believe? Watch: the time is coming—in fact it is here—for you to be scattered, each in a different direction, and leave me alone. But I am not alone, because the Father is with me. I have told you all this so that in me you may find peace. In the world you will find suffering; but courage! I have conquered the world."

17

Jesus spoke all this and lifted his eyes skyward, saying, "Father, my time has come. Glorify Your son so that Your son will glorify You, according as You have given him authority over every living thing, so that to everything You have given him, he may give life everlasting. That is what everlasting life is: for them to know You as the one true God and know the one You sent, Jesus the Anointed. I glorified You on the earth, completing the work You gave me to do. And now glorify me, Father, in Your own sight, with the glory I had in Your sight before there ever was a world.

"I have manifested Your name to the persons whom You gave me out of the world. They were Yours, and You gave them to me, and they have kept Your words. Now they have realized that everything You gave me comes from You; because the words You gave me, I have given them, and they accepted them and truly understood that I came forth from You, and believed that You sent me.

"I ask You for their sake, not for the world's sake but for the sake of those You have given me, because they are Yours, and all that is mine is Yours and what is Yours is mine, and I have been glorified in them, and I am no longer in the world, but they are in the world, while I am coming to You, holy Father: preserve them in Your name which You have given me, that they may be one, as You and I are. When I was with them I preserved them in Your name that You have given me, and guarded them, and none of them was lost except the son of perdition, so that the scripture could be fulfilled. But now I am coming to You, and I say these things in the world so they will have my joy completed in them. I have given them Your words, and the world has hated them because they aren't of the world, just as I am not of the world. I am not asking You to take them out of the world, but to keep them from the Evil One. They are not of the world, just as I am not of the world. Consecrate them to the truth. Your words are truth. Just as You sent me into the world, I also sent them into the world. And I consecrate myself to them, so that they will also be consecrated to the truth.

"I ask not just for their sake, but also for those who believe in me through their words, so that all people will be one, just as You, Father, are in me and I in You; so that they will be in us; so that the world will believe You sent me. And the glory You have given me, I have given to them, so that they will be one as You and I are one, with me in them and You in me, so that they will be perfected into one, so that the world will realize that You sent me and that You loved them just as You loved me.

"Father, I want these—this gift You have given me—to be with me wherever I am, so that they may witness my glory, which You have given me because You loved me before the beginning of the world. Father of justice, still the world didn't know You, but I knew You, and these people knew that You sent me. And I made known Your name to them, and will go on making it known, so that the love You had for me will be in them, and I will be in them."

18

After saying all this, Jesus went out with his students across the torrents of the Cedron to a place where there was a garden, which he and his students entered.

Judas his betrayer also knew the spot, since Jesus had frequently met there with his students. So Judas, with a band of soldiers and servants of the high priests and Pharisees, comes there with lanterns, torches, and weapons. So Jesus, knowing everything that was about to happen to him, came forward and says to them, "Who are you looking for?"

They answered, "Jesus of Nazareth."

He says to them, "Here I am." Judas his betrayer was standing with them. So when he said to them, "Here I am," they drew back and fell to the ground. So he asked them again, "Who are you looking for?"

They said, "Jesus of Nazareth."

Answered Jesus, "I told you, here I am, so if you're looking for me, let these people go"—that was to fulfill the words he'd said, "I have not lost any of those you gave me." So Simon Peter, who had a sword on him, drew it and hit the high priest's slave and cut off his right ear; the slave's name was Malchus. So Jesus said to Peter, "Put your sword back in its sheath: if this is the cup my Father gave me, shall I not drink it?"

So the band of soldiers and the commander and the servants of the

Jews took Jesus with them and tied him up and brought him first to Annas: he was the father-in-law of Caiaphas, who was high priest for that year. (Caiaphas was the one who advised the Jews, "Better for one person to die for the sake of the people.")

Now Simon Peter and another of Jesus' students were following him. The other student was known to the high priest and came into the high priest's courtyard with Jesus, while Peter stood outside the door. So the other student who knew the high priest came out and spoke to the doorkeeper and brought Peter inside. So the maid watching the door says to Peter, "You aren't one of that fellow's students too, are you?"

He says, "No, I'm not." Now the slaves and servants were standing around; they'd made a charcoal fire, since it was cold, and were warming themselves. So Peter was standing there with them and warming up.

So the high priest asked Jesus about his students and about his teaching. Answered Jesus, "I have publicly spoken to the world: I constantly taught in synagogues and in the temple, where all the Jews gather, and I said nothing in secret. What are you asking me? Ask the ones who heard me what I said to them. See these people? They know what I said."

When he said that, one of the servants standing near gave Jesus a slap, saying, "Is that how you answer the high priest?"

Answered Jesus, "If I said something bad, testify about the evil. If I spoke well, why are you beating me up?" So Annas sent him, still tied up, to Caiaphas the high priest.

Now Simon Peter was standing around and warming himself. So they said to him, "You aren't one of his students too, are you?"

He denied it and said, "No, I'm not."

Says one of the high priest's slaves, a relative of the one whose ear Peter cut off, "Didn't I see you in the garden with him?" Again Peter denied it, and just then a rooster crowed.

So they take Jesus away from Caiaphas to the governor's mansion— it was early morning by now—but they didn't go in themselves so they could eat the seder without being polluted.

So Pilate came out to see them, and he says, "What charge are you bringing against this person?"

They answered him, "If he wasn't doing something wrong, we wouldn't have handed him over to you."

So Pilate said to them, "Take him yourselves and try him by your own law."

Said the Jews, "We're not allowed to kill anybody"—to fulfill the words of Jesus in which he indicated by what death he was going to die.

So Pilate went back into the governor's mansion and summoned Jesus and said to him, "You're the king of the Jews?"

Answered Jesus, "Are you saying this on your own, or did others tell you about me?"

Answered Pilate, "Do I look like a Jew? Your people and high priests handed you over to me. What did you do?"

Answered Jesus, "My kingdom is not of this world. If my kingdom was of this world, my servants would fight to the death for me not to be handed over to the Jews; but in fact my kingdom isn't here."

So Pilate said to him, "So you are a king?"

Answered Jesus, "You say I am a king. What I was born for and what I came into the world for was to testify to the truth. Everyone who is of the truth responds to my voice."

Says Pilate, "What is truth?" And having said that, he went out to talk to the Jews again, and he says to them: "I don't see any charge against him. Now it's customary with you that I let one person go for you at Passover. So do you want me to let the 'king of the Jews' go?"

So they shouted again, "Not him—Barabbas!" (Barabbas was a robber.)

19

So then Pilate took Jesus and had him flogged. And the soldiers, weaving a crown of thorns, put it on his head and wrapped him in a robe of royal purple, and they were coming up to him and saying, "Good day, your majesty, king of the Jews" and then giving him a few slaps.

And Pilate came outside again, and he says to them, "See? I'm bringing him out here to let you know that I see no charge whatever against him." So Jesus came outside, wearing the thorny crown and the purple robe, and he says to them, "Here's the fellow."

So when the high priests and their servants saw him they raised a cry of "Crucify, crucify."

Says Pilate, "Take him yourselves and crucify him; I don't see any charge against him."

Answered the Jews, "We have our law and by that law he deserves to die, because he made himself out to be the son of God."

So when Pilate heard those words he really got scared and went back into the governor's mansion. And he says to Jesus, "Where are you from?" But Jesus gave him no answer.

So Pilate says to him, "You won't talk to me? Don't you know I have the power to let you go and also the power to crucify you?"

Answered Jesus, "You would have no power at all over me if it wasn't given you from above; so that the one who handed me over to you has the greater fault."

From that point Pilate was looking for a way to let him go, but the Jews shouted, "If you let this guy go, you're no friend of Caesar's. Anyone who makes himself out to be a king is speaking against Caesar."

So Pilate, on hearing those words, led Jesus outside and sat down on a podium at the place called Rockstrewn, or in Hebrew, "Gabbatha."

It was the Friday before Passover, about the noon hour, and he says to the Jews, "Here is your king."

They shouted, "Take him, take him and crucify him."

Says Pilate, "What, crucify your king?"

Answered the high priests, "We have no king but Caesar." Then he handed him over to them to be crucified.

So they took Jesus away, and carrying the cross on his back he came out to what they called Skull Place (which in Hebrew is called "Golgotha"), where they crucified him, and with him two others on this side and that, with Jesus in the middle. And Pilate lettered a sign and put it above the cross. It said, JESUS OF NAZARETH, KING OF THE JEWS. So many of the Jews read the sign, since it was a place near the city where they crucified Jesus, and it was written in Hebrew, Latin, and Greek. So the high priests of the Jews were saying to Pilate, "Don't write, 'The king of the Jews'; write, 'This man said, *I am the king of the Jews.*' "

Answered Pilate, "What I have written, I have written."

So the soldiers there where they crucified Jesus took his clothes and made four shares, a share for each of the soldiers, plus the tunic. But the tunic was seamless, woven from top to bottom in one piece. So they said to each other, "Let's not tear it up; we'll roll dice for it to see who gets it," so that the scripture would be fulfilled that says,

> *They divided my clothes among them,*
> *And for my vestments they cast lots.*

So the soldiers did just that.

Among those standing by the cross of Jesus were his mother, his mother's sister, Mary wife of Cleopas, and Mary Magdalen. So Jesus, seeing his mother and the student whom he loved standing near, says to his mother, "Madam, here is your son." Then he says to the student, "Here is your mother." And from that hour on the student took her for his own.

After that, Jesus, seeing that everything had already been accomplished, says, to fulfill the scripture, "I am thirsty." Now there was a jar lying there full of strong wine, so they put a sponge full of the wine on the end of a javelin and put it to his mouth. So when he had taken the wine, Jesus said, "It is finished," and bowed his head and gave up the ghost.

So the Jews, seeing as it was Friday, not wanting the bodies to remain on the cross for the Sabbath, especially since that was an important Sabbath-day, asked Pilate to break their legs and take them down. So the soldiers came and broke the legs of first the one and then the other crucified with him. When they got to Jesus, though, and saw he was already dead, they didn't break his legs, but one of the soldiers stuck a lance into his side, and blood and water came right out. And the one who saw that has testified about that, and his testimony is true, and he knows that he's telling the truth, so that you will also believe. That happened to fulfill the scripture, "Not a bone of his shall be broken." And again the scripture says elsewhere, "They will look upon the one they pierced."

After that Joseph of Arimathea, a student of Jesus in secret for fear of the Jews, asked Pilate if he could take the body of Jesus, and Pilate agreed. So he came and took his body, and Nicodemus also came, who had come to see him by night before, bringing a mixture of myrrh and aloes, about a hundred pounds of it. So they took Jesus' body and tied it with strips of cloth perfumed with the ointment, the customary way for the Jews to bury somebody. Now at the spot where they crucified him there was a garden, and in the garden a fresh tomb in which no one yet had ever lain. So, what with the approaching Jewish Sabbath and the tomb being near by, they put Jesus there.

20

On the first day of the week, so early it was still dark, Mary Magdalen comes to the tomb and sees the stone taken away from the tomb. So she runs and finds Simon Peter and the other student whom Jesus was close to and says to them, "They've taken the Lord out of the tomb and we don't know where they've put him." So Peter and the other student came out and headed for the tomb. And they were both running, but the other student ran faster than Peter and got to the tomb first, and bent down and saw the wrappings lying there, but didn't go in. So Simon Peter gets there after him and goes into the tomb, and notices the wrappings lying there, and the cloth that had been over his head, which was not lying with the wrappings but rolled up separately in one place. So then the other student who got to the tomb first also went in, and saw and was convinced. (You see, they didn't know yet about the scripture passage that said he was to rise again from the dead.) So the students went back to their houses.

But Mary was standing outside by the tomb crying. So as she was crying, she bent down and looked into the tomb, and she sees two holy messengers dressed in white sitting there, one at the head and one at the foot of where the body of Jesus had lain. And they say to her, "Madam, why are you crying?"

She tells them, "They took my Lord away, and I don't know where they put him." So saying, she turned around, and she sees Jesus standing there, but she didn't know it was Jesus.

Jesus says to her, "Madam, why are you crying? Who are you looking for?"

She, thinking it was the gardener, says to him, "Sir, if you carried him someplace, tell me where you put him and I'll go get him."

Jesus says to her, "Mary?"

She, turning around, says to him in Hebrew, "Rabbuni!" (which means teacher).

Says Jesus, "Don't cling to me, I have not yet ascended to the Father. Go find my brothers and tell them I am ascending to my Father and your Father, and my God and your God."

Mary Magdalen goes and tells his students, "I have seen the Lord!" and what he said to her.

So when it was getting late on that first day after the Sabbath and the doors were shut where the students were for fear of the Judeans, Jesus came and stood in front of them, and says to them, "Peace to you!" And after saying that he showed them his hands and his side. So his students were overjoyed to see the Lord. Jesus said to them again, "Peace to you! Just as the Father sent me, so I send you." And so saying, he breathed upon them, saying, "Receive the sacred breath. Whoever's wrongs you forgive, let them be forgiven; whoever you hold to their wrongs, let them be held."

Now Thomas, one of the twelve, the Twin, as he was known, wasn't with them when Jesus came. So the other students said to him, "We've seen the Lord!"

But he said to them, "Unless I see the nail-marks on his hands, and put my finger on the nailmarks, and put my hand in his side, I will never be convinced."

And a week later his students were indoors again, and Thomas with them. With the doors shut, Jesus came and stood in front of them and said, "Peace to you!" Then he says to Thomas, "Come here with your finger and look at my hands, and take your hand and put it in my side, and don't be a doubter but a believer."

Thomas answered him, "My Lord and my God!"

Says Jesus, "Because you have seen me, you are convinced? How lucky are the ones who never saw but still believed!"

There are many other wonders Jesus worked in the sight of his students which are not written in this book, but this much has been written so that you may believe that Jesus is the Anointed, the son of God, and by believing have life in his name.

21

Afterwards Jesus revealed himself to his students on the Tiberian Sea. This is how he revealed himself: Simon Peter and Thomas the so-called Twin and Nathaniel from Cana, Galilee, and the sons of Zebedee and two more of his students were together. Simon Peter says to them, "I'm going fishing."

They say to him, "We're coming with you too." They went out and got in the boat, and during that night they caught nothing. When it was already morning Jesus stood on the shore; the students, however, didn't know that it was Jesus. So Jesus says to them, "Kids, do you have anything to eat?"

They answered, "No."

He said to them, "Cast your net on the right side of your boat, and you'll find something." So they did, and they couldn't even drag the net any more what with the great mass of fish.

So the student whom Jesus loved says to Peter, "It's the Lord!" Simon Peter, hearing that it was the Lord, put his tunic on and fastened his belt—he had been naked—and threw himself into the sea. The others came with the boat (since they weren't far from shore, only about two hundred feet off), dragging their netful of fish. As they got out onto land they see a charcoal fire there with a fish and a loaf of bread lying on it.

Says Jesus, "Bring some of the fish you just caught." So Simon Peter came up dragging the net full of big fish, a hundred fifty-three of them, and many as they were, the net didn't rip. Says Jesus, "Come have breakfast." None of the students dared to ask him, "Who are you?" knowing that it was the Lord. Jesus comes and takes the bread and gives it to them, and the fish likewise. That made three times already that Jesus revealed himself to his students after rising from the dead.

So when they'd breakfasted Jesus says to Simon Peter, "Simon Johnson, do you truly love me more than these others?"

He says, "Yes, Lord, you know I love you."

He says to him, "Shepherd my lambs." He says to him yet a second time, "Simon Johnson, do you truly love me?"

He says to him, "Yes, Lord, you know that I love you."

He says to him, "Pasture my sheep." For the third time he says to him, "Simon Johnson, do you love me?"

Peter was heartbroken that he could say to him a third time, "Do you love me?" And he says to him, "Lord, you know everything, you *know* that I love you."

Says Jesus, "Shepherd my sheep. Truly, truly I tell you, when you were a young man you used to fasten your own belt and walk around wherever you wished, but when you are an old man you will hold out your hands while someone else fastens your belt and takes you where you don't want to go." He said that indicating the death by which he was to glorify God, and after saying that he tells him, "Follow me."

Turning round, Peter sees the student whom Jesus loved following them, the same who lay with his head on his chest at the supper and said, "Lord who is your betrayer?" Seeing him Peter says to Jesus, "Lord, what about him?"

Says Jesus, "If I wish him to stay till I come back, what is that to you? You follow me." So the word got out among the brothers that that student would never die. But Jesus didn't say to him that he wouldn't die, just "If I want him to stay till I come back, what is that to you?"

It is this same student who bears witness to these things and wrote these words, and we know that his testimony is true. There are many other things that Jesus did, such that if they were written down one by one, I don't think there would be room in the world for all the resulting volumes.

The Epistles

Introduction to the Epistles

While many non-Christians know at least something of the gospels (Muslims go so far as to regard them as sacred books, along with the Torah, the Psalms, and the Koran), perhaps as many, Christians among them, have little or no familiarity with the later parts of the New Testament. For that reason, the Acts of the Apostles, the Epistles and the Book of Revelation require some introducing.

Acts is almost a fifth gospel. While it does not deal with the life and doings of Jesus, it has the following in common with the four gospels:

—It is a historical narrative. It "picks up the story" shortly after the gospel events conclude and describes some of the very early history (the "salvation history") of the Christian church.

—Its author is St. Luke, or whoever it was who actually wrote Luke's gospel.

—We should read the two writings by Luke as the first and second parts of one continuous story. Luke evidently intended us to read them that way.

Acts may not be literal history of the kind we demand from contemporary historians (or used to demand, before Marxist, feminist, and ethnic revisionists seized the academic high ground). In fact, much of Acts resembles some of the popular heroic fiction of its day, right down to the miraculous escapes from various imprisonments and from a storm at sea. But we should not dismiss Acts on the grounds that it does not "keep to the facts." That simply was not its overriding purpose.

Christians widely refer to Acts as "salvation history," meaning that it is the narrative of how the early church came to understand what it was that Jesus had given them. As Acts tells it, the aid of the Holy Spirit, which is the gift that Jesus gave us as he himself departed, brought Christians to the knowledge that they had been saved by God, acting through the person of His Son. To early (and contemporary) Christians this overwhelms such questions as, "Did they really escape from jail like that?"

Thus, despite the resemblance to Hellenistic "drugstore paperback" novels, Acts is really the history of a spiritual development. For that reason, the book concludes without telling us what becomes of St. Paul. In a popular adventure story, such an inconclusive ending would be unthinkable. But in "salvation history," we reach the end of Acts with the journey complete, provided we understand that it is a journey of insight, and not just of derring-do.

It's still a good yarn, and I think readers will enjoy it the most if they read it at one sitting!

The Epistles pose more problems for readers. They are letters whose exact context and purpose is often unclear. Sometimes the language refers to persons and events which scholars, let alone readers, cannot identify.

This often makes them impenetrable. As translator Andy Gaus said to me, "How can people treat these letters to various early Christian congregations in the Mediterranean world, letters often rife with invective or marked by references to mundane everyday details, as if they were disembodied doctrinal pronouncements?"

So we thought it would be well to introduce the Epistles: what they are, who wrote them, when, to whom, and under what circumstances. A little background might explain why these letters are Scripture to Christians, and important history to non-Christians.

The Epistles are some twenty-one letters said to be written by Paul (14), John (3), Peter (2), and James and Jude (one each). Most of them, particularly most of Paul's, are messages to individual congregations in response to local conditions and problems. Others are sermons or theological essays cast in the form of letters (for example, Hebrews). They are important because they give us a glimpse of the formation of Christianity while that formation was taking place: a dramatic picture of the origins of the Western world's principal religion.

Many readers will be surprised to learn that some of Paul's letters—the ones he most probably wrote himself or had a secretary write at his direction—are the earliest Christian documents we possess, which in itself makes them indispensable. Consider the following composition dates, as suggested by recent scholarship:*

---

* In fairness, I should say, "according to those recent scholars I happen to believe." We hear all kinds of differing views of these dates from scholars, commentators, television evangelists, and Main Street cafe philosophers. Andy Gaus himself believes the Gospels and the Epistles are more or less contemporary; his reasons, and the sources he cites, are as good as mine!

GOSPELS

Matthew	roughly 80 A.D.
Mark	roughly 70 A.D.
Luke	roughly 80–90 A.D.
John	roughly 90–100 A.D.

PAULINE LETTERS

Galatians	between 48–55 A.D.
1 Thessalonians	about 51 A.D.
Romans	between 56–58 A.D.
1 Corinthians	about 56 A.D.
2 Corinthians	57 A.D.
Philippians	between 55–63 A.D.

If we take the date of the Passion events, Jesus' crucifixion and resurrection, as being between 35–40 A.D., we can see that the early letters of Paul follow shortly thereafter. They predate the writing of the Gospels by a generation! Even those Epistles that seem to be later (written by anonymous early Christians who, in a literary practice common in that culture, ascribed them to Paul, John, etc.) draw on the remembered mood and feel and context of those first years of the Christian church.

Because of their early composition, the Epistles give us a description of the life of early Christianity. That picture shows not only the problems they faced (persecution, internal division) and their success in spreading rapidly throughout the Hellenistic world, but it also gives us the earliest Christian theology, that is, what those folks believed, what they made of the message Jesus had just given them. Thus, we can read these letters as both spiritual and historical documents. Does any other major religion possess similar writings—texts offering eyewitness glimpses of their time of theological and organizational origin?

I view the Epistles, especially Paul's, as proceeding along two lines: profession and differentiation. They profess what Christians believe and base their lives and hopes on. They do this in part by contrasting or differentiating their belief from other religions, namely Judaism, Greco-Roman paganism, and gnosticism (though they do not refer to the latter by name; the term itself is a modern one).

The first followers of Jesus were Jews. Following soon after them came

Gentiles. Immediately the two ran into problems. Jewish believers, being faithful to the Mosaic law, were horrified at the prospect of breaking bread with non-Jews who did not keep kosher. So the question quickly arose: What kind of religion is this? Is it a linear historical development within Judaism, in which case Gentile converts would have to be be circumcised and keep kosher, or is it something new and universal, an interruption, and remaking, of history?

The Epistles document how the early assemblies eventually opted for the latter and became "Christian" rather than "Jesusite-Jewish." Much bitterness accompanied this process.

As for the vast majority of Jews who remained in their traditional belief, we can only imagine their revulsion at the efforts of Paul and other early missionaries, who traveled from one Jewish community to another preaching the Gospel. The Gospel in part rebukes Judaism; and what is more galling, the rebuke comes from within!

Hostility toward the early church, then, came from Jewish communities unable to bear its blasphemies and lawlessness. Hostility came also from Roman civil authorities, in some cases allegedly instigated by Jewish communities. As a result, persecution is a major theme of the Epistles. Paul himself was repeatedly imprisoned and tortured, and was eventually executed by the Romans under Nero sometime around 65 A.D.

This historical circumstance—namely, that Christianity originated in hostile opposition to its parent religion—has had immense, and alas very cruel, consequences in the ensuing two millennia. We can read about the roots of the problem in these letters!

Another problem came from those Christians who took the overthrowing of the Mosaic law by Jesus to mean total personal license. As Andy Gaus told me, "On the one hand you had Christians who were saying you were damned if you ate pork, while on the other hand you had people saying it was okay for a Christian to sleep with his sister."

Yet another doctrinal problem arose from the syncretistic mania that characterized the religions and cults of the ancient world. Early Christians were evidently enticed to incorporate elements of paganism and/or gnosticism into their religion, and it was necessary to resist that.

The Epistles document how well the early assemblies did resist and hold on to what was uniquely theirs. A reading of these letters (plus the Acts of the Apostles) wonderfully portrays this progress, principally piloted by Paul, through Christianity's first few decades.

Most of the Epistles are not masterpieces of Greek prose, but they somehow convey great power of expression, which Andy Gaus' translation captures marvelously. Any reader concerned with the development of Christianity and with the religious history of the Western world will delight in them. The following are brief introductions to each of the Epistles.

EPISTLES OF PAUL

Romans is the longest and most theological of Paul's letters. Paul wrote it from Greece in or about 57 A.D. to the Christian community in Rome. At the time, Paul planned to take up a collection among the Gentile Christian assemblies of the Mediterranean world for the poor Jewish Christians of Jerusalem. He refers to this charitable effort in several of the Epistles; it runs as a thread through his letters. Romans deals with the "Jewish vs. Gentile Christian" dispute, the question of salvation through adherence to Jewish law versus salvation through belief in Jesus' revelation. Christians today consider it the thorniest Epistle, and disagree about its meaning in all details. It is undeniably a powerful document, however one interprets it.

First Corinthians gives us the best first-hand picture of early Christian life we have. Corinth was a kind of Hellenistic San Francisco—wealthy, cultivated, and civilized. Its citizens knew a highly organized and advanced pursuit of culture, and of pleasure. The painful gap between rich and poor was there too. Corinthian Christians partook of that urban life, sometimes to the detriment of their religious quest. In about the year 56 A.D. Paul wrote to them to address problems doctrinal, factional, liturgical, and even sexual. As is generally true in the Epistles, we do not know all the details of why the letter was written. This makes it all the more interesting to the reader, who gets to imagine just what crisis or problem Paul is referring to in given passages.

Second Corinthians follows a year later. It is Paul's most personal Epistle. Challenges at Corinth force him to assert his authority, to wax persuasive, and to display a flair for old-fashioned polemic. Characteristically, at the same time he somehow manages the feat of writing profound Christian theology.

Galatians' audience was very unlike the Corinthians: not Greeks living in the center of the Mediterranean world but descendants of barbarians living in what is now central (possibly south central) Turkey. Evidently, after being converted, they received visits from missionaries of the "Judaizing Christian" school, who tried to persuade them to observe the Mosaic law by adding circumcision, for example, to their observance of Jesus' teaching. Paul, writing somewhere between 48 and 55 A.D., rejects this proselytizing, letting some heavy broadsides loose in the process.

Ephesians may not be by Paul. One theory is that a secretary or follower of Paul's wrote it, perhaps as late as 80 to 100 A.D. While seemingly addressed to the assembly in Ephesus, it may in fact have been a circular letter—the first "encyclical"—sent out to all the churches in Asia Minor. The topic, certainly, is the unity and mission of the Christian church, rather than any particular doings in Ephesus.

Paul wrote to the Philippians from prison, though we do not know which prison, between 55 and 63 A.D. Philippi, in northern Greece, was the site of the first Christian community in Europe, with Paul making converts there as early as 49 A.D. He evidently approved of the Philippians' religious life and had great affection for them, as this Epistle is joyous and enthusiastic.

Colossians is another prison letter, perhaps dating from the same time as Philippians. Colossae was in Asia Minor, inland from the Aegean sea. Its people appear to have been prone, as was typical in Asia Minor, to cult religions. Certain teachers arose among the Colossian Christians who combined Christian doctrine with some kind of Middle Eastern, possibly gnostic, emphasis on powers or beings who act as intermediaries between the divine and the terrestrial. Paul rejects these powers as unnecessary for Christians, and praises the Colossians for resisting the cultists. He also gives characteristic advice on what constitutes Christian conduct.

First Thessalonians, dating from around 51 A.D., is written to recent converts in Thessalonica (Salonika) in northeastern Greece. In it Paul expresses his happiness over the faith of the assembly, discusses his travel plans, exhorts the faithful to sexual restraint and to charity. He also outlines a doctrine of the resurrection of the dead. As a side note, among fundamentalists and some other Christians the term "the rapture" is heard quite commonly today. It stems from Paul's description in this letter of those Christians who are alive at the Second Coming as being snatched up (Latin *rapiemur*, "we will be snatched up") to join the Lord.

Second Thessalonians seems to follow First Thessalonians, though some scholars say it was written first. Again, there is thanksgiving over the local church's faith. But it deals with a disturbing element: apparently an oracle and/or a forged Pauline Epistle, claiming the Second Coming has already taken place, has surfaced in the community. Christians then as now were perplexed by the question, "Why hasn't the Lord returned yet?" Paul responds to this in chapter 2, which unfortunately is very hard to make sense of.

The letters First Timothy, Second Timothy and Titus pose problems as to date and authorship. Either a) some contemporary calling himself "Paul" is the author, and Paul did not write them because the Greek style is not his and the theory of the church is too developed to be of his time; b) the style is Paul's, the church theory is traditional Essene in model, and Paul is the author; c) Paul didn't write them, but a secretary, acting under Paul's direction, did; or d) they date from a generation or two after Paul, when an editor put them together using traditions about Paul and fragments of actual Pauline Epistles. Whatever the case, these letters warn about false teachers we may assume to have been gnostics. They are also addressed not to whole congregations but to their shepherds or pastors, namely Timothy and Titus. First Timothy contains various exhortations as to conduct and belief. It specifically rejects the teachers of so-called "knowledge" or gnostics. (Some of St. Paul's own language, particularly in First and Second Corinthians, has a gnostic ring to it, speaking as it does of "secret wisdom." This, I think, is due to two factors: first, that gnosticism was part of the theological tendency of the times, and second, as a result of the first, gnostic-sounding language may be almost inevitable in theological writing of that era. However, although we do not know the precise point on the "gnosticism graph" St. Paul occupied, he seems to reject gnosticism, here and elsewhere, in the sense of a theological system that introduces intermediate beings between God and creation. For St. Paul, and for Christians generally, Jesus obviates the need for such beings.) Second Timothy is very personally directed to Pastor Timothy, speaking conversationally with him about Paul's imprisonment and other tribulations. Titus was the pastor of the church on Crete; that letter contains advice about teaching Christian conduct, appointing church leaders, and how to deal with argumentative heretics.

Paul wrote Philemon (likely between 61 and 63 A.D.) as a plea for his disciple Onesimus, a runaway slave, whom Paul is sending back to his master. This brief Epistle is noteworthy in that it lacks any trace of moral opposition to slavery, which opposition is a distinctly modern development, and also in that it gives a very personal and touching picture of Paul's affection for the slave. He even offers to pay the man's debts!

Hebrews is not so much a letter as a sermon written as a letter. Paul is certainly not the author: the Greek is much too good to be his, and the vocabulary and thought are those of an educated Jew from Alexandria, which Paul was not. References to Jewish temple worship may mean that the destruction of the temple by the Romans (70 A.D.) had not yet occurred at the time of writing. Hebrews, long thought to have been addressed to a group of Jewish Christians (hence the title), is directed at people who needed encouragement in their faith. Their problem was not persecution or internal division, but the normal human tendency to wear down over time. The letter achieves and sustains a beautiful rhetorical (in the best sense of that word) level as it puts forth a theology of Jesus' priesthood and Christian faith.

THE CATHOLIC LETTERS

The remaining seven letters are called "catholic" or "universal" because they were written to the early Christian church in general, and not to any one local assembly.

The James of that letter was probably neither of the two apostles named James, but may be another James, a member of Jesus' family whom Matthew and Mark call "brother of the Lord." Its form is very Jewish, being that of a moral exhortation which is common in Jewish "wisdom literature." On the other hand, the Greek style is superb, which leads some scholars to conclude that James didn't write it, and others that James had a trained scribe do it up for him. If James wrote it, it's an early work, since he was stoned to death in 62 A.D. If not, it may be as late as 90–100 A.D.

First Peter is also in excellent Greek of a kind that we may assume was not penned by a poor fisherman from the Sea of Galilee. The letter does mention, however, that it was written with the help of a secretary, Silvanus, so it just may be by the "Rock" himself. If so, it dates no later than Nero's persecution, 63–67 A.D., in which Peter was martyred. If not, it may be one or two generations later. It contains moral exhortation and doctrinal comfort intended to support those suffering persecution.

Second Peter, on the other hand, is not by Peter, and at the outside it may even date from a hundred years after the crucifixion. Internal references suggest its late composition: for example, it refers to the apostles as "our ancestors," as if they are dead and buried at the time of writing. This letter has two purposes: exhortation to grow in faith, love and virtue; and avoidance of false teachers.

The three letters attributed to John have much in common with the Gospel of John in their vocabularly and themes. There is no proof that John the Gospel writer is their author, but their similarities to that Gospel show them to be the products of the "Johannine school" of Christianity. These similaritites include concerns about the nature of Christ, about the importance of mutual love, about the antichrist, and a very Greek interest in the idea of truth.

First John is theology under the form of a letter. Some scholars consider it to be a commentary on the fourth Gospel. Second John and Third John are very short and of the same length, perhaps because they were each written on a single sheet of parchment.

Jude is not by the apostle Jude but perhaps by the Jude whom Matthew and Mark describe as a brother of Jesus. Again, the date and authorship are debated, the Greek is polished, and the apostles are spoken of as belonging to the past. Many scholars call the epistle pseudonymous and date it around 100 A.D. Others say Jude may have lived long enough to write it at about 80 A.D. This short letter directs its readers to resist very gnostic-sounding heresies. It also refers to two Jewish books, the *Assumption of Moses* and the *Book of Enoch*, which both Judaism and Christianity regard as apocryphal.

REVELATION OF JOHN

The Book of Revelation was penned by someone named John who is definitely not the writer of the fourth Gospel. John the Evangelist simply could not have written such bad Greek, laced as it is with outright errors. It is undoubtedly the work of someone for whom Greek was an imperfectly mastered foreign tongue.

But what power it has! The stumbling, incorrect speech of a foreigner can be powerfully affecting. There is a Polish priest at a parish near me who can barely make himself understood in English, but the man is a joy to hear. Something similar is true of Revelation. Its author, suffering along with his fellow Christians under Roman repression, explodes his vision into unforgettable words.

Readers who feel inclined to decipher the symbolism of Revelation may find their task easier if they keep firmly in mind that the author is describing the eventual triumph of the just over the great powers of this world. Rome was the demon then, and many readers will undoubtedly join in the two-thousand-year-old sport of trying to find parallel bad guys in one's own contemporary scene.

Acts, the Epistles, and Revelation will reward all readers, Christian and non-Christian alike. Andy Gaus has made them a pleasure to read, and has even managed to make intelligible sense out of the problematic passages. (Romans here comes to mind; in order to translate it, Andy took a stand on certain issues, such as what Paul meant by *dikaiosune*, normally translated as "righteousness." It's a well-known, much-debated problem. The very least I can say for Andy's interpretation is that it is thoughtful and defensible. It also makes sense and reads well!) So whether you are new to these works, know them well, or fall somewhere in between, read on and enjoy. I am confident you'll be glad you did.

—GEORGE WITTERSCHEIN

Acts of the Apostles

1

Dear Theophilus,

I chose to make my first words about all the things that Jesus came to do and teach, up to the day when, after giving orders by sacred breath to the apostles he chose, he was taken up on high. He also showed himself in the flesh to them after his suffering in many instances, during forty days when he appeared to them and told them of the kingdom of God.

And assembling them, he commanded them not to separate from Jerusalem, but to wait for "the fulfillment of the promise of my Father as you heard it from me: before, John bathed you in water, but now you will be bathed in holy breath before many days have passed."

Those assembled with him asked him, "Lord, in this coming time are you restoring the kingdom of Israel?"

He said to them: "It isn't yours to know what times and occasions the Father has fixed on His own authority; but you will receive power when the sacred breath comes over you, and you will be my witnesses in Jerusalem, and all Judea and Samaria, and to the ends of the earth."

And having said that, he was raised into the air as they looked on, and taken up into a cloud and out of sight of their eyes. And as they were staring into the sky after he had gone, all of a sudden two men were standing beside them in white robes, who then said, "Citizens of Galilee, why are you standing there looking into the sky? He, Jesus, who was taken from you and up into the sky, will come again the same way that you watched him traveling into the sky."

Then they returned to Jerusalem from the mountain called Mount Olive, which is within a Sabbath-journey of Jerusalem [about two-thirds of a mile].* And when they got back, they went up to the upstairs room

* The maximum distance a Jew may travel on the Sabbath.

where they were staying—Peter, John, James, Andrew, Philip, Thomas, Bartholomew, Matthew, James son of Alpheus, Simon the Revolutionary and Jude son of James. All of these were persevering as one in prayer, with various women including Mary the mother of Jesus, and his brothers and sisters.

And on one of those days Peter stood up in front of the brothers and said, with a crowd there in the same place of about a hundred twenty persons: "Gentle brothers, the scripture had to be fulfilled which the sacred breath foretold through the mouth of David, the one about Judas becoming the agent for the capturers of Jesus, because he was numbered among us, and drew the lot of that assignment. He subsequently bought a field with the profits of his crime, where he went down head first and snapped in the middle and poured out all his guts.* And the fact became so well known to all the inhabitants of Jerusalem that that place became known in the dialect of the people there as Akeldamach—that's 'the Blood Property.' After all, it says in the Book of Psalms,

> *Let his quarters be laid waste*
> *And let there be no lodger in them.*

and

> *Let his high office be taken by another.*

Therefore, choosing from those of us men who have been together during all the time that Lord Jesus went in and out among us, starting from the washings of John to the day when he was taken up out of our sight, we must make one of them a witness to the resurrection, together with us." So they nominated two, Joseph "Barsabbas," also called "the Just," and Matthias.

And they said in prayer: "You, Lord, the expert on all hearts, show us which one of these two You chose to occupy the place of that office and

---

* What, was he standing in the middle of an open field and then he fell over and burst apart? Did he fall *from* something, and if so, what? (Actually, it doesn't even say he fell!) Could the murky and roundabout wording be a cushioned way of saying he fell upon his sword? That would at least be psychologically consistent with the account in Matthew (where he hangs himself), and is more likely to make a person's guts spew out than falling out of a tree.

mission from which Judas went out of bounds to travel to a place of his own." And they drew lots and the lot fell on Matthias, and he was voted in beside the eleven apostles.

2

And when the fifty days after Passover were just being completed they were all together in the same place. And suddenly down from the sky came the rush of a driving wind of violent force and filled the whole house where they were sitting, and there appeared to them separate tongues of what looked like fire, which alighted upon each one of them, and they were all filled with holy breath and started speaking in other languages, according as the spirit granted them to speak their mind.

Now among the residents of Jerusalem were pious men of every nation under the sun. So when this clamor arose the crowd came close and was astonished, because each of them heard them speaking in his own language. They were beside themselves with amazement, saying, "Look at them, aren't they Galileans talking, every single one? So how can each of us hear them in the very language we were born to? Parthians, Medes, and Elamites; and inhabitants of Mesopotamia, Judea, Cappadocia, Pontus, Asia, Phrygia, Pamphylia, Egypt and the part of Libya toward Cyrene; and the Romans residing here; some of us Jews by birth and some of us converted Cretans and Arabs—all of us hear them telling in our own tongues of the greatness of God." They were all beside themselves and couldn't figure it out, saying one to the other, "What can this mean?" Others, though, made a big joke of it and said, "That homemade wine sure packs a wallop!"

But Peter, standing with the other eleven, raised his voice and spoke his mind: "Citizens of Judea and residents of Jerusalem, all of you, let this much be known to you and give ear to what I say: these people have not, as you suppose, been drinking—come now, it's nine o'clock in the morning. No, this is what was spoken of by the prophet Joel:

> *And it will be in the final days, so God says,*
> *I will pour a bit of my breath on every living thing,*
> *And your sons will prophesy, and your daughters too,*
> *And your youth will see visions,*
> *And your elders will be caught up in the dreams they dream.*

Even on my slave-boys, even on my slave-girls,
In those days I will pour my breath, and they will prophesy.
And I will show wonders in the sky above,
And signs on the earth below:
Blood and fire and steaming smoke,
The sun turning into darkness
And the moon into blood,
Before the day of the Lord comes, tremendous and manifest,
And it will be all those who call on the name of the Lord who will
be saved.

"Citizens of Israel, listen to these words: Jesus of Nazareth, a man certified to you as being from God by the miracles and wonders and signs that God worked through him there in front of you, as you yourselves know—this same Jesus, by the ordained will and foreknowledge of God, betrayed by the hand of the lawless, you nailed to the cross and destroyed, him whom God raised up, undoing the pangs of death for him because death could not hold him down. In fact, David says of him:

I foresaw my Lord, there with me through everything,
Since he stands at my right, so that I won't be shaken.
That's why my heart was overjoyed
And my tongue was delighted,
And even my flesh will settle down in hope,
Because you will not let my soul slip down to hell,
Nor allow your holy man to see corruption.
You showed me the ways to true Life;
You will fill me with joy at the sight of your face.

"Gentle brothers, I think I may state with confidence about the patriarch David that indeed he died and was buried, and his grave is still with us to this day. So, being a prophet and knowing that God had sworn to him under oath that the fruit of his loins would sit upon his throne, in prophetic foresight he talked about the resurrection of the Anointed, because he 'wasn't allowed to slip down into hell,' nor did his 'flesh see corruption.' This same Jesus was raised up by God, of which fact we are all witnesses. After being exalted to the right hand of God and receiving the sacred breath as promised from the Father, he poured out all this that you see and hear. David never ascended into the skies, but even he says,

> *The Lord said to my lord, Sit at my right,*
> *While I put your enemies under your feet as a footrest.*

"So let all the family of Israel know without fail that God made him both Lord and Anointed, this same Jesus whom you crucified."

It pierced them to the heart to hear that, and they said to Peter and the other apostles, "What can we do, brothers?"

"Repent," said Peter, "and be washed, each one of you, in the name of Jesus the Anointed, for the forgiveness of your wrongs, and receive the gift of the sacred breath. Because the proclamation is for you and your children, and all those far away, whomever the Lord your God may call." And he bore witness to them on many other points and pleaded with them, "Be healed of the deformity of this age." So they received his words and came to be washed; and the souls added that day numbered some three thousand.

Now they were persevering in the teaching of the apostles and in fellowship, with breaking of bread and prayers. But fear struck every heart, so many were the signs and wonders worked by the apostles. Now the believers were all in one place and sharing everything in common: they were selling their possessions and estates alike and splitting it up among all according to who needed it. By day they persevered as one at prayer in the temple, and then at home they broke bread and partook of their food in joy and simplicity of heart, praising God and finding favor with the general populace. And the Lord brought more of the saved to them there every day.

3

Now Peter and John were going up to the temple for three o'clock prayers. And a certain man born crippled from his mother's womb was being carried in, whom they used to set down every day by the temple gateway known as "the Pretty Gate" so he could beg handouts from the people coming into the temple. He, seeing Peter and John about to enter the temple, asked them for some charity. Peter, with John beside him, stared at him and said, "Look at us."

So he kept his eyes on them, expecting to get something from them.

But Peter said, "I have no silver or gold on hand, but what I have I hereby give you: in the name of Jesus the Anointed of Nazareth, get up and walk." And taking him by his right hand he pulled him up. Suddenly his legs and ankles firmed up, and he sprang to his feet and started walking and went into the temple with him, walking and jumping and praising God. And all the people saw him walking around and praising God. Then they recognized him as the same guy who used to sit begging by the Pretty Gate of the temple, and they were beside themselves with astonishment at what had happened to him.

As he took hold of Peter and John all the people ran towards them gawking, onto what was called the Porch of Solomon. Peter, when he saw that, responded to the people: "Citizens of Israel, why are you amazed at this and why are you staring at us as if we'd made him walk around by our own power or piety? 'The God of Abraham and the God of Jacob and the God of your fathers' glorified his boy Jesus, whom you betrayed, disclaiming all ties with him to Pilate's face, when *his* judgment was to let him go. But you said no to his holiness and innocence and asked instead for a murderer to be spared for your sake, whereas you killed the ruler of life whom God then raised from the dead, a fact to which we are witnesses. And on the basis of faith in his name this man that you see and hear before you was made sound by his name, and faith working through him gave him this perfect health before your eyes.

"Now then, brothers, I know that you acted from ignorance, as did your leaders. That's how God fulfilled what He announced beforehand through the mouths of all the prophets: that His Anointed would suffer. So repent and look toward the expunging of your wrongs, so that some time to recover may come to you from the face of God and so that He may send to you Jesus, your predestined Anointed, whom heaven must keep for now until the time when all things are restored as God spoke of them through the mouths of His holy prophets of old. Moses, for instance, said: 'Your God will raise up a prophet among you out of the ranks of your brothers, as he raised me. Listen to him concerning everything he says to you. Someday every soul who does not listen to that prophet will be exterminated from the race.' And all the prophets who spoke, from Samuel and his successors on, also announced these days. You are the sons and daughters of the prophets and the contract God contracted with your fathers when He said to Abraham, 'And in your seed all the lands of the earth shall be blessed.' To you before anyone else

God sent His son after resurrecting him, to bless you by turning each of you from your evil ways."

4

As they were talking to the people, the priests, the templemaster general, and the Sadducees stood over them, offended at their teaching the people and proclaiming resurrection from the dead in Jesus' name, and they laid hands on them and put them in safekeeping overnight—it was evening already. But many of those who heard the word believed it, and the number of the men grew to about five thousand.

It happened on the next day that their leaders, elders and clerks assembled in Jerusalem, with Annas the high priest, and Caiaphas, and John and Alexander and everyone of high-priestly rank; and setting them in their midst they questioned them: "By what power and in whose name did you do this?"

Then Peter filled with the sacred breath and said to them, "Rulers of the people and elders, if we are being called to task today for a good deed toward a sick person that resulted in his being healed, let it be known to all of you and all the nation of Israel that it was in the name of Jesus the Anointed of Nazareth, whom you crucified and whom God raised from the dead, it was in his name that this man became sound before your eyes. He is the 'stone rejected' by you the builders that 'has become the cornerstone,' and there is no salvation in any other, because there is no other name under the sun that is given to humanity for us to be saved by."

Witnessing this extensive speech of Peter's and John's and noting that these were uneducated commoners, they were amazed and recognized them as having been with Jesus, and as they looked at the fellow standing beside them hale and hearty they had no answer to give. So after clearing them from the council chamber they put their heads together, saying, "What do we do with these people? After all, a celebrated miracle has occurred at their hands; it's public knowledge to all the inhabitants of Jerusalem and we can't deny it. But to keep it from being broadcast any farther among the people let's warn them that they'd better not say anything further in that person's name to anyone in the world." And calling them back in, they ordered them not to teach or make speeches anywhere in the name of Jesus.

But Peter and John answered them, "If it is righteous in the sight of

God to listen to you instead of God, then judge as you will. But we can't keep from saying what we saw and heard." So they threatened them some more and let them go, not seeing any way to punish them because of the people, since they were glorifying God for what had happened. After all, this was a fellow more than forty years old on whom the sign of this healing had been visited.

After being let go they went back to their fellows and recounted what the high priests and elders had said to them. And the hearers lifted their voice as one to God, saying: "Master, You the maker of the sky and the earth and the sea and everything in them, who said of Your child by the holy spirit through the mouth of our father David:

> *Why were the nations strutting their stuff*
> *And the peoples wrapped up in nonsense?*
> *The kings of the earth appeared,*
> *And the rulers were gathered in one place*
> *Against the Lord and against the Lord's anointed!*

They really were gathered in that city against Your holy child, Jesus whom You anointed: Herod and Pontius Pilate, together with the nations and peoples of Israel, to do what Your hand and Your will had predestined to happen. And now, Lord, look down and see the threats they make and give Your slaves the strength to speak Your word right out in public; reach out Your hand so that healings and signs and wonders will be performed through the name of Your holy child Jesus." And when they were done petitioning, the place where they were gathered was shaken. And all of them were filled with the sacred breath and spoke the word of God in public.

The multitude of the believers were of one heart and soul, and none of them called any of his possessions his own, everything was held in common. And with tremendous force the apostles used to give their testimony of the resurrection of Lord Jesus; that was a great joy for them all. And no one among them was needy, because those who were owners of lands and houses sold them and brought the proceeds of the sale and laid it at the feet of the apostles to be given out to each of them according to who needed it. Joseph, the one called Barnabas by the Apostles—that translates as "Son of Consolation"—a Levite of Cyprian blood, who had a field, sold it and brought the money and laid it at the feet of the apostles.

5

But there was a man named Ananias with his wife Sapphire who sold a property and pocketed some of the proceeds, with the knowledge of his wife, and brought part of it and laid it at the feet of the apostles.

But Peter said, "Ananias, why did Satan so fill your heart that you could lie to the holy spirit by pocketing some of the proceeds from that land? If you wanted to keep it, couldn't you have kept it, or sold it and done with the proceeds as you wished? Then why did you take it into your heart to do a thing like this? You didn't lie to other people but to God." Ananias, on hearing those words, fell down and expired, and a great fright arose among all the listeners. Then some of the younger hands got up and wrapped him up and took him out and buried him.

There was an interval of maybe three hours and then his wife, knowing nothing of what had gone on, came in the room. So Peter met her with the words, "Tell me, is this how much you sold the land for?"

"Yes," she said, "that's how much it was."

Said Peter to her, "Then why did you make an agreement to play games with the spirit of the Lord? Do you hear the feet of those who buried your husband, just on the doorstep, coming to carry you out too?" And she fell down suddenly at his feet and expired. So the young men came in and found her dead and took her out and buried her next to her husband, and a great fear came over all the assembly and all those who heard about these things.

Through the hands of the apostles came signs and wonders aplenty among the people, and often they were all together, unified in spirit, on the Porch of Solomon, and none of the others dared to join them, but the people magnified their name. New believers in the Lord were being added apace, masses of men and women, to the point where people were bringing the sick outside and setting them down on cots and pallets so that when Peter passed by at least his shadow would fall on one of them. And the masses from the cities around Jerusalem came in, bringing the sick and those who were troubled by unclean spirits, all of whom were cured.

Then the high priest and all those with him, the prevailing sect of the Sadducees, filling with zeal, laid hands on the apostles and put them in public safekeeping. But a messenger of the Lord, coming by night and opening the doors of the jail, led them out, saying, "Go now and stand in the temple saying to the people all the words of Life."

On hearing that, they went into the temple by the light of early dawn and started teaching. When the high priest and those with him arrived they called the supreme council together and all the elders of the sons of Israel and sent word to the prison to have them brought in. But when the servants went in they couldn't find them in the jail. So they went back and reported, saying, "We found the prison sealed with absolute security and the guards standing at the doors, but when we opened up inside we found nobody there."

When the templemaster general and the high priests heard those words, they were at a loss what to make of them. Then someone else showed up and reported to them, "Guess what? The men you put in prison are standing in the temple teaching the people." Then the templemaster general went in with his servants and led them away, but not roughly, because they were afraid of being stoned by the crowd.

After leading them off they stood them in front of the supreme council, and the high priest asked them, "Didn't we give you an order ordering you not to teach in his name? And here you've filled all Jerusalem with your teaching, and now you're trying to bring this fellow's blood down on our heads!"

Peter and the apostles answered, "God must be obeyed over mankind. The God of your fathers raised up Jesus, whereas it was your handiwork to hang him on the tree. God raised him to His right hand as a ruler and savior who would give Israel a change of heart and the forgiveness of her wrongs. And we are the witnesses to what I have just said, and so is the sacred breath that God gave to those who obey Him."

Hearing that, they gnashed their teeth and wanted to do away with them. Then a certain Pharisee name of Gamaliel stood up in front of the supreme council, he being a legal scholar esteemed by all the people, and after ordering the people in question to be put outside for a bit, he said to them: "Fellow Israelites, be careful what you're going to do with these people. After all, Theudas rose up once upon a time and pretended to be somebody special, with adherents numbering some four thousand men. He was executed, and all those who believed in him broke apart and came to nothing. After him, Judas of Galilee came along around the time of the census and assembled a small nation behind him. And he perished, and all who believed in him were scattered. And this time, I'm telling you, keep away from these people and leave them alone. Because if this is a human will or human deeds, it will break down, whereas if it's from God, you won't be able to break them down or you'll turn out to be fighting God."

They agreed with him; and calling the apostles in, they flogged them, ordered them not to speak in the name of Jesus, and let them go. They for their part went out of the council chambers rejoicing that they had been thought worthy of being castigated for his name, and all day long in the temple and also at home, they never stopped teaching and declaring the good news of the anointed Jesus.

6

Around that time, as more students were being amassed, there was some grumbling among the Greek elements to the effect that their widows were being overlooked by the Hebrews in the distribution of day-to-day assistance. Calling the students in en masse, the twelve said, "It isn't appropriate for us to put the word of God aside and wait on tables. So consider, my brothers, which seven men among you, witnesses full of spirit and wisdom, we shall entrust with this charge. But as for us, we will stick to prayer and the service of the word." And those words found favor with the whole crowd, and they picked out Stephen, a man full of faith and holy spirit, and Philip and Prochorus and Nicanor and Timon and Parmenas and Nicolaus, a new convert from Antioch. These they presented to the apostles, who prayed and laid their hands on them.

And the word of God grew, and the number of disciples in Jerusalem was massive indeed, and a great crowd of the priests were obedient to the faith.

Now Stephen, full of grace and power, was working great signs and wonders among the people. Some people from the so-called Freedom Synagogue and the Cyrenian and Alexandrian and Cilician and Asian synagogues stood up to debate with Stephen, but they were no match for the wisdom and spirit with which he spoke. So they came up with some men who would say, "We heard him say blasphemous things about Moses and God." And they incited both the people and the elders and canon-lawyers, and they came after him and seized him and haled him before the supreme council. They also put up false witnesses saying, "This fellow here never stops saying things against this holy place and against the Law. Why, we heard him saying that Jesus of Nazareth would

take this place apart and replace the morals handed down to us by
Moses." And as they stared at him, all of them sitting in supreme council
saw his face like the face of an angel.

7

Said the high priests, "Is that how it is?"

He said, "My dear brothers and fathers, listen: The God of glory
appeared to our father Abraham, when he was in Mesopotamia before
settling down in Charran, and said to him, 'Leave your land and your
relations behind and come here to the land that I will show you.' Then
he left the land of the Chaldeans behind and settled down in Charran.
And from there, after his father's death, he moved to this land which now
you inhabit. And he gave him no estate in it for himself, nor the right to
set foot upon it, but promised to 'give it into his possession, and to his
seed after him,' this when he had no child. And, so God said, his seed
'would be in a foreign land, where they will enslave them and insult them
forty years. And the race they are enslaved by I will judge,' God said; 'and
afterwards they will come forth and worship me in this place.' And He
gave him circumcision as a condition, and so he fathered Isaac and
circumcised him on the eighth day, and Isaac fathered Jacob, and Jacob
the twelve patriarchs.

"And the patriarchs, jealous of Joseph, sold him off to Egypt. And God
was with him and pulled him out of all his sufferings and gave him
wisdom and favor with the Pharaoh, the king of Egypt, who made him
superintendent over Egypt and over all his house. Then the famine came
over all Egypt and Canaan, with tremendous suffering, and our fathers
couldn't find nourishment. Jacob, hearing there was grain in Egypt, sent
our fathers out first. And Joseph was recognized once again by his
brothers, and Pharaoh learned the secret of Joseph's origins. So Joseph
sent word and called to him Jacob his father and his relations, all seventy-
five souls. And Jacob came to live in Egypt, and he and our fathers ended
their lives there, and were transported to Shechem and put in the tomb
that Abraham bought for a sum of silver from the sons of Emmor in
Shechem.

"As the time grew near for the fulfillment of what God had promised
to Abraham, the people grew and teemed in Israel, until 'another king
took over Egypt, who hadn't known Joseph.' He, as a way to get round

our people, forced our fathers to abandon their young so they couldn't propagate. At that point Moses was born, and he looked very sweet to God. He was brought up for three months in his father's house, but when he was abandoned, Pharaoh's daughter took him in and raised him as her son. So Moses was educated in all the learning of the Egyptians, and was powerful in his words and in his actions. But when his fortieth year came round, the thought rose in his heart to look after his brothers and sisters and the sons and daughters of Israel. And seeing someone being mistreated, he came to his defense and took the side of the injured party by striking the Egyptian. He thought his brothers would understand that God was giving them salvation through his hands, but they didn't understand. The next day he appeared in the midst of their fighting and tried to make peace among them, saying, 'Gentlemen, you are brothers: why do you harm each other?'

"But the one who had harmed his fellow pushed him away, saying, 'Who made you ruler and judge over us? Are you going to kill me the same way you killed that Egyptian yesterday?'

"At those words, Moses fled and became a resident of the land of Madian, where he fathered two sons. And when forty years had come and gone, there appeared to him in the desert of Mount Sinai a holy messenger in the flame of a burning bush. Moses was amazed to see the vision; as he came closer to examine it, there came the voice of the Lord: 'I am the God of your fathers, the God of Abraham and Isaac and Jacob.' Moses, all atremble, didn't dare to even think.

"Then the Lord said to him, 'Untie the shoes from your feet: the place you are standing on is holy ground. I have looked down and seen the sorry state of my people in Egypt and have heard their groans, and I came down to rescue them. And now come along, I'm sending you to Egypt.'

"This same Moses whom they rejected saying, 'Who made you our ruler and judge?', God sent him to be ruler and redeemer by the hand of the holy messenger that appeared to him in the bush. He led them forth, working signs and wonders in the land of Egypt and in the Red Sea and in the wilderness for forty years. It is this Moses who said to the sons and daughters of Israel, 'God will raise you up a prophet out of the ranks of your brothers, as He raised me.' It is he who came to have a conference in the wilderness with God's messenger speaking to him on Mount Sinai and then with our fathers, he who received words of life to give to us—which our fathers didn't want to be obedient to: no, they pushed it away, and in their hearts they were 'back in Egypt' as they said to Aaron, 'Make us gods to travel at our head, because this Moses who led us out of Egypt, we don't know what's become of him.' And they made a calf at that time and brought sacrifices to the idol and rejoiced in the work of their hands.

"But God turned and gave them orders to bow before the army of the sky, as is written in the Book of Prophets:

> *Were your slaughters and sacrifices brought to me*
> *For your forty years in the wilds, house of Israel?*
> *No, you took over the altars of Moloch*
> *And the star of your God, Raiphan,*
> *Images you made so you could worship them.*
> *And now I will uproot you farther than Babylon.*

"The tent for the Ark of the Covenant was there among your fathers in the wilderness just as the one who spoke to Moses had commanded it to be made, according to the design that Moses had seen. Our fathers in turn brought it here with Joshua in the process of gaining control over the peoples whom God drove away from the face of our fathers. That went on till the time of David, who came into favor with God and asked that he might provide the house of Jacob with better quarters. Finally Solomon built a temple for it. But the Most High does not dwell in man-made things, just as the Prophet says:

> *'The sky is my throne,*
> *The earth is the footrest for my feet,*
> *What sort of house will you build me?' says the Lord,*
> *'Or what will be my place of refreshment?*
> *Didn't my hand make all these things?'*

"Thick-skulled and uncircumcised of heart and ears, you are always flying in the face of the holy spirit, just like your fathers before you. Which of the prophets did your fathers not persecute? Indeed, they killed those who foretold the coming of the just man of whom you now have become betrayers and murderers, you who accepted the law as the dispensation of God's messengers but still don't keep it."

Hearing that, they were aroused in their hearts and ground their teeth at him. Full as he was of the sacred breath, he stared into the sky and saw the glory of God and Jesus standing to the right of God and said, "Now I can see the skies opening and the son of humanity standing to the right of God." Letting out a great yell they stopped their ears and rushed at him in a pack and dragged him outside the city and began stoning him. And the witnesses laid their cloaks at the feet of a young man named Saul. And they threw stones at Stephen as he called on God and said, "Lord Jesus, receive my soul." Sinking to his knees he shouted loudly, "Lord, don't hold this crime against them," and so saying he collapsed.

8

Saul, then, was a party to his execution. And on the same day there was a great persecution against the assembly in Jerusalem, and they all scattered across the regions of Judea and Samaria, except for the apostles. God-fearing men laid Stephen to rest and mourned over him. But Saul went on insulting the assembly, going from house to house, dragging away men and women and packing them off to jail.

So those who had scattered went their way bringing the good news of the word. Philip, going down to the Samaritan city, proclaimed the Anointed to them. And the crowds paid attention to the things said by Philip, united in listening and watching the signs he performed: many of them had unclean spirits who cried with a loud voice and left them, many of the lame and paralyzed were healed. And there was great joy in that city.

Now there was a man name of Simon there in that city performing magic and amazing the people of Samaria, making himself out to be someone important, whom all from lowest to highest followed, saying, "This is the power of God that is called the Great." They followed him because he had been amazing them with his magic for quite a while. But when they believed Philip as he brought the good word of the kingdom of God and the name of Jesus the Anointed, both men and women came forward to be washed. Even Simon himself was convinced, and after being washed he became devoted to Philip, and he was beside himself witnessing the great signs and powers performed.

Hearing that Samaria had received the word of God, the apostles in Jerusalem sent Peter and John to them, who, as they went down there, prayed for them that they might receive the sacred breath. (At that point it had alighted on none of them, they had only been washed in the name of Lord Jesus.) Then they put their hands on them, and they were receiving the holy breath. So Simon, seeing that the breath was given by the laying on of hands of the apostles, brought them money, saying, "Give me this power so that whoever I lay my hands on will receive the holy breath."

But Peter said to him, "You and your silver can go to perdition for thinking to buy the gift of God with money. You have no part or portion in this word because your heart isn't straight before God. So renounce this evil of yours and ask the Lord if perhaps this thought in your heart may be forgiven you, because I see you headed for the gall of bitterness and the bonds of dishonesty."

Answered Simon, "Pray for me, all of you, to the Lord that none of what you have said may come upon me."

So they, after bearing witness and speaking the word of the Lord, returned to Jerusalem, and also brought the good news to many villages in Samaria.

Now a messenger of the Lord spoke to Philip saying, "Get up and travel south to the road leading from Jerusalem down to Gaza, which is deserted." And he stood up and got on the road. And an Ethiopian man came along, a eunuch and a potentate in the service of Candace, queen of the Ethiopes, who was in charge of all her treasures and who had come to Jerusalem to worship and was now returning, seated on his carriage and reading the prophet Isaiah. And the spirit said to Philip, "Go over there and stick close to that carriage." Philip, running closer, heard him reading aloud from Isaiah the prophet and said, "Do you really know what you're reading?"

He said, "How can I without someone to explain it to me?" And he asked Philip to climb aboard and sit with him. Now the passage in scripture he was reading was this:

> *Like a sheep to the slaughter he was led,*
> *And like a lamb voiceless at the sight of the shearer,*
> *He did not open his mouth.*
> *By his humility his punishment was increased.*
> *Who will explain his generation?*
> *For his life has been taken from the earth.*

Responding to that, the eunuch said to Philip, "If I may ask you, who is the prophet saying that about? About himself, or about someone else?" Opening his mouth and starting from that passage, he gave him the good news about Jesus. Then as they were traveling down the road, they came upon some water, and the eunuch says, "Look, water! What prevents me from being washed now?" And he ordered the carriage to halt, and both of them went down to the water, Philip and the eunuch, and he bathed him. But when they came up out of the water, a spirit of the Lord snatched Philip away and the eunuch saw him no more, but went his way rejoicing. Philip, on the other hand, turned up in Azotum, and as he passed through he brought the good news to all those towns till he got to Caesarea.

9

Saul, meanwhile, still snorting threats and murder at the disciples of the Lord, went to the high priest and asked him for letters to the synagogues in Damascus, so that if he found any of them on the street, he could tie them up, men and women alike, and bring them back to Jerusalem.

In the course of his journey he happened to be nearing Damascus when suddenly a bolt of light from the sky enveloped him in a blaze. And dropping to the ground he heard a voice saying to him, "Saul! Saul! Why are you persecuting me?"

He said, "Who are you, Lord?"

"I am Jesus," he said, "the one you are persecuting. But now get up and go into town, and you will be told what you have to do."

The men traveling with him stood speechless, hearing the voice but not seeing anyone. Saul then raised himself up off the ground, but when he opened his eyes he couldn't see a thing. So they took him by the hand and brought him into Damascus. And for three days he couldn't see and didn't eat or drink.

Now there was a certain disciple in Damascus name of Ananias. And the Lord said to him in a vision, "Ananias?"

He said, "Here I am, Lord."

And the Lord said to him, "Go down to the alley called Straight Street, to the house of Jude, and ask for Saul of Tarsus, because he in his prayers saw a man name of Ananias coming in and laying his hands on him so he could see again."

Answered Ananias, "Lord, I've heard from many people about that man and all the evil he did to your holy ones in Jerusalem. And here he has authority from the high priests to seize all who call upon your name."

Said the Lord to him, "Get going, because he is my tool of choice to hold up my name in front of nations, kings, and the sons and daughters of Israel. I will show him how much he must suffer for my name."

Ananias then went and entered the house and put his hands on him, saying, "Brother Saul, the Lord has sent me, Jesus who appeared to you on the way you were going, so that you may see again and be filled with the sacred breath." And as soon as he said that, it was like the husks came off his eyes and he could see again; and he got up, and went down to be bathed, and took food and regained his strength.

He stayed with the other followers in Damascus for some days and immediately started proclaiming Jesus in the synagogues, saying he was the son of God. All who heard were astonished, and they were saying, "Isn't this the same man who ravaged the people in Jerusalem who called upon that name, and had come here for the purpose of bringing them in chains back to the high priests?" But Saul only grew stronger, and confounded the residents of Damascus by affirming that Jesus was the Anointed.

After a number of days had passed, the Jews plotted to kill him. Their plot became known to Saul, but they were watching the gates day and night so they could get him. So his disciples got him over the wall by night by lowering him in a basket.

Arriving in Jerusalem he tried to join the followers, but they were all afraid of him and didn't believe he really was a follower of Jesus. But Barnabas took him and brought him to the apostles and explained to them how on the road he saw the Lord, and that he spoke to him, and how in Damascus he had spoken publicly in the name of Jesus. And he was with them, going in and out around Jerusalem, speaking publicly in the name of the Lord. And he talked and debated with the Greek Jews; they, however, attempted to kill him. The brothers, though, when they found out, brought him down to Caesarea and sent him out to Tarsus.

So the assembly throughout all Judea and Galilee and Samaria was at peace, founded on and proceeding in the fear of the Lord; and by the advocacy of the holy spirit it grew apace.

It happened next that Peter, passing through everyplace, went down to see the holy ones living in Lydda. He found there a fellow name of Aeneas who had been lying on his cot for eight years because he was paralyzed. And Peter said to him, "Aeneas, you are cured by Jesus the Anointed. Get up and make your own bed." And he stood right up. And he was seen by all the inhabitants of Lydda and Sharon, who then turned back to the Lord.

Now in Joppa there was a woman disciple name of Tabitha, which in translation means "Gazelle," who was full of good works and charities which she performed. Around that time she happened to take sick and die. And they washed her and laid her in an upstairs room. Lydda being near to Joppa, the disciples, hearing that Peter was there, sent two men to him begging him, "Don't refuse to come this far to us." So Peter got up and went with them. On his arrival they led him up to the upstairs room, where he was surrounded by all the widows crying and showing him the tunics and cloaks that Tabitha had made while she was with them. After throwing everybody out, Peter then sank to his knees and prayed; then turning back to the body he said, "Tabitha, get up!" She opened her eyes and, seeing Peter, sat up. Giving her his hand, he raised her to her feet and, calling the holy men and widows, he presented her to them living. The fact became known throughout all Joppa, and many put their faith in the Lord. And he ended up staying for a number of days in Joppa with a certain Simon the Tanner.

10

Now there was a certain man in Caesarea name of Cornelius, captain of the so-called Italian Squad, religious and God-fearing, as was all his household, performing many charities for the people and asking God's help at all times; around three o'clock he saw clearly in a vision a messenger of God coming into his house and saying to him, "Cornelius?"

He, staring at the other and flying into a panic, said, "What is it, Lord?"

He said to him, "Your prayers and charities have come to the attention of God on high. And now send men to Joppa and fetch a certain Simon who is called Simon Peter. He is staying as a guest with a certain Simon the Tanner, who has a house by the sea."

When the messenger went away who had spoken to him, out of those who were devoted to him he called two of his servants and a God-fearing soldier and explained the whole thing to them and sent them off to Joppa.

The next day, while they were coming down the road and getting near the town, Peter went upon the roof to pray around the hour of noon. And he got hungry and wanted to taste some food. While they were preparing something, a rapture came over him: and he sees the sky opening and a sort of table-setting coming down, like a giant tablecloth being draped over the four corners of the earth, containing all the quadrupeds and serpents of the land and birds of the air. And a voice came to him: "Get up, Peter; slaughter and eat."

But Peter said, "No way, Lord: I never ate such foul and unclean stuff in all my life."

And the voice came yet a second time to him: "Don't you make dirty what God made clean." All this happened three times, then suddenly the table-setting was taken back up into the sky.

Just as Peter was wondering to himself what the vision he'd seen was all about, the men sent by Cornelius to look up the house of Simon stood at the gate and called out, inquiring if the Simon called Simon Peter was visiting there. As Peter was thinking hard about the vision, the spirit said to him, "Here are three men looking for you. Get up and go down and set out with them unhesitatingly, because I have sent them."

Peter then went down to see the men and said, "Here, I'm the one you're looking for; what is the reason that brings you here?"

They said, "Cornelius the army captain, a just and God-fearing man, as all the Jewish nation will attest, was instructed by a holy messenger to summon you to his house, and hear from you what you have to say." So he invited them in and entertained them.

The next day he got up and went forth with them, and some of the brothers from Joppa went with him. The day after that he reached Caesarea. Cornelius was expecting them and had called in his relatives and closest friends. So when Peter finally came in, Cornelius was there to meet him and fell at his feet and bowed before him. Peter pulled him up, saying, "Stand up, I'm just another human being." And conversing with him he came inside, where he finds many people gathered. And he said to them, "You understand that it's considered immoral for a Jewish man to associate or visit with anyone of another race. But God showed me never to call any human being foul or unclean, which is why I came when summoned with no argument. So: I'd like to know for what reason you sent for me."

And Cornelius said: "Four days ago to the hour I was praying, at three o'clock in my house, and all of a sudden a man stood in front of me in a shining robe, and he says, 'Cornelius, your prayer was heard and your charities reached the attention of God. So send to Joppa and ask for the Simon who is called Simon Peter, who is visiting in the house of Simon Tanner by the sea.' So I sent for you immediately, and you did well to come. So now we are all here before God to hear all the orders given you by the Lord."

Peter opened his mouth and said, "I have truly found out that God is no respecter of persons, but that in every race the one who fears Him and practices justice is acceptable to Him. He sent His word to the sons and daughters of Israel, bringing the good news of peace through Jesus the Anointed, who is the Lord of all. You know the word that has been said throughout all Judea, starting from Galilee after the washing that John announced: about Jesus of Nazareth, how God anointed him in sacred breath and power, how he went round doing good and healing all those overpowered by the devil, because God was with him. And we are witnesses of all he did in the country of Judea and in Jerusalem. Him whom they killed by hanging on the tree, God raised on the third day and allowed to become visible, not to all the people, but to those witnesses handpicked by God—us—who have eaten and drunk with him after his resurrection from the dead. And he commanded us to proclaim to the people and bear witness that he is marked by God as judge of the living and the dead. All the prophets bear witness to him, that everyone who believes in him finds forgiveness for their wrongs in his name."

Even as Peter was saying these things, the sacred breath came upon all the hearers of the word. And those with Peter who were faithful to circumcision were stunned that the gift of the sacred breath should be showered upon even the Gentiles when they heard them speaking in tongues and glorifying God. Then Peter answered, "Can anyone stop the water from washing these ones who received the sacred breath the same as us?" And he ordered them to be washed in the name of Jesus the Anointed. Then they asked him to stay for a few days.

11

So the apostles and brothers across Judea heard that the Gentiles too had received the word of God. So when Peter came up to Jerusalem, the circumcised ones had reservations about him, saying, "You went into the houses of foreskinned men and *ate* with them!"

And Peter started in and expounded it to them from beginning to end, saying: "I was in the town of Joppa praying, and in my rapture I saw a vision, a sort of table-setting coming down from the sky, like a giant tablecloth being let down from the sky over the four corners of the earth, and it came down towards me. And staring at it I perceived and saw the quadrupeds of the earth and the wild beasts and snakes and the birds of the air. Then I also heard a voice telling me, 'Get up, Peter; slaughter and eat.'

"I said, 'No way, Lord, nothing foul or unclean ever entered my mouth.'

"Again there was a voice from the sky answering, 'Don't you make dirty what God made clean.' This happened three times, and then the whole thing was pulled back up into the sky. And just at that very instant three men who had been sent from Caesarea to see me came up to the house where we were. And the spirit told me to go with them unhesitatingly. So these six brothers came with me and we went to the man's house. He reported to me how he'd seen a holy messenger standing in his house and saying, 'Send to Joppa and fetch the Simon known as Simon Peter, who will say things to you by which you and all your house will be saved.' As I started to speak, the sacred breath came over them just the way it came over us in the beginning, and I was reminded of the words of the Lord in which he said, 'John bathed in water, but now you will be bathed in holy breath.' So if God gave the same gift to them that he gave us who believe in Lord Jesus the Anointed, who am I to hinder God?"

On hearing that they quieted down and glorified God saying, "Even to the Gentiles, then, God gave the gift of turning their hearts around toward Life."

Now some of those who had been put to flight by the persecution that started over Stephen went on as far as Phoenicia, Cyprus and Antioch, speaking the word to no one but Jews alone. But there were some of them, Cyprian and Cyrenian men, who went to Antioch and also spoke to the Greek Jews, bringing the good news of Lord Jesus. And the Lord's hand was with them, and there were a great number who believed and turned back to the Lord. Word of them reached the ears of the assembly in Jerusalem, and they sent Barnabas out to journey as far as Antioch. Arriving and seeing the grace of God, he was very happy and he exhorted them all to wait for the Lord with resolute hearts, since he was a good man, full of holy spirit and faith. And a substantial crowd was delivered to the Lord. And he went out to Tarsus to look up Saul, and on finding him brought him to Antioch. And it turned out he spent a whole year gathering with them in their assembly and teaching a sizable crowd, and that the disciples in Antioch were the first to bear the name of "Christians."

Around that time some prophets from Jerusalem came down to Antioch. One of them name of Agabus stood up and signaled by means of the spirit that a great famine was going to come upon all the inhabited world, which came true during the reign of Claudius. So the followers decided to send something, depending how well off each one of them was, to aid their brothers and sisters living in Judea—which they did, sending word to the elders by way of Barnabas and Saul.

12

Along about the same time Herod the king laid hands with evil intent on some of the assembly. He killed James the brother of John by sword. Seeing that that was fine with the Jews, he seized Peter for good measure—and this was during the days of Passover—and after seizing him put him in jail, assigning four teams of four soldiers each to guard him, intending to bring him up before the people after the Passover. So Peter stayed in jail, while fervent prayers to God were offered by the assembly on his behalf.

When Herod was getting set to arraign him, that night Peter was sleeping between two soldiers, bound with two chains; and guards were keeping watch in front of the door. And all of a sudden a messenger of the Lord stood over him, and a light shone in his cell. Poking Peter in the ribs he pulled him up, saying, "Get up at once!" And the chains fell off his hands.

Said the messenger to him, "Put on your belt and tie your sandals." So he did. And he says to him, "Put your cloak on and follow me." And he followed him and didn't know that what he was doing with the messenger was really happening: he thought he was seeing a vision. Going past the first guard, then the second, they came to the iron gate that gave on the city, which opened for them by itself; and after they went outside, they went along one block, and suddenly the messenger withdrew from him.

And Peter, coming to himself, said, "Now I know truly that the Lord sent His messenger and snatched me from the hands of Herod and from all the expectations of the Jewish people." Taking it all in, he went to the house of Mary the mother of John, called John Mark, where a number of them were gathered praying. When he knocked at the door of the gate a maid name of Rhoda came out to answer, and when she recognized Peter's voice she was so overjoyed she didn't open the gate, but ran inside and told them that Peter was standing in front of the gate. They said to her, "You're crazy!" But she insisted that it was so. They said, "It's his guardian angel." Meanwhile, Peter kept knocking, so when they opened up and saw him they were beside themselves. Waving his hand at them to be silent, he explained to them how the Lord brought him out of jail and said, "Report this to James and the brothers," then went away and proceeded to another place.

When daylight came there was no small disturbance among the soldiers as to what in the world had become of Peter. Herod, after looking for him and not finding him, sentenced the guards and ordered them taken away, and then went from Judea down to Caesarea and stayed there.

Now he had had a grudge against the people of Tyre and Sidon. But they came to him as one and after first winning over Blastus, the keeper of the royal bedchamber, they sought peace, since their country got its food from the king's country. So on the appointed day Herod, dressed in a kingly robe and seated upon the podium, made a public address to them. And the people cried, "This is a god's voice, not a man's." At once a messenger of the Lord struck him down for not giving glory to God, and after being infested with consumptive worms he breathed his last.

But the word of God grew and multiplied, while Barnabas and Saul returned to Jerusalem after accomplishing their mission, bringing along John Mark.

13

Now in Antioch in the local assembly there were prophets and teachers: Barnabas, Simeon known as Simeon Niger, Lucius the Cyrenian, Manaen, who grew up with Herod the governor, and Saul. In the course of their fasting and devotions to the Lord the sacred breath said, "Now set apart Barnabas and Saul for me for the work I have called them to." Then, after fasting and praying and laying their hands on them, they sent them off.

So they, dispatched by the sacred breath, went down to Seleucia, and sailed off from there to Cyprus. And when they got to Salamis, they proclaimed the word of God in the synagogues of the Jews; and they also had John Mark as an assistant. Traversing all the island as far as Paphos they came upon a certain magician and Jewish pseudoprophet name of Bar-Jesus, who lived with the vice regent Sergius Paulus, a man of discernment. He, calling in Barnabas and Saul, desired to hear the word of God. But they were opposed by the "Elymas" or magician, as his title would be translated, as he tried to turn the vice regent away from the faith. So Saul (also called Paul), filling with the sacred breath, stared at him and said: "Son of the devil, full of every trick and sleight of hand, enemy of all justice, will you never stop perverting the straight ways of the Lord? And now see how the Lord's hand is against you: you will be blind and will not look upon the sun for the time being." Instantly he was befallen by mist and darkness and needed guides to lead him around by the hand. Then the vice regent, seeing what had happened, came to believe, being astounded by the teaching of the Lord.

Setting out from Paphos, those with Paul went to Perge in Pamphylia, while John Mark withdrew from them and returned to Jerusalem. The others, going on from Perge, arrived at Pisidian Antioch and went into the synagogue on the Sabbath day and took their seats. After the reading of the Law and the Prophets, the synagogue leaders sent word to them, saying, "Gentle brothers, if you have any words of encouragement for the people, speak!"

Paul, standing up and motioning for silence, said: "Israelites and God-fearing men, give ear: the God of this people Israel chose our forefathers and exalted His people during their residence on Egyptian soil, and with His upraised arm brought them forth from it, and fed them some forty years' time in the desert. And after destroying seven nations in the land of Canaan He bequeathed the land to them for some four hundred and fifty years. And later He gave them judges in a line down to Samuel the prophet. And from that point on they asked Him for a king, and God gave them Saul son of Kish, a man from the tribe of Benjamin, for forty years. Then He replaced him, raising up David for their king, of whom He said in witness, 'I came up with David the son of Jesse, a man after My own heart, who will do all My biddings.' From his seed, as promised, God brought Israel a savior in Jesus, after John, in advance of his arrival, had proclaimed the washing of a changed heart to all the people of Israel. As John was completing his course, he used to say: 'What do you imagine me to be? That's not what I am. But watch: after me comes someone whose sandals I am not worthy to untie from his feet.' Gentle brothers, sons of the race of Abraham and those among you who fear God, the word of this salvation was sent forth to us. Indeed, the inhabitants of Jerusalem, ignorant of him and of the voices of the Prophets they read every Sabbath, still fulfilled them in condemning him. And not finding any capital charge against him they asked Pilate to have him executed. Then, when they had fulfilled everything written about him, they took him down from the tree and put him in a tomb. But God raised him from the dead, and he appeared over many days to those who had come from Galilee up to Jerusalem with him, and who are now his witnesses to the people.

"And we are now giving you the good news that the promise to your fathers has come true, because God has fulfilled it for his children completely by raising up Jesus, as is written even in the second Psalm:

> *You are my son,*
> *Today I have fathered you.*

"Since He raised him from the dead, never again to return to corruption, so He has said, 'I will give you the trusted holy things of David.' For this reason He also says elsewhere, 'You will not permit your holy man to undergo decay.'

"David, after all, when he had served his race by the will of God, was laid to rest and gathered to his fathers and underwent decay. But he whom God raised underwent no decay. So let it be known to you, brothers, that through him the forgiveness of your wrongs is announced to you. And all the things you could not be acquitted of in the law of Moses, every believer *is* acquitted of, in him. Watch out, then, so that what is said in the Book of Prophets doesn't come upon you:

> *See, you scoffers,*
> *And be amazed, and be obliterated,*
> *Because I am doing a deed in your day,*
> *A deed you will never believe if someone recounts it to you.*"

As they were going out, they begged to have these things said to them on the following Sabbath. When synagogue was dismissed, many of the Jews and worshipful converts followed Paul and Barnabas, who spoke to them and persuaded them to remain in the grace of God.

The following Sabbath, practically the whole town was gathered to hear the word of the Lord. The Jews, however, seeing the crowds, were filled with jealousy and blasphemously contradicted the things said by Paul. And Paul and Barnabas, having spoken freely, said: "It was necessary for you to be told first of the word of God. Since, however, you reject it and don't deem yourselves worthy of everlasting life, we hereby turn to the Gentiles, because the Lord has so commanded us:

> *I have put you there to be a light of nations,*
> *So that you may be for salvation to the ends of the earth.*"

The Gentiles, when they heard, rejoiced and praised the word of the Lord, and as many believed as were destined for everlasting life. And the word of the Lord was carried through the whole country. But the Jews incited the respectable women worshipers and the chief citizens of the town and stirred up persecution against Paul and Barnabas, and they threw them out of those regions. They, after shaking the dust off their feet at them, came to Iconium. And the disciples were filled with joy and sacred breath.

14

It happened in Iconium in the same way that they went into the synagogue of the Jews and spoke so well that a great multitude of Jews and Greeks alike came to believe. But the unconvinced Jews rose up and blasted the souls of the Gentiles against the brothers. So they spent some time there, speaking freely for the Lord, who testified to the words of His grace and permitted signs and wonders to be performed through their hands. So the population of the town was split, and some were with the Jews, others with the apostles. But when the impetus arose among both Jews and Gentiles, along with their leaders, to do violence to them and stone them, they fled when they found out about it to the Lycaonian towns of Lystra and Derbe and their surroundings, and there they were spreading the good news.

And there was a certain helpless man in Lystra sitting on his feet, a man born lame from his mother's belly who had never walked. He listened to Paul speaking, who, staring at him and seeing that he had the faith to be saved, said in a loud voice, "Stand up straight on your feet!" And he jumped up and started walking around. And the crowds, seeing what Paul had done, lifted their voices, saying in Lycaonian, "The gods came down to us in the shape of mortals!" And they were calling Barnabas "Zeus" and Paul "Hermes" (since he was the bearer of the word). And the priest of Zeus's temple, which was just outside the town, was bringing bulls and garlands to the gate, getting ready to sacrifice with the crowds.

When they heard that, the apostles Barnabas and Paul, ripping their garments, leapt into the crowd, shouting, "Gentlemen, why are you doing all this? We too are suffering mortals just like you, bringing you the good word to turn from this nonsense back to the living God 'who made the sky and the earth and the sea and everything in them,' who in previous generations allowed all the nations to go their own way, and did not do His good works leaving no trace, but gave you showers and fruitful seasons from the sky, filling your hearts with nourishment and good cheer." And saying that, they barely stopped the crowd from sacrificing to them.

But Jews from Antioch and Iconium came after them, and after winning over the crowds and stoning Paul, they dragged him outside the town, thinking him dead. But as the disciples surrounded him, he stood up and went back into the town. And the next day he went out with Barnabas to Derbe.

And after bringing the good news to that town and making disciples of a number of them, they returned to Lystra, Iconium and Antioch, strengthening the souls of the disciples, encouraging them to remain in the faith and saying it is through much suffering that we must enter the kingdom of God. And handpicking elders for them in each assembly, with fasting and prayer they entrusted them to the Lord in whom they had believed. And going through Pisidia they came to Pamphylia, and after speaking the word in Perge they journeyed down to Attalia. And from there they sailed off to Antioch, where they had been given over by the grace of God to the work they had completed. On arriving and gathering the assembly, they reported all that God had done with them, and that he opened to the Gentiles the door of faith. And they spent a considerable time with the disciples.

15

And some people coming down from Judea started teaching the brothers: "If you aren't circumcised by the custom of Moses, you can't be saved." There being no little division and argument between them and Paul and Barnabas, they arranged for Paul and Barnabas and a few more of them to go see the apostles and elders up in Jerusalem about this argument. So those sent by the assembly set out through Phoenicia and Samaria recounting the conversion of the Gentiles and brought great joy to all the brothers and sisters. Arriving at Jerusalem they were received by the assembly and apostles and elders, and they reported what God had done with them. But some of the Pharisee party who were believers stood up and said, "They have to be circumcised; we have to proclaim and keep the law of Moses."

And the apostles and elders gathered to see about this matter. After much debate Peter stood up and spoke to them: "Brothers, you already know that since the old days God chose me from among you for the Gentiles to hear word of the good news from my mouth and believe. And God, the knower of hearts, testified to them, giving them the sacred breath the same as us; and making no distinction between us and them He cleansed their hearts with faith. So now why are you trying to make God put the yoke [of the whole Mosaic law] around the necks of the followers, which neither our fathers nor we were able to bear?* Yet by the grace of Lord Jesus we believe we will be saved the same as they."

* Peter is circumcised, but he doesn't keep the rest of the Mosaic law very keenly, as Paul sharply points out in Galatians (page 351).

Silence came over the whole crowd, and they listened to Barnabas and Paul recounting what signs and wonders God had worked among the Gentiles through them. After they finished speaking James responded: "Brothers, listen to me: Simon has recounted how God has, for the first time, looked among the Gentiles for a race to take and put His name upon. And this accords with the words of the prophets, just as it says:

> *Afterwards I will return*
> *And rebuild the tent of David that is fallen,*
> *And reconstruct its shattered pieces,*
> *And raise it up straight.*
> *So that the rest of humanity will seek out the Lord,*
> *And so will all nations over whom My name has been invoked,*
> *Says the Lord, making these things known since time began.*

"For which reason my judgment is not to trouble those of the Gentiles turning back to God [about circumcision]. But we should write to them saying to avoid the pollution of idolatrous sacrifices and unchastity and meat of strangled animals and blood, since Moses has people proclaiming his word from city to city since time immemorial and is read in the synagogues every Sabbath."

Then the apostles and elders, with all the assembly, decided to choose some of their men to send to Antioch with Paul and Barnabas—Judas known as Judas Barabbas, and Silas, a leader among the brothers—after writing in their own hand:

"From the apostles and elder brothers

"To the brothers among the Gentiles across Antiochia, Syria, and Cilicia:

"Greetings. Since we heard that some of us came out and disturbed you, shattering your souls with words which we didn't order them to say, we decided after reaching unanimous accord to choose men to send to you, along with our beloved Barnabas and Paul, persons who have committed their souls on behalf of our Lord, Jesus the Anointed. Therefore we have sent Jude and Silas to report these things verbally to you themselves. Namely, it was decided by the holy spirit and us to put no further burden on you beyond these which can't be done without: to stay clear of sacrifices to idols, and blood, and strangled meat, and unchastity, from all of which it would be good for you to keep away. Stay well."

So they took their leave and went down to Antioch, and gathering the multitude, gave them the letter. When they read it they were delighted by its encouragement. Both Jude and Silas, also being prophets themselves, offered the brothers many words of encouragement and support, and after passing some time, took their leave from the brothers in peace to go back to those who sent them; while Paul and Barnabas stayed in Antioch, teaching and spreading the good news of the Lord, along with many others.

After some days Paul said to Barnabas, "Now let's go back and visit the brothers in every city where we proclaimed the word of the Lord, and see how they're doing." Barnabas wanted to take John Mark along too. But Paul thought rather, after he left them behind in Pamphylia and didn't help them with the work, they shouldn't take him along. There developed such acrimony that they separated from each other, with Barnabas taking Mark along and sailing for Cyprus, while Paul, selecting Silas, went forth, commended to the grace of the Lord by the brothers. And he was going through Syria and Cilicia, lending support to the assemblies.

16

He then arrived in Derbe and Lystra, and there was this disciple there name of Timothy, son of a woman of Jewish faith, though his father was Greek, who was vouched for by the brothers in Lystra and Iconium. Paul wanted him to come along with him, so he took and circumcised him because of the Jews who were in those parts: they all knew his father was Greek. So as they traveled through the towns, he transmitted to their keeping decisions and judgments made by the apostles and elders in Jerusalem. So the assemblies were consolidated in faith and increased in number day by day.

They then went on through Phrygia and the area of Galatia, being forbidden by the holy spirit to speak the word in Asia. As they came near Mysia they tried to travel to Bithynia, but the spirit of Jesus wouldn't let them. So passing Mysia by they went down to Troy. And a vision in the night appeared to Paul: the shape of a Macedonian man was standing there and pleading with him, saying, "Go through to Macedonia, come help us!" As soon as he saw the vision we were anxious to go out to

Macedonia, gathering that the Lord had called us to bring the good news to them.*

Putting off from Troy we headed straight for Samothrace, and for Neapolis the following day, and from there to Philippi, which is a principal city of part of Macedonia, a colony. We were in this city, spending several days. On the Sabbath day we went out along the river, where we understood there would be a prayer service, and sitting down we talked to the assembled women. And a certain woman name of Lydia, a seller of purple cloth of the town of Thyateira who revered God, was listening, as the Lord opened her heart to pay attention to the things said by Paul. When she and all her household had been washed, she pleaded with us, saying, "If you consider me faithful to the Lord, come and stay at my house." And she twisted our arms.

It happened as we were going off to prayer that a certain maid possessed by a Pythian snake-oracle came our way, who provided her masters with a lot of business by prophesying. She started following Paul and us around, shouting, "These people are servants of God the Most High, who are announcing to you the way of salvation." She kept doing that for many days. Paul, getting worn out, turned to the spirit and said, "I command you in the name of Jesus the Anointed to come out of her." And it came out of her at that time. Her masters, seeing that their business expectations had disappeared, laid hands on Paul and Silas and dragged them downtown to see the rulers, and arraigning them before the magistrates general they said, "These people are disrupting our city; they're Jews, and they're proclaiming moral laws which we as Romans are not allowed to accept or practice." And the crowd rose up against them, and the magistrates, ripping their clothes, ordered them to be beaten with sticks, and after giving them many blows they threw them in jail, passing word to the jailer to guard them securely. He, on receiving this order, threw them into an inner cell and secured their feet with shackles.

Around midnight Paul and Silas were praying to God in hymns of praise, while the other prisoners were listening to them. Suddenly an

---

* We? This jolting introduction of the first-person perspective continues sporadically through to the end of the book. The explanation has been offered that some new item of source material such as a travel diary starts coming into play at this point; but it could be simply that Luke joined Paul's party at this point, so that his information from now on is firsthand whereas what came before was reported by others.

earthquake arose, strong enough to shake the foundations of the prison. All the doors instantly flew open and everyone's shackles fell off. The jailer, starting from sleep and seeing the doors of the jail opened, drew his sword and was going to do himself in, thinking the prisoners had escaped. Then Paul in a loud voice called, "Don't do anything bad to yourself, we're all here."

Asking for light, he sprang inside, and fell all atremble at the feet of Paul and Silas. And bringing them outside he said, "Masters, what must I do to be saved?"

They said, "Believe in the Lord Jesus, and you will be saved with all your household." And they spoke the word of the Lord to him, including all the members of his household. And taking them along at that hour of the night, he bathed their bruises, and he and all of his came forward to be washed without delay. And he brought them to his house and spread the table for them, and he rejoiced with all his household, having placed his faith in God.

When it was daylight the magistrates sent the bailiffs saying, "Let those people go."

The jailer reported those words to Paul: "The magistrates have sent word to let you go. So now come out and go your way in peace."

But Paul said to them, "After flogging us in public without our being sentenced, and we Roman citizens, they threw us in jail, and now they're throwing us out again on the sly? Oh no they don't: they can come and let us out in person." The bailiffs reported this conversation to the magistrates, who got scared when they heard that they were Roman citizens. And they came and pleaded with them and brought them out and asked them to leave the city. After getting out of jail they went to Lydia's house and saw the brothers and sisters, and encouraged them, and departed.

17

Taking the road through Amphipolis and Apollonia they came to Thessalonica, where there was a synagogue of the Jews. As was usual with Paul, he came to see them and for three Sabbaths made his case to them on the basis of the scriptures, disclosing it and laying it before them: "The Anointed had to suffer and rise again from the dead, and the Anointed is Jesus, whom I proclaim to you." And some of them were won over and became followers of Paul and Silas, and so did a whole crowd of religious Greeks, and influential women in no small numbers. But the Jews in their jealousy, picking up some villainous men off the street and manufacturing a crowd, alarmed the city; and they descended on Jason's house and said they wanted him to hand them over to the people. But when they couldn't find them, they dragged Jason and some of the brothers before the city councillors, crying, "Those people who've been turning the world upside down, now they've come here too, and Jason's been harboring them. And all of these people fly in the face of the decrees of Caesar by making another king for themselves in the person of Jesus." And they made a disturbance in the crowd, and the city councillors were also disturbed to hear all this; and after exacting a heavy bail from Jason and the others, they let them go.

Wasting no time, the brothers sent Paul and Silas out to Berea by night, and on arriving they went down to the synagogue of the Jews. These were better people than the ones in Thessalonica: they received the word with all eagerness, looking through the scriptures daily to see if all that was so. Thus many of them came to believe, and so did a fair number of well-thought-of Greek women and men.

But when the Jews from Thessalonica found out the word of God was being broadcast by Paul in Berea, they came there too, shaking up the crowds and making a disturbance.

Then the brothers hastily sent Paul off to go travel till he got to the seashore, while Silas and Timothy stayed behind where they were. They then made arrangements and got Paul headed for Athens, and taking the message to Silas and Timothy to join him there as soon as they could, they went back.

In Athens, as Paul took in their ways, the spirit within him was incensed to find the city so given to idolatry. So he started speaking in the synagogue to the Jews and the other worshipers and in the marketplace daily to the passersby. And some of the Epicurean and Stoic philosophers debated with him, and some of them said, "What is this dilettante trying to say?" Others said, "He seems to be introducing new gods from other countries," because he was bringing the good news of Jesus and the resurrection. Taking him in hand they brought him up to the Areopagus, saying, "May we ask what this new teaching is as propounded by you? You're bringing in something foreign to our ears, so we want to know what this is all about." (For all the Athenians and resident aliens, there was no better fun than talking or hearing of some novelty.)

Taking a stand in the middle of the Areopagus, Paul said: "Citizens of Athens, I see you are believers in spirits of every kind. In fact, as I was passing through and looking over your places of worship, I came across an altar on which was written: TO THE UNKNOWN GOD.

"What you worship unawares, then, is what I am here to proclaim to you. The God who made the world and everything in it, being Himself the Lord of earth and sky, is not a tenant of any man-made temples, and does not need anything that mortal hands can help Him with, since He Himself is the giver to all of life, breath, and everything. And out of one substance He made all the human race to live on every surface of the earth, drawing up stated seasons and boundaries to their dwelling, that they might seek God, and see if in fact their groping hands might find Him, since after all He is very close to every one of us: we live in Him and move in Him and are in Him.

"As indeed some of your own poets have said,

We are of his lineage too.

"So if we're of the lineage of God, we shouldn't think that any gold or silver or stone, the impress of human skill and hard thought, is comparable to the divine. To be sure, God overlooks the previous times of ignorance, but now He commands the world—everyone, everywhere— to repent, because He has fixed the day on which He is going to judge the world's population, justly, using the man He ordained, whose credentials he showed to all by raising him from the dead."

When they heard "raising from the dead," some of them started jeering, but others said, "We'd like to hear some more about this from you." And so Paul left the gathering behind. A number of men became his followers and were won over, among them Dionysius Areopagita and a woman named Damaris and various others with them.

18

After that, withdrawing from Athens he came to Corinth. And he came across a certain Jew there named Aquila, Pontic by race and having recently emigrated from Italy with Priscilla his wife as a result of the order of Claudius that all Jews should withdraw from Rome. And he fell in with them, and since he shared the same trade with them, he stayed and worked there—they were tentmakers by trade. He argued in the synagogue every Sabbath and convinced both Jews and Greeks.

By the time Silas and Timothy came down from Macedonia, Paul was engaged in the word, witnessing to the Jews that the Anointed was Jesus. But when they rejected his words with foul curses, he shook the dust off his clothes and said to them, "Your blood be upon your own heads, it won't be on mine. I'm turning to the Gentiles from now on." And moving on from there he went into the house of someone named Titus the Just, who worshiped God and whose house was next door to the synagogue. Crispus, the chief of the synagogue, put his faith in the Lord, along with all his household, and many of the Corinthians, when they heard, were convinced and came forward to be washed.

Then the Lord said to Paul by night in a vision: "Don't be afraid, speak up and don't be silent, because I am with you, and no one will set upon you to harm you, since there are many of my people in this city." So he resided a year and six months there, teaching the word of God among them.

Then when Gallio was vice regent of Achaea, the Jews rose up against Paul en masse and took him before the bar saying, "This guy is convincing people to worship God in an unlawful way."

As Paul was about to open his mouth, Gallio said to the Jews, "If there has been some crime or underhanded foul play here, my Jewish friends, I'll support you to the extent of the law; but if it's a dispute about words and expressions and the laws among your kind, see to that yourselves, I don't want to be the judge of those things." And he drove them away from his podium. So they all took hold of Sosthenes the chief of the synagogue and beat him in front of the regent's podium, which made no difference to Gallio.

After Paul had spent quite a few days with the brothers and sisters, he took his leave and sailed out to Syria, and with him Priscilla and Aquila, who had had his head shaved in Cenchreae in accordance with a religious vow he'd taken. They touched down in Ephesus, where he left them. He then went to the synagogue and started disputing with the Jews. They asked him to stay for a longer time, but he didn't say yes; instead he took his leave, saying, "I will come back this way and see you again, God willing," and set off from Ephesus. And touching down in Caesarea, he went up and said hello to the assembly, and went down to Antioch.

And after passing some time he set out and went systematically through the Galatian and Phrygian countryside lending support to all the disciples.

Now a certain Jew name of Apollos, Alexandrian by race, a man skilled with words, arrived in Ephesus, a mighty man of the scriptures. He was drilling people on the way of the Lord and steaming with the spirit as he spoke and taught accurately all about Jesus, himself understanding nothing beyond the washing of John. And he started to make an address in the synagogue, and Priscilla and Aquila, after hearing him, got in touch with him and expounded the Way of God to him in more detail. Since he was planning to pass through Achaea, the brothers wrote a recommendation to the disciples to receive him. He arrived and had many discussions with the ones who had come to believe through grace. Forcefully he confuted the Jews in public, proving by the scriptures that the Anointed was Jesus.

19

It happened while Apollos was in Corinth that Paul, passing through the upland regions, came down to Ephesus and found a group of followers there and said to them, "Did you believe and receive the sacred breath?"

They said to him, "We never even heard that there was a sacred breath."

And he said, "In whose name were you washed?"

They said, "The washing of John."

Said Paul, "John washed with the washing of a changed heart, teaching the people to believe in the one who would come after him, that is, Jesus."

Hearing that, they came forward to be washed in the name of Lord Jesus. And as Paul laid his hands on them the sacred breath came upon them, and they started speaking in tongues and prophesying. They were all men, about twelve of them.

Going into the synagogue, he was giving speeches there for three months, arguing with them and convincing them about the kingdom of God. But as some of them stiffened in their unbelief and started insulting the Way in front of the whole crowd, he withdrew from them and took his disciples with him, conversing with them daily in the school of

Tyrannus. This went on for two years, till all the inhabitants of Asia had heard the word, Jews and Greeks alike.

Deeds of extraordinary power were done by God through the hands of Paul, to the point where handkerchiefs and aprons that had touched his skin were carried away and placed upon the sick, whose ailments then departed, and whose evil spirits were eliminated.

Now some of the Jewish exorcists traveling around tried invoking the name of the Lord Jesus on those with evil spirits, saying, "I command you by Jesus, the one whom Paul proclaims." There was a certain Jewish priest named Scevas who had seven sons who were doing that. But the evil spirit answered them, "I know Jesus and I've heard of Paul, but who are you?" And jumping all over them, the man who had the evil spirit wrestled them to the ground and so overpowered them that they had to run naked and bleeding from the house. That story became known to all the Jews and Greeks living in Ephesus, and fear overcame them all and they glorified the name of Lord Jesus. And many of the believers came along confessing and saying openly what they'd done. And many of those who had practiced occult arts collected their books and burned them in front of everyone, and they estimated the value of the items and it came to fifty thousand silverpieces. Thus according to the power of the Lord the word grew and was strengthened.

When those things had been accomplished, Paul decided in the spirit to travel to Jerusalem, passing through Macedonia and Achaea, saying, "After I've been there I also have to see Rome." After sending into Macedonia two who were in his service, Timothy and Erastus, he himself stayed for a while in Asia.

Around that time there was no small disturbance about the Way.* In particular, a certain Demetrius, a master silversmith who provided artisans with a lot of work making silver Temple of Artemis souvenirs, called together his people and others of the same trade and said: "Gentlemen, you understand this business means our livelihood, and you see and hear how not only in Ephesus but in almost the whole of Asia, this Paul has been winning over and convincing a substantial crowd, saying the gods made by human hands aren't really gods. This presents

---

* "The Way" is what Christianity calls itself at this point; the word "Christian" comes later and may originally have come from outside as an insult meaning "Messiah freaks," though it appears in the First Epistle of Peter (page 438).

the threat not only that our position will suffer degradation, but that the whole Temple of the great goddess Artemis will come to nothing, and she will be stripped of her majesty, she whom all Asia and the world adores."

Listening and filling up with rage, they started shouting, "Long live Artemis of Ephesus!" And the city was filled with chaos, and they all rushed in a pack to the stadium, dragging with them Gaius and Aristarchus, Macedonian traveling-companions of Paul's. Paul wanted to go face the people, but his followers were holding him back. Some of the Roman provincial officials who were friends of his sent word to him begging him not to show up in the stadium: various people were shouting this and that, and the whole assemblage was confused, with most of them not knowing what they were there for. Out of the crowd they agreed on Alexandrus, whom the Jews put forward. So Alexandrus waved his hand for silence to reason with the people. But when they realized he was a Jew, with one voice they all shouted "Long live Artemis of Ephesus!" for about two hours.

After settling the crowd, the town clerk says, "Citizens of Ephesus, is there anyone in the world who doesn't know the city of the Ephesians as the keeper of the temple of mighty Artemis and the flame of the divine? Just because that is true beyond question, it's important for you to control yourselves and not do anything rash. Look, you dragged these people here who have not robbed our temples or blasphemed our goddess. So if Demetrius and his colleagues have some score to settle with anyone, the courts are in session and the vice regents are around, they can bring charges against each other. If you have anything in mind beyond that, it will be taken care of in the legitimate assembly. Remember, we face the threat of being accused of a breach of the peace on account of today's proceedings if there is no charge obtaining on the basis of which we can account for a gathering like this." And so saying, he dismissed the assemblage.

20

After the ruckus blew over, Paul sent for his followers with words of encouragement and said goodbye and set out to travel to Macedonia. After passing through those parts and offering the people many words of encouragement, he came to Greece. When after three months a plot on the part of the Jews arose against him as he was about to put off for Syria, he took a mind to return through Macedonia. This was also approved by Sopater Pyrrhi of Berea, the Thessalonians Aristarchus and Secundus, and Gaius of Derbe and Timothy, and the Asians Tychicus and Trophimus, who accordingly went on ahead and were waiting for us in Troy. We sailed out from Philippi after the days of unleavened bread and within five days joined them in Troy, where we spent seven days.

On the day after the Sabbath, as we were gathered to break bread, Paul was having a talk with the others, since he would be leaving the next day, and he kept the conversation up till midnight (there were plenty of lanterns in the upstairs room where we were gathered). And there was this teenage kid name of Eutychus, sitting by the door and dropping into deep sleep as Paul talked on and on, who in the soundness of his sleep fell three stories down to the ground and was pulled lifeless from the floor. Paul came down and fell upon him and threw his arms around him, saying, "Don't make an uproar, the breath of life is still in him." Then he went back up and broke bread and satisfied his palate and conversed till dawn, at which point he left. Then they went and got the boy, who was alive, and were relieved no end.

We then got on board first and put off for Assos, planning to pick up Paul from there; as he'd arranged it, he was going to walk. So when he joined us in Asson, we took him along and we went to Mitylene. And sailing off from there we reached a point opposite Chios the next day; on the following day we landed at Samos, and on the day after that we came to Miletus. Paul, it seems, decided to sail past Ephesus, so as not to be delayed in Asia, because he was trying to make good time so as to be in Jerusalem if possible for the day of Pentecost.

Sending from Miletus for the elders of the assembly in Ephesus, he said to them when they arrived where he was:

"You already know how ever since the first day I set foot in Asia I have been with you all the time, slaving for the Lord in all humility and through all tears and trials that have faced me in the plots of the Jews, and how I let no expediency hold me back from proclaiming to you and teaching you in public and in private houses, bearing the word to Jews and Greeks alike of turning back to God and of faith in our Lord Jesus.

"And now you see me constrained by the spirit to travel to Jerusalem, knowing nothing of what awaits me there except that the holy spirit assures me in every city that chains and suffering await me. But I put no value on my life except to finish my course and the service I took on from Lord Jesus, to insist on the good word of the grace of God.

"And now here we are, and I know that all of you will not see my face again, you whom I have passed among, spreading the word of the kingdom. For which reason I would like to affirm that no one's blood is on my hands, because I did not flinch from conveying the whole will of God to you. Watch yourselves and all the flock over whom the holy spirit has made you overseers, to shepherd the assembly of God, which he gave his own blood to possess. I know that after my departure vicious wolves will come upon you who will have no mercy on the flock. And some of your own men will stand up speaking distortions and lining the disciples up behind them. So stay awake and keep in mind how for three years day and night I did not rest from my tearful concern for every one of them. And now I commend you to God and the word of His grace, powerful to build and bestow its estate on all who have been sanctified. Silver and gold and fine clothes meant nothing to me. You know yourselves that my needs and the needs of those with me were seen to by the service of my two hands. I always gave you an example of how you must work hard reaching out to the sick and remember the words of Lord Jesus, who himself said, 'Good fortune is more in giving than in receiving.' "

And so saying he got down on his knees with them all and prayed. And there was a lot of wailing on everyone's part, and they were falling around Paul's neck and kissing him, grieving above all over the words he'd said, that they would never see his face again. Then they escorted him down to the ship.

21

When we came to set sail after saying goodbye to them, we headed in a straight line for Cos, then the next day to Rhodes, and from there to Patara, and on finding a ship crossing to Phoenicia, we boarded it and sailed off. After coming into view of Cyprus and leaving it on our left we sailed to Syria and landed in Tyre, since that's where the ship was going to unload its cargo. Looking up the disciples there he stayed for seven days, while they told him through the spirit not to go up to Jerusalem. And when we came to finish our days there, they all came out with women and children to escort us out of town, and we knelt down on the beach and prayed; then we said goodbye to one another and boarded the ship, while they went back to their own homes.

We, however, concluding our voyage from Tyre, arrived in Ptolemais, and after greeting the brothers and sisters we stayed there one day with them. Setting out the next day, we got to Caesarea and went to the home of Philip the evangelist, who was one of the seven, and stayed with him. He had four unmarried daughters, all given to prophecy.

As we were staying there several days a prophet name of Agabus came down from Jerusalem, and when he came to see us he took Paul's belt and tied his hands and feet with it, saying, "The sacred breath says: the man whose belt this is will be tied like this by the Jews in Jerusalem, who will betray him into the hands of Gentiles." When we heard that, both we and the people who lived there urged Paul not to go up to Jerusalem.

Then Paul answered, "What are you doing crying and wearing away my heart? I am ready not only to be imprisoned in Jerusalem but to die there for the name of Lord Jesus." Since there was no persuading him, we kept quiet and said, "Let the Lord's will be done."

Some days later, after making provisions, we were going up to Jerusalem. Along with us came some of the followers from Caesarea, who brought us to stay with a certain Mnason the Cypriot, a follower from way back. Then when we got to Jerusalem, the brothers and sisters were happy to take us in.

The next day Paul went in with us to see James, and all the elders were there. And after greeting them he explained all the details of what God had done among the Gentiles through his service.

On hearing it they praised God, and also said to him, "You will observe, brother, how many tens of thousands of believers there are among the Jews, all of them diligent observers of the Law. But what has reached their ears about you is that you teach rebellion against Moses, telling those Jews who were among Gentiles not to circumcise their children or walk in the ways of our traditions.* So what does this mean? Everyone will hear that you've come. So do what we tell you: we have four men who have taken a holy vow upon themselves. Take them along and go to be blessed with them and pay for them to have their heads shaved, and then everyone will know that what they heard about you

---

* The rumor is correct: Paul *is* in rebellion against Moses when he says things like "food doesn't change our standing with God" (page 318) and "if when God called you, you were uncircumcised, don't get circumcised" (page 316).

means nothing and that in fact you keep and walk in the ways of the Law. As for the believing Gentiles, we wrote to them our decision that they should keep away from meat sacrificed to an idol, and blood, and strangled meat, and whoring."

So the next day Paul took the men with him and went to be blessed with them, and went into the temple announcing the term of purification that had been fulfilled by each man, till they had all made their offerings.

When just about a week had gone by, the Jews from Asia, seeing him in the temple, stirred up the whole crowd and laid hands on him, shouting, "Men of Israel, help! This is that fellow who's been teaching everybody everywhere to go against our people, our Law, and this holy place, and to top it off he's brought Greeks into the temple and defiled this holy place." (You see, they'd already seen Trophimus the Ephesian in the city with him, and they thought Paul had brought him along into the temple.) So the whole city was in a commotion, with all the people running out into the streets, and they laid hands on Paul and dragged him outside the temple and shut the doors abruptly behind him.

As they were thinking about killing him, word reached the colonel commanding the division that all Jerusalem was in an uproar. He, taking along soldiers and captains, ran right down without delay; and when they saw the colonel and the soldiers, they stopped beating Paul. Then the colonel drew near and took hold of him and ordered him bound with two chains, and inquired who he was and what he'd done, but different people in the crowd shouted different things. Since he couldn't establish the truth what with all the noise, he ordered him to be brought back to camp. When they got to the steps, though, he ended up being carried by the soldiers because of the vehemence of the crowd: a mass of people were following them, yelling "Get him!"

As he was about to be led into camp Paul says to the colonel, "May I say something to you?"

He said, "You know Greek?! Aren't you the Egyptian who a while back raised an army of four thousand assassins and led them out into the desert?"

Said Paul, "I am a Jewish person, from Tarsus, Cilicia, not a citizen of some obscure town. I beg you, let me speak to the people." He agreed, and Paul, standing on the steps, waved his hand for silence, and when a great silence came over them, raised his voice, saying in the Hebrew language:

22

"Brothers and fathers, listen to what I tell you now in my defense."
Hearing that he was speaking to them in the Hebrew language they paid
more attention. And he says, "I am a Jewish man, born in Tarsus, Cilicia,
raised in that city, schooled at the feet of Gamaliel in all the niceties of
our ancestral Law, a person fired up for God—just as all of you here
today are—who hounded the Way to death, chaining and putting in jail
both men and women, as the high priest and all the council of elders can
testify for me, since I obtained letters from them before traveling to see
their brothers in Damascus, so I could also bring the people there back
in chains to Jerusalem to be punished.

"It happened as I was traveling on and nearing Damascus, around
noon, that suddenly a mighty light from the sky enveloped me in a blaze,
and I fell on the ground and heard a voice saying to me, 'Saul, Saul, why
are you persecuting me?'

"I answered, 'Who are you, Lord?'

"And he said to me, 'I am Jesus of Nazareth, the one you're persecuting.' Those with me observed the light but didn't hear the voice of the
one speaking to me.

"So I said, 'What shall I do, Lord?'

"And the Lord said to me, 'Get up and travel on to Damascus and there
you will be told about everything that has been arranged for you to do.'
Since I couldn't see after the glory of that light, I came to Damascus with
my comrades leading me by the hand.

"A certain Ananias, a man respectful of the Law, whom all the Jews
who live there will vouch for, came to me and stood over me, saying,
'Brother Saul, see again.' And that very minute I could see him. And he
said, 'The God of our fathers destined you to be informed of His
intentions, to look upon the Just One and to hear the voice of his mouth,
because you will be his witness to all the world of what you have seen and
heard. And now what are you waiting for? Stand up and go bathe and
wash your wrongdoing away as you call upon his name.'

"It happened that when I returned to Jerusalem and was praying in the
temple, I went into a rapture and saw him telling me, 'Quick, get out of
Jerusalem in haste, because they won't accept testimony about me from
you.'

"And I said, 'Lord, they already know how I had those who believed in you jailed and flogged in the synagogues, and that when they shed the blood of your witness Stephen, I was standing there in person and going along with it and watching the coats of his killers.'

"And he said to me, 'On your way! I am sending you far among the Gentiles' "—they got as far as that word and then raised their voices saying, "Get that so-and-so off the face of the earth, it isn't right to let him live!" Amid their screaming and ripping their garments and throwing dust into the air, the colonel ordered him led into the camp, saying he should be examined under the lash to find out the reason why they were shouting at him like that. But as they exposed him to the lash, Paul said to the presiding captain, "Are you allowed to flog a Roman citizen who hasn't been tried and sentenced?"

When he heard that, the captain went to report that to the colonel, saying, "What are you going to do? This guy's a Roman citizen."

So the colonel came over to him and said, "Tell me, are you a Roman citizen?"

And he said, "Yes."

Answered the colonel, "I bought my citizenship for a hefty sum."

Said Paul, "And I was born with mine."

So right away the ones who were going to interrogate him drew back, and the colonel got scared, realizing that this was a Roman citizen and he'd had him tied up.

The next day, trying to establish exactly what it was the Jews were accusing him of, he untied him and ordered the high priests and supreme council to assemble, and bringing in Paul he set him there before them.

23

Fixing his gaze on the supreme council Paul said, "Brothers, I have lived my life in all good faith before God up to the present day." The high priest Ananias ordered those standing next to him to hit him in the mouth. Then Paul said to him, "*You* will be struck by God, you crumbling wall! You sit there judging me by the law and then you order me struck in defiance of the law?"

The bystanders said, "Are you going to vilify the high priest of God?"

Said Paul, "Brothers, I didn't know he was the chief priest. After all, it is written, 'You shall not speak evil of the ruler of the people.' "

Knowing that one party was Sadducees and the other Pharisees, he proclaimed before the supreme council, "Brothers, I am a Pharisee and the son of Pharisees, and I'm being condemned for my hope in the resurrection of the dead."

When he said that, the Pharisees and Sadducees split into factions and the masses were divided, because while the Sadducees say there is no resurrection, nor are there any angels or spirits, the Pharisees admit both. There was a lot of shouting, and some of the canon-lawyers on the Pharisee side stood up and shouted defiantly, "We don't see anything wrong with this person, whether the spirit or an angel spoke to him."

Amid growing dissension the colonel, afraid that Paul would be torn apart by them, ordered his men to come down and take him out of there and back to camp. The following night the Lord stood over him and said, "Courage! Just as you bore witness to me in Jerusalem, now you must go to Rome and bear witness."

When daylight came the Jews held a gathering where they swore a curse on themselves if they should ever eat or drink again before they saw Paul dead. There were more than forty who took that oath together, and they went to see the high priests and elders saying, "We have sworn a mighty oath to let nothing cross our lips till we see Paul dead. So now you go notify the colonel and the supreme council to bring him down here, saying we're going to find out more particulars about him. We'll be prepared to get rid of him before he even gets here."

The son of Paul's sister, hearing of the plot, showed up at the camp and went in and brought word to Paul. Paul called one of the captains over and said, "Take this lad to see the colonel, he has something to tell him."

The captain took him in tow and brought him to the colonel saying, "The prisoner Paul called me over and asked me to bring this lad to see you so he can say something to you."

Taking him by the hand and withdrawing to private quarters he asked, "What message do you have for me?"

And he said, "The Jews have planned to ask you tomorrow to bring Paul down before the supreme council, saying they're going to inquire further particulars about him. Don't believe them. There's a plot against him on the part of forty of their men who have sworn a curse on themselves if they ever eat or drink again before they see him dead, and now they're in readiness awaiting your orders." So the colonel in turn let the lad go, ordering him "not to let slip to anyone that you made known these things to me."

And calling in two of his captains he said, "Get two hundred soldiers ready to travel as far as Caesarea, with seventy horsemen and two hundred lancers, by nine o'clock tonight; also provide a couple of animals to seat Paul on so we can deliver him in safety to Felix the commander." Meanwhile, he wrote a letter in the following form:
"From Claudius Lysias
"To the honorable commander Felix:
"Greetings: As this man had been seized by the Jews and was about to be killed by them, I intervened with my forces and pulled him out, learning that he was a Roman citizen. In an effort to find out what charge they were indicting him on, I brought him down to their supreme council, and found that he was accused on the basis of questions involving their law but had no charge against him worthy of death or imprisonment. Being informed, however, that a plot against the man was afoot, I sent him to you, ordering his accusers also to say what they have to say about him in front of you."

So the soldiers, as they were ordered, took Paul in hand and brought him by night to Antipater. The next day they left the horsemen to go on with him and returned to camp. The horsemen came to Caesarea and handed over the letter to the commander, to whom they also presented Paul. He, after reading it and asking what province he was from, and being answered "Cilicia," said, "I'll hear you out when your accusers show up," and ordered him held in the governor's mansion belonging to Herod.

24

Five days later the high priest Ananias came down with some of the elders and an attorney named Tertullus and filed charges against Paul with the commander. Once he had been called in, Tertullus opened the prosecution by saying, "Since we have lived very much in peace under you and many wrongs have been righted for our people through your kind concern, we receive these things, most honorable Felix, with the utmost gratitude. So that I may not harangue you at length, I beg you to listen to us briefly with the fair-mindedness you are known for. You see, we found this man to be a plague, stirring up revolution among all the Jews across the world, and a kingpin of the Nazarene cult, and even trying to profane our temple, and so we arrested him; you can ask him yourself to find out about all the things we charged him with." And the Jews chimed in, saying all these things were so.

Answered Paul, as the commander signaled him to speak: "Since I understand you have been judge over these people for many years, I am encouraged to make my defense; I beg to inform you that it's no more than twelve days since I went up to Jerusalem to worship. And they did not catch me either in the temple arguing with anybody or assembling a crowd of people in the synagogues or in the middle of the city, nor can they prove the things they're accusing me of right now. I grant you this much: that according to the Way, which they call a cult, I worship the God of our fathers, believing in all the things about the Law and everything written in the Prophets, having indeed the same hope in God that these people themselves abide in, that there will be a resurrection of the innocent and the guilty. In the meantime I cultivate a blameless conscience toward God and other people at all times. I came here for the first time in several years to perform charities for my people and make offerings, which they saw me doing in the temple in all purity, with no crowds and no noise; in fact some of the Asian Jews saw me who should be here in front of you accusing me if they had anything on me. Or let these people themselves say what crime they uncovered when I stood before the supreme council, unless it's about the one outburst I uttered as I stood among them, namely, 'I'm being judged by you today for the resurrection of the dead.' "

Then Felix put the others off, and having learned in more detail about the Way he said, "When Lysias the colonel comes down here, I will decide your case," and ordered the captain to keep him under lenient treatment and not to prevent any of his people from taking care of him.

After a few days, Felix came by with Drusilla, his wife, who was Jewish, and summoned Paul and heard from him more about the belief in Jesus the Anointed. As he discussed justice, self-control and the judgment to come, Felix, getting scared, answered, "Go on your way for now, I'll find another time to call you back," hoping at the same time that Paul would slip him some money, for which reason he kept sending for him repeatedly and talking with him.

After two years had passed Felix was replaced by Porcius Festus, and to curry favor with the Jews, Felix left Paul locked up.

25

So Festus, after arriving in the province, went up to Jerusalem from Caesarea three days later, and the high priests and most prominent Jews swore affidavits to him against Paul, and begged him as a special favor to send him to Jerusalem, having formed a plot to kill him on the way. Festus answered that he was keeping Paul in Caesarea and that he himself would be traveling out there before long. "So whoever is influential among you," he said, "let them all come down here and, if there's anything wrong with the man, accuse him."

After spending no more than eight or ten days among them he went back down to Caesarea, and the next day, sitting on his podium, he ordered Paul brought in. As soon as he appeared he was surrounded by the Jews who had come down from Jerusalem, bringing all sorts of grievous charges to bear which they weren't able to prove, while Paul said in his defense, "I did no wrong to the law of the Jews, nor to the temple, nor to Caesar."

Festus, wishing to gain favor with the Jews, answered Paul saying, "Do you want to go up to Jerusalem and be judged about these matters in my presence there?"

Said Paul, "I am standing before the bench of Caesar, and that is where I must be judged. I did no wrong to the Jews, as even you can see very well. If I should be guilty and if I've done something deserving of death, I won't beg to be spared from dying; but if there's nothing behind what these people are accusing me of, no one can throw me to them as a sop: I appeal to Caesar!"

Then Festus, after talking with the rest of the council, answered, "You have appealed to Caesar, to Caesar you shall go."

After some days had passed, Agrippa the king and Bernice arrived in Caesarea and paid their respects to Festus. And as he was staying there several days Festus brought up the subject of Paul to the king, saying, "There is a prisoner left over from Felix's term, whom the high priests and elders reported to me when I was in Jerusalem, seeking judgment against him. I answered them that it isn't customary with us Romans to give a person up before the accused has seen his accusers face to face and had a chance to defend himself against the charge. So when they assembled here, I didn't delay, but on the next day mounted the podium and ordered the man brought in, against whom his accusers, when they stood up, brought no charge of a kind that would strike me as wicked; instead, they had some kind of dispute with him concerning their own mumbo-jumbo and a certain Jesus who had died and who Paul said was alive. Not knowing what to make of the dispute on those subjects, I said if he wanted he could go to Jerusalem and be tried there on those matters. However, when Paul appealed to be committed to the judgment of Augustus, I ordered him held till I could send him to Caesar."

Agrippa then said to Festus, "I'd like to hear from this person myself."

"Tomorrow," he said, "you shall hear him."

The next day, after Agrippa and Bernice had arrived with much pomp and circumstance and gone into the auditorium, with some colonels and men of influence in the city and Festus had given the order, Paul was brought in. And Festus says: "King Agrippa and all you gentlemen who are with us today, here you see the one about whom all the Jews interceded with me an masse, both in Jerusalem and here, shouting that he mustn't be allowed to live any longer. I, however, did not uncover anything worthy of death that he'd done, but when this man himself appealed to Augustus, I decided to send him.

"What I don't know is exactly what to write to my lord about him, which is why I brought him here with all of you present, especially you, King Agrippa, so that when the interrogation is done I'll have something to write; after all, it seems senseless to me to send somebody as a prisoner without also indicating the charges against him."

So Agrippa said to Paul, "Do you wish to tell us about yourself?"

26

Then Paul, stretching out his hand, made his defense: "As for all the things I'm accused of by the Jews, King Agrippa, I consider myself particularly lucky to be defending myself before you today, since you are familiar with all the customs and matters of debate among the Jews, for which reason I beg you to hear me out patiently. First of all, my life from childhood on, starting from the beginning among my people and in Jerusalem, is well known to all the Jews who know me from back then, if they wish to testify about it: namely, that I lived according to the most exact conception of our religion as a Pharisee. And now I stand accused of hoping for the fulfillment of the promise made by God to our fathers, the same promise that our twelve tribes worship day and night in the hope of seeing it fulfilled; for that hope I am accused by the Jews, your majesty. Why is it considered incredible to you all if God should raise the dead?

"Now I at first felt obligated to do all sorts of things against the name of Jesus of Nazareth, which in fact I did in Jerusalem; and after receiving authority from the high priests I shut many of the faithful up in jail; and when they were killed, I assented to it. And by punishing them repeatedly in all the synagogues I kept trying to make them renounce their faith, and in my immoderate fury towards them I hounded them as far as the outlying cities.

"On one of those days as I was traveling to Damascus with the authority and permission of the high priests, at midday along the road I saw, your majesty, a light from the sky of greater brightness than the sun, enveloping me and those who traveled with me in its light. As we all fell to the ground I heard a voice saying to me in the Hebrew language, 'Saul, Saul, why are you persecuting me? Isn't it hard to keep throwing yourself backward against the prod?'

"I said, 'Who are you, Lord?'

"And the Lord said, 'I am Jesus, the one you're persecuting. But now get up and stand on your feet, because the reason I appeared to you was to appoint you my assistant and my witness, both as to what you just saw and what you will see of me in the future, as I deliver you from your own people and from the Gentiles I will send you among, hoping that their eyes may open, and that they may turn from darkness back to light and from the power of Satan back to God and find forgiveness for their wrongdoing and a place among the blessed through their faith in me.'

"For which reason, King Agrippa, I did not disregard the heavenly vision, but brought the word, first to those in Damascus and in Jerusalem, then to all the country of Judea and the Gentiles: to repent and turn back to God, doing the deeds that go with a change of heart. Because of that the Jews seized me in the temple and tried to dispose of me. Receiving protection from God, I have stood, up to the present day, bearing witness to great and small without distinction, talking about what the prophets, and also Moses, said would happen, about how the Anointed would suffer and how as the first to be resurrected from the dead he would proclaim a light to his people and the Gentiles."

When he had made this defense, Festus said in a loud voice, "You're crazy, Paul. All that reading and writing has tipped you over the edge of madness."

"No, I'm not crazy, honorable Festus," said Paul: "I'm speaking words of truth and prudence. Certainly the king to whom I speak so freely understands about these things; I doubt that any part of all this has been lost on him, because none of this happened off in a dark corner. Do you believe, King Agrippa, in the prophets? I know you do."

Agrippa said to Paul, "In a little while you'll persuade *me* to become one of those 'Christians'!"

Said Paul, "I would pray to God that in a little while or a long while not only you but all who hear me today might become just as I am, except without these chains!"

And the king stood up, and the governor and Bernice, and the others sitting with them, and withdrawing by themselves they said to each other, "This person isn't doing anything worthy of death or imprisonment."

Agrippa said to Festus, "This guy could have been let go if he hadn't appealed to Caesar."

27

When it was decided that we would sail to Italy, they handed Paul and some other prisoners over to a captain name of Julius of the squad of Augustus. Boarding a ship from Adramyttium which was bound for parts in Asia, we sailed off, with Aristarchus, a Macedonian from Thessalonica, on board with us. The next day we landed at Sidon, and Julius, treating Paul benevolently, allowed Paul to go see his friends and be cared for. Putting off from there we sailed around Cyprus, because of the wind's being against us, and sailing across the sea of Cilicia and Pamphylia, we reached Myra, in Lycia. And there the captain, meeting with an Alexandrian ship sailing for Italy, moved us onto it. And after sailing slowly for quite some days and barely getting to Cnidus, with the wind keeping us back we sailed below Crete, passing Salmone. And just coasting by it we came to some place called Fairhavens, with the city of Lasea near by. Seeing that a lot of time had passed and sailing was already risky, since it was already past the fast days [of Yom Kippur and into October], Paul spoke to them in warning: "Gentlemen, I see that this voyage is going to involve injury and a lot of damage, not just to the cargo and ship, but to our lives." But the captain listened to the ship's owner and the pilot more than to what Paul said. And since the harbor wasn't well set up for wintering over, the majority chose the course of sailing off from there, to see if they could make it as far as Phoenix to spend the winter, that being a port in Crete looking to the northwest and southwest.

With a gentle southerly wind blowing, thinking they had seized the advantage, they lifted anchor and coasted closer to Crete. Not long afterwards a wind sprang up from the other direction, a typhoon wind called a nor'easter. With the boat caught up in it and unable to withstand it, we gave up and were carried along by the wind. Then as we rounded a little island called Cauda we barely managed to get hold of the lifeboat; and after hauling it up they took the precaution of tying ropes around the ship, and fearing that they might run aground on the Great Sandbank, they lowered the gear and so were carried along.* The next day, as we were severely storm-beaten, they threw some things overboard; and the day after that with their own hands they threw all of the ship's furniture overboard. With no sun and no stars visible for several days, and no small storm prevailing, it got to the point where all hope was stripped away of our being saved.

There being a great shortage of food, Paul then stood up in their midst and said, "Well, gentlemen, you should have listened to me and not sailed off from Crete to face this damage and loss. And now I advise you to take heart, because there will be no loss of life among you except for the ship. You see, last night a messenger of the God whom I belong to and whom I serve stood by me and said, 'Don't be afraid, Paul: you must and will stand before Caesar. And do you know what? for your sake God has spared all those sailing with you.' So take heart, gentlemen, because I trust in God that it will turn out the way I have been told: we're bound to run onto some island."

Then as the fourteenth night fell since we had been drifting on the Adriatic, about midnight the sailors suspected they were drawing close to some kind of land. And on sounding the depths they read twenty fathoms; then after a short interval they sounded again and read fifteen

---

* Either they lowered the sails or they let down a "drift anchor," which drags along behind a ship and steadies its course.

fathoms, and fearing that we might be wrecked somewhere on rocky ground they cast four anchors from the stern and prayed for day to come. Then when the sailors tried to flee the ship and were lowering the lifeboat into the sea on the pretext of letting down more anchors farther out from the prow, Paul said to the captain and the soldiers, "If these guys don't stay with the ship, you'll never make it." Then the soldiers cut the lines to the lifeboat and let it fall away.

At the point where it was just about to be daylight, Paul called on everyone to take some food, saying, "Today as you start the fourteenth day, you remain without food, taking nothing, for which reason I beg you to take some food. It's for your own good, because not a hair on any of your heads will be lost." Having said that and taking a piece of bread, he thanked God in front of them all and broke it and began to eat. And with their spirits rising all the rest of them also took some food themselves. (In all there were two hundred seventy-six souls on the ship.) Then after filling up on the food they lightened the ship by throwing the grain into the sea.

So when day came, they didn't recognize the country, but they noticed a bay with a beach that they thought they would bring the ship up onto if they could. And drawing up the anchors all round they entrusted the ship to the sea, at the same time detaching the crossbars joining the rudders and running up the foresail to the breeze; so they reached the shore. And coming upon a spot with water on either side, they ran the ship aground: the prow got stuck and remained immovable, while the stern was broken off by the force of the waves. The soldiers had the idea of killing the prisoners so none of them would swim away and escape. But the captain, who wanted to save Paul, hindered them in this project and ordered those who could swim to dive off first and go on land and the rest to come either on planks or on something else from the ship, and in this manner all arrived safely on land.

28

And once they were safe they found out the island was called Malta. The natives showed us most unusual kindness: they lit a bonfire and brought us all close to it on account of the impending showers and the cold. Then after Paul had gathered quite a bundle of sticks and put them on the fire, a viper fleeing from the heat fastened onto his hand. When the natives saw the beast hanging from his hand, they started saying to each other, "Clearly this guy is a murderer whom justice would not allow to live even when saved from the sea." So he shook the beast off into the fire and suffered no ill effects, while they were expecting that he would break out in an inflammation or suddenly drop dead. But after they watched and waited a long time and nothing bad happened to him, they changed their minds and started saying he was a god.

In the parts around that place were some estates belonging to the ruler of the island, name of Publius, who put us up for three days and entertained us agreeably. It happened that Publius's father was lying in bed, kept down by fevers and dysentery; Paul went in to see him and, after praying, laid his hands on him and healed him. After that had happened, all the other people on the island with infirmities came to him and were cured. They honored us with many presents and, when we sailed off, added various things for our needs.

Three months later we sailed off in a ship that had wintered on the island, an Alexandrian ship with the insignia of Castor and Pollux. And landing at Syracuse we stayed three days. Casting off from there we reached Rhegium. And one day later with a southerly wind blowing, we got to Puteoli, where we found some brothers and were invited by them to stay for a week. And so we came to Rome. And the brothers there, hearing about us, came out to meet us as far as Appian Market and Three Taverns. Seeing them, Paul thanked God and took heart.

When we got into Rome, Paul was allowed to stay by himself with the soldier guarding him. Three days later he happened to call together the most prominent of the Jews, and when they were assembled he started speaking to them, "I, gentle brothers, having done nothing against our people or ancestral customs, was given over in chains from Jerusalem into the hands of the Romans, who after interrogating me would have let me go on the grounds that there was no capital offense to be found in me. But when the Jews objected, I was obliged to appeal to Caesar— not that I have anything to accuse my people of. So the reason I asked you to come see me and talk with me is because it is for the sake of the hope of Israel that I wear these chains."

And they said to him, "We didn't receive any letters about you from Judea, nor did any of the brothers there show up to bring word or say anything bad about you. So we propose to hear from you what you think, since one thing we do know about this sect is that it is spoken against everywhere."

Having agreed with him on a day, more of them came to him at his reception, to whom he bore witness, expounding the kingdom of God, convincing them about Jesus on the basis of Mosaic Law and the Prophets, from morning till evening. And some were convinced by what was said, while others didn't believe. They left in disagreement with each other, Paul saying one last word: "The holy spirit spoke well through Isaiah the prophet to your fathers, saying:

> *Go to these people and say:*
> *With your ears you hear and never understand,*
> *And when you look, you look and never see,*
> *For the heart of these people was dulled,*
> *And with their ears they heard dimly*
> *And they kept their eyes closed*
> *Lest they should see with their eyes,*
> *And hear with their ears,*
> *And understand with their hearts,*
> *And lest they should come back, and I should heal them.*

"So let it be known to you that this the salvation of God has been sent to the Gentiles—and they *will* listen!"

So he stayed for two whole years in his own rented quarters and received all those who came to see him, proclaiming the kingdom of God and teaching about Lord Jesus the Anointed, in all openness and without hindrance.

The Letter from Paul to the Community in

Rome

1

From Paul, slave of Christ Jesus, apostle called and dedicated by God to the good news of His that was promised in advance by His prophets in the holy scriptures: about His son, born (physically) of David's seed, the set-apart son of God empowered with the spirit of holiness by his resurrection from the dead, Jesus Christ our Lord, from whom we receive grace and a mission to make obedient to faith all the world's peoples on behalf of his name, you also being among those called by Jesus Christ;

To all in Rome who are beloved of God and called to holiness:

Grace to you and peace from God our Father and Lord Jesus Christ.

First of all I thank my God through Jesus Christ for all of you because your faith is reported abroad in all the world. God, whom I worship in my spirit in the good word of His son, is my witness to how uninterruptedly I keep you in mind, asking all the time in my prayers that somehow sometime I may be guided aright in God's will to come to you. In truth I long to see you and pass on some spiritual gift to you to strengthen you, indeed to feel with you the comfort of our faith in each other, both yours and mine. I want you to know, brothers and sisters, that I have planned to come see you many times and always been diverted so that I could reap some harvest among you but also among the rest of the world's peoples: I have obligations to the Greek-speaking world and to other foreigners, to the learned and ignorant alike. Such is my eagerness to bring the good word also to you in Rome.

After all, I'm not ashamed of the good word: it is God's power to save, for everyone who believes: the Jews above all but also the Gentiles, since within the good word, God's just nature is revealed by faith for faith's purposes, just as it is written: "The just man shall live by faith."

For we see God's wrath unfolding from the sky upon all the impiety and injustice of people who are unjustly suppressing the truth, when in fact God's knowledge is evident to them, God Himself having revealed it to them. After all, since the creation of the world, the invisible in Him, including His timeless power and divinity, has been observable to those who examine His creations, which leaves those people with no excuse: knowing God, they did not glorify Him and praise Him as God, but lost themselves in speculation and let the spark go out in their foolish hearts.

Saying "we are wise," they took leave of their wits and threw over the glory of God incorruptible for the likeness of a corruptible image: human beings or birds or beasts or serpents. In return God left them to their filthy behavior, with the drives of their heart, to degrade them physically in their own sight. Some of them threw over the truth of God for lies, honoring and worshiping the created over the Creator (be He blest for all ages indeed). In return God gave them over to dishonorable passions, with their women exchanging the natural usage for the unnatural one, and the men likewise leaving the natural usage of women behind and heating up with an appetite for each other, men performing indecent acts with men and storing up the reprisals that must follow on the sinfulness amongst them. And as they didn't keep God steadily in mind, God left them to their unsteadiness of mind to do things that decency forbids, filled as they were with all kinds of unlawfulness, meanness, greed, and evil, rampant with envy, murder, discord, treachery, and disorderly conduct: rumormongers, character assassins, God-haters, criminals, haughty, boastful, fabricators of evil stories, disobedient to parents, with no comprehension, no cohesion, no affection, no compassion. Even knowing the verdict of God that those who act like that are worthy of death, they not only go ahead but also support one another's actions.

2

That means you have no excuse, you out there condemning all the world! In condemning your fellow, you convict yourself of the same crime, since you the accuser do same things. And we know that the judgment of God is in line with the truth by going against those who do such things. Consider this, you out there accusing those who do such things and doing them yourself: will you be able to run from the judgment of God? Or do you scorn God's abundant kindness, His long-suffering nature, His patience, not realizing that God's kindness is supposed to lead you to repentance; whereas with your callousness and unrepentant heart you are storing up wrath for the Day of Wrath, the day of revelation of the outcome of God's justice as He "gives to each according to his deeds": to those who persisted in the good work, seeking glory, honor and immortality, He will give life everlasting; on those who dwell in contention and who obey not the truth but their own unlawful desires, He will vent His anger and fury. Suffering and oppression waits for every human soul that performs evil deeds, especially the Jew but also the Gentile; honor and peace for every doer of good, especially the Jew but also the Gentile. God is no respecter of persons.

Those who sinned lawlessly will also perish lawlessly, and those who sinned under the law will be judged by the law, because it's not those who hear the law who are innocent (after all, when pagans with no law do what the Law says, simply by nature, then in the absence of the law they are a law to themselves: they show the effects of the law written on their hearts, as attested to by their consciences and the things they say criticizing one another's actions or defending them) on the day when God will examine what people are hiding, in line with the good word I have brought you through Jesus Christ.

On the other hand, if you call yourself a Jew and rest on the foundation of the Law and boast in God and know His will and try to do the most important things, being instructed by the Law, you're sure that makes you a "guide for the blind, a light to those in darkness, an instructor of the ignorant, and a teacher for beginners," since in the Law you have the outlines of knowledge and truth. So in teaching others will you not teach yourself? After preaching, "You are not to steal," you steal? You say "Don't commit adultery" and commit adultery yourselves? Expressing horror of things idolatrous, you steal things from temples? You who glory in the Law, you dishonor God by your violation of the Law. "Because of you the name of God is blasphemed among the Gentiles," as it is written.

Now circumcision is good for something if you keep the Law. But if you are a violator of the Law, that makes your circumcision uncircumcised. Whereas if someone else in their uncircumcised way keeps the just commands of the Law, shouldn't that person's lack of circumcision count the same as circumcision? Indeed, the physically uncircumcised person who keeps the Law will one day sit in judgment upon you who have undergone instruction and circumcision only to become a violator of the Law. In the end, it's not who is manifestly a Jew or who is circumcised in the outward physical sense, but who is Jewish inside and who is circumcised at heart, spiritually and not literally, who earns the praise, not of the world but of God.

3

Then is there any advantage in being Jewish, or any use for circumcision? Yes, quite a lot in every way. For one thing, it was to them that the words of God were entrusted. Some didn't believe, but so what? Does their lack of faith invalidate the good faith of God? No, never! It must be that God is truthful even if every human being is a liar, so that, as scripture says, "You will be justified in your words, You will win when charges are brought against You."

But then if our wrongdoing only shows all the more the just nature of God, what shall we conclude? That God has no right to react with anger (as I imagine people saying)? No, never! How would God ever judge the world on that basis? "But," you say, "if by my lying the truth of God is increased, to His greater glory, how can I still be condemned as an evildoer?" Isn't that like what people insultingly say of us and some people (who deserve to be condemned for it) even claim that we say ourselves: "Let's do evil so good will come of it?"

So what shall we say? Are we [Jews] above the rest? Not at all. After all, we have already charged Jews and Gentiles alike with being under the power of sin, as it is written:

> *There is not one innocent, not even one,*
> *No one who understands,*
> *No one seeking God.*
> *All declined into uselessness together*
> *With no one practicing kindness,*
> *Not a single one.*
> *Like an open grave is their open mouth:*
> *They use their tongues for treachery,*
> *And inside their lips is snake venom,*
> *They whose mouth is crawling with curses and bitterness,*
> *Whose feet are swift to shed blood.*
> *Confusion and consternation follow them everywhere,*

And the road of peace is one they never knew.
The fear of God isn't there before their eyes.

Now we know that everything the Law says is said to those under the Law to end all discussion and make the whole world accountable to God; certainly no living thing is exculpated in His eyes by the works of the Law, since through the Law we get the perception of sin.

But now, without the Law's help, God's uprightness has been shown forth, as attested by the Law and the Prophets, a godly uprightness through faith in Jesus Christ which is for all believers. For one is no different from another: all did wrong and missed out on the glory of God, and are being cleared of guilt as the gift of God's own good will, through redemption in Christ Jesus, of whom God made a propitiatory sacrifice that is offered through our faith in his blood; a sacrifice in which God shows His fairness by canceling the sins of the past as a gesture of His good-natured tolerance, wishing to show these times of ours His justice in action—that He himself is just and counts among the just those who go by the faith of Jesus.

So where is our glory in this? Nowhere. Through what law was this? The law of pious deeds? No, the law of faith. We hold that a person is made acceptable by faith without performance of the Law. Is God only the god of Jews? Not Gentiles too? Of course Gentiles too! It's one and the same God who will acquit the circumcised on the basis of faith and the uncircumcised through the action of faith. So with faith are we setting law aside? No, never! We're upholding law.

4

Now then. What shall we say was the experience of Abraham, who was (physically) our forefather? Because if Abraham was made upright by his good works, that's to his credit, but not with God. What does the scripture say: "Abraham had faith in God, and that counted toward his good standing." Now if someone has done something deserving, that person's pay doesn't count as a favor but as an obligation. But if someone has done nothing deserving but puts faith in Him who confers good standing on the unholy, that faith counts toward his good standing. Thus David describes the good fortune of the person on whom God confers a good standing not backed up the person's deeds:

How lucky those whose lawlessness was forgiven,
Whose wrongful deeds were covered up!
How lucky the man whose sins the Lord isn't counting!

Now is this blessing for the circumcised or also for the uncircumcised? Well, we said Abraham's faith "counted toward his good standing." So how did it count? With him circumcised or still with his foreskin? In fact, he wasn't circumcised, he still had his foreskin. And he was given circumcision to be the sign and seal of the good standing of his faith, which he already had in his uncircumcised state—which makes him father of all those who have faith amid their lack of circumcision and for whom it will also "count toward their good standing," as well as being father of a "circumcision" not just for those from that tradition but also for those who follow the pathway of a faith preceding circumcision, as shown by our father Abraham.

It wasn't through the Law, after all, that the promise came to Abraham and his seed that made him the inheritor of a world: rather, it was through the good standing of his faith. If inheritance [of Abraham's promise] were governed by the Law, then faith would turn out to be empty and the promise meaningless. For the Law brings down wrath, whereas when there is no law there is also no violation of it. Therefore, [the inheritance of Abraham's promise] comes on the basis of faith, to make it more of a gift—which means the promise is firm for all the descendants, not just descendants of the Law but also the descendants of Abraham, who is father of us all—just as it is written: "I hereby make you father of many nations" in the eyes of that God in whom he placed his faith, who brings the dead back to life and calls what has no being into being.

He placed his faith, then, in a hope where there was no hope and became the father of many nations, in line with what was said: "So numerous will be your descendants"; and he didn't falter observing his own lifeless eighty-year-old body and the withered womb of Sarah. For the sake of God's promise he didn't hesitate for lack of faith but took on the power of faith and gave glory to God, satisfied that what He promises He can also fulfill. And that's why it "counted toward his good standing."

The part about "counting toward his good standing" wasn't written just about him: it goes for us too. It will also count toward our good standing if we place our faith on Him who raised our Lord Jesus from the dead, Lord Jesus who was betrayed on account of our guilt and resurrected on behalf of our acquittal.

5

Being acquitted, then, on the basis of faith, we are at peace with God through our Lord Jesus Christ, through whom we have access to this grace that we stand in, glorying in the promise of God's glory—but not in that alone. No, we also glory in our suffering, knowing that suffering brings endurance, endurance brings steadfastness, and steadfastness brings hope. And our hope does not come to grief, because our hearts are flooded with God's love through the holy spirit given to us.

Indeed, weak as we were, Christ died for us godless people at the appointed time. Most people would scarcely die for an upright person. Or someone might brave death on behalf of the good. But it confirms God's love for us that Christ still died for us when we were evildoers. And now that we stand acquitted in his blood, how much more shall we be saved through him from God's fury. After all, if when we were God's enemies we were reconciled with Him through the death of His son, how much surer we are, once reconciled, to find salvation in his life—to be not just saved, but exulting in God through our Lord Jesus Christ, through whom this reconciliation was tendered to us.

Because of this, just as through one man sin came into the world and through sin came death, so death spread through all mankind, seeing as how all sinned. Now before the Law came there was sin in the world, but it didn't count as sin without any law being there. Instead, death reigned from Adam to Moses even over those who had not done any wrong to parallel the transgression of Adam, who was a symbol of things to come.

Not that the forgiveness was only as great as the transgression. If through one man's transgression everyone died, how much more did everyone overflow with God's grace and the free gift of the grace of one man, Jesus Christ. Nor was it just one man's sin that occasioned the gift. No, the judgment of the one led to condemnation, while the forgiveness of many transgressions led to a verdict of innocent. Because if by one man's sin death became king through that one man, how much more shall those who keep drawing on the overflowing grace and freely conferred good standing reign in true life through one man, Jesus Christ. So then, as one man's transgression worked to the condemnation of every human being, so one man's acquittal was for every human being, letting them enter upon true Life free and clear. You see, as through one man's disobedience the rest were classed as evildoers, through one man's obedience the rest were classed among the just. Law came in to multiply transgressions. Where sin has been multiplied, grace has been showered, so that as sin was king in the land of death, grace might reign in justice for an eternity of Life through Jesus Christ our Lord.

6

What shall we say then? Should we stay in sin so as to multiply grace? No, never! We who died to sin, how can we live in it anymore? Or are you unaware that all of us who were initiated into Christ Jesus were initiated into his death as well? By being initiated into his death, we were buried with him, so that just as Christ was raised from the dead through the glory of his Father, so we might walk in the freshness of a new life. Because if we have grown into the likeness of his death, we shall do the same with his resurrection.

This much we know: that the old us was crucified with him, that sin's body was destroyed to keep us from being the slaves of sin any more, since in dying a person is cleared of sin. So if we died with Christ, we trust that we will live with him too, knowing that Christ once raised from the dead dies no more: death no longer rules him. What died, died to sin at the same time; what lives, lives to God. Consider yourselves likewise dead to sin but alive to God in Christ Jesus.

Therefore, let's not let sin rule in our mortal body, making us obey the body's passions. Neither must you furnish your arms and legs to sin as instruments of mischief. Instead, furnish yourselves to God like people restored to life from the dead, and furnish your arms and legs to God as instruments of what is right. Remember, sin no longer rules you, because you are no longer under the law, but under grace.

What does that mean? Shall we sin away, since we aren't under the law but under grace? No, never! Don't you know that once you pledge to something the obedience of a slave, you are really its slave as long as you keep obeying? Either you're enslaved to sin to do death's work or you're enslaved to obedience to do virtue's work. Thanks be to God! You were once slaves of sin, but then you listened with your heart to the character of teaching presented to you; so you were set free from sin and you enslaved yourselves to virtue.

I use these commonplace terms [like "slave" and "slavery"] to emphasize the weakness of your flesh. Just as you furnished your arms and legs in bondage to uncleanness and lawlessness, with lawlessness resulting, so now furnish your arms and legs in bondage to virtue, with sanctification resulting. After all, when you were slaves of sin, you were free of virtue's control. And what fruits did your labors bring back then? The kind you are now ashamed of, the kind whose end is death. But now, set free from sin and enslaved to God, the fruits of your labors are toward sanctification and their end is Life everlasting. For the wages of sin is death, but the charity of God is everlasting Life in Christ Jesus our Lord.

7

Or don't you know, brothers and sisters (since I'm speaking to people who know the law) that the law only governs a person as long as that person lives? The wife with a husband over her is bound to her man by law. But once the man dies, she ceases to be governed by the law concerning her husband; so that while her husband lives she will be called an adulteress if she becomes another man's wife. But if the man dies, she's free of the law, so that she isn't an adulteress for being another man's wife. Which means, my brothers and sisters, that you also were rendered dead to the Law, through the body of Christ, so that you could belong to another, the one raised from the dead, so that we might yield a harvest to God. When we were in the flesh, you see, the ravages of sin occasioned by the Law were operating in all our members, yielding a harvest of death. But now, having died, we are out of the purview of the Law that kept us down, so that we are slaves in the newness of the spirit and not in the ancientness of the written word.

What shall we say then? That the Law is sinful? No, never! But I would never have known sin if not for the Law: I wouldn't have known what covetousness was if the Law hadn't said, "You are not to covet." But sin, taking its cue from the commandment, put all kinds of covetousness to work within me. After all, without law, sin is dead. I once lived without law, but when the commandment came along, sin came to life—while I died, and in my case the life-bringing commandment ended up bringing death, because sin took the commandment as an occasion to delude me and used it to do me in. So that the Law, basically, is holy, and the commandments are holy, just and good.

So then it was this goodness meant my death? No, never! It was sin that, wishing to look like sin, used goodness to do the work of death in me, so that sin might reach the height of sinfulness with the command-ments' aid.

We know, after all, that the Law is spiritual, while I am fleshly, sold out to sin. Why, I don't even recognize my own actions: what I want to do, I don't do; what I hate doing, I do. Now if I'm doing what I don't want to do, I'm agreeing with the Law and saying it's right. And in that case my actions are no longer my own but those of the indwelling fault within me.

For I know that what dwells in me—that is, in my flesh—is not good. Wanting what's good, it seems, comes naturally, but doing it does not. So I don't do the good thing I intend; instead, the bad thing I want to avoid is what I do. But if I'm doing what I don't want to do, my actions are no longer my own but those of the indwelling fault within me. In fact I find that it is a law for me, when I want to do the right thing, that evil comes naturally. I more than consent to the Law in the inner me. But then I see another law in my veins battling against the law of my mind and taking me captive under the law of sin, the one in my veins. What a miserable wretch I am! Who will snatch me from the clutches of this body of death? Give thanks to God through Jesus Christ our Lord! So that's how it is, even for me: with my mind I am bound to the law of God, with my flesh I am bound to the law of sin.

8

Now then: no condemnation awaits those in Christ Jesus, because the law of the spirit of true Life in Christ Jesus freed you from the law of sin and death. To make up for the impotence of the law, the place where it was weakened by the flesh, God sent His own son in the fleshly likeness of sin and then sentenced sin in person to die for its sins, so that the stipulations of the Law might be fulfilled for you who go by its spirit without going by it physically. Those who go by the flesh have their minds on the flesh; those who go by the spirit have their minds on the spirit. Having your mind on the flesh is death, while having your mind on the spirit is life and peace. Therefore, worrying about physical factors is inimical to God: it's not subordinate to the law of God, it can't be. So those who are on the physical level can't please God.

But you are not on the physical but on the spiritual level, as long as a holy spirit dwells within you. If someone doesn't have the spirit of Christ, that person isn't Christ's. If Christ is in you, the body is a corpse, dead for sin's sake, but the spirit is a life lived for justice's sake. And if the spirit of the one who raised Jesus from the dead is housed within you, He who raised Jesus from the dead will also make your mortal bodies alive with the indwelling spirit within you.

There you have it, brothers and sisters: we have an obligation, and not to the flesh to live by the flesh; because if you live by the flesh you will die. But if with the spirit's aid you kill off your body's way of acting on its own, you will truly live. Remember, all those who are led by the spirit of God are God's sons and daughters. You didn't receive an enslaving spirit dragging you backwards into fear, you received the spirit of adoption by God, the spirit in which we cry "Papa! Father!" This spirit corroborates the testimony of our own spirit that we are children of God. And if we are children, the inheritance is also ours: the inheritance of God, which we will share with Christ, if we're willing to suffer with him in order to be glorified with him too.

In fact I would say that the sufferings of this present time don't count beside the glory waiting to be revealed to us. The expectations of the created world are turned upon the revelation of the son of God. Creation, it seems, has been taken over by emptiness, not willingly but because its superior put it in that position, with the hope that that same creation will be set free from the slavery of decay into the glorious freedom of being children of God. For we know that the whole of creation hasn't stopped groaning and laboring together as one right up to the present day. And not just creation: we too, having had a sample of the spirit, groan amongst ourselves as we wait for the adoption as God's children that will ransom our bodies [from this captivity].

In fact, it is hope that saved us. Now if what you hope for is in front of you, that isn't hope. How can you "hope" for what's before your eyes? But if we hope for something that is out of sight, we keep steadily waiting for it.

In just such fashion the spirit compensates for our weakness: of course we don't really know how to pray correctly, but the holy spirit itself intercedes for us with groans unutterable; and the Examiner of hearts knows what the spirit has in mind, because it is God's will that he should plead on behalf of the holy ones.

Now we know that for those who love God everything works to the good, those that are called according to God's plan. Because those whom He knew from the first, He also chose in advance to be modeled on the image of His son, making him the firstborn among many brothers and sisters. Those whom He chose in advance, He also called; those whom He called, he also cleared of guilt. And those whom He cleared of guilt He also glorified.

What shall we say in the face of all this? If God is for us, who is against us? If He didn't spare His own son but delivered him up for our sakes, how will He not lavish upon us, besides His son, everything else as well? Who will bring charges against God's chosen ones? It's God who declares them innocent; who will condemn them? Christ, who died or rather was resurrected, it is he who is on God's right hand and who pleads our case. Who will come between us and Christ's love? Suffering, anguish, persecution, hunger, lack of clothing, danger, the sword? As it is written:

> *For your sake we are slain the whole day through,*
> *We count as sheep for the slaughter.*

But amidst all this we win out because of the one who loved us. Indeed I am convinced that neither death nor life nor angels nor dominions, nor the present nor the future nor miracles nor the heights nor the depths nor anything else in creation will ever be able to come between us and the divine love found in Christ Jesus our Lord.

9

I'm not lying but speaking Christ's truth, corroborated by the holy spirit speaking in my conscience, when I say that my heart is full of tremendous grief and constant pain. I would have prayed for myself to be barred from Christ forever if that would have helped my brothers and sisters who are of the same stock as I physically, namely Israelites, the ones to whom the sonship of God and the glory and the covenants and the lawgiving and the worship and the promises belong, from whom the patriarchs came, even Christ being one of them physically, God be blessed who is above all things forever, amen.

Now the word of God cannot possibly have failed. It seems that not all who are *from* Israel are *of* Israel, nor are all the children of Abraham his "seed," since it says "Through Isaac a race shall be named for you." That means it isn't Abraham's physical children that are children of God, it's the children of the promise that count as his "seed," because the words of the promise say "I will come back this time next year, and Sarah will have a son."

That's not the only example. There's also Rebecca, whose children were both sired by one man, Isaac our forefather: with them still unborn, and not having done anything good or bad—so that God's plan according to His choice would prevail—it was said to her, based not on her good deeds but His own decree, that "the greater shall be the slave of the lesser," as it is written: "I showed Jacob love and rejected Esau."

What shall we say then? Not that there is injustice on God's part, surely? No, never! It is as He says to Moses: "I will pity whomever I please and have compassion on whomever I like." So that's how it is: it's not a matter of our wanting or striving but of God's mercy. It's as the scripture says to Pharaoh: "I have raised you high just so I can make you an example of My power and spread My name through all the earth." That's how it is: He pities whomever He pleases and hardens whatever heart He chooses.

"Well then," you say, "how can a person still be blamed? After all, who can withstand His will?" But just a minute: you there, who are you to talk back to God? Is it for the sculpture to say to the sculptor, "Why did you make me like this?" Or doesn't the potter have the right to use his clay to make, from the same pile, one pot for elegant purposes and another for the homeliest uses? Because if God, even when He decided to show His anger and display His power, still had great patience in putting up with the vessels of wrath intended for destruction, doesn't He also mean to display His abundant glory upon the vessels of His mercy that He prepared for glory, namely us whom He summoned from among Jews and Gentiles alike? As it says in the Book of Hosea:

> *I will call a people not my own, my people;*
> *And the unloved, beloved.*
> *And it will be in the same place where they were told*
> *"You are no people of mine"*
> *That they shall be called children of a living God.*

And Isaiah shouts for Israel:

> *Though the numbers of sons and daughters of Israel be as the sands*
> *of the sea,*
> *A handful will be saved.*
> *Completing and condensing, the Lord will settle accounts upon*
> *the earth.*

And as Isaiah says earlier:

> *If the Lord of Heaven's Armies had not left some seeds of us alive,*
> *We would have ended up like Sodom, we would have been like*
> *Gomorrah.*

What shall we say then? That peoples who had not sought good standing were put in good standing, a good standing based on faith; while Israel, trying to achieve good standing legally, couldn't keep up with the law. Why was that? Because they weren't going on faith, but supposedly on their good deeds, so they knocked against "the stone of offense," as it says:

> *I hereby set down in Zion a stone of offense and a rock of stumbling;*
> *Those who place their faith in it will not be sorry.*

10

Brothers and sisters, all the good will in my heart goes out to them, [my fellow Jews,] as also my prayers go to God for their salvation. I will say this for them, that they have a godly zeal: their zeal just isn't guided by knowledge. Knowing nothing of God's justice, they've tried to establish their own justice and have been insubordinate to the justice of God. Christ is what the law aims at: for every believer to be on the right side of [God's] justice.

Moses, after all, describes the good standing based on the Law, saying: "The person who does these things shall be given life by them." But the good standing based on faith speaks as follows: "Do not say in your heart, Who will ascend into heaven?"—that is, to bring Christ down—or

"Who will descend into the depths?"—that is, to raise Christ from the dead. What instead does it say? "It is close to you, this word: in your mouth and in your heart." That ["word"] means the word of faith that we proclaim. Because if you admit with your lips that "Jesus is Lord" and believe in your heart that God raised him from the dead, you will be saved. The belief of the heart puts you in the right, while the profession of the mouth brings salvation, since scripture says, "Everyone who places their faith on him will not be sorry." You see, there is no difference between Jew and Greek, there is just one Lord of everyone, sharing his wealth with all who call upon him, since "All who call upon the name of the Lord will be saved."

"But," you say, "[as for the Jews,] how could they call on his name without believing in him first, and how could they believe in him without hearing about him, and how could they hear about him without someone bringing the word, and how could they bring the word if not enough people have been sent out? Scripture is right: 'How precious' indeed 'are the feet of those who bring the good news'!"

But it's not as if all who heard the good news accepted it. Isaiah is also right: "Lord, who believed through hearing us?" Belief does come from hearing, and hearing comes through the word of Christ.

And furthermore, I say, did they really not hear? I would say rather that

> *Across the whole earth their voice has gone forth,*
> *And their words as far as people dwell.*

And I would add, didn't Israel already know? It's Moses who originally says:

> *I shall make you jealous of a non-people,*
> *Toward a senseless people I will stir your envy.*

Isaiah is even so bold as to say,

> *I will be found among those not seeking me,*
> *Being clear to those not asking me questions.*

To Israel he says:

> *All day I spread my hands out*
> *Toward a people who believe nothing and contradict everything.*

11

But wait: did God reject His own people? I should hope not! I too am an Israelite, of the seed of Abraham, of the tribe of Benjamin. No, God did not reject His people whom He had previously recognized. Or don't you know what scripture says about Elijah, how he puts in a word with God against Israel?

> *Lord, they killed Your prophets,*
> *They uprooted Your altars.*
> *I am the only one left*
> *And they want my life.*

But what is the divine response to that?

> *I saved [for myself] seven thousand men*
> *Who didn't bend their knees before Baal.*

In the same way, in the present instance a handful have come through according to the selection of God's grace: by His grace, meaning not through their good deeds; or else that wouldn't be grace any more.

What does that mean? That what Israel looked for, it never got hold of. A chosen few got hold of it; the rest were too stone-hearted, as it is written:

> *God laid upon them a darkening spirit*
> *To keep their eyes from seeing and their ears from hearing,*
> *From that day to this.*

And David says:

> *Let their banquet-table become a snare and an entrapment,*
> *To their confusion and punishment.*

Let their eyes be too darkened to see
And let their backs be always bent over.

But wait. Did they stumble so as to fall [and never get up]? I should hope not! Rather, by their transgression, salvation came to the Gentiles so that the Jews would then want it for themselves. Now if their transgression enriched the world and their diminution enriched the Gentiles, what richness when they come into their own!

I say to you the Gentiles: however much I may be an apostle to the Gentiles, I consider my service glorious if ever by any means I can make my own kind jealous [of salvation] and save a few of them that way. Because if their act of rejection led to world reconciliation, what will their act of acceptance do—will it be anything less than death brought back to life again?

If the first bit tastes sacred, the rest of the dough will be the same. From a holy root, holy branches. And maybe some branches did break off, and maybe you, the wild olive, were grafted on there and tapped into the richness of the true olive's roots; but don't laugh at the fallen branches. Remember in your smugness that you are built upon the roots and the roots are not built upon you. You may say, "These branches were broken off so I could be grafted on," and you may be right: their lack of faith broke them off, while your faith has put you there. But don't be too proud, watch out. If God didn't spare the original branches, it's possible He also won't spare you. You should see in all this both God's goodness and His severity: severity toward those who have fallen away, God's goodness towards you, if you also persist in goodness; otherwise, you too will be cut down, and the others, if their lack of faith doesn't prove permanent, will be grafted right back on. God certainly has the power to graft them back on. After all, if you were lopped off from your own natural wild olive and grafted, out of line with nature, onto the fine olive, how much easier it will be to graft those others back onto the true olive which is naturally their own.

I don't wish, brothers and sisters, to withhold from you this secret, so that you don't get lost in your own speculations: this partial resistance we see in Israel has come about so that the Gentiles may come into their own, so that all Israel can be saved. Thus scripture says:

From Zion the rescuer will come;

He will remove the impieties heaped upon Jacob.
And this shall be my covenant with them:
That I will take away their sins.

So according to the good word the Jews may be enemies towards you,
but according to God's choice they are still beloved because of their
forefathers: there is no taking back the blessings and calling of God.
Once you had no belief in God, but now you have been shown mercy
through their disbelief; similarly, they didn't believe in the mercy shown
you, so that now it's their turn to be shown mercy. You see, God has
trapped us all in our unbelief, because He wants to have mercy on us all.

Oh, the depths of the wealth and wisdom and knowledge
    of God!
How unexaminable His decisions,
How untraceable His paths!
Who ever knew the mind of the Lord?
Who ever acted as an adviser of His?
Who ever gave Him something
And is entitled to be paid back?
Since from Him and through Him and toward Him is how
    everything goes;
Let His be the glory for all ages indeed.

12

So I beseech you, brothers and sisters, by the mercy of God to deliver
your bodies up to God as a living sacrifice, holy and pleasing to Him,
your conscious way of worshiping. And don't follow the outlines of the
present age, but be so completely changed by the renewal of your mind
as to ask what God's will is, what is good and acceptable and perfect.

For one thing, I am telling everyone among you, by means of the grace
bestowed on me, not to have grand self-conceits beyond a proper self-
conception, but to aim for a conception that shows perception, each
according to the measure of faith that God apportioned you. You see,
just as in one body we have many organs, and all the organs don't have
the same function, in the same way, there's many of us, but we are one
body in Christ. So we are all parts of one another, having such talents as

we have been graced with, each one differently: perhaps showing the proportions of your belief in prophecy, perhaps serving in [community] services, perhaps teaching in [religious] education, perhaps lending your voice to bolster the community; for those who dispense charity, acting natural; for those who preside, acting responsible; for those who remember the needy, acting cheerful.

Love is no empty show. Keep on despising meanness and clinging to goodness, living in brotherly love with each other, honoring others above ourselves, not shirking responsibility, being aflame with the spirit, being slaves of the Lord, rejoicing in hope, enduring amid troubles, persisting in prayer, sharing to meet the needs of the holy ones, making the effort to be hospitable. Bless your persecutors, bless and do not curse them. Rejoice with the happy, weep with the sorrowful. Always treat each other as equals, don't get the idea that you're too good to mix with common folk. Don't get lost in your own cleverness. Never return evil for evil toward anyone; have the best intentions for all the world to see. In so far as it's up to you, be at peace with all the world. Getting revenge is no good, dear friends, leave that to the wrath of God, as scripture says:

Settling accounts is My business:
I will give what is due, says the Lord.

Instead, [as scripture also says,]

If your enemy is hungry, give him bread;
If he's thirsty, give him water.
So doing you will heap coals upon his head.

Don't let evil conquer you: let it be you in your goodness who conquer evil.

13

Every soul amongst you must be obedient to superior authorities. Remember, there is no authority except from God, and the existing authorities are put there by God. That means the rebel against authority is going against God's plan, and those who do so are writing their own sentence. Those in power, after all, are a threat not to good deeds but to evil deeds, so if you want to have nothing to fear from the authorities, just do good, and they will have nothing but praise for you. You see, authority is God's servant for your own good. If you do evil, on the other hand, watch out; there's a reason why it carries a sword: it is also God's avenging servant, visiting His wrath upon the evildoer. Therefore obedience is a necessity, not just because of God's wrath but because of your own conscience. By the same token, pay your taxes: those who faithfully do just that are public servants of God. Pay everyone what's owed them, tax for tax, toll for toll, respect for respect, honor for honor.

The only debt you should owe to anyone is that of loving one another: if you love your fellow man, you've fulfilled the law, since everything about how "You are not to commit adultery, you are not to murder, you are not to steal, you are not to covet" and any other commands you could name is all summed up in the words "You are to love your neighbor as yourself." Love doesn't do evil to a neighbor; therefore, love is what makes the law complete.

Keep in mind what times these are, because it's already time for you to be roused from your slumbers: already salvation is nearer than when we first came to the faith. The night is far gone, the day is approaching. Then let us put the works of darkness aside and put on the armor of light. Let us walk decently as if in the light of day and not go in for wild parties and drinking-bouts, sleeping around and debauchery, and jealousy and ill will. Instead, be clothed in the Lord Jesus Christ and don't let your body's desires lead you around.

14

If someone is weak in the faith, have consideration, don't cause them mental perplexities. One person confidently eats anything he likes, another has qualms about eating anything but vegetables. The former shouldn't put down the latter because of what he doesn't eat, while the latter shouldn't condemn the former because of what he does eat, since God is on his side. Who are you to scold the servants that aren't your own? They have the same master to stand or fall by as you do. And stand they will, since the Lord has power to make them stand.

[To take another example,] one person attaches importance to this day or that day, while another person's observance is the same for every day.

Let each find fulfillment in his own conception. The person who observes particular days does it for the Lord. The person who eats freely does that for the Lord too: it's his way of thanking God. The person who avoids certain things likewise avoids them for the Lord and also gives thanks to God. None of us live for ourselves, none of us die for ourselves. If we live, we live for the Lord. If we die, we die for the Lord; so whether we live or die, we are the Lord's. That's why Christ died and came back to life: to be Lord of both dead and living.

You there, how can you condemn your brother? And you, how can you put your brother down like that? We shall all be brought before the bench of God, as scripture says:

> *I am alive, says the Lord:*
> *every knee will bend before Me*
> *and every tongue will acknowledge God.*

In short, each of us will have to make our own accounting to God.

So let's stop judging each other. Instead, use your judgment to avoid giving offense or creating quandaries for your brother. Now I know and have confidence in Lord Jesus that nothing is unclean of itself, except to someone who considers it unclean, in which case it is unclean—for him. If what you eat troubles your brother's mind, right there you're not going by the rule of love. Don't let your diet be the undoing of someone whom Christ died to save. So avoid letting your goodness be misinterpreted. Remember, the kingdom of God isn't eating and drinking, it's right living and peace and joy in the spirit of holiness. Whoever is Christ's slave in this matter is someone God can be happy with and the rest of the world can trust.

In short, pursue the ends of peace and of building each other up. Don't let dietary considerations undo the work of God. Everything may be clean, but it's evil for the person who eats it in an offensive spirit. Better not to eat the meat or drink the wine or whatever else your brother is offended by. As for the faith that you have, keep that between yourself and God. The person is in luck who doesn't condemn himself for what he samples. On the other hand, the person with doubts about something who eats it anyway is guilty, because he isn't acting on his faith, and any failure to act on faith is a sin.

15

So it is for the strong to bear with the weaknesses of the less strong and not just please ourselves. Let each do what will please his neighbor with good and constructive intentions. Christ, after all, didn't please himself either: as scripture says, "The insults of those who insult you have fallen on me." What was written back then was written for our edification now, so that, by means of our own endurance and the consolation of the scriptures, we may hold fast to our hopes. May the God of endurance and consolation grant it to you to be united in spirit with each other in Jesus Christ's way, so that unanimously as with one mouth you may glorify God the Father of our Lord Jesus Christ.

For that reason, take each other in, just as Christ took you in with a view to God's glory. Because Christ, I tell you, acted as the servant of Mosaic law so as not to make a liar of God, so as to confirm the promises given to the Jewish patriarchs while giving the other nations cause to glorify God for His mercy, as scripture says:

> *For this I will acknowledge you among the nations*
> *And sing hymns to your name.*

And it says further:

> *Give praise, all you nations, to the Lord,*
> *And let all peoples honor him.*

And also Isaiah says:

> *He shall be the root of Jesse,*
> *And the one who arises to rule the nations,*
> *On whom nations put their hopes.*

May the God of hope fill you with all joy and peace to go with your faith, so that you may overflow with hope in the power of holy spirit.

Now I have confidence, my brothers and sisters, in relation to you that you yourselves are full of goodness and well along in all matters of knowledge, fully able to counsel one another. Yet I have written you rather boldly in some places as a reminder to you on account of God's having given me the grace to be Christ's delegate sent to the Gentiles, the celebrant of the good word of God, so that the offering of the Gentiles might be deemed acceptable, sanctified in holy spirit. That gives me reason to boast in Christ Jesus when it comes to the things of God. I won't even venture to say what Christ hasn't done through me to bring the Gentiles into line, with words and deeds, with the power of signs and wonders, with God's spirit in me strong enough for me to carry the good news of Christ from Jerusalem all the way round to Illyricum, my policy in these matters being to bring the good news to where Christ's name was never heard, and not to build on other people's groundwork. As the scripture says,

> *Those who weren't given the word about him will see for themselves,*
> *And those who have not heard will understand.*

It's because of that that I've been prevented so many times from coming to see you. But now that my work is done in this part of the world, and I still have the desire to come see you after all these years, I'm hoping that when I travel to Spain I can visit you passing through and you can help me with provisions for my journey that way after I have first had the fulfillment of seeing you.

Right now I'm traveling to Jerusalem to bring assistance to the holy ones there: Macedonia and Achaea have been so kind as to take up a collection for the poor among the Jerusalem faithful, on the grounds that they owe something to those people. After all, if the Gentiles took a share of their spiritual gifts, they owe it to them to look out for their physical needs as well. So once I finish with that and sign over this bounty to them, I'll be off for Spain, stopping on the way to see you. I know that when I come I will be coming to you in the fullness of Christ's blessing.

I'm asking you, brothers and sisters, in the name of our Lord Jesus Christ and by the love of the spirit, to stand by me in my fight with your prayers on my behalf to God that I may slip through the fingers of the unbelievers in Judea and that this assistance of mine to Jerusalem may prove most welcome to the holy ones there. That way I can come to you joyfully and, by God's leave, share some relaxation with you. The God of peace be with all of you, let it be so.

16

I'd like to introduce Phoebe, our sister [in the faith], who has been of service to the assembly in Cenchreae [and is bringing this letter]. You are to give her, [as a sister] in the Lord, a reception worthy of the holy ones and come through for her in any matter where she needs you, since she herself has come through for many others including me.

Say hello to Priscilla and Aquila, my fellow-workers in Christ Jesus, who put their necks on the line in defense of my life, to whom I send not only my own thanks, but those of all the Gentile congregations as well. Also say hello to the group [that meets] at their house. Say hello to my dear friend Epaenetus, who was our first score for Christ in Asia. Say hello to Maria, who has worked so hard for you. Say hello to Andronicus and Junias, who are family of mine and fellow prisoners too, noted among the apostles: they were in Christ even before I was.

Say hello to Ampliatus my dear friend in the Lord. Say hello to Urbanus, our fellow-worker in Christ, and Stachys, my dear friend. Say hello to Apelles, trusty in Christ. Say hello to the people from Aristoboulos's house. Say hello to Herodion, who is family of mine. Say hello to those of Narcissus's people who are in the Lord. Say hello to Tryphaenas and Tryphosa, who work hard in the Lord. Say hello to dear Persis, who did so much work in the Lord. Say hello to Rufus, chosen in the Lord, and his mother, who is really mine too. Say hello to Asyncritus, Phlegon, Hermes, Patrobas, Hermas and our other brothers who are with him. Say hello to Philologos and Julias, Nereas and his sister, and Olympas and the other holy ones with her. Greet each other with the kiss of holiness. All the congregations of Christ send their greetings to you.

And now I ask you, brothers and sisters, to watch out for people who cause divisions and disturbances against the teaching you were taught: stay away from those people. People like that aren't slaves of Christ our Lord but of their own bellies, and by talking nice and being well-spoken they fool innocent-hearted people. Now it has gotten around to everyone how loyal you are, and that makes me rejoice for you, and I want you to be experts in goodness and inexperienced in evil. The God of peace will smash Satan to the ground at your feet, and soon. The grace of our Lord Jesus be with you.

My fellow-worker Timothy says hello, and so do Lucius, Jason and Sosipater, who are part of my family. (I, Tertius, the person taking this letter down, send you my greetings in the Lord.) Greetings to you from Gaius, who has been host to me and the whole assembly; greetings also from Erastus the city treasurer and his brother Quartus.

To Him who can make you stand tall according to the good word I have brought and the message of Jesus Christ, in line with the revelation of a secret denied to the endless ages but now made public through the writings of the Prophets and communicated by the command of the everlasting God to all nations to bring them to the obedience that comes from faith—to Him, the one wise God, through Jesus Christ, be the glory for ever, let it be so.

The First Letter from Paul to the Community in

Corinth

1

From Paul, called to the apostleship of Christ Jesus through God's will, and Brother Sosthenes;

To the assembly of God in Corinth, made holy in Christ Jesus called to holiness, together with all who call upon the name of our Lord Jesus Christ in every place, theirs and ours;

Grace to you and peace from God our Father and Lord Jesus Christ.

I thank my God continually for you, seeing the grace of God given you in Christ Jesus, how you came to share his wealth in every way in all kinds of words and knowledge, while the witnessed word of Christ was imparted to you so firmly that you have every gift you need as you await the revelation of our Lord Jesus Christ, who will also confirm your blamelessness on the day of our Lord Jesus Christ. Through God you were called into the fellowship of His son Jesus Christ our Lord, and God keeps His word.

I am asking you, brothers and sisters, in the name of our Lord Jesus Christ, to be in agreement, all of you, and not to have divisions among you, but to perfect yourselves in being of one mind and opinion. In fact, I was informed about you, my brothers and sisters, by some of Chloe's people, to the effect that you have factions. What I mean is that each of you says, "I'm on Paul's side," "I'm on Apollos's side," "I'm on Peter's side," "I'm on Christ's side." Can Christ be so fragmented? Was Paul crucified for you, were you washed in the name of Paul? Thank God I didn't baptize any of you except Crispus and Gaius, so no one can say they were washed in my name. (Well, I also baptized Stephen's household, but beyond that I don't think I baptized anyone else.) Christ didn't send me to wash people but to bring the good word, and not with cleverness of language, so as not to trivialize the cross of Christ.

For the meaning of the cross is utter nonsense to those who are lost forever, but to us who are saved it is the power of God. After all, it is written:

> *I shall wipe out the wisdom of the wise,*
> *And set aside the cleverness of the clever.*

Where *are* the wise? Where are the legal experts? Where are the great debaters of our age? Didn't God already make a dunce of the world's wisdom? Since, according to God's wisdom, the world didn't recognize God because it was too wise, God decided to use the very foolishness of His doctrine to save those who placed their faith in it. Now Jews always want to see signs from heaven, while Greeks want to see wisdom. Then we come bringing the word of Christ crucified, which is a sticking-point with the Jews* and utter nonsense to the Gentiles, though to you who have been called, Jews and Greeks alike, it is Christ, God's power and God's wisdom. That's because the foolishness of God is wiser than all human beings and the weakness of God is stronger than all human beings.

For instance, brothers and sisters, look at who among you has been called: most of you aren't scholars by nature, most of you aren't powerful, you aren't mostly from the best families. But God chose the foolishness of the world to put the wise to shame, and God chose the weakness of the world to put the strong to shame, and God chose the low-born nothings of the world, the nobodies, to replace the somebodies, so that no living creature would act too proud before God. It is because of Him that you are in Christ Jesus, who was born imbued with wisdom for us from God, wisdom and innocence and holiness and redemption, so that, as it is written: "Let the boaster boast in the Lord."

2

Likewise, when I came to you, brothers and sisters, I didn't come with any great excess of rhetoric or learning in announcing to you the mystery of God. After all, I didn't think I knew anything more than any of you except for Jesus Christ, and a crucified Jesus Christ at that. And I have

---

* Being crucified makes their vaunted Messiah look like the scum of the earth, as well as a dismal failure at leading his people to the expected Messianic victory. Besides, it says in the Bible that "anyone hanged on a tree is accursed" (Deuteronomy 21:23).

come through a lot of weakness and fear and trembling on my way to you. And my words and my message didn't consist in persuasive, wise-sounding phrases but in a show of spirit and power, so that your faith wouldn't be in human wisdom but in God's power.

We also talk of "wisdom" among the spiritually advanced, but we don't mean the wisdom of the present age or of the ephemeral powers that rule this present age: we mean God's wisdom, kept hidden as a secret, which God planned out before all ages for our glory, and which none of the rulers of the present age recognized. Certainly if they'd recognized it, they wouldn't have crucified the Lord of glory. But it's as scripture says:

> *Eye never saw and ear never heard,*
> *And into human heart there never entered*
> *What God has prepared for those who love Him.*

Our revelations came from God through the spirit, since the spirit plumbs all depths, even those of God. What human being has ever known what it is to be human if it isn't the human spirit within [that knows that]? Likewise, matters of God can only be known by means of the spirit of God. But that's what we were given: not a spirit of this world but a spirit coming from God, so that we would appreciate the gifts God has graced us with, the same ones we keep speaking of, in words informed not by worldly wisdom but by spirit, putting spiritual matters in spiritual terms. The purely material person has no use for the spirit of God: it's all nonsense to him and there's no way he can understand it, because it has to be discerned spiritually. The spiritual person, on the other hand, discerns everything and is seen through by nobody. As it says, "Who ever knew the Lord's mind, who ever instructed him?" And yet we possess the mind of Christ.

3

As for me, brothers and sisters, I haven't previously been able to speak to you as spiritual persons but only as people on the physical level, babies in Christ. I gave you milk, not solid food, because you weren't ready. As a matter of fact, you still aren't ready now, you're still on the physical level. Any place where you have rivalry and factions among you, aren't you acting purely physical and conducting yourself like humanity in general? Where you have one person saying, "I'm on Paul's side," and another saying, "I'm on Apollos's side," aren't you being all too human?

So what is Apollos? What is Paul? Servants who brought you to the faith, each doing the job the Lord gave us. I planted, Apollos watered, but God made it grow. So that neither the planter nor the waterer matters, but only God who makes things grow. Planter and waterer are all the same, and each will receive his own reward for his own labors. You see, we are God's fellow-workers, while you are God's farm, what God has built up.

By the grace of God given to me, like a wise architect I laid a foundation. Someone else can then build upon it, as long as each one watches how he builds. That means no one can lay another foundation besides the existing one, which is Jesus Christ. Perhaps what someone has built on the foundation is of gold, silver, and precious stones, or perhaps it is of wood, grass, and reeds; but everyone's work will be seen for what it is: that will all be made clear on the Great Day, since the fire will reveal it, and the fire will test each one's work to see what it's made of. If someone's work is still standing the way he built it, he will be rewarded; if someone's work burns down, he loses—but he himself will still be saved, saved by the fire, as it were. Don't you know you are God's temple and the spirit of God lives in you? If someone tears down the temple of God, God will tear him down too, because the temple of God is holy, and that's what you are.

Don't any of you fool yourselves: if any of you think you're "wise" in the current sense, get dumb if you ever want to be wise. The wisdom of this world is nonsense to God, whom scripture describes as "the one who catches the crafty in their tricks," also saying, "The Lord knows the thoughts of the wise and how shallow they are." Which means no one in the world should be too proud: because everything is yours—Paul, Apollos, Peter, the world, life, death, the present, the future—it's all yours, and you are Christ's, and Christ is God's.

4

Let people think of us as assistants of Christ and managers of God's secrets. Now where I come from, managers face questioning eventually, to see if they turn out to be trustworthy. Now I couldn't care less if I am judged by you or any human court. Nor will I judge myself. In fact, I don't have anything on myself, but that doesn't clear me: my judge is the Lord. Which means don't make any premature judgments till the Lord comes who will illuminate the dark hidden places and bring to light the intentions in our hearts. And then each will get his praise from God.

I have put all this, brothers and sisters, in terms of myself and Apollos for your benefit, so you can take a lesson from us in sticking to the letter: that way no one among you will get inflated above the rest and put down his fellow. Who says you're so special anyway? What do you own that wasn't given you? If it was given to you, why do you put on airs as if it wasn't given to you? You're already full, you already found riches, without our help you already won the kingdom. Would that you *had* won the kingdom! That would make us kings as well as you. As it is, I think God has singled us apostles out to be the very lowest, marked for death, so as to make a spectacle of us before the world, angels and mortals alike. We are fools for Christ's sake, you are wise in Christ. We are weak, you are strong. You are glorious, we are unworthy of respect. Even now we go hungry and thirsty and without clothing and undergo punishments and disruptions and wear ourselves out working with our hands. They insult us, and we bless them; they persecute us, and we put up with it. They slander us, and we are supportive of them. We've become scapegoats for the world, everybody's floorsweepings, and so we remain.

I don't write this to embarrass you, but as a reminder to you, who are like dear children to me. Because you may have tens of thousands of pupils in Christ, but few founding fathers, and I fathered you in Christ Jesus by bringing you the good word. So my advice to you is to become imitators of me. For that reason I have sent to you Timothy, my beloved child, trusty in the Lord, to remind you of my ways in Christ, the same as I teach everywhere in all the assemblies. My not coming to you personally has occasioned much empty-headed speculation among some of you, but I *will* come to you, and soon, if the Lord wills, and then the inflated ones can show not how great their words are, but how great their power is; because that's where the kingdom of God lies: in power, not in words. What do you want? Shall I come to you as a big stick or in love and a spirit of gentleness?

5

Now then. Word reaches me of a filthy thing among you, and such filth as you don't even see among the pagans, a man actually taking up with his father's wife. And are you even proud of it, instead of being horrified and casting out from your midst the author of such a deed? Now I may be physically absent but I am present in spirit, and being present I have already pronounced judgment on the one who did something like that. In the name of our Lord Jesus, with all of you assembled and my spirit present with the power of our Lord Jesus, cast such a person out and let the devil take his flesh; with luck, his spirit can still be saved on the Day of the Lord.

It isn't good, your boasting and bragging. Don't you know a little leaven renders the whole batch un-kosher? Clear away the old leaven, so that you'll be a new batch, now that you're kosher for Passover. And in fact Christ was sacrificed for our Passover, so now we no longer celebrate it with the old leaven or the leaven of evil and treachery but with unleavened sincerity and truth.

I wrote you in my letter not to deal with whoremongers, meaning not the whoremongers of the general world—or the greedy or the extortionists or the idol-worshipers of the general world, for that matter—because then you would have to exit completely from the world. What I wrote you to do was to break off relations if any so-called "brother" is promiscuous or greedy or an idol-worshiper or a character assassin or a drunk or an extortionist; don't even eat a meal with such a person. After all, is it up to me to bring the outside world to justice? But will you *not* regulate those within? "Cast out the evildoer from your midst."

6

Can any of you who has a score to settle with a brother be so shameless as to have the matter heard by a lawless court and not by the holy ones? Or don't you know that the holy ones will judge the whole world? And that if you are to be the judges of the world, those lower courts are beneath you? Don't you know that we will judge the angels? But you can't judge things here on earth! So if you have law-cases here on earth, you put the very people in charge who count for nothing among your number? I say to your shame, is no one among you wise enough to render judgment in a case involving your brothers? So instead, brother files suit with brother in the court of the unbelievers?

To be sure, it's already a step backward for you to have court-cases like that amongst you. Why don't you just suffer the wrong? Why don't you just live with being cheated? Instead, you yourselves cheat and do wrong, including to your brothers and sisters.

Don't you know that lawless people won't inherit God's kingdom? Don't fool yourselves: no whoremongers and no idol-worshipers, no adulterers, no decadent people, no man-lovers, no thieves, no greedy people, no drunkards, no slanderers, and no extortionists will inherit any kingdom of God. And some of you were people like that. But you've been cleansed now, you've been made holy now, you've been cleared now in the name of the Lord Jesus Christ and in the spirit of our God.

Maybe "I can do whatever I want," but not everything is advisable to do. Maybe I can do whatever I want, but I don't want something doing whatever it wants with me. "Food is made for bellies, and bellies for food"—all right, but God will make an end to both, and in any event the body is *not* for whoring but for the Lord, and the Lord is for the body. God raised the Lord and by His power will raise us too. Don't you know that your bodies are parts of Christ's body? Shall I take part of Christ's body and make it part of a whore's body? God forbid! Don't you know that if you take up with a whore, you are one with her in body? That's what it says: "The two shall become one flesh." Whereas if you stick with the Lord, you are one with him in spirit.

Run from promiscuity. Any other sin a person commits is outside his body, but by illicit sex acts a person sins against his own body. Or don't you know that your body is a temple of the holy spirit within you, given to you by God, and that you don't belong to yourselves? No, you were bought for a price. Then make your bodies glorify God.

7

To answer what you wrote me last, the ideal for a man would be never to touch a woman. But what with the temptations of whoredom, each man had better have his own woman and each woman her own man. The man should do his duty by his wife, as she by her husband. The woman isn't privileged to her own body, her husband is; likewise, the man isn't privileged to his own body, his wife is. Don't deprive each other, unless you make an agreement for a fixed term to use the extra time for prayer. But then get back together again: you don't want Satan to put you to the test, knowing your lack of self-control. My own opinion—this is not a command—is that I would like for everyone to be like me. But each has his own gift from God; one person like this, another like that.

I say to the unmarried and the widowed: you would do well to remain [single] like me. If they can't hold out, let them get married, because it's better to get married than to burn right up. To the married ones I command, or rather the Lord commands, that a woman is not to separate from her husband. If she does separate anyway, let her remain unmarried or make up with her husband. Also, a man is not to leave his wife.

Now the rest is me speaking and not the Lord. If one of our brothers has a wife not in the faith and she's willing to stay with him, he shouldn't leave her. If a woman has a husband not in the faith and he's willing to stay with her, she shouldn't leave her husband. Such a wife makes the unbelieving husband holier, as the believing husband also makes the unbelieving wife holier. If that weren't so, your children would be unclean, whereas in fact they are holy. But if the unbelieving spouse moves out, let them go; the believing brother or sister is not further bound in such a case: it is in peace that God has called you. After all, how can you know, wife, if you'll be able to save your husband; and how can you know, husband, if you'll be able to save your wife?

If not each with what the Lord gave you, then each as God has called you, so you should continue, and that is my instruction to all the assemblies. If someone circumcised was called, he shouldn't put it back on. If someone who has been called still has his foreskin, he shouldn't get circumcised. Circumcision means nothing, having a foreskin means nothing; what counts is keeping the commands of God. Whatever station a person was called in, there they should remain. If God called you as a slave, don't let that bother you (though if you can manage to become free, all the better). The slave with a calling in the Lord is the freedman of the Lord, as the free man with a calling is a slave of Christ. You were bought for a price. Don't become the slaves of the world. Each in the station where he was called, brothers and sisters, there let him remain as far as God is concerned.

About [celibate spiritual] "brides" I have no command from the Lord, but I'll give you my opinion as one whom the merciful Lord has rendered trustworthy: I think it's a good thing in the present necessity, it's good for a person to be that way. If you have such a bond with a woman, don't move to break it off. If your bond is broken with a woman, don't look for a wife. But if you do get married, that's not a sin, and if your former partner in celibacy gets married, she isn't sinning either. Such people will have fleshly troubles of their own, but I will let them off.

I tell you, brothers and sisters, time is short. From now on, those with wives had better act as if they had none, mourners as if they weren't mourning, the happy as if they were not rejoicing, buyers as if they didn't own, and those who use the world as if they weren't making full use of it; because this form of the world is passing away.

I would like you to be free of worries. The unmarried man worries about the Lord's business, how to make the Lord happy. After he marries, he worries about the world's business, how to make his wife happy. So he's divided. The unmarried woman and the "spiritual bride" also worry about the Lord's business, how to be holy in body and spirit. But after she marries she worries about the world's business, how to make her husband happy. I say this for your benefit, not to put a collar around your necks, but to make you decorous and well-grounded in the Lord, without distractions.

If anyone thinks he's being unfair to his spiritual bride, and she's not getting any younger, then if that's how things must go for her, let her do what she wants, let them get married, there's no sin. But if another stands firm in his heart and feels no compulsion, because he has control over his own will, and it is the decision of his heart to maintain the celibate relationship, he would do well to do so. So the one who marries his "spiritual bride" does the right thing, and the one who doesn't, does even better.

A woman is bound as long as her husband lives. But if the husband has gone to his rest, she's free to marry whom she wishes, as long as she marries in the Lord. But she's better off if she just stays as she is, in my opinion. And I think I also have a spirit of God.

8

Now when it comes to meat butchered under pagan auspices,* I know

---

* Which could include most of the meat at market.

we all share an understanding. But understanding gets inflated; it's love that's constructive. If someone thinks he knows something, he still doesn't know the way he ought to know. Whereas if someone loves God, that person is known by Him.

So about eating the paganly butchered meat: we know that none of the pagan gods in the world exist and there is no God but one. And even if there are many "gods" talked of either in the sky or on earth, so that there are all these "gods" and "lords,"

> Still for us there is one God the Father,
> From whom everything comes and toward whom we are going,
> And one Lord Jesus Christ,
> Through whom came everything, and we come through him.

But not all people have this knowledge. Some, reverting to pagan customs recently discarded, may actually eat the meat in honor of the pagan deity, and their religious understanding, being weak, is corrupted. Food doesn't give us standing with God: we don't lose by not eating something, nor do we gain by what we do eat. Make sure your dietary freedom doesn't set a trap for those of weaker religious understanding. If you were seen eating a meal in a pagan temple by someone who doesn't have your insight, wouldn't his weaker understanding be influenced in the direction of eating pagan sacrifices? In such a case the weak person is being done in by your insightfulness, this brother of yours for whom Christ died. By thus wronging your brothers and sisters and hitting them hard in the weak points of their understanding, you are doing wrong to Christ. Therefore if food puts my brother in a quandary, I'll do without meat forever rather than create quandaries for a brother of mine.

9

You think I'm not my own man? I'm not a real apostle? I've never seen Jesus our Lord? Are you not the results of my work in the Lord? If I'm not an apostle for other people's purposes, I certainly am to you. You are the seal of my apostolate in the Lord.

To those who are calling me into question, my answer is this: don't we have a perfect right to ask for food and drink? Don't we have a perfect right to have a wife from among the faithful traveling round with us, as do the other apostles and the brothers of the Lord and even Peter? Only I and Barnabas are expected to work for our upkeep? Who ever went to war and paid his own wages? Who ever planted a vineyard and never ate any of the fruits? Who ever kept a herd of sheep and never drank any of its milk?

Am I just saying this in my human way, or doesn't the Law say that? After all, it says in the Law of Moses, "You are not to muzzle the threshing ox." Now is God just concerned about the oxen, or is He always saying everything for our benefit? It was for our benefit, surely, that it was written: "The ploughman must plough in expectation of return, and the thresher must hope to have his share." If we sowed a spiritual crop among you, is it too much to ask that we should reap our physical needs? Others *do* partake of that right among you, shouldn't we do so more than anyone? Yet we never made use of any such rights, we just got along somehow through everything, because we didn't want to have any obstacles to the good news of Christ.

Don't you know that the people who tend the holy places eat of the holy offerings, and those who are stationed at the altar get a share of what is sacrificed? That was also the Lord's instruction to those bringing the good word, that they should live off the good word.

But I've never taken advantage of any such rights. And I'm not writing this to make what goes for the others go for me: on the contrary, I would rather die than give up to anyone the glory of what I've done. If I come bringing the good word, I have nothing to be proud of: that is a necessity with me. I'm in deep trouble if I don't bring the good word. If I did this willingly, I could expect a reward; but if unwillingly, I've simply been entrusted with a job. So what is my reward in that case? It has been my reward that in bringing the good word I have made the good word free of charge to the point of not taking advantage of my rights as contained in the good word.

Free before all men, I bound myself a slave to all, hoping to win the greatest number. With the Jews I acted Jewish to win over Jews; with the keepers of the Law I acted like a keeper of the Law, though I'm not a keeper of the Law myself. To those who had no law, I acted like a person with no law (though I'm not devoid of the law of God so much as informed by the law of Christ), so that I can win over the ones with no law. With the squeamish ones I acted squeamish to win over the squeamish ones. I have been everything to everybody, so that I can at least save some of the people. I do it all for the good word, to be a partner in it.

Don't you know that the runners in the stadium all run, but only one takes the prize? So run like you're going to win. Everyone who enters a contest practices total self-control: they do it to win laurels that fade; we do it to win laurels that don't fade. I for my part am running in no random fashion and fighting without pulling any punches. I punish my body and drag it around in chains, because after preaching to others I can't myself fail to pass muster.

10

I want you to be aware, brothers and sisters, that our fathers all went forth under the cloud and all passed through the sea and all were washed and initiated into the way of Moses in the cloud and in the sea. And they all ate the same spiritual food and all drank the same spiritual drink, since they drank from a spirit-stone that kept reappearing for them: that stone was Christ. But God wasn't happy with most of them: He left them lying in the wilderness.

What they were is an example for us, so we won't get cravings for evil like the cravings they had. Don't be idol-worshipers like some of them, as scripture says: "The people sat down to eat and drink and stood up to play." Let's avoid acts of lewdness, as some of them engaged in lewdness and twenty-three thousand fell in a single day. Let's not try Christ's patience, as some of them did and were killed by the snakes. Don't grumble, as some of them grumbled and were killed by the destroyer. Those things happened to them as an example and were written as a reminder to us who find ourselves face to face with the end of time. Which means if you think you're standing, be careful you don't fall. No trials have come upon you except on a human scale. God keeps good faith and will not allow you to be tried beyond what you can bear, but will always furnish, along with the trial, the means of withstanding it.

For that reason, dear friends of mine, shun the worship of pagan gods. I speak to you as sensible people; you judge whether I'm right. The benediction cup that we bless, isn't it a share in the blood of Christ? The bread that we break, isn't it a share in the body of Christ? The whole lot of us are one loaf, one body, since we all share that one loaf. Look at Israel ("Israel" in the geographic sense). Aren't those who eat the sacrifices part of the temple community?

So what am I saying? That there's anything special about "pagan sacrifice meat," or that any of the pagan gods are real? No, I'm saying that what the people are sacrificing is being sacrificed to demons and not to God, and I don't want you to be part of demon society. You can't drink the cup of the Lord and the cup of demons, you can't have your share at the table of the Lord and at the table of demons. Do we want to make the Lord angry? Are we stronger than him?

Everything is permissible but not everything is advisable. Everything is permissible, but not everything is constructive. Don't have yourself in mind, any of you; have the other person in mind.

Whatever they sell at the butcher's, eat it with no scruples of conscience; because "The earth is the Lord's, with all that it is full of." If someone not of the faith invites you over and you feel like going, eat whatever is put in front of you without scruples of conscience. But if someone says to you, "This is pagan sacrifice-meat!" don't eat it, for the sake of that person and for conscience's sake. I don't mean your conscience, I mean the other person's. Why, basically, should my own freedom be judged by someone else's conscience? If I gratefully eat what's before me, why should I be vilified for what I thank God for?

So whether you eat or drink or do whatever, do all for the glory of God. Let Jews, Greeks, and the assembly of God find no fault with you, just as I myself please everyone in all matters and don't look out for my own interest but that of all the others, to save them. Follow my example, as I follow Christ's.

11

I commend the way that you mind me in all matters and keep my transmissions as I transmitted them to you. Now, I'd like you to know that every man is headed by Christ, every woman is headed by her husband, and Christ is headed by God. Any man praying or prophesying with something on his head is insulting his superior. Any woman praying or prophesying with her head uncovered is dishonoring *her* superior. It's exactly the same as if she were bald. In fact, if a woman isn't going to cover her head, she should shave it too! If a woman is ashamed of shaving her head and being bald, then she could cover herself.

You see, whereas the man shouldn't have his head covered because he's God's image and glory, a woman is her husband's glory. Man, after all, was not made from woman, woman was made from man. Remember also that man wasn't created for woman, woman was created for man. For that reason, a woman had better wear her authority on her head for the sake of the angels. But in the Lord, woman is not isolated from man nor man from woman. Just as woman came from man, man comes through woman, and all comes from God. Judge for yourselves: is it suitable for a woman to be bareheaded when she's praying to God? Doesn't nature herself teach you that it's a disgrace for a man to grow his hair long, while growing her hair long is a woman's glory? That's because long hair is given to a woman to stand for a head-covering. If anyone wishes to make trouble about this, well, it's just not our custom [for women to be bareheaded at meeting], nor that of the assemblies of God.

As I give these instructions, I cannot praise the way that, when you get together, it's more to the bad than to the good. First of all, when you get together there are divisions among you, or so I hear and I believe at least part of it. But there would have to be factions among you, to show who among you can be counted on. So: there you are in one place, but scarcely "eating the Lord's supper." When you're eating, each person quickly reaches for the dinner he brought with him, and one person is starving while the other is drunk. Don't you have houses to eat and drink in? Or do you look down on the assembly of God and want to embarrass those who have nothing? What can I say to you? Shall I praise you? I can't praise you for this.

I, after all, received from the Lord what I have also transmitted to you: that Lord Jesus, on the night he was betrayed, took bread, gave thanks, and broke it, saying: "This is my body, which is for you. Do this in my memory." The same with the cup, after the dinner, saying: "This cup is the new agreement sealed in my blood: every time you drink, do this in my memory." So every time you eat this bread and drink this cup, you are announcing the death of the Lord till he comes back, which means that whoever eats the bread or drinks the cup of the Lord improperly is guilty of the body and blood of the Lord. Each person should examine himself and eat of the bread and drink of the cup accordingly. The person eating or drinking compounds his guilt with every swallow by seeing no body of Christ there. That's why so many among you are sick and weak and a considerable number are dying. If we police ourselves, we won't be judged. But when we are judged by the Lord we are being disciplined so that we won't finally be condemned with the rest of the world.

So, my brothers and sisters, when you get together to eat, wait for everyone else to arrive. Anyone who is hungry should eat at home, so that the way you act at meeting incurs no guilt. As for the rest, when I come I will give you instructions.

12

Concerning spiritual practices, brothers and sisters, I do not wish to leave you in the dark. You know how, when you were pagans, you were led astray toward speechless idols, which is why I want you to know that no one speaking in a godly spirit says "Jesus be damned!" and no one can say "Jesus is Lord!" if not in a holy spirit.

There are differences among gifts, but the spirit is the same. And there are different modes of service, all to the same Lord. And there are differences in activities, but it is the same God who activates them all in everyone. Each person has a chance to show forth the spirit for the common good. One person is given words of wisdom through the spirit, another is given words of knowledge in line with the same spirit, another is given faith in that same spirit, someone else is given the gift of healing by power of this one same spirit, and others have gifts of summoning power, prophesying, or testing [the holiness of] spirits. One has the gift of different kinds of tongues, while another has the gift of interpreting tongues. All these things are energized by one and the same spirit, who allots, in his discretion, to each person whatever he wishes to.

Just as the body is one but has many organs, and all the organs of the body, many in number, make one body, so too with Christ: in one spirit we too were all baptized into one body, whether Jews or Greeks, or slaves or free, and we all drank one spirit. And the body, you see, isn't one organ, it's many organs. If the foot says, "I'm not a hand, so I'm not part of the body," isn't it still part of the body anyway? And if the ear says, "I'm not an eye, so I'm not part of the body," isn't it still part of the body anyway? If all the body were eyes, where would hearing be? If it were all ears, where would smell be? As it is, God put each of the organs in the body right where He wanted it. If all the organs were the same, where would the body be? In fact, there are many different organs but one body. It's impossible for the eye to say to the hand, "I don't need you for anything," or for the head to say to the foot, "I don't need you for anything." On the contrary, the most important organs of the body are of necessity the most delicate, and the parts we consider less respectable we clothe with special respect, and we give the less decent parts a decency that our more decent parts have no need of. In fact, when God put the body all together, he gave special attention to the parts of least importance, so there would be no division in the body, but instead all the parts of the body would be united in their concern for one another. And if one part suffers, all the parts suffer with it, and if one part exults, all the parts rejoice with it.

And you are Christ's body, the various parts of it, placed by God in various positions in the assembly: apostles first, prophets second, teachers third, then miracle-working, healing by grace, volunteer work, administration, and the various kinds of tongues. Is everyone an apostle? Is everyone a prophet? Is everyone a teacher? Is everyone a miracle-worker? Does everyone have the gift of healing? Does everyone speak in tongues? Does everyone interpret tongues? Insist on the best gifts.

And what is more, I will show you a way par excellence:

13

If I speak the tongues of mortals and angels, but have no love, that makes me a trumpet-blast or a cymbal-crash. And if I have the gift of prophecy and know all the mysteries and possess all knowledge and have faith enough to move mountains, but have no love, I'm nothing. And if I turn all my possessions into bread for the poor and deliver up my body for my greater glory hereafter, but have no love, it does me no good.

Love can wait; love has a heart. Love doesn't begrudge, doesn't brag, isn't inflated, doesn't act crude, doesn't take advantage, doesn't pick fights, doesn't plot evil, and takes no delight in doing harm, but delights together in the truth. It is always accepting, always believing, always hoping, always enduring.

Love never fails. Prophecies? They will be disproven. Tongues? They will be stilled. Knowledge? It will be superseded. For we know in part and prophesy in part, but when perfection comes, the partial will be abolished. When I was a baby, I talked like a baby, felt like a baby, thought like a baby. Now that I'm a man, I've put the baby things away. You see, for now we look as if in a mirror, shrouded in mystery; but then we will see face to face. Now I partly discern; but then I will perceive the same way that I was perceived all along. And so we have faith, hope and love, these three: but the greatest of these is love.

14

Make love your goal. And be eager for spiritual practices too, especially prophesying. The person speaking in tongues, after all, is speaking to God and not to the other people, since no one can hear what he says: the spirit makes him talk in mysteries. The person prophesying, on the other hand, does speak to the other people and says constructive words of encouragement and consolation. What the person speaking in tongues says is constructive only for himself; what someone says in prophesying is constructive for the assembly. I'd like for you all to speak in tongues, but I'd like even more for you to prophesy. Prophesying is better than speaking in tongues, unless the tongues are translated, so that the assembly gets something constructive from it.

Now brothers and sisters, if I come to you speaking in tongues, what good will I be to you if I say no words of revelation or knowledge or prophesy or instruction? It's the same with the voices of inanimate instruments like flutes and harps: if I don't make the sounds distinctly, how will anyone make out what I'm fluting or harping? And if a trumpet doesn't give a clear blast, who will ready themselves for battle? And the same with you: if you don't use your tongue to say something good and clear, how will anyone know what you said? You're talking to the air! There are who knows how many languages in the world, and not one of them is unintelligible. So if I don't know what force the utterance has, I'm a foreigner to the person speaking, and the person speaking is a foreigner in my eyes. The same with you: in your devotion to spiritual practices, always strive for the ever greater building-up of the assembly.

So then: the person speaking in tongues should pray to be interpreted, because if I pray in tongues, my spirit may be praying, but my mind produces nothing. What does that mean? That I pray with my spirit, but I pray with my mind too. I sing hymns with my spirit, but I also sing hymns with my mind.

Suppose you speak a blessing in tongues: how will the person filling the position of the common man* say Amen to your benediction if he doesn't know what you're saying? You may be giving a fine blessing, but the others get nothing out of it. God be praised, I speak in tongues more than any of you, but at meeting I'd rather say five words with my mind for the instruction of others than thousands of words spoken in tongues.

Brothers and sisters, don't be children emotionally. Be babes in arms at evildoing, but have the sensibilities of mature adults. It is written in the Law:

> *In alien languages, on the lips of outsiders,*
> *That is how I will speak to this people.*
> *And they still won't listen to me, says the Lord.*

What it comes down to is that speaking in tongues is a sign for the unbelievers, not the believers; while prophesying is for the believers, not the unbelievers. So then, suppose the whole assembly is gathered in one place, and all are speaking in tongues, and then in come some outsiders or non-believing people; won't they say you're all mad? By contrast, if everyone is prophesying, and an outsider or non-believing person comes in, is engaged in discussion by everybody, has his ideas challenged by everybody, and sees the secrets of his heart being brought to light, then he will fall on his face and worship God, declaring, "You really do have God among you!"

So what does that mean, brothers and sisters? When you get together, everyone has a song to sing, teaching to impart, a revelation to share, tongues to speak in, or interpretation to give; but all in the most constructive way, please. If anyone is going to speak in tongues, make it just two or at the most three people, one at a time, with one person interpreting. If someone has no interpreter, he shouldn't speak in the assembly, but keep it between himself and God. Prophets, also just two or three, should speak, while the others offer their comments. If a revelation comes to someone seated, the person before should stop talking. Certainly you can all prophesy one by one, so that everybody learns something and everybody receives encouragement. Prophetic

---

* This could mean either "the impartial onlooker" or "the person sitting in the visitors' seat."

spirits can and should be controlled by their respective prophets, if God is not the god of pandemonium but of peace.

As in all the assemblies of the faithful, the women are to keep silent at meeting. They are not permitted to speak; no, let them obey, as indeed the Law says. If they want to know about something, let them ask their own husbands when they get home, because it's a disgrace for a woman to speak in the assembly. Did the word of God come from you, or are you the only ones it has found its way to?

If any among you consider yourselves a prophet or spiritual person, be informed that what I'm writing you is a command of the Lord: whoever ignores it will be ignored.

In short, my brothers and sisters, put the emphasis on prophesying, but there's nothing wrong with speaking in tongues too; only, everything decently and in good order, please.

15

I remind you, brothers and sisters, of the good news that I brought you the good news of, which you accepted and now live within, and through which you are being saved, if you keep to the same words in which I brought you the good word—and if you don't, you never believed for real. Now among the first things I transmitted to you, as I received them, were these: that Christ died for our sins according to the scriptures and that he was buried and that he is risen on the third day according to the scriptures, and that he appeared to Peter and then the Twelve. Next he appeared to over five hundred of the faithful at once, of whom most are still with us though some have gone to their rest. After that he appeared to James and all the apostles. Last of all he appeared, so to speak, to the runt of the litter, me.

And I really am the last and least of the apostles, not worthy to be called an apostle at all, because I persecuted the assembly of God. But by God's grace I am what I am, and his grace toward me wasn't for nothing; no, I toiled more than all the others—not I, actually, but the grace of God that is with me. But whether it was I or one of the others, that is the message we bring and that is what you put your faith in.

Now if the message is that Christ is risen from the dead, how can some of you say that there is no resurrection of the dead? If there is no resurrection of the dead, then Christ isn't risen either. And if Christ isn't risen, our message is worthless and so is your faith, and we turn out to be perjuring ourselves about God, because we're contradicting God by our testimony that He raised Christ, whom He can't have raised if the dead are never raised. If the dead are never raised, Christ also isn't risen. But if Christ isn't risen, your faith is worthless, you're still there in your sins, and so those who died in Christ were lost forever. If our hope in Christ is only for this life alone, we are the most pathetic people in the world.

But in fact Christ *is* risen from the dead, a prototype of all the dead. Since through one human being came death, so through another human being comes the resurrection of the dead. Just as all die in Adam, all will be brought to life in Christ. Each in his proper order: Christ as a prototype, then Christ's people, upon his coming; then the end, when he hands the kingdom over to God the Father, so that He may abolish all thrones, dominions and powers. He then must rule till he "has put all his enemies beneath his feet." The last enemy destroyed will be Death. For He "placed everything below him, underneath his feet." Now when it says everything was placed below him, that obviously excludes the One who originally placed everything there below him. When He has put everything below him, then he, the son, will be placed below the One who placed everything below him, so that God will be all in all.

Tell me, what are they doing when they hold proxy baptisms on behalf of departed souls? If the dead still aren't going to be raised, why have baptisms for them? What are *we* risking our necks for every minute? I die every day, brothers and sisters, I swear it by whatever credit I may take for you before Christ Jesus our Lord. If on the human level I fought with wild beasts at Ephesus, what good does that do me? If the dead aren't raised, well—"eat and drink, for tomorrow we die." Don't be fooled: "Evil talk corrupts good morals." Have the decency to sober up and keep from sin, because some of you have no knowledge of God, I say to your shame.

"But," someone will say, "how are the dead raised? What body do they come with?" Fool, what you sow doesn't come to life without dying first, and what you sow is not the physical form that will develop but just a bare seed of, say, wheat or whatever other crop. It is God who then gives it whatever physical form He decided on, and to each of the seeds he gives its own physical form. Not all flesh is the same kind: in fact, human flesh is different, cattle's flesh is different, bird-flesh is different, the flesh of fishes is different. Likewise, there are heavenly bodies and earthly bodies. But the shining of the heavenly bodies is one thing, and the shining of the earthly bodies is another. The shining of the sun is different, the shining of the moon is different, the shining of stars is different. Indeed, one star differs from another in its shine. That's what the resurrection of the dead is like: it is sown amid decay, and rises up imperishable; it is sown amid rejection, and rises up in glory; it is sown in sickness, and rises up in strength; the animal body is sown, the spirit body rises up.

If there is an animal body, then there is a spirit body too. That's also what scripture says: "(the first) man (Adam) became a living creature," while the ultimate Adam, [Christ,] became a lifegiving spirit. But the spirit body isn't first: first comes the animal body, then the spirit body. The earlier human being* is of the clay of earth, the later human being** is from heaven. As the one earthen man is, so are the other earthen ones; and as the heavenly man is, so are the heavenly ones. And as we bore the mark of our earthliness, we will also bear the mark of our heavenliness.

What I'm telling you, brothers and sisters, is that flesh and blood cannot inherit God's kingdom, nor can corruption inherit incorruptibility. Listen, I will tell you a secret: not all of us will die, but all of us will change—in an instant, in the twinkling of an eye—at the sound of the last trumpet. For it will sound, and the dead will rise up immortal, and we will be transformed; because this perishable stuff must put on imperishability, and this mortal stuff must put on immortality. When this perishable stuff puts on imperishability, and this mortal stuff puts on immortality, then it will be as the words are written:

> *Death was absorbed into Victory.*
> *Death, where is your victory?*
> *Death, where is your sting?*

The sting of death is sin, and the empowerment of sin is the Law. Thanks be to God for giving us the victory through our Lord Jesus Christ.

In short, my dear brothers and sisters, be firm, immovable, contributing generously to the Lord's work always, knowing that your labors

---

* Adam as prototype of all who belonged to the animal humanity of the old order.
** Christ as prototype of all who now belong to the spiritual humanity of God's new order.

don't count for nothing in the Lord.

16

Now about the collection for the [Jerusalem] holy ones, what I instructed the congregations in Galatia to do, you should do also. Sunday by Sunday each of you should put aside in storage whatever you feel guided to contribute, so that the collection doesn't have to be taken up when I come. When I show up, I will send whoever you trust, equipped with letters from me, to convey your kindness to Jerusalem. If the occasion warrants my coming in person, they can travel with me.

I will come see you when I get across Macedonia. You see, I'm passing through Macedonia now, so maybe I could stay with you a while and even spend the winter, so that you can help me on my way wherever I go next. Rather than seeing you right away but only in passing, I hope to spend some time with you if the Lord permits. I'm staying in Ephesus from now till Pentecost. A door, it seems, has opened for me here—great and full of potential, with many people blocking the way.

If Timothy arrives, make sure he needn't dread coming to you, because he performs the Lord's work just as I do. Let no one disregard him. Send him well equipped and in peace on his way back to me. I'll be waiting for him with the other brothers. Concerning Brother Apollos, I pleaded with him left and right to bring the other brothers and come see you. And still it wasn't his decision to come now; he will come when he finds a better time.

Keep awake, stand firm in the faith, act like men, be strong. Let all your doings be done with love.

I have a request of you, brothers and sisters: you know the household of Stephen, how they were the first ones in Achaea, and how they turned themselves over to the service of the holy ones. I ask you to give your obedience to people like that and to every fellow-worker and laborer. It has been my joy to have Stephen and Fortunatus and Achaicus here; they've helped make up for my missing the rest of you. They've eased my spirit and no doubt yours. Give people like that your recognition.

The congregations of Asia say hello to you. Very best wishes to you in the Lord from Aquila and Priscilla and the congregation centered around their house. All the brothers and sisters say hello to you. Greet each other with a holy kiss.

Here I, Paul, greet you in my own hand. If anyone won't make friends with the Lord, let them be damned. *Marana tha* [Come, Lord]! The grace of our Lord Jesus be with you. My love to all of you in Christ Jesus.

The Second Letter from Paul to the Community in
Corinth

1

From Paul, apostle of Christ Jesus through God's will, and Brother Timothy;

To the assembly of God in Corinth, together with all the holy ones in all Achaea:

Grace to you and peace from God our Father and Lord Jesus Christ.

Blessed be God, the Father of our Lord Jesus Christ, the father of compassion and God of all encouragement, who encourages us in our troubles so that we can encourage those in trouble by means of the encouragement with which we ourselves have been encouraged by God. Because just as the sufferings of Christ abound to our benefit, so through Christ our encouragement abounds. Are we oppressed? It's for your advancement and salvation. Are we consoled? It's for the sake of your consolation, put to use in the steadfast endurance of the same sufferings that we too have suffered. And our hopes for you are firm and strong, knowing that as you have a membership in the sufferings, you also have a membership in the consolation.

I don't want you unaware, brothers and sisters, of the troubles that overtook us in Asia: we were well and truly pressed beyond endurance, to the point where we didn't see how our lives could go on. But we already carry our own death-decree within us, so that our faith won't be in ourselves, but in God who raises the dead, who rescued us from all that impending death and will do so again, on whom we have placed our hopes of being rescued with the assistance of your prayers for us, so that what God grants us in the face of many requests will make many thank God on our behalf.

If we have anything to boast of, it is the testimony of our conscience that we made our way through the world, and especially towards you, wrapped in the simplicity and sincerity of God: in God's grace, not in mortal cleverness. And in fact what we are writing you now is nothing other than what you read and understand it to be. Actually, I hope you'll understand us completely (as I think you have so far understood us partly), since we are what you can claim, and you are what we can claim, on the day of Lord Jesus.

And in this confidence I meant to come see you before, to give you another dose of grace: I was going to go to Macedonia by way of you and then see you on my way back from Macedonia so you could help me on my way to Judea. So when I made those plans do you think I was kidding around? Are the plans I announce just strategies on the lowest level, so that with me yes is really no? God is my witness that what we say to you is never yes-and-no. After all, the son of God, Jesus Christ, whom we have proclaimed among you, I and Silas and Timothy, *he* was never a yes-and-no person but is himself the essence of Yes, since each of God's promises finds in him its confirming Yes. Thus through him comes also our Amen to God unto His glory. The same God who confirms us with you in Christ and who anointed us, has also put His seal on us and given us the spirit in our hearts as a surety.

I call God as witness to my soul that I didn't come to Corinth at that point, because I didn't want to be too hard on you. We are not here to supervise your faith—you're in the faith already—but to collaborate in your joy.

2

You see, what I decided in my own mind was not to come see you again in a mood of grief. Because if I grieve you, who can give me joy but the one I have aggrieved? And I wrote you that letter* so that I wouldn't arrive only to be given grief by those who should make me happy, since I am sure about all of you that my happiness is happiness for all of you. Suffering greatly and anguished at heart, I wrote you through my many tears, not to give you grief but to let you see the love I have especially for you.

If anyone has given offense, it's not me that they have offended, but in a way—not to press the point too hard—all of you. It's enough for that person to have been censured by the majority, so much so that it is now

---

* A letter now lost, falling between First and Second Corinthians, which must have been a scorcher.

rather for you to be magnanimous and supportive and not to overwhelm that person with additional opprobrium, which is why I encourage you to use love towards him. After all, I wrote to find out how solid you were, whether you were obedient all the way. If you forgive a person for something, so will I. And what forgiveness that involves on my part, if any, is for the sake of your standing before Christ, that we may not become too tempting a prey for Satan, whose intentions, after all, are known to us.

Anyway, I went on to Troy to bring the good news of Christ, and though a door was opened for me in the Lord, my spirit found no ease as I waited in vain for Titus my dear brother, so I took leave from those people and went on into Macedonia.

Thanks be to God who always parades us in Christ's triumph and broadcasts the fragrance of knowledge by means of us in all parts of the world, since we are the sweet fragrance of Christ rising to God from among the saved and the lost, a fragrance which for some comes from death and brings death, while for others it comes from life and brings life. And who has any power in the face of these things? Unlike many others, we are not diluting the word of God, but speaking as sincerity dictates, speaking in Christ the word of God as if under His watchful eye.

3

Are we starting to commend ourselves again? Surely we don't need letters of commendation either to you or from you, like some others use? You are our letter, written down upon our hearts, known and read by all the world, showing them all that you are a letter of Christ for which we were the secretary, written down not in ink but in the spirit of a living God, and not upon stone tablets but on the flesh-and-blood tablets of the human heart.

Such is the confidence we have before God because of Christ. Not that we have any status of our own to claim anything on our own merits: our status comes from God, who in fact gave us the status of servants under a new contract—not in writing, but a contract of spirit. Because the letter kills, while the spirit gives life.

If the service of death carved in letters of stone was born in such glory that the sons of Israel could not look straight at the face of Moses because his face shone with such glory, temporary though it was, how can the service of the spirit fail to be one of even greater glory? If it was glory to serve what condemned you, how much more will it overflow with glory to serve what declares you innocent. In fact, there is no glory in the glories that were, in relation to this all-surpassing glory. If what is ephemeral passes through glory, how much more does what is permanent remain in glory.

Having hopes of such nature, we can then act with great confidence, not like Moses, who put a veil upon his face so the children of Israel couldn't watch his glory fading to its end. Ah, but their senses must have become very dull, since right up to the present day their reading of the Old Testament is still veiled with the same veil, which has not been unveiled again, because it takes Christ to set it aside. Even today whenever the books of Moses are read amongst them, it is with a veil lying on their hearts. "Every time he returns toward the Lord, the veil is lifted." Now "the Lord" is the spirit. And where the spirit of the Lord is, that is freedom. And all of us, mirroring with unveiled faces the glory of the Lord, are being reshaped into that image, changed from glory to glory as if by the Lord's spirit.

4

So, now that we have our mission as it has been mercifully granted to us, we don't quit. No, having washed our hands of what is hidden in shame, we don't operate by trickery nor doctor the word of God; instead, we operate in the openness of truth, commending ourselves to every human conscience before God. If there is anything veiled about our good news, it is veiled for those who are lost, those for whom the god of these times, [Satan,] has blinded the senses of the unbelievers to keep the illumination of the good news of the glory of Christ (who is God's image) from dawning upon them.

Certainly we are not bringing word of ourselves, but of Jesus Christ the Lord, we being only your slaves for Jesus' sake. Because the same God who said, "And now from the darkness, the light will shine," shone in our hearts to throw the light of the knowledge of the glory of God on the face of Jesus Christ.

We keep this fortune in pots of clay, so that the surpassing power of it may be God's and not anything coming from us; while in all things we are pressed hard but not suppressed, at a loss but never at a total loss, pursued but not forsaken, downed but never destroyed, carrying around in our bodies the death Jesus was put to, so that the true life of Jesus will also be there in our bodies for all to see. In fact, while we live we are constantly being given over to death because of Jesus, so that the true life of Jesus may also be clearly seen in our mortal flesh. Which means that death is at work in us while life is working in you.

Having the same spirit of faith and going by the words of scripture: "I believed, therefore I spoke," we also "believe, and therefore we speak," knowing that He who raised Lord Jesus will also raise us up with Jesus and put us there next to you. Really, this is all for your sake, so that grace, increasing the gratitude of the many it is bestowed upon, may overflow to the greater glory of God.

That's why we don't quit: even if our outer self is falling apart, our inner self is renewed with every passing day. These current little troubles of ours operate beyond measure to bring us an immeasurable load of everlasting glory. Meanwhile we keep our eyes, not on what we see, but on the unseen, since what we see is temporary, while the unseen is eternal.

5

We know, after all, that when this earthly tent that houses us on earth is struck, that we have housing from God, a dwelling no hands ever shaped, everlasting in the skies. In the meantime we groan with the desire to put on our habitation from heaven, so that we won't end up naked when we take off the other one. Indeed, while still in this tent of ours we groan with oppression, wishing not to take anything off but to put something more on, so that our mortality might be swallowed up by life. It is God who has put us in this very situation, and who also has given us the spirit as our surety.

So, taking heart always in the knowledge that while we reside in our bodies we are on leave of absence from the Lord, we go by faith and not by appearances. We feel strong, thinking it would be better to move out of our bodies and take up residence in the Lord. Consequently, whether we're moving in or out, we consider it important to make him very happy with us, since all of us must stand in the open before the tribunal of Christ so that each may get what he deserves for the use he made of his body, either good or bad.

So, knowing the fearsome might of the Lord, we can make other people believe us, but before God we stand revealed. Actually, I hope to be revealed as well in the state of your characters. We aren't saying that to you to pat ourselves on the back but to give you occasion to be proud of us, so that you'll have something to say to the others, the proud faces with nothing in their hearts to be proud of. After all, if we are mad, that is for God; what wits we have about us are for you. Christ's love, you see, urges us on in our conviction that one died for all, therefore all died. And it was for all that he died, so that the living would no longer live for themselves but for the one who died and was raised for them. Which means from now on we no longer know anyone as a creature of flesh and blood. In fact, even if we knew Christ as a flesh-and-blood creature, we no longer know him that way. So that anyone who is in Christ is a new creation. The old has passed away: look, there's something new here; and it's all from God, who reconciled us to Himself through Christ and put us in the service of reconciliation, because God was in Christ, reconciling a world to Himself, not counting their violations and instilling in us the words of reconciliation.

So we are ambassadors on Christ's behalf as if God was advising you through us. We pray on Christ's behalf: be reconciled with God; for our sake He cast the one who knew no sin in the role of Sin, so that we may become God's righteousness in him.

6

As your colleagues, we beseech you not to let the grace of God you receive be for nothing. After all, it says:

> *At the appointed time I gave ear to you,*
> *And in the day of salvation I helped you.*

But this is it: the duly appointed time! This is it: the day of salvation!

For ourselves, we keep from giving offense of any kind, so as not to besmirch the good work: instead, we show ourselves God's servants in everything: in our long endurance, in our sufferings, in our need, in our dilemmas, amid beatings, amid jailings, amid uprisings, in toil, during sleepless nights, during hungry days, in purity, in knowledge, in patience, in gentleness, in holy spirit, in unfeigned love, in words of truth, in the power of God, by taking up the arms of justice in our right hand and our left, through glory and dishonor, through slander and praise, sometimes called swindlers and sometimes honest men, sometimes unknown and sometimes known, and sometimes about to die, though you see we're alive. They punish us but it doesn't kill us; we are saddened and still always rejoicing; we are poor and share our wealth with many; we have nothing, but everything is ours.

We have spoken openly to you, Corinthians, and opened up our hearts. We are not closed to you: it is your own feelings that are closed. Return our favor, I say to you as my children, and open up your hearts too.

Don't forge bonds with unbelievers. What connection do just actions have with lawlessness? What do light and darkness have in common? What agreement does Christ have with Beliar? What does the believer share with the unbeliever? Do heathen idols sit well with a temple of God? Because we *are* a temple of God's life, just as God has said:

> *I will live and walk among them*
> *And I will be their God and they will be My people.*
> *Therefore leave the others behind*
> *And go off by yourselves, says the Lord,*
> *And keep uncleanness from touching you;*
> *And I will accept you as Mine.*
> *And I will come to be your Father,*
> *And you will come to be My sons and daughters,*
> *So says the Lord omnipotent.*

7

With promises like these in hand, dear friends, let us wash off all our dirtiness of flesh and spirit, making our holiness perfect in the fear of God.

Make room for us [in your hearts]. We never abused anyone or corrupted anyone or did anybody out of anything. I don't say this to condemn you; as I have told you before, you are so much in our hearts that we live and die with you. I have a lot of confidence in you; I take a lot of pride in you. It fills me with consolation and makes me overflow with joy in the midst of all my troubles.

And so when we went on into Macedonia, there was no rest for our bones but only suffering everywhere: outward battles, inward fears. But God, who brings relief to the lowly, brought relief to us too with the arrival of Titus: not just that he was there, but also that he was so gratified with you, telling me of your fondness for me, your sincere regrets and—to increase my joy—your zeal on my behalf.

Actually, if I shocked you with my last letter, I am not sorry. Even if I were sorry, I see how that letter, even if it shocked you at the time, I'm still happy about it now: not that you were shocked, but that you were shocked into repentance. It was God's kind of shock you suffered, so that you took no loss because of us. God's kind of shock makes you revert toward irreversible salvation, whereas the world's kind of shock brings death. For instance, look here how much this very experience of being shocked in God's way inspired you with concern, then the wish to defend yourselves, then indignation, then fear of God, then motivation, then zeal, then punishment for the offender! In every way you have shown your integrity in this matter. Therefore, as far as what I wrote you, the point was not the offender and the point was not the offended: the point was for you to show your concern for our relations toward you before God. And on that count we feel much better.

To add to our satisfaction, it made us enormously happy to see the happiness of Titus, how he came away from you all so refreshed in spirit, because that means I hadn't made a fool of myself by bragging to him about you: instead, just as all of what I said to you was the truth, so my boasting about you to Titus turned out to be the truth too. And his feelings about you were especially warm as he detailed how obedient you all were, with what fear and trembling you received him. I rejoice to see I can count on you at all times.

8

We want you to know, brothers and sisters, what grace God has spread among the assemblies of Macedonia: for amid trials and sufferings their overflowing joy and deep-down poverty redounded to the richness of their simplicity. Yes, they did as much as possible—indeed more than possible, by my reckoning—voluntarily and with much satisfaction begging of us the grace of sharing in this service toward the [impoverished Jerusalem] holy ones. It wasn't that we were expecting it: they right away gave of themselves to the Lord and as through God's will, which led me to ask Titus, seeing how he had already made such a beginning, if he would also carry out this work of grace for you.

But since you have so much in every way, in faith and words and knowledge and all concern and in our love that is amongst you, you should also give freely in this work of grace. I don't say this as a command but because of the eagerness others have shown and to test the nobility of your love. You know, after all, the grace of our Lord Jesus Christ: that he was a rich man who became poor for you, so that his poverty could make you rich. I will in fact give you my opinion about this: this is a good thing for you, those of you who have been getting ready for a year now, both in action and in planning. But now take your actions to their conclusion, so that the eagerness of your desire is matched by your coming forward with what you have; since as long as the willingness is there, what you have is the appropriate gift, not what you don't have. After all, their relief should not be your distress; things should balance. At this particular time what you have left over makes up for their shortages, so that next time what they have will make up for your shortages: that way there's a balance. As it is written: "The one with much didn't have too much, the one with little didn't have too little."

Thanks be to God for putting so much concern for us in Titus's heart that he was not only receptive to our advice, but in his eagerness was already setting out on his own to see you. We sent along with him a brother whose spreading of the good word is esteemed among all the congregations and was also handpicked by them to be our companion in this work of grace that we have attended to—which arrangement is toward the Lord's greater glory and also in line with our own preference for settings things up so that no one will make slanderous remarks about the size of the fortune we are administering: we want our good intentions to be clear, not just to the Lord, but also to the world. Besides the others, we sent along another brother of ours whom we have found to be responsible in many matters on many occasions and who is even keener about this responsibility because of his great confidence in you. As for Titus, he is my associate and fellow-minister to you; as for the other brothers, they are delegates of their congregations and part of the glory of Christ. So let the confirmation of your love (and of our boasting about you to the others) be further confirmed in the sight of all the congregations.

9

Concerning this service to the Jerusalem holy ones I scarcely need write to you, since I know your eagerness and indeed have boasted about you to the Macedonians—"Achaea started getting ready last year!"—so that your zeal has infected most of them. I sent the abovementioned brothers so that my boasting about you should not come up short in this respect, so that after I said you were prepared, the Macedonians coming with me should not find you unprepared, thereby embarrassing us, not to say you, in this matter. Therefore, I thought it necessary to ask those brothers to go see you first and get your promised blessings together, so that it will be ready, looking like the fruits of your good will and not of our greed.

It's like this: the one who sows stingily will also reap but sparingly, while the one who sows with open-handed gratitude will also have a harvest to be grateful for. Each according to the decision of his heart, not glumly nor under constraint, since "God loves a cheerful giver." And God has the power to heap every grace high for you, so that at all times and in all ways you can meet your own needs and still have lots left over for every good work, as scripture says:

> *He scattered freely and gave to beggars.*
> *His justice prevails for ever.*

He who provides "seed to the sower and bread for the eating" will also provide for your sowing many times over and make the fruits of your just actions grow tall. Keep getting richer in every way, aiming for the total simplicity that makes you an agent of thanksgiving to God. Because the attention paid to these charitable offices has the effect not only of relieving the holy ones' difficulties but of heaping high the gratitude of many toward God. By proving trustworthy in this service you will be glorifying God with your submission in the faith to the good word of Christ and the openness of your sharing with them and with everyone, while they will pray to be allowed to see you someday because of the extraordinary grace of God upon you. Thanks to God, who gives us gifts beyond telling for free.

10*

And now I, Paul, beg your pardon by the gentleness and fairness of Christ if I am humble face to face among you, then show you my strength from far away. Don't make me, I pray, show my strength when among you: I think I can still face with confidence the ones who take the position that we are as fleshly as the rest. We walk around in the flesh, but we do not fight by the flesh's rules, because the weapons for our battle aren't physical, but they have power from God to storm fortresses, knocking down old arguments and every edifice raised against the knowledge of God, taking all intellects captive to the obedience of Christ, and making ready to punish any disobedience, once your obedience is established.

Look matters in the face: if anyone is sure of himself that he is Christ's, let him consider himself again and see that however much he is Christ's, so are we. And if I take some extra credit by reason of the authority given us by the Lord, not to tear you down, but to build you up, I'm not embarrassed to do so. I don't want to be thought of as terrorizing you with my letters. "His letters," some say, "are weighty and strong, but he has a weak physical appearance, and at speaking he's nothing much." Let those people be assured that what we are on paper in our letters from afar is what we will also prove to be in action when we show up.

To be sure, we wouldn't dream of putting ourselves alongside some of those self-aggrandizers or comparing ourselves with them. They set themselves up as a standard to measure themselves by and use themselves as a point of comparison for themselves—they make no sense. We, on the other hand, don't make claims we can't measure up to: we measure up to the standard God set for us as a measure, namely that of reaching you [with the good news]. It's not as if we never came to you before and now we're overstepping ourselves: in fact, we were the first to come to you bringing the good news of Christ. We're not taking immoderate credit for other people's labors. What we hope is that with

---

* From this point on, after bringing his disputes with the Corinthian assembly to a magnanimous conclusion, Paul proceeds to get angry as a bear all over again. It's not so hard to imagine Paul as having mood swings as it is to imagine him sending a letter that makes no sense as a whole. Some commentators have theorized that there was a shuffling of manuscripts and that chapters 10 to 13 are really part of "*that* letter," the scorching First-and-a-Half Corinthians mentioned on p. 334.

your growing faith, our stature among you will increase—by our own standards—giving an extra boost to our efforts to bring the good news to outlying areas beyond you; we don't want to take credit for work already done by someone else's standards. "If you seek glory, seek glory in the Lord," because it isn't the person who stands behind himself who can be trusted: it's the person whom the Lord stands behind.

11

I need for you to put up with a little of my foolishness: come, please put up with me! Because I am guarding you with a godly jealousy, having undertaken to deliver you, still pure and virginal, to one man: Christ. And I am afraid that, as the snake fooled Eve with his bag of tricks, your sensibilities too might somehow be corrupted, losing their Christ-oriented simplicity and purity. It seems that if someone comes along bringing the message of some other "Jesus" than the Jesus we brought word of, or conferring some other "Spirit" than the one that was given you, or bringing some other "good word" than what you received before, that's just fine with you.

In fact, I don't see how those "real live apostles" [who are doing all this] have anything on me. I may be a beginner in public speaking, but not as regards my knowledge, as I have demonstrated to you in every way in the sight of all.

Or did I do wrong when I humbled myself to build you up, charging nothing for the good news of God I brought you word of? I shook down the other congregations to pay the cost of our mission to you, and when I was there with you I didn't put the bite on anyone even when I was running low. Instead, my needs were met by brothers coming from Macedonia, while in every way I kept myself from leaning on you. And I plan to keep it that way. By Christ's truth that is in me, no one in the whole region of Achaea will ever be able to take that boast away from me.

Why have I done this? Because I *don't* love you? God knows the truth.

What I've been doing, I plan to keep doing, so as to close the avenue to those who seek an avenue for showing that we are simply the same [kind of "professional evangelizers"] as they pride themselves on being. In fact, that kind are fake apostles, con artists turning into "missionaries of Christ." And that's no surprise: if Satan himself can turn into an angel of light, is it any great matter for his servants also to turn into "servants of justice" (who will finally get what their deeds deserve)?

Again I say, let no one think I've lost my wits, or if they do, then take me, witless as I am, while I too do a little bragging. What I say now is not on the Lord's authority: I'm just talking in my foolish way while the boastful spirit is upon me. If so many others take pride in worldly things, I can take pride in them too. After all, you in your wisdom are very good at putting up with fools: you put up with people who enslave you, who eat you out of house and home, who take money from you, who condescend to you, who slap you in the face. I'm ashamed to speak of it; it makes us look anemic.

Whatever challenge they make—I say in my foolishness—I can make too. They're Hebrews? So am I. They're Israelites? So am I. Seed of Abraham, are they? So am I. Servants of Christ, are they? Let me throw caution to the winds and say I'm even more so: outstanding in my labors, conspicuous for my jail terms, pre-eminent in beatings suffered, familiar with death sentences. Five times the Jews gave me nine-and-thirty lashes; three times I was beaten with sticks, once with stones. Three times I was shipwrecked, spending a night and a day adrift on the face of the deep. Besides, all the traveling, danger of war, danger from robbers, danger from my own kind, danger from the Gentiles, danger in the city, danger in the wilderness, danger on the sea, danger from false brothers, with toil and labor, many sleepless nights, hunger and thirst, often not enough to eat, cold and lack of clothing. And besides all those externals, there is the preoccupation of every day: my deep concern for all the assemblies. Who is sick without my being sick too? Who is scandalized without my turning red?

If I must boast, let me boast of everything that is weak about me. God, who is also the father of Jesus, knows—let Him be praised for ever—that I'm not lying. In Damascus, King Areta's provincial governor stationed guards around the city of Damascus to catch me, but I was lowered out a window and over the wall, hidden in a basket, and thus slipped through his hands.

12

I have to boast, though no good comes of it, and now I get to the visions and revelations of the Lord. I know a person in Christ who fourteen years ago—whether in or outside his body I don't know, only God knows—was snatched up all the way to third heaven. And I know that the person in question*—whether in or out of his body, I don't know, only God knows—was transported into paradise and heard ineffable things spoken which it is not for mortals to utter. About that person I can boast; as for myself, I have only weaknesses to boast of.

However, if I want to boast, I'll be no fool, I'll be saying the truth. But I'll spare you for now: I don't want people to look beyond what they see in me or hear from me or judge me by the grandeur of those revelations. For just that reason, to keep me from being arrogant, I was given a thorn in the flesh, a messenger that Satan sends to cudgel me so I won't get too arrogant. On this account I three times prayed the Lord to make it go away. And I have been told: "Enough that you have my grace: power is perfected in infirmity."

So now I am glad to boast of my weaknesses, so that the power of Christ may settle down upon me. Therefore I'm pleased with sicknesses, indignities, need, persecution and oppression, if it's for Christ. When I am infirm, then I am powerful.

I'm really losing my mind, but you force me to it: I ought to have received more support from you. I was every bit as good as those "real live apostles" even if I'm nothing at all. The signs of an apostle were duly performed among you with the greatest patience: signs and wonders and powers. In what way were you ranked below the other assemblies—unless it's that I personally never took anything from you? Can you forgive me that crime?

This is now the third time that I'm getting ready to come see you and I'm still not going to take anything from you, because I don't want what you have, I want you. The parents' treasure should go to their children, not the children's treasures to their parents. I am glad to spend till I'm spent out if it's for your souls. Should I be loved less for loving you too much? At any rate, I never leaned on you. Instead, being a person who stops at nothing, I used my tricks to catch *you*. Or did I use any of the people I sent to you to get after your money that way? I asked Titus to go see you and sent the other brother with him: did Titus go after your money? Don't we walk in the same spirit? And along the same path?

* The person in question is probably Paul himself, both because he seems to be offering this experience as one of his credentials and because he remembers so exactly that the incident happened fourteen and not "about fifteen" years ago.

By now it must seem to you that we're acting defensive. Before God we say in Christ: it is all, dearest friends, for your own benefit. I am afraid, you see, that I might come and find you not the way I want you, and also have you find me to be not what you want. There could be discord, jealousy, hot tempers, arguments, denunciations, rumors, egotism, rebellion. I don't want to come and have God humiliate me in front of you and be dismayed to see all the former sinners who have never repented of the uncleanness and the lewd and disorderly behavior they engaged in.

13

This is the third time I'm coming to see you, and then "all testimony will be taken on the word of two or three witnesses." Having been with you twice and being away from you now, I say in advance as I have said before to the former sinners and all the rest: the next time I come I will spare nobody, in case you need any demonstration of the Christ who speaks in me and who is not helpless before you but powerful within you. He was crucified out of weakness, but lives by the power of God, and we are also weak in him, but we will live with him by means of God's power over you.

Examine yourselves: are you in the faith? Check yourselves out. Or do you not think of yourselves as having Jesus Christ in your midst? Because if not, you have failed. And I hope you know that we have not failed. So we pray to God that you may do nothing wrong, but not so that we will look successful: if you do the right thing, it's fine if we look like failures. In any event, we have no power against the truth but only for the truth. We are glad to be weak while you are strong: we pray for that, for your maturation. That's why I'm writing this before I arrive, so that when I'm there I needn't make summary use of the authority given me by the Lord, which is to build you up and not to tear you down.

For the rest, brothers and sisters, be happy, keep growing, urge each other on, be united in spirit, keep the peace, and the God of love and peace will be with you. Greet each other with the holy kiss. Greetings to you from all the faithful.

The grace of our Lord Jesus Christ and the love of God and the fellowship of the holy spirit be with you all.

The Letter from Paul to the Community in
Galatia

1

From Paul, apostle sent not by men nor by any man but by Jesus Christ
and God the Father who raised him from the dead; and all the brothers
with me;

To the assemblies of Galatia;

Grace to you and peace from God our Father and Lord Jesus Christ, who
gave himself for our sins to pull us clear of the evil present age according
to the will of God our Father, glory be to Him forever and ever, let it be
so.

I am amazed how quickly you turn away from the one who called you
in Christ's grace towards another "good word"—not that there really is
any other: it's just that there are these people confusing you and trying
to distort the good word of Christ. Don't let them: if we ourselves or a
messenger from the sky should bring you a different "good word" from
the one we brought you, let that person be damned. As we have said
before, I will say again right now: if anyone brings you a different "good
word" than was transmitted to you before, let him be damned!

In short, do I want the world to believe me or do I want God to believe
me? And am I trying to please the world? If I ever did please the world,
I wouldn't be Christ's slave.

Because, let me tell you, brothers and sisters, the good news reported
abroad by me is not a human thing: I didn't get it from any person, I
wasn't taught it, it's through revelation from Jesus Christ. Now you've
heard about my conduct back in my Jewish days, how I was the champion
persecutor of the assembly of God and laid it waste, and was also deeper
into Judaism than many of my contemporaries in my generation, being
an absolute zealot for the traditions of my forefathers.

But when it pleased God, who marked me out from my mother's
womb onward and called me through His grace, to reveal His son in me
and send me bringing the good word of him to the Gentiles, I did not

349

immediately confer with my own flesh and blood, and I did not go up to Jerusalem to see the apostles who had come before me: instead, I headed for Arabia and came back later to Damascus. Then three years later I went up to Jerusalem and looked up Peter and stayed with him for two weeks, but I didn't see any of the other apostles except James the brother of the Lord. What I'm writing you now, I hereby swear before God that it is no lie. So then I headed for the regions of Syria and Cilicia. I wasn't known by sight to the Judean assemblies in Christ: all they heard was, "Our former persecutor now bears the faith abroad that he used to attack," and they glorified God because of me.

2

Then fourteen years later I went up to Jerusalem again with Barnabas, taking Titus along as well. This time I went there by divine instruction. And I discussed with them the good word I have been bringing to the Gentiles, including a private meeting with the so-called "church pillars," [James, Peter, and John,] just in case I was headed for a pit or had already fallen in. But in fact they didn't even pressure Titus my companion, who is Greek, to get circumcised. What we had trouble with were bogus "brothers" coming in to spy on the freedom that we have in Christ Jesus, hoping to enslave us again—though we never bowed to their demands for a minute, wanting the good word to remain with you in all its truth.

And on the part of those who were supposedly big names—what they were in the past makes no difference to me, God is no respecter of persons—at any rate, they brought up no issues; on the contrary, seeing how I am entrusted with bringing the good word to the foreskinned world as Peter is to the circumcised world (because the same one who operated in Peter to bringing about the mission to the circumcised world also operated in me to go to the Gentiles), and recognizing the grace given to me, James and Peter and John, the so-called "church pillars," gave their hand to me and Barnabas in fellowship, we bound for the Gentiles and they for the circumcised world. We were only supposed to remember the poor [among the Jerusalem faithful], that's all, which is just what we hastened to do.

But then when Peter came to Antioch, I challenged him to his face, because he was acting inexcusably. You see, before some of James's people showed up he had been eating together with the Gentiles. But then when they showed up, he stopped doing that and kept away from them, deferring to the representatives of the circumcised world. Furthermore, he was joined in the act by the other Jews there, to the point where even Barnabas was misled into being part of the performance. But when I saw how they had lost their footing in the truth of the good word, I said to Peter in front of everybody, "If you're a Jew who lives like a Gentile and doesn't follow the Jewish ways, who are you to impose Judaism on the rest of the world?"

We're Jews by birth, not of "sinful heathen stock," but we also know that no person is cleared of wrongdoing by the works of the Law, only through the faith of Jesus Christ. Accordingly we put our faith in Christ Jesus, to be cleared of wrong by faith in Christ and not by the works of the Law, since the works of the Law don't confer innocence on anything alive. If we are sinners for seeking exoneration in Christ, is Christ then the servant of sin? No, never! After all, if I reinstate the law which I abolished, I also name myself as a violator of it. Through the Law I became dead to the Law so I could be alive to God. I have been crucified with Christ: from now on I live no more, instead Christ lives in me. Even the life I have in the flesh, I now live by the faith of the son of God, who loved me and laid himself down for me. I am not going to turn the grace of God aside, because if exoneration comes through the Law, then Christ died for no reason whatever.

3

O mindless Galatians, who cast this spell on you, you in whose presence the crucifixion of Jesus Christ was described in full? Just tell me one thing: was it through performing the Law that the spirit came to you or through hearing and believing? Can you be so senseless as to finish on the physical level what you started on the spiritual level? Have you come so far for nothing? Really? Nothing at all? And the One who provides the Spirit to you and activates His powers among you, does He go by your performance of the Law or on the basis of your having heard and believed?

Just as Abraham "believed in God," and that "counted toward his uprightness," you know then that those who go by the faith are the children of Abraham. The scripture saw how God would clear the Gentiles of guilt, and gave Abraham the good news early: "You shall become a blessing to all nations." Those who go by belief, then, are blessed along with the believing Abraham.

Whereas those who go by performing the Law are under a curse, for it says, "Accursed all those who do not stick to the written letter in the book of the Law and do just that." That the Law makes no one virtuous in God's eyes is clear, because, "the virtuous shall live by faith." But the Law doesn't go by faith; instead: "who does these things shall find life in them." Christ ransomed us from the curse of the Law by becoming a cursed thing for us (since it says, "Anyone hanged on a tree is accursed"), wishing the blessing of Abraham to go out to the other nations in Christ Jesus so that we might receive the promised spirit through faith.

Brothers and sisters, this is a homely way to put it, but once a person's testament is in force, no one sets it aside or puts anything in. Now the promises made to Abraham were also made to his seed. It doesn't say "to his seeds," as referring to many, but as referring to one: "to your seed as well," which means Christ. And I tell you this: a testament once made operative by God cannot be set aside by a law that comes along four hundred thirty years later rendering its promises no longer valid. If our inheritance is based on the Law, it isn't based on the promise. But it was through a promise that Abraham was favored by God.

So what is the Law for? Laid down for the purpose of creating violations, until that seed should come to whom the promise was made, it was ordained by angels in the hands of an intermediary. But there is no such thing as an "intermediary" between one person and himself, and God is One.* Does that mean the Law is against the promises of God? No, never! If we had ever been given a law that could bring life to us, then exoneration really would be based on law. But the scriptures locked up everything in the jail of sin, so that the promise given to the believers would be based on the faith of Jesus Christ.

So before the faith came we were in the custody of the Law, imprisoned awaiting the faith that would later be revealed, which means the Law was there to hold our hands on the way to Christ, so that we could then be made holy on the basis of faith. But now that the faith is here we aren't schoolchildren any more: you are all sons and daughters of God

---

* This sentence is murky but may mean that the Law was a two-party transaction, a contract between God and man, while God's promise to Abraham was really a one-party transaction, God's unilateral commitment to Himself.

by virtue of your faith in Christ Jesus, since all of you, when you were initiated into Christ, also clothed yourself in Christ. There are no Jews and no Greeks, no slaves and no free men, no male and no female now that you are all one in Christ Jesus. If you are Christ's, then you are Abraham's seed, with a claim to the promised inheritance.

4

Let me say this: as long as the heir is underage, he is no different from a slave, even if he's the owner of it all. Instead, he's ruled by regents and executors for the term specified by the father. The same with us: when we were babies, we were the slaves of cosmic elements, but when the time was ripe, God sent forth His son, born of woman, born under the Law, to ransom those under the Law, so we could undergo adoption as His children. And since you're His children, God also sent down the spirit of His son into our hearts crying "Papa! Father!" Which means you're not a slave any more, but a son: and son also means heir of God.

But whereas before you served gods that don't exist in reality, because you didn't know God, now that you do know God, or rather are known by Him, how can you go back to those poor sick "cosmic powers" that you're so anxious to be enslaved by all over again? You busy yourselves counting days and months and seasons and years*—it makes me afraid I have toiled for you in vain.

Be more like me, brothers and sisters, since I have already become like one of you. You were more than fair to me when bodily weakness first brought me to you with the good news, and despite the dilemma you faced in view of my physical condition, you didn't put me down or spit me out. Not at all: you received me like a messenger of God, like Jesus Christ himself. So where is your radiance now? Why, back then I swear you would have ripped your eyes out to give them to me if you could have. I'm your enemy now for telling you the truth, is that it? It's not good the way those people want you: they're trying to cut you off so you'll have to turn to them. (It's nice to be wanted and all—in a good

---

* Note that these worshipers in Galatia aren't just *reverting* to pagan arts like astrology and numerology, they're apparently trying to *combine* them with Christianity—"the secret wisdom of Jesus can be seen in the stars," or something like that. See George Witterschein's introduction.

way—and not just when I can come to see you.) But my children! whom now I bear again in suffering till Christ emerges full-blown among you, I wish I could come see you now and change my tone of voice, because I just don't know what to do with you.

Tell me, those who wish to be under the Law, didn't you ever *hear* the Law? Because it says that Abraham had two sons, one by a slavegirl and one by a free woman. The one by the slavegirl was fathered in the normal manner, but the one by the free woman was promised [by God], which is a metaphor: the two women are the two Testaments. The first comes from Mount Sinai and bears children into slavery: that's Hagar ("Hagar" is actually the name for Mount Sinai in Arabia), and it corresponds to the present Jerusalem in servitude with its children. The other is Jerusalem again, the free Jerusalem that is our own mother, since it is written:

> *Rejoice, sterile one who never gave birth,*
> *Cry aloud and shout, you who never were in labor,*
> *Because many are the children of the barren one,*
> *More than of the one with a husband.*

You then, brothers and sisters, are children of Isaac's kind, children of the promise. But just as back then the natural-born one persecuted the one of spiritual origin, so it is now. But what does scripture say? "Throw the slavegirl out and her son with her: the slavegirl's son shall not share the inheritance with the free woman's son." So then, brothers and sisters, we are not the slavegirl's children, we are the free woman's children.

5

Christ used his freedom to free us too. So stand tall and don't yoke yourselves again to any forms of slavery. See here: I, Paul, am telling you that if you go on getting circumcised, Christ won't be able to help you at all. I avow again to every circumcised man that he is then obligated to perform the entire Law. You are annulled from Christ, you who are trying to be found innocent through the Law: you've fallen out of divine favor. The hope of being found innocent that *we* are counting on is by virtue of a spirit based on faith. Remember, in Christ Jesus, circumcision or having a foreskin doesn't count: what counts is faith energized by love.

You were running well: who cut you off from following the truth? Their persuasive words don't come from the One who called you. "A little leaven gets into the whole batch." I have confidence in the Lord about you, that you won't embrace those other views. The person disturbing you will pay for the crime, whoever he is. But as for me, brothers and sisters, if I were still preaching the Mosaic law, would I still be persecuted like this? Why, no: the sticking-point of the cross would be cleared away. Those people who are upsetting you [about circumcision] should go get something else cut off!

After all, you were called to freedom, brothers and sisters, just not a freedom that opens the gate to fleshly desires. Instead, let love make you slaves of one another, since all the Law is fulfilled in the one saying, "You are to love your neighbor as yourself." If you attack one another and bite one another's heads off, watch out that you don't get devoured by one another. No, I say: be guided by the spirit and you won't end up doing whatever your body wants. What the flesh desires is against the spirit, while what the spirit desires is against the flesh, because the two are opposed to each other—which keeps you from doing what you mean to do. But if you're led by spirit, you aren't under the Law. Now it's very clear what the deeds of the flesh are: lewd behavior, uncleanness, wildness, idol worship, witchcraft, making enemies, strife, jealousy, hot tempers, arguments, divisions, factions, envy, drunkenness, bacchanals and the like, about which I declare to you now as I declared before that those who do such things will not inherit God's kingdom. The fruits of the spirit, on the other hand, are love, joy, peace, patience, kindliness, goodness, faith, gentleness, and self-control. There is no law against things like that. Those who belong to Christ have crucified the flesh along with its passions and cravings. If we live by spirit we also walk by spirit: let's not be full of hollow pride, facing each other down and viewing each other with jealousy.

6

Brothers and sisters, if a person is caught in some violation, you as spiritual persons are to set that person right in a spirit of gentleness, making sure in the process that you are not tempted yourself. Help bear one another's burdens, and that way you will fulfill the law of Christ. Anyone who thinks he's something special, which he isn't, is just fooling himself. Let each examine his own deeds and then he can at least take credit for his own deeds and not other people's. Each person will have his own load to carry.

Let those who are instructed in the word share all good things with their instructor. Don't be fooled: you can't play games with God. What a person sows he will also reap. If you cultivate your flesh, the harvest of your flesh will be decay; if you cultivate your spirit, the harvest of your spirit will be life everlasting. Let's do the right thing and not lose heart: we will reap the harvest in our own due season if we don't give up. So then while we have time, let us do good to all, especially our family-members in the faith.

(Here I am writing in my own hand—notice the large letters?) Those who want to keep up appearances physically are only making you get circumcised so they themselves won't be persecuted about the cross of Christ. In fact the circumcised ones don't even keep the Law themselves. They just want *you* to be circumcised so they can boast of controlling your physical condition.

Far be it from me to boast of anything unless of the cross of our Lord Jesus Christ, through whom the world has been crucified to me and I to the world. Remember, circumcision doesn't count, nor does having a foreskin: what counts is being a new creation. And those who proceed by that standard, peace upon them, and mercy on the Israel of God.

In the future, let no one cause me grief. I already bear the wound-marks of Jesus on my body.

The grace of our Lord Jesus Christ be with your spirits, brothers and sisters, let it be so.

The Letter from Paul to the Community in
Ephesus

1

From Paul, apostle of Christ Jesus through God's will,
To the holy ones in Ephesus and the faithful in Christ Jesus:
Grace to you and peace from God, our Father and the Father of our Lord Jesus Christ.

   Bless God the Father of our Lord Jesus Christ, who blessed us in Christ among the heavenly with every spiritual blessing, accordingly as He chose us in Christ before the creation of the world to stand before Him holy and spotless in love, and preselected us for adoption as His children through Jesus Christ and for Jesus Christ. That was in accord with His intention to increase the praise of His glorious grace, which He has graced us with in His beloved son. For in His son we find ourselves redeemed through his blood and our violations paid for with the wealth of grace that He has lavished upon us in His total wisdom and good judgment. In the process He has let us in on the secret of His intentions, the decision He long ago made for Himself about how to administer the culmination of time: namely, that under the heading of Christ everything in the skies and on the earth should be summed up: in him. It is also through him that we are included in God's promises, chosen for that purpose by the One who manipulates all things according to the pleasure of His will, destined to be part of the luster of His glory, we who have long since put our hopes in Christ. And it was in him that you too, who heard the words of truth, the good news of your salvation, and believed in it, it was in him that you received the seal of the spirit of the promise, that holy spirit which is the surety of our promised inheritance, of being ransomed and signed over to God, to the further increase of His glory and praise.

   Therefore, since I too have heard of the faith among you in Lord Jesus and of the love you have shown to the holy ones, I never cease to thank God for you, remembering you in my prayers that the God of our Lord

Jesus Christ, the Father of glory, may give you the spirit to find wisdom and revelation in the knowledge of Him, brightening the eyes of your heart to let you see what His calling means, what hopes it contains, what a wealth of glory He means to distribute among the holy ones, and what an overwhelming power He exerts on us believers by activating the controlling force of His might. He activated it in Christ by raising him from the dead and setting him at His right hand in the heavens above and beyond all dominion and authority and power and lordship and every name that is named, not only in this age but in the coming ones. And so He "placed everything beneath his feet" and made him the head on the highest level for the assembly, which is his body: the completion of him who completes all in all.

2

And you were once dead, with all the offenses and wrongdoing that was part of your lives, going the way of this passing world, the way of the Prince of Flying Things, the same spirit now working in the family of unbelievers. And our former behavior once put all of us in that class, with our fleshly cravings forcing us to do the will of our bodies and our mental fixations, so that we were children born to God's wrath, just like the rest. But God, rich in mercy, because of His love that He felt for us, dead in our sins though we were, He brought us back to life along with Christ—it is grace that has saved you—and raised us along with Christ and set us there in the heavens beside Christ Jesus, so that the coming ages might be shown the surpassing wealth of His grace by His kindness toward us in Christ Jesus. Yes, it is grace that has saved you through faith. It didn't come from you: the gift is God's. Nor is it based on your deeds, so that no one should act too proud. We are, after all, of His making, created in Christ Jesus for the good work that God prepared for us to give our lives to.

Therefore remember that once you were paganism in the flesh, the "foreskinned world" (as you were called by those who call themselves "circumcised" in their manufactured, corporeal way). That was because at that time you were without Christ, alien to the citizenship of Israel and foreigners to the promises of God's covenant, without hope in a world without God. But now you who were off in the distance have come close in the blood of Christ. He is our peace, who joined the two in one and tore down the intervening fence along with the enmity it physically represents, nullifying the law of dogmatic commandments so that he could make peace by reshaping both [Jew and Gentile] as one new person in himself and then reconciling the two, now incorporated as one, to God through the cross, taking the enmity to death with him as he died. And he came forth to bring the good news: peace to you out there and peace to those right here, because through him both can gain entrance to see the Father in one spirit.

In short, you aren't foreigners or resident aliens any more: you live with your fellow citizens, the holy ones, as members of the household of God, built on the foundation of the apostles and prophets, Christ Jesus himself being the cornerstone on which the entire building is constructed and rises into a holy temple in the Lord, in which you are also built into the structure so as to be in spirit a settlement of God.

3

On that account, I Paul, am the prisoner of Christ Jesus: it's because of you the Gentiles. You may have heard how the plan of God's grace picked me to come to you, and how God's secret was made known to me by divine revelation. I briefly wrote you of that before: read that and you can get an idea of my insight into the secret of Christ, a secret not revealed in previous generations to the sons of humanity, which has now been revealed in the spirit to his holy apostles and prophets: that the other nations are made part of the inheritance and part of the body and partners in the promise in Christ Jesus by the terms of that same good word whose servant I became through the free gift of God's grace, given me by His activating power.

I, the last and least of all holy ones, was granted the favor of giving the Gentiles the good news of the inestimable wealth of Christ and of opening their eyes as to what kind of secret plan God, the Creator of all, has kept hidden from past centuries, to reveal it now to the celestial powers and principalities, God's assembly being the showpiece of the many-faceted wisdom of God, as seen in the plan God made centuries ago involving Christ Jesus our Lord, who gives us confidence and makes an opening for us by means of the conviction that comes through faith in him. That is why I pray not to lose heart amid my sufferings for you, which are your glory.

On that account I bend my knee before the Father from whom all citizenship in the skies and on the earth receives its name, praying that He may grant you, out of His rich glory, to be confirmed in power in your inner selves through His spirit, and that with faith's aid Christ may settle down in your hearts, so that thus rooted and grounded in love you may have the power to comprehend, along with all the faithful, the length and breadth and height and depth of it all, and to know what surpasses knowing: the love of Christ. Thus may you be filled with every fullness of God.

To Him who can do more than anything—things way beyond what we ask for or dream of—by the power activated in ourselves, to Him be the glory in the assembly and in Christ Jesus for all generations forever and ever, let it be so.

4

So I, the prisoner of the Lord, am asking you to behave as is worthy of the calling you were called to, with all humility and gentleness, with patience, putting up with each other charitably, studiously preserving unity of spirit in the common bond of peace.

> One body and one spirit, as you were called with the same hopes
>   for your calling,
> One Lord, one faith, one cleansing,
> One God and Father of all,
> Who is over all and through all and in all.

Each of us has been given grace according to the measure of Christ's free gift. That's why it says:

> *He ascended to the heights and took captivity captive;*
> *He gave gifts to the world.*

What does "ascended" mean if not that he had also descended to the lower regions of Earth? The one who descended is the same as the one who ascended higher than the heavens, so as to fulfill all things. And it was he who gave us the apostles, the prophets, the heralds of the good news, the shepherds and the teachers for the training of the holy ones in the work of service, to build up the body of Christ until we all arrive at the unity of belief in, and perception of, the son of God, and add up together to one perfect man, some portion of the maturity of the fullness of Christ. Then we won't be babies anymore, drifting and blown around by every doctrinal wind amid all the fallaciousness, the treachery that works by deceitful dodges; instead, firm in the truth of love, we will make everything grow towards him who is the head: Christ, by whose guidance the entire body, fitted and bound together with all sorts of connective equipment, gets together to do what's good for the body as a whole—each member in due proportion, so that the body builds itself up in love.

Therefore I say and testify in the Lord that you must not walk the path the pagans walk in their emptiness of mind, dim of perception and excluded from the life of God by the ignorance among them and the stoniness of their hearts—they who feel no pain any more and have given themselves over to shameless behavior, engaging in all kinds of filthy behavior insatiably.

That's not the Christ you were taught. Didn't you ever hear or receive instruction about him, how the truth is there in Jesus: how you must put away—along with your old behavior—your old selves, corrupted by desires that lead you on, and must be rejuvenated in the spirit of your senses and put on your new selves, made to God's order in virtue and the holiness of truth.

So put away all dishonesty and "let each of you speak the truth with your neighbor," because we are parts of each other. "Be angry but do no wrong." Don't let the sun set on your anger or you'll make an opening for the Father of Discord. Anyone who is stealing must stop stealing and instead work with his own hands to earn all the good things of life so he'll have something to give when someone else needs it. Let all ugly words be forbidden to go out of your mouth; instead, let it be something good that will speak constructively to people's needs and bring grace to your listeners. And don't make trouble for the holy spirit of God, who gave you your seal for the day of redemption. All bitterness and hot tempers and rage and yelling and cursing must be removed from you, and every evil besides. Be decent towards each other, compassionate, doing things for each other, as God did something for you by giving you Christ.

5

So, as beloved children of God, take after Him and walk in love like the love Christ showed for you, laying himself down as a contribution and sacrifice to rise as a sweet-smelling fragrance to God.

Let all lewd behavior, uncleanness and greed be completely unheard of among you, the way it should be among holy ones, and the same goes for shameful, vapid, or insincere speech—things that aren't becoming—where instead there should be blessings and thanksgiving. Be conscious of this: that anyone lewd or unclean or given to the idolatry that is greed is disinherited of the kingdom of Christ and God. Make no mistake, deceived by someone's empty words: those things bring down the wrath of God upon the children of disobedience. So don't be their fellows in guilt. After all, back then you were the darkness, but now in the Lord you are a light. Walk like children of the light (since the light bears fruit in all kind of goodness, rightness and truth), looking to see what best pleases the Lord. And don't join in the fruitless works of darkness, but rather expose them to the light. Because their doings in secret are too shameful even to name, but when it is all examined under the light it comes to light, and all that comes to light *is* light, which is why it says,

> Sleeper awake!
> Rise up from the dead,
> And Christ will shine down upon you.

So look closely at how you live: not like the witless but like the wise, finding a way to turn the time to profit in these evil days. So don't be foolish, but understand what the will of the Lord is. And don't be always drunk on wine, which brings a loss of self-control, but be filled with the spirit, speaking to each other in psalms and hymns and religious songs, playing and singing to the Lord with your hearts, always thanking God the Father for everything in the name of our Lord Jesus Christ. Be subject to each other out of respect for Christ, with wives subject to their own husbands as to the Lord, since the wife is headed by her husband, just as the head of the assembly is Christ, the savior of the whole body. But as the assembly is subordinate to Christ, so women should be subordinate to their husbands in everything.

Men, love your wives, just as Christ loved the assembly and laid himself down for it, to make it holy, cleansing it with the washing of water and saying of the word, so as to provide himself with a glorious assembly that would have no blotches or wrinkles or anything like that but instead be holy and spotless. That's how men should love their wives: like their own bodies. The man who shows love to his wife shows love to himself. After all, no one ever hated his own flesh; no, we nourish it and cherish it, just as Christ does with his assembly, because we are parts of his body. "On this account a man shall leave father and mother and stick with his wife, and the two shall become one living thing." There is a great secret here; I apply it to Christ and the assembly. But also to each of you: you should love your wife the same as yourself, but let the wife know her husband is boss.

6

Children, obey your parents in the Lord; that's only just. "Honor your father and your mother," that's the first commandment in the covenant, "that you may do well and be long-lived upon the earth."

And parents, don't make your children resentful, but bring them up with discipline and mindfulness of the Lord.

Slaves, obey your earthly masters with fear and trembling in the simplicity of your hearts as if obeying Christ, not doing a superficial job to meet human standards but doing the will of God from your soul like slaves of Christ, serving with good will as if you were serving the Lord and not a human being, knowing that any person who does something good will be repaid by God whether slave or free. And masters, act the same way toward them, leaving aside intimidation, knowing that their Master and yours is in heaven and there is no respecting of persons with Him.

For the rest, be empowered in the Lord and in the force of His strength. Put on the armor of God so that you can stand up against the dodges of the devil. Because our fight is not against flesh and blood but against the Powers, Dominions and World Rulers of this present darkness, against the spirits of evil high in the skies. Therefore take up the armor of God so that you can stand up against the evil day and accomplish everything without falling down. Therefore stand forth with the truth like a belt around your waist, having put on the breastplate of justice and sandaled your feet in readiness on behalf of the good news of peace, brandishing amidst it all the shield of faith, with which you can make all the flaming missiles of the Evil One fall spent to the ground. And reach for the helmet of salvation and the sword of the spirit, which consists in the word of God.

Amid all your prayers and petitions, keep praying at all times in the spirit, and spend your nights the same way, persevering in prayer for all the holy ones—and for me too, that I may be given the words to open my mouth so that I can freely make known the secret of the good news (for which I serve as ambassador in chains), that it may give me the confidence to say what I should.

So that you too can find out about me and how I'm doing, all that will be communicated to you by Tychicus, a beloved brother and trusty servant in the Lord whom I sent to you for just that purpose, so you could find out about me and relieve your hearts.

Peace with faith to the brothers and sisters, from God the Father and Lord Jesus Christ. Grace be with all whose love for our Lord Jesus Christ is safe from death's decay.

The Letter from Paul to the Community in
Philippi

1

From Paul and Timothy, slaves of Christ Jesus;

To all the holy ones in Christ Jesus living in Philippi, with their overseers and church-servants:

Grace to you and peace fom God, Father to us and to Lord Jesus Christ.

I thank my God each time I remember you in my constant prayers on your behalf; and my prayers are made joyful by your having been part of the good news from day one to the present day, since I am convinced of this if anything: that the One who began this good work among you will carry it right through to the day of Christ Jesus.

It is only right that I should have such feelings for you all when you have kept me in your hearts and shared in the grace shown me amid my chains as also amid my efforts to defend and strengthen the good word; and indeed God is my witness that with the heart of Christ Jesus I long to see you. And this I pray: that your love may more and more be bursting with knowledge and many-faceted perception, so that you can sort out what's important and be sincere and blameless for the day of Christ, yielding, with the help of Christ Jesus, a full harvest of just actions to the greater glory and praise of God.

One thing I want you to know, brothers and sisters, is that what has happened to me has served if anything to advance the cause of the good word, to the point where my chains have spread the fame of Christ through all the ruling house and all its attendant crowd, with the greater part of the brethren in the Lord so won over by my chains that they speak the word more fearlessly than ever. Some do so, to be sure, for spiteful and contentious reasons; but others proclaim the Messiah in good faith, acting from love, knowing that I am poised to defend the good word, whereas those who are there for partisan reasons proclaim the Messiah in a way that isn't clean, as if to add an extra rancor to my chains.

But so what? as long as one way or another, for devious or truthful reasons, Christ is being proclaimed; and that makes me happy.

And I will also be happy in the future, because I know that—with your prayers and contributions of the spirit of Jesus Christ—what happens to me will be towards salvation, in line with my expectation and hopes that I will come to no shame, and that, on the contrary, now as much as ever, my body will serve the greatness of Christ for all to see, whether in life or in death.

Understand that for me, Christ is the only life, and death means getting ahead. But being alive physically means my labors can bring fruit, so I don't know which to choose. I am pressed from both sides. I have the longing to break away and be with Christ: that would be vastly more desirable. But on your account, persisting in the flesh is more necessary. And in that conviction I *know* that I will still be here for you all and will keep on working for your advancement and joy in the faith, so that I may make you burst with the glorious feeling of Christ Jesus by coming again to see you.

Just act like a community worthy of the good news of Christ, so that whether I come and see you or whether I'm far away, what I hear about you is that you are standing firm, united in spirit, not at all abashed by your enemies, striving as one, joined by your belief in the good news, the belief that is the sign of their destruction and your salvation—in both cases coming from God; since you were given the gift of being for Christ, not just believing in him but also suffering for him and facing the same battle that you saw me face and now hear that I am faced with again.

2

So if there is any consolation in Christ, if there is such a thing as the solace of love, if there is any sharing of the spirit, or if there is pity and mercy anywhere, then make my joy complete by holding to the same convictions, having the same love, as soulmates with the same ends in mind, never acting contentiously or out of vanity, but humbly giving others a higher status than yourself, not with each person looking out for himself but with each of you looking out for the others too.

Keep the same spirit amongst yourselves that is also in Christ Jesus:

> Who, though in form divine,
> Held being equal to God as nothing to cling to,

But emptied himself and took the form of a slave,
Made in the likeness of humankind,
And, being seen as a human figure,
He humbled himself by being obedient unto death,
And not just death, but the cross;
Wherefore God also raised him up on high
And bestowed on him the name above all names
So that in the name of Jesus every knee would bend,
Whether celestial, earthly, or below the earth,
And every tongue confess that Jesus Christ is Lord,
To the greater glory of the Father, God.

Therefore, dear friends, just as you always obeyed before, not just in my presence but now even more in my absence, work with alarmed urgency to bring about your salvation, for it is God within you who motivates both your intentions and your actions on behalf of what He deems good. Do it all without grumbling and second thoughts, so that you'll be blameless and guileless, spotless children of God amid a generation of moral hunchbacks and perverts, among whom you will shine like the lanterns of the universe, holding to the word of Life (and allowing me to claim, on the day of Christ's return, that I did not lose my way or labor for nothing). But even if I myself end up being sacrificed in the course of offering up the service and sacrifice of your faith, I am glad for myself and glad for all of you, so do likewise: be glad for yourselves and glad for me.

I hope in Lord Jesus to send Timothy to you soon, that I too may have the satisfaction of knowing how you are. No one I have of his soul-stature shows such genuine concern on your behalf; they all want what is theirs, not what is Jesus Christ's. You know how solid he is, how he has served me like a child serving his father in the work of the good news. So he is the one I hope to send you as soon as I see how things are going to turn out for me—but I am convinced in the Lord's name that I will soon come myself.

I found it necessary to send back to you Epaphroditus, my brother, colleague, and comrade-in-arms, whom you had delegated to supply my needs: he missed all of you so much and was so dispirited because you had heard that he was sick. And indeed he was sick, near to death. But God had mercy on him—and not just him; He also had enough mercy on me not to give me grief upon grief. So I was all the more anxious to send him, so that you could have the joy of seeing him restored, and I could have one grief less. So receive him in the Lord's name with all joy, and make a place of honor for people like him, because in the work of Christ he came near death and put his life on the line to do what the rest of you couldn't do by way of giving me service.

3

For the rest, my brothers and sisters, be happy in the Lord. If I write the same things to you over and over, it's no extra trouble for me, and for you it gives greater certainty.

Watch out for those dogs, those evil operators, those ax-wielding circumcisionaries! In fact, we are the circumcised ones, serving the spirit of God and glorying in Christ Jesus and having a conviction not written on our flesh [by circumcision], even if my convictions *are* written on my flesh. And by the way, if anyone thinks he is conviction in the flesh, I am more so: circumcised the eighth day, of Israel's race, Benjamin's tribe, Hebrew born of Hebrews, in matters of the Law a Pharisee, by inclination a persecutor of our assembly: so that as far as the virtue of fulfilling the Law goes, I couldn't be faulted.

But what was a plus for me then, I now consider a minus because of Christ, though actually I consider everything a minus, so surpassing is the knowledge of Christ Jesus my Lord, for whom I already wrote off everything as a loss and consider it a pile of manure as long as I gain Christ and find a place in him, not with my good standing based on the Law but with a standing that comes through the faith of Christ, the standing God confers upon faith, so as to make me know Christ and the power of his resurrection and my participation in his sufferings. Thus, by sharing in the form of his death, I may yet attain to being resurrected from the dead.

Not that I've already got it or that I'm already perfect; rather, I'm pursuing something I hope to catch, much as I have been caught by Christ. Brothers and sisters, I don't think of myself as having reached my goal, all I think is this: that, forgetting what lies behind me and reaching out for what lies ahead, I pursue the prize I have set my sights upon, namely the higher calling of God in Christ Jesus. Those of us who are perfected should all see things this way. Even if you see things another

way, this is what God will reveal to you. Just be sure to proceed by the
same path that has brought us this far.

Join together in following my example, brothers and sisters, and
observe those who go by the model that you have in us: because there are
many others, as I have said to you many times and now say through my
tears, who are enemies of the cross of Christ, who are headed for
perdition, who deify their bellies and glory in their swinishness, because
their minds are here on earth. But our citizenship is valid in the skies,
from which we also expect that a savior will come, Lord Jesus Christ,
who will reshape our wretched bodies to match his glorious body by the
indwelling power of the One who has so much power that He can make
all things subject to Christ.

4

And so, brothers and sisters whom I cherish and long for—my crowning
joy—keep steady in the Lord, dearest friends.

I call on Euodia, and I call on Syntyche too, to keep your mind on your
common goals in the Lord. As a matter of fact, I also ask my distinguished
colleague if you would look after them, since they both fought for the
good word beside me, along with Clement and those other fellow-
workers of mine whose names are in the Book of Life.

Be happy in the Lord at all times. Again I say, be happy. Your decency
deserves to be known to all the world. The Lord is near. Never worry
about any matter, but make it all a prayer and a petition, giving God
thanks and making your requests known to Him. And the peace of God
surpassing all conception will stand guard over your hearts and thoughts
in Christ Jesus.

For the rest, brothers and sisters, ask yourselves: What is true? What
is modest? What is just? What is pure? What is friendly? What makes
a good reputation? Is there anything virtuous or praiseworthy here?
Those are the things to think about. Remember what was taught and
conveyed to you and what you heard from me and what you saw in me:
act like that, and the God of peace will be with you.

It gave me great joy in the Lord to see how your concern for me
blossomed once again, after that first time when you had the concern but
no chance to act on it. I don't mean to sound deprived: I have learned to
get along with whatever circumstances I am in. I know what it means to

live humbly, and what it means to have everything. I am schooled in the
mysteries of each and every circumstance: feasting and starving and
having everything and having nothing. I have the strength for it all
because of the one who empowers me.

At any rate, you did a fine thing by making my troubles your own. Do
you know, Philippians, that when I was coming from Macedonia, back
when the good news was first coming out, that none of the assemblies
made it their rule to give something for something received except for
you alone? Even when I reached Thessalonica, you not just once but
twice sent something along to help with my needs. Not that I'm looking
for gifts: no, I'm looking for you to bear the kind of fruit that will add to
your standing. I have received your whole gift and I have plenty now,
having had the fulfillment of receiving from Epaphroditus what came
from you: a sweet fragrance floating upward, a proper sacrifice, well-
pleasing to God. My God will supply all your needs with the wealth of
His glory in Christ Jesus. To God our Father be the glory forever and
ever, let it be so.

Convey my greetings in Christ Jesus to each of the holy ones. The
brothers and sisters here with me say hello. Greetings to you from all the
holy ones, especially those of the imperial household.

The grace of Jesus Christ be with your spirits.

The Letter from Paul to the Community in

Colossae

1

From Paul, apostle of Christ Jesus through the will of Christ, and Brother Timothy;
To the holy and faithful brothers and sisters in Christ living in Colossae: Grace to you and peace from God our Father.

We thank God the Father of our Lord Jesus Christ at all times in our prayers concerning you, for we have heard of your faith in Christ Jesus and the love you show toward all the holy ones for the sake of the hope stored up for you in the skies, of which you were told in the truthful words of the good news when it came to you. In fact throughout the world the good news has been bearing fruit and growing apace, and so it has done among you since the first day you heard of, and truly understood about, this grace of God from the teaching of my dear fellow-worker Epaphras (who is a trusty servant of Christ on your behalf and who has described to us how much love issues from your spirit).

And therefore we, ever since the first day we heard about you, have never stopped praying and petitioning that you may be filled with the consciousness of Christ's will, with all wisdom and spiritual understanding, so that your path is worthy of the Lord and completely to his liking, bearing fruit in all good works and with growing consciousness of God, empowered by the strength of His glory with all needed powers of endurance and patience, and joyfully thanking God the Father, who gave you the right to be granted your portion alongside the rest of the holy ones, standing in the light.

> He: who snatched us from the powers of darkness
> And put us instead in the kingdom of the Son of His love,
> From whom comes our redemption and forgiveness of
>   wrongdoing,
> Who is the image of God the invisible,

And firstborn of all creation,
Since in him were created all things
In the skies and on the earth,
The seen and the unseen,
Whether thrones, lordships, sovereignties, or powers:
All were created through him, and with him in mind.
And he himself is before all things
And all things are contained in him,
And he is the head of our assembly's body.
He is the beginning, firstborn from among the dead,
So that among all persons he might have first place,
Because in him all fullness thought it good to dwell,
Using his aid to reconcile all things to him,
(Peacemaker through the blood he shed upon the cross),
Yes, all things, whether upon the earth or in the skies.

And you, who were once aliens and enemies to good sense, given over to doing evil, were reconciled by him through the death of his fleshly body, which enabled you to stand in holiness, spotless and blameless in his sight, as long as you stand founded and firm in your belief, unwavering in the hope given you by the good news that you heard, the same that has been proclaimed throughout all creation under the sun and which now counts me, Paul, as its servant.

Now I welcome what happens to me for your sake: my own flesh is catching up on the sufferings of Christ by my sufferings for the sake of his body, which is his assembly. It is Christ's assembly whose servant I have become by taking on the assignment to you that God gave me of fulfilling the word of God, the secret hidden from former ages and generations. But now the secret has been revealed to His holy ones, to whom God wanted to show the wealth of glory contained in this, His secret plan for the Gentiles: that you should have Christ among you, your hope of glory. He is the message that we bear and bring to every person's attention, as we instruct each person in all wisdom, wishing to see every person be perfect in Christ. That is what I labor for, struggling on with an inner strength from him that operates in me very powerfully.

2

And I want you to know how much I worry about both you and the group in Laodicia, and about many other people who have never physically seen my face, hoping that your hearts will be consoled, as you hold steady in love on the way to all the riches of a mature understanding and knowledge of God's secret, Christ, in whom all treasures of wisdom and knowledge lie hidden.

I say this so that no one will deceive you with fancy oratory. Even if I am absent physically, still I am there with you spiritually, rejoicing to see you so together and solid in your belief in Christ.

So now that you have accepted Christ Jesus the Lord, keep going his way, rooted in him and built upon him and confirmed in the faith as it was taught you, bursting with gratitude. Watch out for anyone who might string you along with philosophizing and empty pretense of purely human origin, having to do with "the elements of the cosmos" and having nothing to do with Christ, since in him the whole fullness of divinity bodily resides, and you are now filled with him, the head of all authority and power. And because of him you are also circumcised with a circumcision that is not created artificially by taking off part of the fleshly body, but with the circumcision of Christ, by being buried with him in a baptism in which you are also resurrected with him by faith in the efficacy of God who raised him from the dead.

And you, who were dead in your sins and uncircumcised in your flesh, he raised you back to life again with him, freely letting us off for all our transgressions. He obliterated the arrest warrant with our names on it that had been in force against us, with all its dogmas, hauled it right out of the way and nailed it to the cross. Stripping the principalities and powers bare, he showed them up for what they were and paraded them as captives in his triumph.

Don't let anyone call you to account about your food or drink or your observances of the feast days, the new moons, and the sabbaths. Those things are just the shadows of what was to come; the actual body is Christ. Let no one put you in your place with a show of piety and devotion to angelic ministers he claims to have seen on his inner journeys, being vainly inflated in his earthly mind and not having control of his head, which should allow the whole body, fitted and connected with joints and ligatures, to keep growing with the growth of God.

When you died with Christ, you got away from "cosmic elements." Now that you live again, why let the world make rules for you like "Don't touch this and don't taste that and don't come close to the other"—about things that are there to be consumed and used up—on the basis of purely human commands and teachings? There may be a measure of wisdom in their artificial devotions and humble piety and denial of their bodies, but as far as curbing fleshly indulgence, it has no value.

3

So now that you have been brought back to life along with Christ, aim for the heights, where Christ sits at the right hand of God. Keep your mind on the heights, not here on earth. You died, remember, and your life is hidden with Christ in God. When Christ, your life, is fully revealed then you yourselves will also stand fully revealed with him in glory.

So kill off every part of you that's bound to the earth: whoring, uncleanness, passions, evil desires, and the idolatry that is greed. These things bring down the wrath of God upon the tribe of the unbelievers. These are things that you too were involved in before, when you lived with them all around you. But now be sure to clear all anger, willfulness, meanness, cursing and foul language out of your mouths. Don't lie to each other, now that you've cast off your old self and the conduct that went with it and put on your new self, which is renovated to be made more perceptive, using as a model the image of its Creator, for whom there are no Gentiles and no Jews, no circumcision and no foreskins, and no foreigners, barbarians, slaves, or free men, but instead Christ is all in all.

And so, as God's holy and beloved chosen ones, wrap yourself in the guts of compassion, good will, humility, gentleness and patience, putting up with one another and being gracious towards each other when someone is involved with someone else in a dispute. Just as the Lord was gracious to you, that's how you should act toward others. One thing above all else: love, which is a link to perfection. And let the peace of Christ be in charge of your hearts, that peace to which you were called all as one body. And be thankful.

May the word of Christ settle in with you abundantly as you teach and admonish each other in all wisdom, singing psalms and hymns and religious songs to God from the grace of your hearts. And anything whatever that you do, in word or in deed, let it all be in the name of Lord Jesus, giving thanks to God the Father through him.

Women, be obedient to your husbands as becomes those who belong to the Lord. Men, love your wives and don't be nasty to them. Children, obey your parents in every way, since that is proper among the Lord's people. Parents, don't keep badgering your children until they lose heart.

Slaves, be obedient in every way to your earthly masters, not with a superficial job that looks good to human eyes, but with simplicity of heart and fear of the Lord. Whatever you do, let your work come from your soul as if serving the Lord and not a human being, and remember that you will be repaid by the Lord with the inheritance [of his kingdom]. Be slaves of Christ the Lord. Whoever does wrong will find his misdeeds coming back to him: there is no respecting of persons there. Masters, show fairness and impartiality to your slaves, knowing that you also have a Master in heaven.

4

Persevere in prayer, staying awake to do it and giving thanks; at the same time pray for us too, that God may open to us a door for the word, for telling the secret of Christ (the secret for whose sake I lie in chains), so that I can reveal it as it ought to be told. Deal wisely with the rest of the world, taking advantage of what time there is. Always make your words graceful and well-suited to the point, so that for each person you know what answer to give.

As for me, that will all be related to you by our dear brother Tychicus, a trusty servant and fellow-slave in the Lord, whom I sent to you precisely so you could find out how I am and so he could relieve your minds; along with him I sent our dear and faithful brother Profitabilis, who is one of you. They will tell you all about how things are here.

Greetings to you from Aristarchus, my fellow captive, and from Mark, the cousin of Barnabas (about whom you were given instructions to welcome him if he comes your way), and also from Jesus "the Just," these being the only ones of Jewish origin to work beside me for the kingdom of God: they have been a great comfort to me. Greetings to you from your own Epaphras, a slave of Christ Jesus who is always fighting for you with his prayers that you may stand perfected and fulfilled in everything that is the will of God. I can vouch for him that he takes great pains on your behalf and for the people in Laodicia and Hierapolis. Greetings to you from our dear friend Doctor Luke and from Demas.

Say hello to the brothers and sisters in Laodicia, and to Nympha and the group that meets at her house. Also, after this letter has been read to you, arrange for the assembly at Laodicia to have it read to them too, while you also read the letter sent to Laodicia. And say to Archippus, "Remember the mission you have taken on in the Lord's name and be sure to carry it through."

Greetings to you in my own hand,

PAUL

Remember my chains. Grace be with you.

Thessalonica

1

From Paul, Silas and Timothy,

To the Thessalonian assembly in God the Father and Lord Jesus Christ: Grace to you, and peace.

We thank God constantly for all of you, remembering you in our prayers, thinking over and over of your deeds of faith and labors of love, and your steadfast clinging to the hope given us by our Lord Jesus Christ, with which we can face our God and Father. And we know, brothers and sisters loved by God, that He has chosen you, and that when we brought you the good news, for you it wasn't just words: it was power, holy spirit, and real results; you know as well as we do what our presence among you has meant to you.

And you followed our example and that of the Lord, accepting the word, and all the sufferings that go with it, in the joy of the holy spirit, so much so as to make you a model for all the believers in Macedonia and Achaea. After all, the word of the Lord that started with you has resounded forth not just in Macedonia and Achaea: no, your faith in God has spread to all parts of the world. In fact, by now we have no need to mention it, since everyone else is already saying it for us: what kind of inroads we made with you, how you turned to God, leaving your idols behind to serve a true and living God while waiting for His son to return from the skies, the one whom God raised from the dead, Jesus, who pulls us out of the path of the approaching fury.

2

After all, you know yourselves, brothers and sisters, that it was not for nothing that we made our approach to you. After all we went through and the indignities we suffered, as you know, in Philippi, our God still gave us the courage to speak the good word of God to you—another great struggle. That's because what we espouse is not based on foolishness or skullduggery and is not a trick: instead, we speak the good word in the same form in which we have been entrusted with it by God's approval, not so as to please the world but so as to please God, the examiner of our hearts. Thus we were never the ones for flattering words, as you know, nor for covert moneygrubbing, as God is our witness; nor were we looking for glory from anyone, whether from you or from others. We could have acted important as Christ's emissaries, but instead we were as gentle in your midst as a nurse with her own children, so drawn to you that we felt like transmitting our very souls to you, and not just the good news of God: that's how dear you were to us. You recall, brothers and sisters, with what toil and weariness we labored day and night so as not to burden any of you [with our upkeep] while we proclaimed to you the good news of God. You are my witnesses and God is too, as to how impeccably pious and proper we were towards you the believers: you know how we treated each of you like a father his children, exhorting you, encouraging you, and formally calling upon you to live in a manner worthy of God, who is summoning you to the kingdom of His glory.

And thus we too thank God continually that when the audible word of God was transmitted from us to you, you did not take it to be the word of mortals, you took it for what it really is: the word of God, now activated within you the believers. That is shown by the way your experience, brothers and sisters, has mirrored that of the assemblies of God located in Judea who belong to Christ Jesus: you have had to undergo the same things at the hands of your countrymen that they have undergone at the hands of the Judeans. Ah, the Judeans, they who killed Lord Jesus and the prophets and who have hounded us from pillar to post, displeasing to God and at odds with all the world—and who now, to complete their wrongdoing once and for all, are trying to stop us from speaking to the Gentiles and saving them! But the wrath of God has caught up with those people at last.

As for us, brothers and sisters, we have felt terribly separated from you these last days (physically, not in our hearts), and we were extremely anxious to come see you face to face as we so much desired. In fact we would have come to you—I, Paul, made such plans not once but twice—if our way had not been blocked by Satan. After all, what hope, what joy or crowning glory do we have to show Lord Jesus when he comes again, if not you? You are our glory and our joy.

3

Finally, unable to stand it any longer, we decided to stay behind in Athens by ourselves while we sent Timothy, our brother and God's fellow-worker in spreading the good news of Christ, to give you support and strengthen the courage of your faith so you would not come unglued in these troubled times. After all, you know as well as we do that such troubles lie before us: indeed, when we were there with you, we told you in advance that we would have to suffer, which is just what has happened, as you know. That's why I couldn't stand it any longer and sought to get word about the state of your faith, fearing that the Tempter might have tempted you and our work might have come to nothing.

But when Timothy came back just now from seeing you, bringing us the good news of your faith and love and reporting that you remember us always in a kindly light and long to see us just as much as we long to see you, we were much encouraged (in the midst of all our suffering and need) to hear of your continued faith: it makes us come alive again to know that you stand firm in the Lord. Indeed, how can we thank God enough for you, seeing with what joy you have caused us to rejoice before our God? Night and day we pray as hard as we can to see your faces once again and remedy any weaknesses in your faith.

May God Himself, our Father, and our Lord Jesus clear a path for us to come see you. May the Lord also increase without limit your love for each other and for all people, so as to match our love for you, and may He give your hearts the strength to stand in faultless sanctity before God our Father upon the return of our Lord Jesus with all his holy attendants, let it be so.

4

One more thing, brothers and sisters, we ask and implore of you in the name of Lord Jesus: you have learned from us the way to live and how to please God, and in fact you are living that way, but now go even farther. After all, you know the principles we instilled in you through Lord Jesus. Remember, it is God's will that you should be consecrated to Him and keep away from lewd behavior, with each of you knowing enough to keep to what is his in holiness and honor (not in lustful passion like pagans who know nothing of God), and with no one overstepping the line and taking advantage of his brother in such matters, because the Lord is there to settle all these scores, as I already told you and spelled out for you. God didn't summon you to uncleanness, but to holiness. That means that anyone rejecting this is not rejecting a human being but God, who puts His holy spirit into you.

When it comes to brotherly love, you don't need me to write and tell you about it, God has already taught you directly to love each other, and so you have acted towards all the brothers and sisters in the whole of Macedonia. But I urge you, brothers and sisters, to go even farther and consider it a point of honor to keep the peace and mind your own business and work with your hands, the way we instructed you, so as to behave reputably toward the rest of the world and not lack for anything.

Now then: we don't want to leave you wondering, brothers and sisters, about those who have gone to their rest, so that you won't be grief-stricken in the same way as the others who don't share our hopes. Because if we believe that Jesus died and rose again, then God, using Jesus, will also bring the other sleepers along with him. We tell you this as the word of the Lord: we, the living who have been left here to await the coming of the Lord, will not get there before the dead. The Lord himself, amidst a shouted command, an archangel's voice, and the trumpet of God, will come down from the sky, and those who died in Christ will be the first to rise; then we who have been left alive will be snatched up in the clouds alongside them, moving through the air on our way to meet the Lord. And so we will be with the Lord forever. So comfort each other with these words.

5

As for the times and seasons, brothers and sisters, you need nothing written to you, you yourselves know very well that like a thief in the night is how the Day of the Lord will come. Just when they're saying, "Ah, peace and security!" that's when suddenly there will come upon them a destruction like the labor-pains of a woman with a child in her belly, and no way will they escape it. But you, brothers and sisters, are not in such darkness that the day should come upon you like a thief and catch you. You, after all, are all children of the light and the sunshine; we don't belong to the night or the darkness. Well then, let's not be asleep like the others, but stay wakeful and sober. For it is at night that the sleepers sleep and at night that the drinkers get drunk. But let us who belong to the day stay sober, dressed in the breastplate of faith and love and the helmet of our hope of salvation, because God did not put us here as objects of His anger, but to take ownership of us by salvation through our Lord Jesus Christ, who died for us so that whether sleeping or waking we might live together with him. So comfort each other and give support to one another, as in fact you are doing.

And now we ask you, brothers and sisters, to recognize those who labor among you and preside over you in the Lord and give you admonitions and to hold them in the most loving esteem because of the work they do. Live in peace with each other. We urge you, brothers and sisters: speak up to those who are wasting their lives, comfort the faint-hearted, put up with the weak, have patience with everyone. Be careful that no one returns evil for evil: always pursue goodness, towards each other and everyone else.

> Always be happy,
> Constantly pray.
> For all things be thankful,
> Since God wants that for you in Christ Jesus.
> Don't let the spirit ever go out
> Or prophecy ever come to scorn:
> Examine all things, and stick with the good,
> And from every form of evil keep away.

May the God of peace Himself sanctify you to perfection, and may your spirit, soul and body be preserved with faultless integrity upon the coming of our Lord Jesus Christ. Trust him who has called you: he will also follow through.

Brothers and sisters, pray for us.

Say hello to all the brothers and sisters with a holy kiss. Swear by the Lord that this letter will be read to all the brothers and sisters!

The grace of our Lord Jesus Christ be with you.

Thessalonica

1

From Paul, Silas and Timothy,
To the Thessalonian assembly in God the Father and Lord Jesus Christ:
Grace to you and peace from God our Father and Lord Jesus Christ.

We owe it to God to thank Him at all times for you, brothers and sisters: that's only right, when your faith keeps growing and growing and every single one of you abounds with such love for one another that we ourselves brag about you to the other assemblies of God: your steadfastness, your faith amid all your persecutions and the troubles you must bear. That steadfast faith proves that God has decided justly in deeming you worthy of the kingdom of God that you are suffering for. What, after all, could be more just than for God to repay your tormentors with torment and bring relief to you the tormented and to us? And He will, when Lord Jesus is revealed coming down from the sky with the messengers of his power, in flaming fire, meting out punishment for those who did not recognize God and who did not listen to the good word of our Lord Jesus: they shall pay the penalty of eternal damnation (far from the Lord and from the glory of his power) when he comes on that day to be glorified among his holy ones and to be the wonder of all believers, [including you] since you believed the testimony we gave you. Which is why we are always praying for you that our God may make you worthy of His calling and powerfully bring to fruition all your good intentions and your deeds of faith, so that the name of our Lord Jesus may be glorified among you and you may be glorified through him by the grace of our God and Lord Jesus Christ.

2

We urge you, brothers and sisters, as regards the coming of our Lord Jesus Christ and our [hopes of] being reunited with him, not to let your minds come easily unhinged and not to be terrified by any intuition, utterance, or even letter supposedly from us, that states that the Day of the Lord is already upon us.

Don't let anyone fool you by any means: Not till the great loss of faith has first come! Not till the Lawless One, the Son of Perdition has been revealed, who will oppose and put himself above every known "god" or devotion and finally enthrone himself in God's temple, pretending that he himself is God! (Don't you remember how I told you that back when I was still there with you?) What's keeping him? Why hasn't he been revealed in due course? Now you know: the essence of his lawlessness is already at work, but the one who has restrained him up till now still has to get out of the way. And then the Lawless One will be revealed, the one whom Jesus will destroy with the breath of his mouth and supersede by manifesting his own presence, that same one who has Satan working within him so that he can come along with all sorts of powers and false signs and omens and every sort of wrong to deceive the lost souls who were not instilled with the love of truth that would save them. For that, God sends upon them a deceiving force to make them believe in lies, so as to condemn all who wouldn't believe in the truth but preferred iniquity.

But we owe constant thanks to God on your behalf, brothers and sisters loved by the Lord, because God chose you as His consecrated portion, to be saved by holiness of spirit and faith in the truth. That is what He summoned you to through our spreading of the good word: to a glorious transfer of your ownership to our Lord Jesus Christ.

And so, brothers and sisters, stand firm and hold fast to the traditions you have been taught, whether verbally or in our letters. May our Lord Jesus Christ himself and God our Father, who has shown us His love and given us eternal consolation and good hope in His grace, encourage you in your hearts and support you in all your good words and deeds.

3

For the rest, pray for us, brothers and sisters, that the word of the Lord may spread and be glorified as has been the case with you, and that we may be delivered from the hands of screwed-up, evil people. The faith is not everyone's to have. But you can have faith in the Lord, who will support you and guard you from evil. And we have confidence in the

Lord about you, that what we have instructed you is what you are doing and will continue to do. May the Lord direct your hearts toward love of God and Christ-like endurance.

We command you, brothers and sisters, in the name of our Lord Jesus Christ to cut yourselves off from any brother who is living a disorderly life that is not in accord with the principles transmitted to them by us. You yourselves know that you're supposed to follow our example. When we were among you, did we hang around expecting that someone would feed us for free? No, we toiled and labored night and day so as not to be a burden to any of you, and not because we didn't have a right to do so, but so as to make an example of ourselves that you could follow. And in fact when we were there with you, this was our command to you: "If any will not work, neither let him eat." But now we hear that some of you are hanging around doing nothing and getting in other people's way. And we command and exhort those people in the name of Lord Jesus Christ to settle down and earn the bread that they eat.

As for you, brothers and sisters, keep doing the right thing and don't give up.

If anyone will not obey what we say in our letters, mark that person as someone to be avoided so as to shame him. And don't treat him as an enemy but admonish him as a brother. May the Lord of peace Himself give you peace at all times and in all ways. The Lord be with you all.

Greetings to you in my own handwriting, which is a mark of all my letters: this is what my writing looks like.

PAUL

The grace of our Lord Jesus Christ be with you all.

The First Letter from Paul to
Timothy

1

From Paul, apostle of Christ Jesus as commanded by God our Savior and Christ Jesus our hope;
To Timothy, our very own child in the faith:
Grace, peace and mercy from God the Father and Christ Jesus, our Lord.

[You recall] how I asked you to stay there in Ephesus, while I traveled on to Macedonia, so you could give certain people instructions not to meddle with the teachings and not to waste time on endless mythologies and genealogies, which lead to empty speculations and not to the faith in which God's plan is found. What the teaching aims at is the love that comes from a clean heart and upright sensibility and a faith without pretense; but some have moved away from these things and turned to empty speechifying in their desire to be "teachers of the law"—in fact they have no notion what they're saying or what their solemn assurances are about.

As for the Law, we know that it is good if a person uses it lawfully, knowing what the Law is there for: not for the just, but for the lawless and disorderly, the impious and sinful, the unholy and irreligious, father-killers and mother-killers, murderers, people who commit lewd acts and sleep with other men, slave-traders, liars, oath-breakers, and everything else contrary to the healthful teaching that is in line with the glorious good word of blessed God, the word that has been entrusted to me.

I thank the source of my power, Christ Jesus our Lord, that he thought me trustworthy enough to enlist in his service someone who used to be a blasphemer, persecutor, and criminal—except that I have been shown mercy on the grounds that I acted ignorantly in my unbelief. And then the overflowing grace of our Lord brought me faith and the love to be found in Christ Jesus. It is a reliable saying, worthy of everyone's acceptance, that Christ Jesus came into the world to save evildoers, I being chief among them. But I was shown mercy so that Christ Jesus could make me the chief example of all his forbearance, as a model for all the others who would make him the basis of their faith in everlasting life. To the King of the ages, imperishable, unseen, unique God, be honor and glory forever and ever, let it be so.

This is my charge to you, young Timothy: to be guided by the prophetic words that have been spoken over you and to fight the battle of goodness in light of them, keeping the kind of faithfulness and upright sensibility that others have repudiated at the cost of a shipwrecked faith—among them Hymenaeus and Alexander, whom I had to cast out to Satan until they learn to stop speaking such blasphemies.

2

I urge you first of all, then, to offer petitions, prayers, requests, and thanksgiving on behalf of all persons, for kings and all those in high places, so that we can lead a quiet and tranquil life of the greatest piety and purity, as is good and proper in the eyes of our savior God, who wants all people to be saved and come to the perception of truth.

> One God,
> And one mediator between God and humankind,
> The human Christ Jesus,
> Who gave himself as a ransom for all,
> Bearing witness at the chosen moment.

That is what I am here for, as a herald and emissary—I speak true, this is no lie—to be a teacher for the Gentiles in truth and good faith.

So then: I would like to see in each location the men praying with upraised holy hands, free of anger and dissension, with the women correspondingly in neat and tidy costumes, dressing themselves modestly and prudently, not in braids and curls and pearls and gold and expensive fabrics, but clothing themselves in good works, as befits women for whom godly reverence is a command. A woman should quietly receive instruction in complete obedience. I will not allow a woman to be a teacher nor act superior to a man: instead, she should be quiet and peaceable. After all, Adam was shaped first, and Eve second.

And it wasn't Adam who was deceived: the woman was deceived and is therefore in a state of transgression, but she shall be saved because of her childbearing function, the ones who continue in faith and love with a clear head. Those are words to count on.

3

Anyone who yearns to be a church-supervisor has set his sights on a noble task. Accordingly, the supervisor has to be someone above reproach: a one-woman man, sober, responsible, orderly, hospitable, and able to teach, not a boozer or a brawler, but instead reasonable, peaceful, and free of greed, a good head for his own household who keeps his children in line, respectable in every way. (If someone can't head his own household, how will he care for an assembly of God?) He should not be a newcomer who might get puffed up and fall into the devil's hands. He must also have a good reputation with the outside world, so as not to fall into disrepute and the traps of the devil.

For church-servants, the same: decent, not two-faced, not overly fond of their wine, not greedy and dishonest, but possessing the secret of the faith with a chaste sensibility. And they should be examined first and then serve if there's nothing wrong with them. Their wives should likewise be decent, not given to gossip, sober, trustworthy in every way. A church-servant should be a one-woman man, a good father to his children and a good head for his own household. Those who serve well make a special place for themselves and become especially confident of their faith in Christ Jesus.

I write these things to you in the hope of coming to see you very soon. But in case I am delayed I want you to know how people are to behave in God's house, which is what the congregation of the living God is: pillar and foundation of the truth. And as all concede, the secret of our worshipfulness is mighty:

> Made manifest in flesh,
> Made righteous in spirit,
> He appeared to his messengers,
> Was proclaimed to the nations,
> Was believed in by the world,
> Was raised high in glory.

4

The Spirit expressly says that in later times some will abandon the faith to follow misleading spirits and the teachings of demons with burned-out consciences, who in a show of dishonest language forbid marriage and say to avoid certain foods which God created to be gratefully partaken of by the faithful who perceive the truth: that all God's creation is good and none of what we gratefully receive should be rejected instead, not when it is made holy by God's word and the grace we say over it.

That is what you should present to the brothers and sisters in order to be a good servant of Christ Jesus, raised on the words of faith and sound teaching that you have devoted yourself to. As for unhallowed myths and old wives' tales, avoid them.

Train yourself in the art of reverence. Physical exercise is only useful in a limited way, while reverence is useful toward all ends because it carries the promise of life both present and future: those are reliable words, worthy of everyone's aceptance. In fact, that's why we toil and struggle: because our hope is in the living God, the savior of all humanity, especially the faithful.

Command these things and teach them. Don't let anyone look down on you for being young, but make yourself an example for the faithful by your speech, your behavior, your love, your faith, your purity. Until I arrive devote yourself to reading, giving advice, and teaching. Don't forget the gift within you that was given you by prophecy with laying-on of hands by the elders. Keep these things in mind and have them around you so that your advancement will be evident to all. Attend to yourself and to the teachings, and keep on with them: by doing that, you will save both yourself and those who listen to you.

5

With an older man use no shock tactics, but appeal to him as a father; appeal to younger men as your brothers, to older women as mothers, and to younger women in utter chastity as your sisters.

Do right by those widows who are really widowed. But if any widow has children or grandchildren, let them first learn to be decent to their own family and give something back to those who came before: that is what is expected in the sight of God. A real widow who has no one puts all her hopes on God and keeps to her petitions and prayers night and day; the one who's wallowing in luxury is already dead before she dies. And you must remind them of these things to keep them above reproach. Anybody who won't look after his own kind, especially his own family, has denied the faith and is worse than an unbeliever.

A widow whose name goes on the rolls should be no less than sixty years old and have been only one man's wife. Her good works should be well attested: Did she raise children? Did she lodge travelers? Did she wash the feet of holy persons? Did she lighten others' sufferings? Was she devoted to good works in general?

Avoid [enrolling] younger widows: when their lust gets the better of their spirit of Christ, they'll want to get married again, which is a crime because then they're doing so in the face of a prior vow [of celibate widowhood].* At the same time their idleness leads them to stick their head in at this door and that; and they're not just idle but gossipy and nosy too, saying things that shouldn't be said. Younger women, then, should re-marry, have children, run households, and offer no opening to the adversary who would slander us. I say this because some have already fallen in line behind Satan. If any woman among the faithful has widows in the family, she should help them herself, and not burden the community, which can then help those who are really widowed.

Elders who fill their position well should be regarded with double respect, especially laborers in the fields of word and doctrine. After all, scripture says, "Don't muzzle the threshing ox," and "The worker is worth his wages." Against an elder no charges should be lodged that are not "on the word of two or three witnesses." Those who do go wrong should be publicly reproved, to give the others a scare. I call on you by God, Christ Jesus and his chosen messengers to maintain all this without fear or favor and not to do anything for personal reasons. Don't be too quick to lay hands on anyone [and ordain him], or you'll end up sharing the blame for someone else's wrongdoing. Keep your hands clean.

Don't keep to drinking just water: add a little wine to soothe your stomach and help with your frequent illnesses. Some people's sins

---

* Note that Paul's idea of "real widows" virtually amounts to an order of nuns: they need character references, they apparently must take vows of celibacy, and they have a liturgical function, to serve as the community's lightning-rod of prayer.

conspicuously lead them to their doom, while other people's only catch up with them later. Likewise, good works stand out, but even those that don't cannot stay hidden forever.

6

All those who are slaves beneath the yoke should consider their respective owners worthy of the highest esteem, so that people won't blaspheme the name of God or our teaching. Those whose owners are among the faithful should not look down on them for being brothers, but serve them all the better, since those who benefit from their good work are dear friends and partners in the faith.

That is what you should teach and call upon people to do. Anyone who meddles with the teachings and doesn't come back to the healthful words of our Lord Jesus Christ and what reverence teaches, is too puffed up to understand anything; he saps his strength in debates and verbal battles, and the results are envy, strife, blasphemy, evil suspicions and the constant friction that exists among people of corrupted minds who are devoid of honesty and thinking of piety as a source of profit.

And actually there is great profit in piety—for those who can make do with what they have:

> Remember, we brought nothing into the world,
> Since we also can take nothing out again.
> With something to eat and something to cover us,
> We'll have enough.

By contrast, those who want to be rich fall into a temptation and a trap and are prey to many desires that are stupid and destructive and drag people to ruin and perdition. For at the root of all evils is money-love, an appetite that has already caused some to wander away from the faith and expose themselves to troubles aplenty.

> Not you, though, godly person: flee such things.
> Seek after justice, reverence and faith,
> Love and endurance and a gentle touch;
> Fight the good fight of faith.
> Reach for the everlasting life you were called for,

The same to which you pledged that noble pledge,
With all those witnesses standing around you.

I charge you by God, the Lifegiver to all things, and by Christ Jesus, who swore out so noble a deposition before Pontius Pilate, to keep the commandment and be spotless and irreproachable till the appearance of our Lord Jesus Christ, which will be shown to us in His own time by

The blessed and sole Potentate,
The King of all who are kings
And Lord of all who are lords,
The sole Possessor of immortality,
Housed in light to which there is no approach,
Whom no human being has seen or ever could,
His is the honor and ruling power forever indeed.

Tell those who are rich—in this life—not to act too high and mighty, and not to set their hopes on the uncertainties of money, but on God, who provides us richly with everything for our enjoyment. Tell them to do good, to get rich in good deeds, and to be generous and sharing, storing up something good to build on for the future, so that true Life will be within their grasp.

Please, Timothy, guard what has been handed down to you by fending off all the godless prattle and contradictions of false "knowledge," which some have adhered to, losing the way of the faith.

Grace be with you.

The Second Letter from Paul to
Timothy

1

From Paul, apostle of Christ Jesus by God's will in accord with the promise of life in Christ Jesus;
To his beloved child Timothy:
Grace, mercy and peace from God the Father and Christ Jesus our Lord.

I thank God (whom I worship with a clean conscience as my ancestors did before me) as I keep you incessantly in mind in my prayers night and day, longing to see you, remembering your tears when we parted and longing to make my joy complete by seeing you again, recalling the faith without pretense that is in you, the same that lodged first in your grandmother Lois and your mother Eunice, and which I am convinced is also in you.

For that reason I am reminding you to keep rekindling that gift of God that is in you because of the laying-on of my hands. Remember, God didn't give us a cowardly spirit: He gave us a spirit full of power, love and good sense. So don't be ashamed of our Lord's testimony or of me his prisoner, but suffer along with the good word with a power from God,

> Who saved us
> And called us with the call of holiness,
> Not because of our deeds
> But according to His own inclination and grace
> Bestowed upon us in the person of Christ Jesus
> Before the dawn of time,
> But only manifested now
> With the appearance of our savior Christ Jesus,
> Annihilating death and bringing the light of imperishable life
>   through the good word—

to which I was assigned as herald, emissary and teacher. That is also the

395

reason why I am suffering these things. But I'm not ashamed, because I know Who I have put my faith in and I am confident that He can watch over everything that is in my keeping until that day off yonder. Take an example from the health-giving words you heard me speak in the faith and love of Christ Jesus. Guard this fine thing in our keeping with the holy spirit that lives inside you.

You no doubt know that all the people from Asia went off and left me, including Phygelus and Hermogenes. The Lord be merciful to Onesiphorus and his household: he did many things to give me relief and was not ashamed of my chains; in fact, as soon as he got to Rome he hastened to look me up and got in touch with me. May the Lord grant him mercy from his own lordly hand on yonder day. And as for all the service he gave in Ephesus, you know about that better than I do.

2

So as for you, my child, take on the power of the grace of Christ Jesus, and what you heard from me through many witnesses, pass it on to trustworthy people who will be capable of teaching others in their turn. Join in the struggle like a good soldier of Christ Jesus. No campaigner gets involved in the business concerns of life: his commander wouldn't like it. And if someone's in a contest, he doesn't get the laurels if he doesn't play by the rules. The toiling farmhand should be the first to eat of the harvest. Understand what I mean? The Lord will give you a grasp of all these things.

Keep your mind on Jesus Christ, risen from the dead, of the seed of David, according to my telling of the good word which has occupied me to the point of my being jailed as a criminal—but they can't lock up the word of God.

Therefore I put up with everything for the sake of the chosen ones, so that they too can win salvation in Christ Jesus, with glory everlasting. Mark my words:

> Because if we suffered along with him, we shall have life along with him,
> If we endure, we shall share in his reign.
> If we reject him, he'll reject us too.
> If we do not trust him, he remains trustworthy.

After all, how can he not believe in himself?

Remind people of these things, calling on them in the sight of God to avoid verbal battles which are of no use except to throw the listeners into confusion. Be at pains to make yourself useful to God: a worker not to be ashamed of, cutting no corners on the word of truth. Steer clear of the ungodly empty theories [of some people]: they lead to more impiety than anything else, and such teachings will eat away at the faith like a cancer. Examples of that are Hymenaeus and Philetus, who wandered afield from the truth when they said that our resurrection has already occurred and who are going around subverting people's faith. But in fact the firm foundation of God bears the inscription: "The Lord knew which were His own," and also "Keep away from wrongdoing, all who call upon the name of the Lord."

Now in a large household you don't just find things of gold and silver, you also find things of wood and pottery, and there's fine china and other dishes not so good. If someone will wash himself of all these things, he can be the fine china, sanctified, just what the Master likes, ready for any good work.

Don't let your youthful desires catch up with you. Pursue justice, faith, love and peace with those whose clear hearts call upon the Lord. Stay away from foolish and unthought-through theories, knowing that they cause fights. A slave of the Lord is not supposed to fight: he's supposed to be gentle with everybody, a good teacher, and long-suffering, someone who gently enlightens those who resist him. You never know: by a gift of God they may yet repent and acknowledge the truth and be clearheaded enough to escape the traps by which the Devil abducts them into the service of his will.

3

You should know that in the days toward the end there will be terrible times: there will be people who are self-serving, greedy, puffed-up, haughty, foul-mouthed, disobedient to parents, ungrateful, irreverent, hardhearted, unyielding, slanderous, out of control, savage, contemptuous of goodness, traitorous, heedless, inflated, pleasure-loving rather than God-loving, keeping a veneer of reverence while denying its essence. Those are the people to avoid!

Some of them even break into houses and kidnap young girls who are then loaded with sins and delivered to multifarious desires, getting in deeper and deeper and unable to see their way to a recognition of the truth. The same way [the Egyptian wizards] Jannes and Jambres contended with Moses, that's how these people contest the truth, people corrupted in mind and unreliable in matters of faith. But they won't get very far: their mindlessness will become apparent to all, as happened to the others before.

You, on the other hand, have been a follower of my teaching, my leadership, and my mission, with trust, patience, love and endurance, amid persecutions and sufferings, like those I encountered at Antioch, Iconium and Lystra; I bore up under those persecutions and was rescued from them all by the Lord. In fact, everyone who tries to live a reverent life in Christ Jesus will be persecuted. Treacherous and deceptive people will get progressively worse, losing their way and misdirecting others.

But as for you, stick with what you were taught and made to believe, knowing who your teachers were and that from babyhood on you have known the sacred writings, which can give you the needed wisdom for salvation through faith in Christ Jesus. All the scripture is divinely inspired and useful for teaching, pointing out faults, giving correction and offering guidance along the paths of justice so that the person who belongs to God may be perfect and full and equipped for every good work.

4

Swear in the sight of God and Christ Jesus, who will judge the living and the dead, and by his coming return and by his kingdom that you will spread the word insistently, at the right time and at the wrong time, exposing faults, calling for improvements and giving encouragement with the patience of a true teacher. Remember, in the time to come they will find healthy teaching intolerable and provide themselves with a host of teachers more to their liking who will massage their ears. They will turn away from hearing the truth and turn toward mythology. You must keep a clear head amidst all that, keep struggling on, and do your job as a messenger of the good word, giving full service.

I, after all, am already on the chopping-block, and the hour of my release has come round. I have fought the good fight, I have finished the race, I have kept the faith. My future holds in store the crown of righteousness, which the Lord who judges justly will give me on that day yonder, and not just me but all who have longed for his return.

Try hard to get here soon. You know, Demas left me behind and went off to Thessalonica. He decided he liked this world better. Kreskes is in Galatia, Titus in Dalmatia. Luke is here alone with me. Go get Mark and bring him with you: he's been of very good service to me. Tychicus I sent to Ephesus. You know the overcoat I left in Troy at Carpus's house? When you come, please bring that, and also my books, particularly the parchments. Alexander Coppersmith has treated me badly over and over. He will receive from the Lord what his deeds deserve. You watch out for him too: he's completely against everything we say.

At my first hearing nobody stood up for me, they all left me in the lurch—may it not count against them. But the Lord was at my side and gave me the strength so that by my efforts the spreading of the word might be carried on until all nations hear. So I was saved from the lion's jaws. I will be saved again by the Lord, from everything evil can do and brought safe and sound into His kingdom above the skies. To Him be the glory for an age of ages, let it be so.

Say hello to Priscilla and Aquila and Onesiphorus's household. Erastus is staying in Corinth. Trophimus was sick when I left him in Miletus. Hurry up and get here before winter. Greetings to you from Eubulus, Pudens, Linus, Claudia and all the brothers and sisters.

The Lord be with your spirit. Grace be with you.

The Letter from Paul to
Titus

1

From Paul, slave of God, sent by Jesus Christ to minister to the faith of God's chosen ones and to their understanding of the truth we revere in hopes of the life everlasting promised by an unfailingly truthful God who has chosen these times to reveal His word in the form of a proclamation entrusted to me by order of God our Savior;
To Titus, my own true child in our shared faith:
Grace and peace from God the Father and Christ Jesus our savior.

The reason I left you behind in Crete was so that you could do whatever clean-up tasks remained, including installing elders on a city-by-city basis, as I instructed you, assuming you find someone that there's nothing wrong with, a one-woman man with children among the faithful who are not notoriously licentious or disorderly. Remember, a supervisor must be God's keeper of the keys: not high and mighty, not hot-tempered, not a drunk, not a brawler, not a greedy schemer; but instead hospitable, eager for the good, sensible, fair, reverent and self-controlled, someone who will hold on to the reliable substance of what was taught him so that he can encourage others with healthy teaching and show the nay-sayers where they're wrong.

And there are a lot of those, flouting authority, talking nonsense, and practicing deception—especially those of Jewish origin. You must put those people in their place: they're leading whole families astray, teaching things they shouldn't be teaching to make a dishonest profit. In the words of one of their own, a spokesman from among them:

Cretans! What liars, what animals, filling their indigent bellies!

This testimony is correct; and that means you must light into them incessantly if they are to grow strong in the faith and not waste their time on Jewish mythology and the commandments of people who have turned their backs on the truth. All things are pure to the pure, while to the corrupted and faithless nothing is pure: the corruption is there in their minds and their perceptions. They say they believe in God, but their deeds deny Him; they're repugnant and unruly and useless for any good work.

2

But as for you, keep saying what healthy teaching requires: that older men should be sober, decent, sensible and robust in faith, love and endurance; similarly, that older women's clothes should match their holiness, and they shouldn't be gossips or drink so much wine as to become enslaved to it, while they should be well versed in the teachings and able to advise the younger women about how to be good to their husbands and children, sensible, chaste, good homemakers—and obedient to their husbands, so the word of God doesn't get a bad name.

As for the younger men, likewise encourage them to show common sense in all matters and set an example for them by your good behavior, the integrity of your teaching and the seriousness of your sound and irrefutable words, so that our adversaries will be embarrassed when they can't say anything bad about us.

Tell slaves to obey their masters in everything, to make them happy and not talk back and not to filch things, but rather to show the utmost good faith, so that they will be in every way a credit to the teachings of God our Savior.

For the saving grace of God appeared to all, disciplining us to forget our irreverence and worldly desires and live sensibly, justly and piously in these times now while we await the hoped-for good fortune and manifest glory of our great God and savior Jesus Christ, who gave himself for us to ransom us from all lawlessness and wash us clean enough to be his own dedicated band, afire to do the right thing. Say these things, urge them upon the people and point out faults with complete authority. Don't let anyone look down on you.

3

Remind them to be subject to power and authority and give their obedience, to be ready for any good work, never to vilify anyone, to be reasonable and not quarrelsome, displaying the greatest gentleness toward all the world. We know: we too were once mindless, unruly and adrift, slaves to our passions and multifarious pleasures, proceeding with spite and envy, hateful and hating one another.

> But then the kindliness of our savior God appeared,
> His love for us humans.
> Not because of any redeeming deeds we did ourselves
> But of His own mercy He saved us
> Through the washing that bestowed new life,
> The renewal brought by the holy spirit,
> Which God poured out upon us richly
> Through Jesus Christ our savior,
> That we might be acquitted by means of his grace
> And be heirs to the hope of everlasting life.

Those are words to count on, and in these matters I want you to be very firm, so that they will be anxious to excel in doing good now that their faith is in God. That's the right way, the way that is good for people; whereas foolish speculations and fables of the forefathers and debates and arguments about the Law are to be avoided: they're useless and idle. A divisive person should be given a first warning and a second warning and then avoided, in the certainty that such a person is beyond reaching and will keep on sinning and writing his own stiff sentence.

When I send Artemas to you—or it may be Tychicus—come quickly and meet me at Nicopolis, where I have decided to stay the winter. Graciously supply all the traveling-needs of Zenas the jurist and Apollos; make sure they have everything they need. Our number must also lead the way in doing good where the need is present, if our work is to bear fruit.

Everyone here with me says hello to you. Say hello to our friends in the faith.

Grace be with you all.

The Letter from Paul to
Philemon

From Paul, prisoner of Christ Jesus, and Brother Timothy;
To Philemon our dear friend and fellow-worker, and our sister Apphia, and our comrade-at-arms Archippus, and the group that meets at your house:
Grace to you and peace from God our Father and Lord Jesus Christ.

As I keep you always in mind in my prayers, I thank my God as I hear of the love and faith you bear toward Lord Jesus and all the holy ones, which allows your shared faith to be put to work in your discernment of every good thing among us that leads to Christ. And I must say that the love within you has been a great joy and consolation to me, since through you the holy ones have received such new life for their old bones, my brother.

Therefore, though possessing broad powers in Christ to command you to do the decent thing, for love's sake I will simply ask you in my capacity as Paul, now an old man and a prisoner for Christ Jesus: I am asking you concerning my pupil, whose faith I have fathered in my chains, Profitabilis, that fellow who was no good to you before but now can do a lot of good for you and me both. I have sent him back to you, and it's like sending you a piece of my heart.

I would rather have kept him here with me, to give me the service that you would wish to give, as I lie in chains for the sake of the good word. But I didn't want to do anything without consulting you, because your contribution should not be forced but freely given.

You see, it's possible that he was lost to you for a while so that you could regain him forever, no more as a slave but as more than a slave: as a brother most dear—certainly to me—who should then be even dearer to you as a person and a brother in the Lord. So if you consider me a partner, receive him as if it were me. If he owes you for any debts or damages, put it on my account. Here you have it in my own hand-writing: I WILL REPAY YOU—PAUL. (Let me not seem to be telling you that I own you.)

My brother, let me profit from you in the Lord. Give this lift to my spirit in Christ's name.

I write to you sure of your cooperation, knowing that you will do what I say and more. While you're at it, prepare me a place to stay: I hope with the aid of your prayers that I will be returned to you.

Greetings to you from Epaphras my fellow-prisoner in Christ Jesus, and from Mark, Aristarchus, Demas and Luke, my fellow-workers.

The grace of Lord Jesus Christ be with your spirit.

The Letter to the
Hebrews

1

At many times and in many ways God spoke to our forefathers through the prophets in ages past. Now at the close of these days He has spoken to us through His son, to whom He gave the inheritance of all things and through whom He created Time:

> The reflection of God's glory, the image of God's substance,
> And the bringer of all things by the word of his power,
> He brought about the cleansing of our wrongs,
> Then took his seat at majesty's right hand on high,
> As much excelling any of the angels
> As the name allotted him surpasses any of theirs.

For to which of the angels did God ever say:

> *You are My son, this day I have begotten you?*

Or

> *I shall be a father for him, and he shall be a son for Me?*

And as He brings His firstborn into the world, He says:

> *Before him shall bow all messengers of God.*

And after saying to the messengers,

> *The one who turns his messengers into winds*
> *And his ministers into tongues of fire,*

He then says to the son,

> *Your throne is God for an age of ages,*
> *And your rod of correction is your kingly scepter.*
> *You always loved justice and hated lawlessness.*
> *And so your God, your God anointed you*
> *With olive of exultation, you more than all your peers.*

And

> *In the beginning, Lord, you laid the earth's foundations,*
> *And it is your hands that have produced the skies.*
> *And though they perish you are always there.*
> *All others age and wear like an old coat,*
> *And like a coat you will bundle them up,*
> *And like a coat they will also be discarded,*
> *But you are always the same, with limitless years to go.*

And to which of the angels has God ever said,

> *Sit at My right*
> *Till I have made your enemies your footrest?*

Aren't the angels just spiritual agents dispatched on missions for the benefit of those who are to inherit salvation?

2

Therefore we must pay more attention to what we have been told, or we could drift off course. After all, if the words brought by the angels of old proved reliable, and every violation and disobedience brought down the appropriate retribution, how shall we go unpunished if we ignored a giant offer of salvation originating in the Lord's own words and confirmed for our benefit by people who heard him speak?—especially after God has stood behind it with such signs and wonders and multifarious powers and influxes of holy spirit as suit His design.

Remember, it is not the angels whom He put in charge of the coming world of which we speak, [but Christ]. For someone somewhere once affirmed:

> *What is a human being that You should remember him?*
> *Or a human child that You should look upon him?*
> *You lowered him just a little below the angels;*
> *With glory and honor You crowned him*
> *And set him with everything underneath his feet.*

Now in the subordination of all things to him nothing was left unsubordinated, yet so far we haven't seen him with the whole world arrayed below him: but we have seen Jesus who was "lowered a little below the angels" by suffering death, now crowned with glory and honor so that by God's grace the death he tasted might be to everyone's benefit.

You see, in order that God (for whom and through whom all things exist) might bring His many children to glory, the captain of salvation, [Christ,] first had to be perfected through suffering: in fact, Christ the sanctifier is of one origin with those he sanctified, for which reason he does not shrink from calling them brothers when he says:

> *I will make Your name known to my brothers and sisters,*
> *With everyone assembled I will sing Your praise.*

And also

> *My trust shall be in Him,*

And also

> *Here I am with the children God gave me.*

Therefore, since those "children" shared a nature of flesh and blood, he closely shared it with them, so that by his death he might render powerless the keeper of Death's power, namely the Devil, and so might buy the freedom of those whom fear of Death had reduced to slavery their whole life long. His concern is not with the angels, not at all; the seed of Abraham is his concern, for which reason he had to be one of us, his brothers and sisters, in every way so he could have the mercy to make a high priest who could be counted on in relation to God, to make an offering in atonement for the misdeeds of his people: after being put to the test by what he went through, he can now help others with their trials.

3

Therefore, holy brothers and sisters, sharers in the heavenly calling, remember the apostle and high priest of our professed faith: Jesus, as faithful to the One who made him as was "Moses in all his house." In fact, Jesus ranks higher in glory than Moses, much as a house deserves respect but the builder deserves more. Every house, after all, is built by someone, but the builder of all things is God. And while Moses was "faithful in all his house" as a servant of the testimony that was to be given, Christ is like a son toward his house, his house being us—that is, if we hold on to the confidence and splendor of our hopes.

Therefore, as the holy spirit says:

> *Today, if you will hear his voice,*
> *Don't harden your hearts with the defiance*
> *That they showed in the desert on the day of the testing*
> *When your fathers tested Me out as an experiment,*
> *And saw what I did for the next forty years.*
> *So I grew embittered with this generation*
> *And said, "Their hearts will go in circles forever.*
> *My pathways have remained unknown to them."*
> *So I swore in My anger:*
> *Let's see if they ever open the door to My comfort and rest!*

Watch out, brothers and sisters, that none of your hearts is ever so evil and faithless as to turn away from the living God. On the contrary, encourage each other to treat every day as the abovementioned "Today..." (since we are partners with Christ now, as long as we follow the matter once begun to a firm conclusion), and not to let any of you be hardened into the kind of sinful self-deception referred to in the words:

> *Today, if you will hear his voice,*
> *Don't harden your hearts with defiance.*

Now then: who was it that heard and defied? Everyone whom Moses brought out of Egypt, wasn't it? Who was God embittered with for forty years? The evildoers, isn't that right, whose lifeless forms were left in the desert? Who did God swear would never find ease through Him if not the disobedient? So we see that it was their failure to trust God: that's why they couldn't "open the door."

4

We must be careful, then, that after being left with the promise that you *shall* "open the door to God's comfort and rest," no one among you ends up having missed your chance. After all, we have been given this happy announcement, but so had they [our forefathers], and the audible word didn't help them if it wasn't mixed with faith in their listening ears. Whereas we *are* "opening the door to comfort and rest" because we did have faith. And so it says:

> *So I swore in My anger:*
> *Let's see if they ever open the door to My comfort and rest!*

even though His labors were over once the world was created. For it says concerning the seventh day: "And God *rested* on the seventh day from all His labors," and then here it says, "they shall never open the door to my comfort and *rest*." Since that leaves others who *will* open the door, while the first hearers of the good news couldn't open the door for lack of faith, God must be setting aside another day, namely the "today" he mentions (speaking through David at a much later date, as mentioned above):

> *Today, if you hear his voice,*
> *Don't harden your hearts...*

If Joshua had given them their rest, David would not be talking here about another day coming afterwards. So there must be a Sabbath's rest still waiting for the people of God, and whoever finds this rest has rested from his own labors as God once rested from His.

Then let us hasten to find that rest, so that no one becomes yet another example of the disobedience of old. For the word of God is living, active,

more cutting than any double-edged sword, and penetrating enough to
sever soul from spirit and marrow from bone, while it judges the
thoughts and passions of our hearts. No part of creation is hidden from
Him; everything lies bare with the truth wrung out of it in the eyes of
Him to whom we are accountable.

Therefore, since we have a great high priest who has passed through
the skies and beyond, Jesus the son of God, let us hold to the truths we
profess. After all, we do not have a high priest who can't sympathize with
our weaknesses: without doing wrong, he has still faced all the same
temptations. Then let us confidently draw near to the throne of grace
and receive the mercy and find the grace that can give us timely aid.

5

You see, every human being chosen to be high priest represents
humanity in relation to God by bringing gifts and sacrifices to make up
for people's misdeeds, and he is able to sympathize with their ignorance
and error because he's also subject to weakness and so consequently
obliged, while he makes propitiation for the people's misdeeds, to do the
same for his own. Also, one doesn't bestow such an honor on oneself but
is called by God just as Aaron was.

Likewise, it wasn't Christ who gave himself the glory of becoming
high priest but the One who said to him:

You are My beloved son; today I have engendered you,

as he also says elsewhere:

You are a priest forever, of the order of Melchisedek—

a priest who in his earthly days offered prayers and supplications, with
tears and loud cries, to the One who could save him from death, and was
heard because of his reverence, and who, son though he was, learned
obedience from the things he went through, and once perfected became
responsible for the everlasting salvation of all who obey him, having
been installed by God as high priest of the order of Melchisedek.

Upon this subject, we have much to say and no clear way to say it, since
you have grown too stunted of hearing. In fact, though by this time you

should be teachers of the word yourselves, it seems you need someone to teach you the fundamentals of the most basic pronouncements of God all over again, and you have come to need milk and not solid food. Now anyone who takes milk is inexperienced in matters of morality: he's just a baby. Solid food is for adults, who by conditioning have acquired senses trained to distinguish right and wrong.

6

And for their sakes we prefer to omit mention of the basics of Christ and go onward, without re-laying the foundations—turning away from the works of death, trusting God, the teachings about washing and laying on hands, the resurrection of the dead, the eternal judgment. And with God's permission we will do just that.

The fact is, it is impossible for those who have once seen the light and sampled the free gifts of heaven and received a share of holy spirit and tasted God's noble word and the wonders of the world to come, if they then fall away, to be renewed and find repentance: they're re-crucifying the son of God on their own and making a laughingstock of him. The earth that drinks the rain that keeps falling on it and sprouts vegetation useful to those who cultivate it receives a blessing from God. But if it brings forth thorns and thistles, it's good for nothing and on the edge of the damnation that finally leads to the fire.

Now we confidently believe the best and most salutary things about you, dear hearts, even if we're talking like this. After all, God is not so unjust as to overlook your actions and the favors you've done and are still doing for the other holy ones, thus showing love for His name. We fervently wish to see each of you showing the same determination to fulfill the dream and reach the goal, so that you don't slack off, but follow the example of those whose faith and patience have given them a claim to the promised rewards.

You see, when God gave His promise to Abraham, having no greater to swear by, He swore by Himself, saying

> *Without fail I shall bless you with blessings*
> *And multiply you many times over,*

and sure enough, Abraham's patience earned him his reward. Now when people swear, they swear by something greater than themselves, and the oath is meant to confirm their words beyond all negation. So God, wishing to make even clearer to the promised heirs of His reward how unalterable His intentions were, introduced an oath into the proceedings, so that those two irreversible transactions, [the promise and the oath,] which God couldn't possibly lie about, would give us firm assurance, we who rush to clutch the safety of the dream lying there up ahead, the dream we hold on to as the sure and solid anchor of our souls, which can go behind the curtain [and into the Holy of Holies,] where our forerunner Jesus went on our behalf, high priest in the order of Melchisedek forever.

7

This Melchisedek, you see, was "king of Salem, priest of God the most high, who met Abraham coming back from the slaughter of the kings and blessed him; and Abraham gave him the tenth part of everything there." First of all, his name means "king of justice." Then he's called "king of Salem," [but Salem means "peace," so] that's "king of peace." He has no father or mother or ancestry of any kind. There is no start to his days nor end to his life. And in all these things he resembles the son of God, remaining priest in perpetuity.

And see how great he is, so great that "*Abraham* gave him the tenth part" of his spoils, Abraham the patriarch! Now to be sure, those sons of Levi who take the priesthood on are also commanded by the law to collect a tenth from the people, that is to say, their own brothers, though those brothers are just as much issued from the loins of Abraham as they are. But now this person not of their ancestry collected a tenth from Abraham and blessed him, the recipient of God's promise. Now beyond all dispute it is the lesser who is blessed by the greater. And while in other cases it is mortal men who receive the tithes, in this case he is described [by the Bible] as being still alive. So you could say that Levi, the receiver of tithes, paid tithes of his own through Abraham, since he was already present in the loins of the patriarch when the latter encountered Melchisedek.

Now if perfection came through the priesthood of Levi, which was after all the basis for the people's being given the law, what further need would there be for another priest to arise "from the order of Melchisedek"? Why not just say, "from the order of Aaron"? After all, a change in the priesthood necessarily brings a change in the law, and the person that all this applies to, [Christ,] belonged to another tribe, none of whose members ever tended the altar: as everyone knows, our Lord appeared from the tribe of Judah, a tribe that Moses never mentioned in speaking of priests. It becomes even clearer [how great the change is] when after the fashion of Melchisedek another priest arises who isn't there by virtue of the earthly commands but by the power of a life that is indestructible, as the Bible witnesses:

> *You are a priest* forever *in the order of Melchisedek.*

What we have here is the repeal of the pre-existing commandment on account of its weakness and uselessness—in fact, the law never perfected anything—coupled with the introduction of a nobler hope that lets us come nearer to God.

And all this with no lack of oaths being sworn. And where others had become priests with no oaths being sworn, for him an oath was sworn by the One who said to him:

> *The Lord swore and will never take it back:*
> *You are a priest forever.*

The result is that Jesus is the co-signer of a new and better agreement [between God and humanity]. Also, while all those others became priests because death wouldn't let their predecessors stay on, he, by remaining forever, possesses a priesthood beyond infringement, which also means he can permanently save those who pray to God through him, since he is always alive and ready to intercede [with God] on our behalf.

It was just such a high priest we needed: holy, free of evil, unblemished, with no ties to wrongdoing, higher than the high heavens, who has no daily need, like other high priests, of offering sacrifice first for his own misdeeds and then for the people's: no, he did that once and for all by sacrificing himself. You see, the old Law installed high priests who were human beings with weaknesses, but the sworn word [of God] that came after the Law has installed the Son in all his eternal perfection.

8

Summing up what has been said, we have the kind of high priest who could and did take his seat at the right of majesty's throne in the skies, attending to the holy things and tending the true tabernacle erected not by mortals but by the Lord.

Now every high priest is installed to offer gifts and sacrifices, which means he needs to have something that he can offer. Actually, Jesus wouldn't be a priest at all on the earth, where we already have priests to offer the gifts prescribed by law. (Of course those priests worship using but a semblance and shadow of heavenly things, in line with the injunction given to Moses when he was getting the Tent of Meeting finished: "Be sure," it says, "that you make everything according to the plan that was shown to you up on the mountain.") But the service Jesus has now entered upon is of a different order, inasmuch as he becomes the go-between for the new and better agreement, founded on new and better promises.

You see, if there had been no fault to find with the old agreement, there would have been no room for another one. But God certainly sees a fault when He says to His people:

> *And now the days are coming, says the Lord,*
> *When I will ratify a new agreement*
> *Covering the house of Israel and the house of Judah.*
> *Not like the agreement that I made with their fathers*
> *On the day I raised my hand and led them out of the land of Egypt,*
> *For they haven't kept to My agreement,*
> *And I have not taken good care of them, says the Lord.*
> *For this is the agreement I will agree on with the house of Israel*
> *When those days are done, says the Lord:*
> *I will make laws for their minds*
> *And write them on their hearts.*
> *And I will be a God of theirs,*
> *And they will be a people of Mine.*
> *And each one will not have to lecture his neighbor,*
> *Nor each instruct his brother, saying "Know the Lord."*
> *They'll know Me, all from the smallest to the greatest.*
> *For I shall be merciful about their injustices,*

And their misdeeds I shall think no more of.

Calling this the "new" agreement already makes the first one the "old" one. And something so antiquated and creaky won't be around much longer.*

9

Now the old agreement included decrees about the worship to be offered and a holy place here in the world. One tent was set up which had the candelabra and the table and the loaves spread out, and that tent was called the Holy. Then, beyond a second curtain, was another tent called the Holy of Holies, with a gilded altar for the incense and the "Ark of the Covenant," the chest all covered with gold containing the golden urn with manna in it and the staff of Aaron that blossomed and the tablets with the commandments, topped by the figures of glorious cherubim in whose shade is God's Mercy-seat—things of which this is not the time to speak in detail.

At any rate, with all this in place, the first tent has priests constantly going in and out performing the various devotions, while the second tent is entered just once a year and only by the high priest, who never enters without bringing blood to offer for himself and for the people's heedless errors—whereby the holy spirit makes it clear that the pathway of the holy ones is not yet fully shown as long as the first tent remains standing. That comparison is meant for us here in the present and applies to all the offerings and sacrifices people bring which can do nothing to develop the worshipers' consciences—all about foods and drinks and washing different things, earthly points of law only in force till the time of the great overhaul.

But now Christ is here, and as high priest of those who are now the good, he passed through the greater and more perfect Tent not made by any hands—at any rate no creature's hands—and with no blood of goats or calves, but bringing his own blood, he went once and for all into the holy places after winning our redemption forever. And think: if the blood of goats and bulls or the ashes of cows is sprinkled on the unclean

---

* In fact, Judaism is still with us.

and makes them acceptable again, rendering their bodies clean, how much more shall the blood of Christ—who, of his everlasting spirit, laid himself down before God without blemish—yes, how much more shall the blood of Christ wash our thinking so as to turn from deadly behaviors and toward the worship of the living God.

That's why Christ is here as the bringer of the new order, so that, now that his death is accomplished (thus redeeming the transgressions still in arrears from the old order), those who are called to the everlasting inheritance may now receive their promised reward.

You understand that in any case of a will or testament, the death of the will's author is a necessary condition, because wills are for the dead: as long as a person lives, his will has no force. Which is why even the previous contract was not entered into without bloodshed. Thus Moses, when he had finished telling the people about the commandments of the old Law, took the blood of calves and goats with water and red wool and hyssop and sprinkled the holy book itself and all the people with it, saying

This is the blood that seals the contract that God ordered you to make.

And he likewise sprinkled blood on the Tent of Meeting and all the sacred vessels. In fact, almost everything in the Law uses blood for cleansing, and without bloodshed no wrongs are forgiven.

But if the shadowy representations of heavenly things were cleansed by rites like these, the heavenly things themselves demanded sacrifices of a different order. It was not into a man-made sanctum that Jesus went, no mere copy of the real thing, but into heaven itself, to show himself before the face of God on our behalf.

Nor did he go there to sacrifice himself over and over, like the high priest who enters the holy place year after year, bringing another's blood with him; otherwise he would have gone through the same sufferings since the world's creation. Instead, he has been revealed by his sacrifice to cancel out your guilt, now, just this once, towards the close of time. And the same way that human beings have one death, and after that comes the judgment, so Christ was sacrificed once to take away the sins of many, and will have sin out of the way the next time he appears to those who are waiting for him to bring them to salvation.

10

Since the law offers only a shadowy glimpse of better things to come and does not show the full picture of things, its sacrifices offered the same way every year in perpetuity cannot possibly perfect those who seek its aid. If it did, wouldn't they then stop offering the sacrifices, on the grounds that the worshipers were clean now and felt no more consciousness of wrong? But they don't stop, and that fact is an annual acknowledgment of wrong. It's just impossible for blood of bulls and goats to take the wrongdoing away.

That's why Christ comes into the world saying,

> *Sacrifices and offerings were not what You wished,*
> *But You fashioned a body for me.*
> *Burnt offerings for sin didn't meet with Your approval.*
> *So then I said, "Here I am, God:*
> *There is a chapter of the Book that speaks of me,*
> *And here I am to do Your will."*

Notice he starts out saying, "Sacrifices and gifts and burnt offerings for wrongdoing were not what you wished or approved," meaning the ones offered under the old Law. Then he says, "Here I am to do your will." So he's abolishing the old standard [of offerings and sacrifices] and establishing the new standard of doing God's will, the same will through which we have been made holy by the body of Jesus Christ, offered once and for all.

And while every other priest stands there conducting the same services day after day and repeatedly offering the same sacrifices which can never root out the faults they atone for, here is a priest who offered a single sacrifice for all sins forever, then took his seat at the right hand of God to await the future time when "his enemies would be made into a footrest for his feet." That is because with one sacrifice he perfected the sanctified ones for all time. The holy spirit bears witness to all this by having said:

> *This agreement shall I ratify with them*
> *When those days are done, says the Lord,*

Making laws for their hearts
And writing them on their minds,
And their misdeeds and lawlessness I shall think no more of.

But if everything is forgiven, there are no more offerings to bring in reparation.

And so, brothers and sisters, having confidence in the entryway to God's inner sanctum provided by the blood of Jesus, a new and living entryway that he made for us through the curtain—meaning the curtain of his flesh—and having so great a priest for the house of God, let us approach with true hearts and abundant faith, with hearts sprinkled to rid them of their evil outlook and bodies washed in the water of purity; let us hold on to the unswerving expression of our dream, since the promiser can be trusted; and let us think about how we can spur each other on in expressions of love and good works—certainly not by staying away from meeting, as some habitually do—but by giving encouragement, more and more as you watch the great day getting nearer and nearer.

Remember, if we knowingly choose wrong after gaining knowledge of the truth, we cannot offer sacrifice for our sins—that's over and done with—we can only expect a fearful judgment and the heat of the fire waiting to consume the forces of opposition. After all, if someone who breaks the law of Moses is put to death without pity "on the word of two or three witnesses," imagine how much worse punishment someone deserves for trampling on the son of God, taking the blood that consecrated the new agreement and treating it like dirt, and roughing up the spirit of grace. We know who said

Revenge is Mine, I will pay what is due,

and also

The Lord shall judge His people.

A fearful thing, falling into the hands of the living God!

Think back to the days when you first saw the light and had to withstand such a round of sufferings: some of you were exposed to insults and injury in full public view, others shared in the sufferings of those so mistreated. And you suffered for those who were in jail and accepted the impounding of your possessions with joy, knowing that you had a better and more lasting fortune elsewhere. So don't throw your confidence away: it has a great reward attached to it. Patient endurance is what you need to do the will of God and reap the promised reward.

What does it say?

> *Just a little, a little bit longer,*
> *And he who is coming will come without delay.*
> *The just man who belongs to Me shall live by his belief,*
> *But if he gives up, in My soul I will not be pleased with him.*

But we are not ones for giving up, which brings destruction, we are ones for believing, which transfers ownership of the soul [to God].

11

Faith is what gives substance to our dreams and allows us to discuss as fact what we cannot see. It is this faith that spoke so well of our ancestors. Faith is what tells us that Time was fashioned by a word of God, so that the visible comes from the invisible. Faith is what made Abel's sacrifice to God better than Cain's; it's what showed Abel to be in good standing, as evidenced by God's reaction to the gifts. And though Abel is dead his faith still speaks to us. Faith is what carried Enoch away without his seeing death ("and he couldn't be found, because God had carried him away"): before his carrying-away we have the [Bible's] testimony that he was well-pleasing to God, and without faith it is impossible to please Him, because one has to come to God believing that He *is* God, the giver of rewards to those who ask Him.

Faith is what gave Noah advance knowledge of things as yet unseen; faith made him obediently build the Ark that saved his family (and by the same token condemned the world), and he thus inherited the virtuous standing with God which faith determines.

Faith is what made Abraham answer when called and go forth to a place which was to be his inheritance: he set out with no knowledge of where he was going. Faith made him migrate to the Promised Land, which wasn't yet his, and live there in tents with Isaac and Jacob, his fellow-heirs of the promise, while he waited for the real city with foundations whose architect and builder would be God. His faith gave Sarah in her barrenness the power to be impregnated by seed when past the prime of adulthood, because he had faith in the One who made the promise. And thus from one man whose life was over came a multitude like the stars in the sky, like the sand at the sea's edge, past all counting.

And in that faith he and his sons all died without seeing the promises fulfilled, only glimpsing them from afar and waving to them, professing themselves to be strangers, short-term residents upon the earth. People who talk like that are obviously looking for their homeland. In their case, if it was the homeland they left that kept filling their thoughts, they could have gone back, they still had time. But no, they're reaching for a better homeland: a homeland in the sky. For that reason God himself is not ashamed to be called on as "the God of Abraham, Isaac and Jacob": He did, after all, build a city for them.

Faith is why Abraham, when put to the test, laid Isaac down and was going to sacrifice his only son, he who had received a promise in which it was said,

Through Isaac a race shall be named for you.

He figured that God could always raise him from the dead again, and so Isaac was, figuratively speaking, restored to him from death. Faith allowed Isaac to speak of things to come in blessing Jacob and Esau. Faith allowed Jacob, a dying man, to bless both sons of Joseph, "supporting himself on his staff as he bowed and adored them." Faith enabled Joseph to give admonitions on his deathbed about the coming exodus of the children of Israel as well as about the disposition of his remains.

Faith is what made the parents of Moses hide him three months long: they simply saw that he was a pretty baby and they weren't afraid of the king's decree. Faith is what made Moses himself, when grown, refuse to be called the son of Pharaoh's daughter, choosing instead to suffer the same torment as all the people of God rather than reap the temporary enjoyment from what would be wrong; to him, it was a wealth greater than all of Egypt's coffers to be reviled for the Messiah's sake, because he was always looking beyond to the recompense awaiting him.

Faith is what made him leave Egypt behind, not fearing the wrath of the king: he persisted in "seeing" the invisible. Faith made him institute

Passover and the smearing of blood to prevent the destroyer of the firstborn from touching the people there. Faith enabled him to cross the Red Sea like dry land, which, when they tried it themselves, caused the Egyptians to drown.

Faith made the walls of Jericho topple after being surrounded for seven days. Faith is why Rahab the whore wasn't killed with the rest of the unbelievers: she gave Israel's emissaries a peaceful reception.

And why should I go on? Time would run out before I told the tales of Gideon, Barach, Samson, Jephthah, David, Samuel and the prophets, who by faith conquered kingdoms, put justice into action, received what they were promised, escaped the jaws of lions, overpowered fire and forced it out, avoided the sword's edge, recovered strength after sickness, were strong in war, and razed the camps of the others to the ground. Wives saw their husbands return from the dead. Others were tortured, refusing to bargain and go free: it was a better life they wanted back. Still others got a taste of mockery and whips, and beyond that chains and imprisonment. They suffered stoning, they were sawed in half, they were stabbed with knives in cold blood, they went round wearing sheepskins and goathides, lacking for everything, pressured and feeling terrible: people whom the world didn't even deserve, wandering around deserted areas, mountains and caves and holes in the ground.

And none of these who bore such witness to their faith ever saw the promise fulfilled, because God kept the best in reserve for us and wouldn't let them reach the goal without us.

12

Well now, with such a swarm of good examples on every hand, let us cast off all our dead weight including the sinfulness that gets into everything, let us run the endurance race that lies before us, taking our cues from the captain and trainer of our faith, Jesus, he who turned from the joy that beckoned to him to endure the death of the cross, caring not a whit how shameful it was, and now sits at the right of the throne of God. Think how much opposition *he* took on from the evildoers who were against him, any time your souls are wearing out and threatening to give way.

You have not yet gone to the wall in your fight against what is wrong. And you have forgotten to take comfort in what is described as part of your being true sons and daughters:

> *Son, do not shrug off the punishments of the Lord*
> *Nor break down under His criticism:*
> *If the Lord loves you, He also disciplines you,*
> *And whips any son whom He accepts as His.*

Stick it out through the punishments visited on you, His children, by God. What son is not corrected by his father? And without this correction, which all the others have shared with you, you would be bastard children and not legitimate. Think: if our earthly fathers held the power of punishment over us and we accepted that, how shall we not recognize the Father of our souls and thereby find Life?

Your other fathers disciplined you for a short time, however they saw fit, but this Father disciplines you for your own good so you can receive His holiness. No punishment seems at the time like something to be happy about; it seems like something to be sad about. Then later it bears a fruit bringing peace to those who are now better trained because of it: morality.

Then pick up those hands hanging slack at your side and straighten the knees that gave under you, and walk straight paths with your feet, so as not to throw the sprain still farther out of joint, but rather heal it. Seek peace with all and the transformation of holiness, without which no one will ever see the Lord. Keep watch in case anyone falls away from the grace of God, in case any roots of bitterness should make trouble when they grow tall and cause the pollution of many, in case anyone should be as lewd and as loose as Esau, who gave away his rights as the firstborn for a single meal. After all, you know that later he wanted to receive Isaac's blessing and was rejected: there was no way to change his mind even though he begged through his tears for a second chance.

You have not come [like Moses] to a palpable mountain with its blazing fire, its darkness and fog and storms and trumpet calls and the sound of a voice, which the hearers begged never to hear speaking again, because the commandment to "stone man or beast that sets foot on the sacred mountain" was too much for them. Indeed, so fearsome was the spectacle that Moses himself said, "I am fearful and trembling."

No, you have come to Mount Zion and the city of God alive, Jerusalem in the sky, with thousands of His messengers and a great crowd assembled for the festival of the first-born sons whose names are recorded in the skies: God, the judge of all, is there, with the souls of those perfected in justice; so is the bringer of the new agreement, Jesus, whose purifying blood is more eloquent than Abel's.*

Make sure you listen to the Person speaking. If our forefathers didn't escape punishment for ignoring one who prophesied here on earth, how will we ever escape punishment for ignoring Him who speaks from heaven, whose voice in those days shook the earth, but about which we are now assured:

One last time I will shake not just the earth, but the heavens too.

The "one last time" makes clear that the things shaken will be transformed as created things, while only the unshakable things remain. For that reason, we who are receiving an unshakable kingdom should give thanks and have the grace to worship God as He desires, with reverence and fear. For "our God is an all-consuming fire."

13

Let brotherly love continue. Don't neglect to offer one another lodging when needed. After all, others before you have given lodging to travelers who turned out to be angels! Remember those in prison as if you were in prison with them; remember those who are mistreated as if you suffered the same things physically.

Show respect for marriage in every way and keep the marriage-bed unspotted, since the lewd and adulterous will be judged by God.

No greedy behavior: just making do with what you have, since He Himself has said

I will not leave you, nor will I abandon you

—which is reason for us to take heart and say

---

* Whose blood cried out from the soil according to the story in Genesis 4:10.

The Lord is my aid, I will not fear.
What can a mere human do to me?

Don't forget your leaders, the ones who told you the word of God:
regard how their way of life has turned out and take an example from
their faith. Jesus is Messiah, yesterday and today the same, now and for
all time. Don't let strange and fancy teachings distract you. The right
thing to steady your heart with is grace, not diets which never helped the
ones who went by them. We eat from an altar forbidden to those who
worship in the Tent of Meeting—where, as you know, the bodies of
those animals whose blood is taken into the holy place by the high priest
are burned outside the camp. Which is why Jesus, when he went to
sanctify the people with his own blood, was put through his sufferings
outside the city gate. Let us now go outside the camp ourselves to meet
him, suffering his injuries; because the city we have here will not stay:
we're looking for the city of the future. Therefore with his aid, let us
bring to God a sacrifice of continual praise, a rich harvest of lips pledging
allegiance to His name. And don't forget about kindness and sharing:
those are just the sacrifices that please God.

Obey your leaders and go along with them. Those people stay up late
at night, holding themselves accountable for the state of your souls. Let
them do it with joy and not with moans and groans: that's not in your best
interests.

Pray for us, since we are confident that we have the right outlook and
are always trying to conduct ourselves well. I especially ask this of you
in hopes that I may not be kept away from you much longer. May the
God of peace, who raised from the dead the great shepherd of the flock,
our Lord Jesus, in the blood that sealed an everlasting contract, now
perfect you in every virtue that will lead you to do His will, and may He
Himself plant within us all that is pleasing in His eyes, through the
agency of Jesus Christ, to whom be the glory forever, let it be so.

I implore you, brothers and sisters, not to reject these words of
encouragement that I have briefly written you. Be aware that our brother
Timothy has been let out, and if he gets here soon enough I'll bring him
with me to see you.

Say hello to all your leaders and all the holy ones. Greetings to you
from those in Italy.

Grace be with you all.

The Letter from

James

1

From James, slave of God and Lord Jesus Christ;
To the twelve tribes which are scattered abroad:
Be happy! An utter joy: so you should consider it, my brothers and sisters, when you are thrown into the midst of trials of every kind, knowing that being tested makes your faith more durable. May your endurance run its course to the finish, so that you may be perfect and perfectly whole, with no deficiencies.

So if any of you lack guidance, ask God, who gives to all freely without begrudging, and you shall receive it. Ask with a faith that has no ifs or buts, because those whose faith is only qualified are like waves of the sea, blasted by the winds and carried away. Such a person had better not think that the Lord will have anything to give a man divided at heart and unsteady in all his paths.

Let the humble brother glory in his high estate; let the rich brother glory in his humbleness, since he will pass on as the flower in the field did, when the sun rose with its burning heat and singed the field, and the flower in the field keeled over, and its face lost all of its charm: thus will the rich man wither away, with all his pursuits.

The man is in luck who endures trials, because if he passes muster he will win the crown of life that God promised to those who love Him.

Let no one who is tempted say "God is tempting me": God is untried in evil and Himself tempts no one. But every person is tempted by greedy desire, which flushes him out and draws him to the bait. So desire gets pregnant and gives birth to sin; and then sin grows up to become the mother of death.

Don't be fooled, my beloved brothers and sisters. Every good giving and every perfect gift is descended from above, from the Father of Lights, for whom there is no changing of phases or cycles of darkening. He intentionally bore us anew by the words of His truth so as to make us a kind of first sample of the harvest of His creatures.

Be sure, my beloved brothers and sisters, that every person should be quick to listen, slow to speak, and slow to get angry, because a man's anger doesn't put him on the right side of God. Therefore, gently putting aside all mudslinging and malicious excesses, let us accept God's implanted word, which can save our souls.

Be people who put the good word into action, not just listeners who are only fooling themselves. Because if somebody is a listener to the word but not a doer, he's like the man who gazed in a mirror at the face he was born with, and after looking himself over went away and immediately forgot what he looked like. But the one who leans down to look at the perfect law of freedom and stays there, who is not a forgetful listener but an active doer, that person will have good luck in whatever he does.

If someone thinks he's religious while deceiving his own heart and not curbing his tongue, that person's religion is meaningless. Religion is something pure and unblemished before God the Father: looking after orphans and widows in their suffering and keeping yourself unspotted by the world.

2

My brothers and sisters, let there be no judging by appearances in the faith of our Lord Jesus, the Anointed of glory. Suppose your congregation is assembled and a man comes in with gold rings and spick-and-span clothing and a poor man also comes in wearing shabby clothes, and you look at the one in glittering clothes and say, "Here's a nice seat for you here," while you say to the poor man, "Stand over there" or "Sit beside me on the ground": aren't you discriminating between them and acting like a judge whose deliberations are foul? Listen, my beloved brothers and sisters, didn't God single out the poor of this world as rich in faith and heirs of the kingdom that He promised to those who love Him? And then you dishonor the poor. But isn't it the rich who use their power against you and the rich again who drag you into court? And aren't they the same ones who drag through the mud that noble name that has been invoked over your heads? You would do well to fulfill instead what according to scripture is the king of laws: "Love your neighbor as yourself." Whereas if you judge by appearances, you are doing wrong, and that same law accuses you as violators. After all, if one keeps the whole Law but breaks just one part, he's committed an offense against all the Law, because the same One who said, "You are not to commit adultery" also said, "You are not to murder." If you don't commit adultery, that doesn't make you a keeper of the Law if you do commit murder.

Whatever you say and whatever you do, do it like people who will be judged by the law of [your new] liberty. Remember, condemnation will be merciless toward those who had no mercy, whereas mercy triumphs over condemnation.

What does it help, my brothers and sisters, if someone claims to have belief but has no actions to show? Can his belief save him alone? If some brother or sister has no clothes or food from day to day, and one of you says to them, "Peace be with you, be warm and eat your fill," but you don't give them any of those bodily necessities, what good does that do? That's what belief is like if actions don't show it: it's dead just by itself.

"Perhaps," someone will say, "one person has the gift of belief while another has the gift of action." Show me how the one person's belief has no relation to his actions, and I'll show you how the second person's actions constitute belief.

If you believe that God is One, that's good: the demons believe that too, and it makes them shudder.

Do you need to be shown, you emptyhead, that belief without actions is no good? Didn't it make Abraham our father upright that he laid his son Isaac down upon the altar? See how his beliefs worked together with his actions, while his actions brought his beliefs to completion? And that fulfilled the scripture saying, "Abraham believed in God, and that counted toward his uprightness," so that he was known as a friend of God. So you see that a person is made upright by actions and not by belief alone. Didn't Rahab the whore achieve uprightness the same way: by her actions of receiving the messengers and slipping them out a back road? As dead as the body is without a soul inside, that's how dead belief is when it's devoid of action.

3

Don't all of you become teachers, my brothers and sisters; remember that our kind will be judged more strictly: we all commit many offenses.

If someone's speech is free of offense, that person is mature enough to keep his whole body reined in. That's true of horses too: once we put bits in their mouths to make them obey us, we can lead their whole bodies around. Or think how ships, which may be huge and driven by stiff winds, are still led around by a tiny rudder, wherever the steersman's impulse wills. Similarly, the tongue is a small part of the body that boasts of greatness. What a great fire and what a forest it catches! Yes, the tongue *is* a fire. A world of injustices is incorporated into our very bodies along with the tongue, which besmirches the whole body and inflames the whole cycle of our existence with a flame from Gehenna. Just think: every kind of beasts and birds and snakes and fish is tamed by, and subject to, the human kind; while the tongue, that disorderly menace full of deadly venom, cannot be tamed by anyone in the world. With one and the same tongue we bless our Lord and Father and then curse the human beings created in God's likeness, the same mouth issuing blessing and curse. That can't go on, my brothers and sisters, not like that. Surely a spring from a single source can't flow sweet *and* bitter? Or is it possible, my brothers and sisters, for a fig-tree to give olives or a grapevine, figs? No it can't, nor can the salt spring give sweet water.

Is anyone among you wise and perceptive? Then show it by your good behavior, acting with the gentleness wisdom brings: or if you do harbor bitter jealousy and rivalry in your hearts, at least don't go against the truth by jeering and telling lies. That's not wisdom descended from above: it's earthly, it's animalistic, it's diabolical. Where you have jealousy and discord, there is constant disruption and every kind of bad goings-on. Whereas wisdom from above is first of all *decent*; besides that, it's peace-loving, reasonable, willing to go along, full of compassion and good results, steady of purpose and sincere. It is the fruit of integrity, peacefully sowing its seed among those who keep the peace.

4

Where do these wars and battles among you come from? Don't they come from the pleasurable desires on the march in your veins? You want something and you don't have it; you're jealous and grudging but no luck; you battle and fight, and still don't get what you want because you haven't asked, or you ask and don't receive because you asked for something bad, to be spent on your dissipations. You turncoats, don't you know that friendship with the world is enmity toward God? So if you want to be the world's friend, that makes you God's enemy. Or do you think it's empty words when scripture says, "With jealous longing He seeks out the spirit He implanted in us?" And then He bestows more grace upon it, which is why it says:

> God is not on the side of the haughty,
> But to the humble He gives grace.

So be obedient to God. Stand up against the devil and he will flee from you; draw near to God, and He will draw near to you. Wash your hands, evildoers; cleanse your hearts, half-hearted ones. Be miserable, grieve and weep! Turn your laughter to grief and your joy into sorrow. Humble yourselves before the Lord, and He will exalt you.

Don't speak evil of each other, brothers and sisters. The one who denounces or condemns his brother is denouncing and condemning the law [of gentleness]. But if you're sitting in judgment on the law, you're not a follower of the law but a judge of it; whereas there is really only one lawgiver and judge who has power to preserve and destroy. Who are you, sitting in judgment on your fellow-man?

And as for you who say: "Today or tomorrow we will travel to such and such a city and stay there a year and do business and make money"—and you have no notion what your life will be like tomorrow! You are a stream of mist, briefly appearing and then gone again. What you should say instead is: "*If the Lord wills*, we will live to do this or that." As it is, you're talking big and putting on airs. But that kind of talking big is always bad. So if you know the right thing to do and don't do it, that counts as doing wrong.

5

And now for you the rich: weep with shuddering sobs at the miseries awaiting you! Your wealth is rotting, your clothes are going to the moths! Your gold and silver is turning to rust, and the rust will be used as evidence against you and consume your flesh like fire. You were storing up wealth while the world was ending. The wages of the workers who harvested your fields and were never paid are screaming aloud, and the field-hand's cry has reached the ears of the Lord of Heaven's Armies.

You lived on the earth amid decadence and waste, feeding your heart's desires just when it was time for the slaughter. You condemned and executed the innocent who couldn't resist you.

So wait patiently, brothers and sisters, for the coming of the Lord. You see how the farmer must wait for the precious harvest of the land, being patient while it is watered by the rains of spring and fall. So wait patiently yourselves and be firm in your hearts, because the return of the Lord is approaching. Don't gripe about each other, brothers and sisters, so you won't face judgment for it. Don't you see? The judge is standing at the door. Take an example, brothers and sisters, from the suffering and patience of the prophets who spoke in the name of the Lord. We hereby congratulate those who endure: you've heard of the endurance of Job and you see what the Lord finally did for him, because the Lord is full of compassion and pity.

Above all, brothers and sisters of mine, don't swear by the heavens or the earth or any other oath. Let your yes be yes and your no be no, so you don't incur judgment.

If any of you are feeling bad, you should pray; if you're feeling good, sing praises. If anyone of you is sick, he should call the elders of the assembly and have them pray over him, applying oil to him in the name of the Lord, and their faithful prayer will save the one who is laid up, and the Lord will put him on his feet. And if there are wrongs that he has done, he will be forgiven them. So admit to each other what you've done wrong, and pray for each other to be healed.

There is great power to the prayers of the just in operation. Elijah was just as human and vulnerable as we are, but he prayed a prayer for it not to rain, and it didn't rain upon the earth for three years and six months. And then he prayed again, and the sky let loose a shower, and the earth blossomed with its produce.

My brothers and sisters, be sure that if one of you strays from the truth and another brings him back, the one who brings back the misguided one from his wandering ways will save his own soul from death: it will "cover a multitude of sins."

The First Letter from

Peter

1

From Peter, apostle of Jesus Christ;
To the chosen ones whose dwellings for the time being are spread across
Pontus, Galatia, Cappadocia, Asia and Bithynia, who were chosen by the
foreknowledge of God the Father, with the sanctifying Spirit leading
them towards obedience to Jesus Christ as they are sprinkled with his
cleansing blood:
Grace to you, and may your peace abound.

Blessed be our God and Father of our Lord Jesus Christ, who of His
great mercy caused us to be born anew into living hope, through the
resurrection of Jesus Christ from the dead, born anew into a promised
inheritance that cannot fade nor stain nor wither, kept safe in the skies
for us, we who are watched over by the might of God, believing in the
salvation ready to be disclosed in the final days. Which are days of delight
for you, even if right now you can't help feeling sad, surrounded by trials
of every kind, which are there so that the solidity of your faith, more
precious than that of perishable gold when it is tested by fire, may show
itself to your praise, glory and honor on the day of revelation of Jesus
Christ. You never saw Jesus Christ, but you love him; and still without
seeing him you believe in him and are delighted with an inexpressible
and exalted joy to be garnering the salvation of your souls that is the
object of your faith. That salvation was the subject of much searching
and scrutinizing by the Prophets, who prophesied about the grace in
store for you, searching for clues as to the identity or nature of the age
for whose benefit the spirit of the Messiah, which was amongst them,
recorded in advance the sufferings of Christ and his ensuing glories. As
they discovered, it was not for themselves, but you that they were the
bearers of this message. Now it has been conveyed to you by those who
spoke in a sacred breath sent down from heaven, bringing you such good
news that the angels bend down in their eagerness to hear it.

433

Therefore, buckle the belts of your minds and stay alert, keeping your hopes to the end on the grace to be brought you on the day when Jesus Christ is revealed. Be like obedient children, no longer shaped by the passions of your former ignorance; and as the One who has called you is holy, be holy yourselves in all your behavior, since it is written: "You shall be holy, because I am holy." And if you address as Father the One who leaves appearances aside and judges each person by his deeds, behave yourself with respect for the term of your earthly residence,

> Knowing that by nothing perishable, like gold or silver, you
>   were ransomed
> From the senseless behavior handed down from your fathers;
> But by blood precious as from an unspotted lamb, from
>   unblemished Christ,
> As determined in advance from the foundation of the world,
> But revealed only now at the close of time,

for your sake, you who through him have become believers in God, who raised him from the dead and bestowed a glory on him that is the reason why your faith and hope is in God.

Now that truthful obedience has made your souls clean enough for sincere brotherly love, love each other constantly with clear hearts, reborn not from a perishable seed but through the imperishable word of a living and lasting God. Thus,

> Every living thing is like grass,
> And their glory is like the flower amid the grass,
> When the grass dried out and the flower keeled over on
>   the ground.
> But the words of the Lord remain forever.

(And that's what the words of the good news are as it has been brought to you.)

2

Then put away all evil and trickery and pretense and envy and speaking evil, and be like newborn babes longing for genuine, undoctored milk that will make you grow toward salvation, "if you have tasted how good the Lord is." Come to him now, the living stone, to humanity a reject, but to God the chosen, precious one, and become the living stones yourselves that build a spiritual house to be used as a holy sanctum where spiritual sacrifices of the kind most acceptable to God can be offered through Jesus Christ. That is why scripture contains the following:

> *I hereby set down in Zion a stone to be the cornerstone, chosen and*
> *precious,*
> *And he who believes in it shall not come to shame.*

So the stone of honor to you the believers is, to the disbelievers, "the stone that the builders rejected" which "ended up being the cornerstone" and "the stone they stumble against and the rock they fall over" for those who were destined to stumble against the word by refusing to accept it.

But you are a chosen race, a royal priesthood, a holy nation, a people ready to be taken over [by God], so that you may tell the world of the powers of the One who called you out of the darkness into this wonderful light. Those who were "no people of Mine" are now God's people; those for whom there was no mercy have now found mercy after all.

Dear friends, I implore you, you who are really short-term residents in a foreign country, to keep away from the physical passions which are always waging a campaign against your soul. Your behavior towards other peoples should be good, so that just as they're denouncing you as evildoers they may take a look at what good you do and end up praising God on the judgment day.

Be obedient to every earthly institution for the Lord's sake: whether to the high station of a king, or to those leaders sent by him to punish evildoers and praise those who do good. Remember, it is God's will that those who do good should shut the mouths of the senseless people and their ignorance and that they should act like free people who never use "freedom" as a cover for evil actions but are really slaves of God. Give honor to all: love brotherhood, fear God, respect the king.

Domestics are to mind their masters with all due respect, and not just if they're kindly and fair but even if they're less than upright. Remember, it brings grace if someone who suffers unjustly bears up under his pains for the sake of a godly attitude. After all, what is glorious about bearing up under punishment when you've done wrong? But if you suffer for

doing good and bear up, that counts as a grace with God.
    That [suffering], actually, is what you were called to:

> Christ suffered too, on your behalf
> and left a tracing behind for you
> so that you could follow his footsteps,
> he who never did wrong,
> nor did any deceit come out of his mouth,
> who, when abuse was hurled, didn't hurl it back,
> didn't answer suffering with threats,
> but commended himself to the One who judges justly.
> He is the one who lifted our sins up,
> in the form of his body, onto the tree
> so that our evildoing selves might pass away
> and we might live doing right.
> He is the one whose bloody bruises have healed you:
> You were like sheep gone astray,
> But now you've come back to the shepherd and guardian of
>   your souls.

3

Women, you likewise are to be obedient to your husbands, so that if some of your husbands aren't convinced by the good word, through the wordless force of the wife's conduct they may be won over when they observe how decent and respectful your behavior is. And let your outer selves not be all braids and curls with gold hanging all over you and an array of wardrobe changes, but let your secret selves in your heart be clothed in what never withers, a gentle and tranquil spirit, which in God's eyes is precious and costly. That's how the holy women of old, whose hopes were in God, adorned themselves: by being subordinate to their husbands. That's how Sarah obeyed Abraham, calling him "lord": you are her daughters when you do good, unworried by possible intimidation.

    The men are likewise to live with their wives, showing understanding for the fragile stuff of womanhood, giving them the share of respect due those who are also heirs of the gift of Life: that way their prayers won't be cut off [from reaching God].

So, in the end let's have everyone united in purpose, joined in feeling, full of brotherly love, rich in compassion, humble of spirit, with no one repaying evil with evil or slander for slander, but giving blessings since you were called so that you could inherit a blessing. As it says:

> *Whoever wishes to enjoy life*
> *And see good days*
> *Should make his tongue refrain from evil*
> *And stop his lips from speaking deceit,*
> *Should incline away from evil and do good instead,*
> *Should desire peace and pursue it;*
> *Because the Lord's eyes are on the just,*
> *And He gives ear to their prayers,*
> *But the Lord's face is against the evildoers.*

And who will do evil to you if you become eager supporters of the good? And even if you did suffer for doing what's right, you would be lucky. "Don't let the fear of them make you scared or disturbed," but treat the Lord Messiah as holy in your hearts and be ready at all times to answer those who ask you to tell them something about the hopes you share. Do so with gentleness and respect, with a good attitude, so that those who speak against you and vilify your fine behavior in Christ will be shown up. And if it finally is God's will that you suffer, better that you suffer for doing good than for doing evil.

> Christ too suffered once because of wrongdoing,
> The just man suffering for the unjust,
> So that, physically murdered but spiritually vivified,
> He might bring you close to God—

for which purpose he came bringing the news even to the imprisoned souls [in hell], the same ones who didn't listen before, as long as God's patience held out, in the days when Noah was getting the ark ready, which only a few would enter—eight souls, to be exact—and pass safely through the water, which is a symbol of how being washed in the Lord saves you now: it's not the removal of dirt from the body, it's a plea to God for a better outlook through the resurrection of Jesus Christ, who is now at the right of God, having entered into heaven to take his place above the angels, the dominions, and the powers.

4

So since Christ suffered physically, you too should be armed with the same insight: that it's the one who suffers physically who is really done with his wrongdoing. That will help you live by the will of God and not by human passions for the rest of your fleshly existence. You've had enough time up till now to do what the pagans like, making the rounds of their lewdness, lustfulness, drunkenness, wild parties, drinking-bouts and unlawful idol-worship. Now they're amazed that you're not tagging along with their outpourings of licentiousness as before, and they're dragging your name through the mud; but they will have to give answer to the one who stands ready to judge the living and the dead. That's the reason the good news was brought to the dead, so that they would face judgment the normal human way but might also be given life by the spirit, which is the way of God.

All things are nearing their end. So keep your wits about you and stay clear-headed for your prayers. The most important thing is keeping your love for each other going continuously, because "love covers a multitude of faults." Happily play host to each other without grumbling. Whatever talent you each were given, put it to one another's service like good managers of the multifarious favors of God. When someone speaks, let it be like God's conversations. When someone helps out, let it be as if with a strength provided by God, so that in all matters God may be glorified through Jesus Christ, to whom belongs the glory and the reign forever and ever, let it be so.

Dear friends, do not be shocked at the firestorm of trials which has come upon you, as if that were a strange thing to happen to you; instead, rejoice in the degree to which you share the sufferings of the Messiah, and on the day that reveals his glory, your joy will be delightful. If you are insulted in the name of Christ, congratulations: the breath of glory, the breath of God is alighting upon you. Let no one among you be punished as a murderer or thief or criminal or meddler in others' affairs. But if you're punished for being one of those "Christians," don't be ashamed. Give glory to God for a name like that.

The time for the judgment has come, starting with us, God's family. But if it starts with us, what will happen at the end to those who didn't believe the good word of God? And as it says, if

> *The just man can barely be saved,*
> *Where does that leave the godless and the sinful?*

Which means that even those who suffer in line with the will of God should make sure their fine actions commend their souls to their trusted Creator.

5

Therefore I call on the elders among you as a fellow elder and witness of the sufferings of the Messiah, and shareholder in the glory still to be revealed: Shepherd your local flock of God not by compulsion, but willingly, in line with God's wishes: not grasping for money, but eager to serve; not lording it over the people who are yours now, but being a model for the flock. And when the Great Shepherd appears you shall have glory's unfading crown.

By the same token, you younger ones must obey the elders. All of you, be dressed in humility towards each other, since God "goes against the haughty and gives favor to the humble."

Be humbled then beneath the mighty hand of God, that He may exalt you in due time; and unload all your worries onto Him, because He's in charge of you.

Stay clear-headed, stay awake. Your adversary the devil, like a roaring lion, is on the prowl looking for somebody to gulp down. So on your side, stand firm in the faith, knowing that your brothers and sisters in the world at large have been undergoing the same range of sufferings. But the God of all graces, Who called you to His everlasting glory in Christ Jesus, after you have suffered a little, will season you, will firm you up, will strengthen you, will give you a foundation. To Him be the ruling power forever, let it be so.

By way of Silas, a brother whom I assume you know and trust, I send these few lines to encourage you and give you evidence that this, [your suffering,] is really God's good will toward you, which you should stand

firm in. Greetings to you from the assembly here in the new Babylon*
and from Mark my pupil. Greet each other with the kiss of love. Peace
to you all in Christ.

* Rome.

Peter

1

From Simon Peter, slave and apostle of Jesus Anointed,

To those who, like us, have been awarded faith by the just actions of our God and savior Jesus Christ;

Grace to you and may your peace abound in the knowledge of God and Jesus our Lord, since in all respects His divine power which we need for our lives and worship is given to us for free by our recognition of the one who called us with a unique glory and special power that allows the richest and greatest of promises to be given us for free, promises by which you can come to participate in divine nature and escape the decay with which willful desire fills the world. Just the reason why you should put forth every effort to make sure your belief has virtue, your virtue has knowledge, your knowledge has self-control, your self-control has endurance, your endurance has a God-fearing attitude, your God-fearing attitude has friendliness, and your friendliness has real love! With these things in your possession and growing with you, you will not be idle or ineffective in your search for the knowledge of our Lord Jesus Christ. In fact, whoever is without these things is shortsighted to the point of blindness and has forgotten all about the way he was washed clean of his former wrongs. Therefore, redouble your efforts, brothers and sisters, to make certain of your being called and chosen: if you do that you will never fall by the wayside—certainly not when you are being so richly provided with an entryway into the everlasting kingdom of our Lord and savior Jesus Christ.

That is why I will always remind you of these things, though of course you know them and feel supported by clear and present truth. Still I think it only right, as long as I am encamped in these bones, to rouse you to mindfulness, knowing how imminent my removal from this encampment is, as our Lord Jesus Christ revealed to me. But I will make efforts to ensure that even after my departure you will keep these things in mind.

After all, we weren't following the lines of some well-composed fiction when we made known to you the power and the second coming of our Lord Jesus Christ: we were eyewitnesses of his grandeur—such as when he took on a splendor and shining from God the Father, and a voice came to him, carried to him on the beams of that magnificent glory: "My son, My beloved son, this is the one with whom I am delighted." And we heard that voice borne from the sky as we were with him on the holy mountain. So now we have even more confidence in the words of the prophets, to which you would do well to turn your attention, as to a lamp shining in a dark place till the day dawns and the morning-star rises in your hearts, keeping in mind first of all that all the prophecies of scripture are beyond the individual to unravel: that's because no prophecy was ever delivered by human intention in the first place: instead, human beings, in a transport of the sacred breath, spoke with a voice from God.

2

But there were fake prophets among the people then, and there will also be fake teachers among you, who will create destructive factions and repudiate the One who bought us and owns us now; in so doing, they will bring their own speedy destruction down upon their heads. And they will have many following along with their debaucheries and will cause the way of truth to fall into disrepute, and they will greedily make their pitch for you with shapely words, though their own guilt has long been pronounced and their destruction awaits with unsleeping eyes.

After all, God didn't spare the angels who went wrong, but tied them up in the darkness of hell and left them to be kept there till the Judgment. He didn't spare the ancient world either, but preserved only eight including Noah, herald of justice, while He brought the cataclysm down upon a world of ungodly people; and He also incinerated the cities of Sodom and Gomorrah, making their condemnation an example of what would happen in the future to the ungodly, while the just man Lot, who had been oppressed by the debauched conduct of his immoral neighbors, was rescued, after that upright man had been visibly and audibly assaulted in his upright soul every day by the unlawful doings of those he lived among. The Lord knows how to free the godly from their trials, while He leaves the wicked in their punishment till Judgment Day, especially those who let their bodies lead them around in their polluted desires and are contemptuous of authority.

Reckless and swell-headed, they have no qualms about blaspheming the powers of heaven, about which the angels would never express any blasphemous judgments in the presence of the Lord, though the angels are much stronger and more powerful than these others.

Like unreasoning animals born by nature to be captured or to die and rot, they blaspheme what they know nothing about, destined to rot in their own corruption, with their lack of integrity receiving its proper reward. They think the middle of the day is a good partytime, those dirty, scabby people indulging their misguided lusts as they feast beside you. Adultery is in their eyes, and their wrongdoing is uninterrupted: they lay traps for unsteady souls and have the hearts of practiced moneygrubbers, children of the curse.

Leaving the straight road they wandered off, following the road of Balaam son of Bosor, who was seduced by the payment promised for his misdeeds, and whose unlawfulness was laid bare when his mute beast of burden spoke up in a human voice and overruled the prophet's foolish plans. These people are wells run dry and clouds that the storm drives this way and that, and the darkness of the underworld awaits them. Speaking the most utter and complete nonsense, they set traps of fleshly passion and lewdness to catch those who have just recently escaped from the circles of people whose behavior is off the track. "Freedom" is what they promise others, though they themselves are the slaves of decay, since what you're defeated by takes you as its slave. In fact, if after the knowledge of our Lord and savior Jesus Christ let them escape the pollutions of the world, they then get trapped in them and defeated by them all over again, in the end they are worse off than before: they would have been better off never knowing the right way of living than to know it and then go against the holy commandments transmitted to them. They're a good example of the truth of the proverb about the dog that returns to its own vomit and the pig that gets bathed so it can roll in the mud again.

3

This, dear friends, is already the second letter I've written you, rousing your well-intentioned minds with the warning to keep in mind what was said before by the holy prophets, as well as the commands that came to you through the apostles from the Lord and Savior, knowing first of all that in the final days schemers will come along with their schemes, following the lead of their greedy desires and saying, "Where is this Second Coming that he promised us? In the meantime our fathers and mothers have died, and the whole world is still just the same as it has been since the beginnings of creation."

Those who would like to think that way are forgetting that there were previous skies, and there was a previous earth, which was from the water and on the water, established by the word of God—that word which also caused the world of that time to be destroyed in a watery cataclysm. The skies and earth we have now, amassed by the same word, are destined for the fire on the day of judgment, the day of destruction for the ungodly.

Let this one thing not escape you, dear friends: that a single day, for the Lord, is like a thousand years, and a thousand years is like a day. The Lord isn't "late" in fulfilling His promise; what some call His lateness is really His patience with you: He doesn't want to lose anybody, He wants repentance to include everybody.

But like a thief, the day of the Lord will suddenly be there, the day when the skies will go bang and vanish, and the heavenly bodies will burn up and dissolve, and the earth and its deeds will be revealed. With everything about to come apart like this, how important it is for you to be on your holiest and most reverent behavior, living in hopes of the speedy arrival of the day of God which is the reason why the sky must burn to cinders and the heavenly bodies melt in the flames: according to God's promise, new skies and a new earth await us, where justice shall reside.

Therefore, dear friends, make every effort so that these things we wait for will find us spotless, unblemished and at peace with God, and consider His lack of haste to be your salvation, just as our dear brother Paul, in his God-given wisdom, has written to you, which is in fact the same way he speaks to this subject in any of his letters where the subject is spoken of. (Admittedly, his letters contain some hard-to-understand parts, which the ignorant and unsteady twist around like the rest of scripture to further their own destructive ends.)

So as for you, dear friends, be warned and keep watch so you won't follow those unprincipled people down the same wrong path and lose your own balance, but will instead grow in the favor and knowledge of our Lord and Savior Jesus Christ. To him be the glory, from now till the first day of eternity, let it be so.

John

1

What was there from the beginning, what we have heard, what we have seen with our eyes, what we observed and felt with our hands concerning the word of Life—a Life that has now appeared, so that we have seen and are reporting and announcing to you the everlasting Life which was there by the Father and became visible to us—what we have seen and heard, we now announce to you, so that you too can have a common bond with us, our bond being with the Father and with His son, Jesus Christ. And what we write to you now is so that your joy may be complete.

And this is the message which we have heard from him and now report to you: that God is light, and there is no darkness in Him anywhere. If we say that we have a common bond with Him but we walk in the darkness, we're lying and our actions are dishonest; whereas if we walk in the light as He is in the light, we have a common bond with each other, and the blood of Jesus His son cleanses us of all our wrongs.

If we say we have no guilt, we're fooling ourselves, and the truth has escaped us. If we admit our guilt, He is trustworthy and fair and will release us from our guilt and cleanse us of everything that isn't right. If we say we haven't done wrong, we're making a liar out of Him, and His word is nowhere within us.

2

My dear children, I write this to you so you won't do wrong, but even if a person does do wrong, we have someone to intercede with God the Father: Jesus Christ, the just. He himself is the propitiatory offering for our offenses, and not just ours but those of all the world.

And the way we can tell if we really know him is by whether we keep his commandments. Anyone saying "I know him" who doesn't keep his commandments is a liar and has no honesty in him. But if someone does keep his word, that person truly has perfect love for God: that's how we can tell that we are part of Christ. The person who says "I'm with Christ" is obligated to look at the path Christ followed and follow it too.

Dear friends, I'm not sending you a new commandment, but the same old one you've had from the very beginning. What is this old commandment? The message that you already received. Yet in a way I *am* sending you a new commandment: something true in itself and true within you, since the darkness is passing and the true light is already shining. Anyone who says he's in the light and treats his brother hatefully has been in the darkness all along. The one who treats his brother with love is in the light to stay and doesn't keep tripping over something inside him. But the one who treats his brother hatefully is in the darkness and walks in the darkness and doesn't know where he's going because the darkness blinded his eyes.

I am writing to tell you, dear children, that your wrongs are forgiven for the sake of his name.

I am writing to tell you older ones that you have known him from the beginning.

I am writing to tell you younger ones that you have conquered the Evil One.

I wrote to tell you children that you know the Father now.

I wrote to tell you older ones that you have known Him from the beginning.

I wrote to tell you younger ones that you are strong, and the word of God is with you to stay, and you've conquered the Evil One.

Don't fall in love with the world or what's in the world. Whoever loves the world has no room for the love of the Father, because everything the world is full of—the greedy desires of the flesh, the greedy desires of the eyes, lavish displays of means—belongs not to the Father but to the world itself. And the world is passing away with all its greedy desires, while the one who does the will of God remains forever.

Dear children, this is the final hour. And just as you heard that the Antichrist was coming, so now we have a host of Antichrists, which is how you can tell the final hour is here. They came *from* us but they were never *of* us: if they were of us, they'd still be here with us. But in fact they're all clearly enough not of our kind. But you have received an anointing from the holy one, and so you all know what's what. I am writing to you, not because you don't know the truth, but because you do know the truth and you know that no lies can be part of it.

And who is more of a liar than someone who says no, Jesus is not the Messiah? There you have the Antichrist, saying no to the Father and the son. In every case, repudiating the son means there's no Father for you either, while accepting the son gives you the Father too. As for you, make sure what you heard from the beginning stays within you. If you keep within you what you heard from the beginning, you also remain in the son and the Father. And that is the promise Jesus promised you himself, this life that lasts forever.

That's what I wanted to write and tell you concerning those who are misleading you. As for you, the anointing you received from Jesus is still within you, and you don't need to have anyone teach you: [the spirit you received with] your anointing teaches you about everything and is always truthful and never lies. So do what it taught you: remain in Christ.

Yes, dear children, remain in Christ, so that when he appears, we will be confident and not shrink away from him upon his return. If you know that he is just, you also understand that everyone who does what is just is born of his lineage.

3

See what love the Father has given us? It's so that we can be called "children of God"—which we are. That's why the world doesn't recognize us, because it didn't recognize Him. Dear friends, children of God is what we now are; it has not yet been revealed what we will be. We know that when it is revealed, we shall be like Him, because we will see Him as He is. And everyone who has such hopes in Him keeps pure, just as He is pure.

Everyone who does wrong is also breaking the law, and wrongdoing is lawbreaking. And you know who it was that appeared to take our wrongs away, and that there is no wrong in him. Anyone who stays with him stops doing wrong; anyone who keeps doing wrong has neither seen him nor gotten to know him.

Dear children, don't let anyone fool you. The one who does what is just, is just, the same as he whom we speak of is just. The person who does what is wrong is of the devil's kind; because the devil has been doing wrong since the very beginning. That's why the son of God appeared, to break up the operations of the devil. Everyone born of God keeps from doing wrong, because the seeds of God remain in him, and he *can't* do wrong, because he's born of God. That's how you can clearly tell the children of God from the children of the devil: anyone who doesn't do what's right isn't of God's kind, as well as anyone who doesn't treat his brother with love.

Yes, this is the message you have heard from the beginning, that we should love one another, not like Cain, who was of the Evil One's kind and slaughtered his brother. And on what account did he slaughter him? Because his own deeds were evil and his brother's deeds were virtuous.

And don't be surprised, brothers and sisters, if you are hated by the world. We know what we've done: we've turned around and gone from death to life; we can tell by our love for our brothers and sisters. Whoever does not love remains in the dead state. Anyone who treats his brother with hatred is a murderer, and you know that no murderer has eternal life lodged within him. We have come to know what love is by the way that special person laid his life down for us, and it's our duty to lay our lives down too for our brothers and sisters. But if someone possessed of worldly means sees his brother in need and shuts him out of his heart, how can the love of God be dwelling within him? Dear children, we mustn't love with words or with our tongue, but in truth and action.

That is how we can be sure that we are motivated by the truth and able to face God with a steady heart. After all, if our own heart knows bad things about us—well, God is greater than our hearts and knows everything. Dear friends, once our own hearts say nothing bad about us, we can have confidence before God and what we ask, we receive from Him, because we're keeping His commands and doing what is most pleasing in His eyes.

And this is His command: to trust in the name of His son Jesus Christ and love each other as he commanded us. If you keep His commands, He lives in you and you in Him, and we can tell that we have Him within us by the spirit He gave us.

4

Dear friends, don't put your faith in just any spirit: test the spirits out to see if they're from God, because many pseudoprophets have come forth into the world. This is how you can tell if it's the spirit of God: any spirit that acknowledges Jesus as the Messiah coming in the flesh is from God, and any spirit that doesn't acknowledge Jesus, isn't from God: it's the spirit of the Antichrist that you heard was coming and which is now in the world already.

You are God's kind, dear children, and you have already triumphed over the others, because the One who is in you is greater than the one who is in the world. The others are the world's kind, which is why they speak the world's language, and the world listens to them. We are God's kind, and those who know God listen to us, but those who aren't of God's kind don't listen to us; on that basis we can tell the spirit of truth from the spirit of error.

> Dear friends, let us show love to one another,
> Because love is from God,
> And all who show love are born of God
> And know God.
> If you show no love, you never knew God,
> Because God is love.
> And this is what revealed the love of God among us,
> That, having one only son, God sent him into the world
> That we might find life through him.
> And what does love consist in?
> Not in the way we have felt love for God
> But in the love He felt for us,
> Sending His only son to be a sacrifice
> In payment for our offenses.

Dear friends, after God showed such love for us, we have a duty to show love for each other too. God has never yet been seen by anyone, but if we love each other, God dwells in us and we have His perfect love within us. We can tell that we are living within Him and He in us, because He gave some of His spirit to us. And we have witnessed and can report that the Father has sent His son to be savior of the world. If someone professes that Jesus is the son of God, God is living in him and he in God. And we have come to know and believe in the love that God shows among us.

God is love, and whoever lives in love lives in God, and God lives in him. What it means to have perfect love is that we will have confidence on the day of judgment that in this world we have been the same way as he [God's son] is. In love there is no fear. Perfect love throws fear right out, because fear will be punished: the fearful person isn't perfect in love. It is our turn to show love, since God loved us first. If someone says "I love God" but hates his brother, he's a liar: after all, if he has no love for his brother, whom he has seen, he can scarcely have love for God, whom he has never seen. And we have this command from Him, that anyone who wants to love God must love his brother too.

5

All who believe that Jesus is the Messiah are born of God and all who love Him who gave birth also love the one He gave birth to. The way we know that we love the children of God is when we love God and do what He commands. That is what our love of God is: it's the way we keep His commandments, and His commandments are not burdensome, because everyone born of God conquers the world. What is the victory we achieve over the world? Our faith.

Who is the conqueror of the world if not the person who believes that Jesus is the son of God? It is he who came through water and blood, Jesus Christ, not just water alone, but water and blood, and the Spirit is our witness because the Spirit is truth. That makes three witnesses: the Spirit, the water, and the blood; and the three make one. If we accept human testimony, God's testimony is much greater, and this is the testimony of God, what He has testified about His son. And the testimony is that God gave us life everlasting, and this life is to be found in His son. If you have God's son, you also have true life, and if you don't have the son of God you have no such life.

I am writing you all this because I want you to know that eternal life is yours; it's for those who put their trust in the name of the son of God. And the nature of the confidence we have in Him is that if we ask something in line with His will, He listens to us. And knowing that He listens to us whatever we ask, we can also count on receiving the requests we have requested from Him.

If anyone sees his brother doing something wrong but not a deadly wrong, he should pray to God, who will still bestow Life on those whose wrongs are not deadly. (Some wrongs are deadly, and I'm not telling you to pray for those.) Every failure of integrity is wrong, but some wrongs are not deadly.

We know that anyone born of God does not keep doing wrong: no, the person born of God never loses God, and the Evil One can't get hold of him. We know that we come from God, while the Evil One has the whole world surrounded. But we also know the son of God is coming who has given us minds to recognize the True One, and we are part of the True One, part of His son, Jesus Christ. This is the true God and life everlasting.

Dear children, please: keep away from false gods!

The Second Letter from
John

From the Elder;
To your noble and God-chosen mother community, with all her children, whom I love—and I am not the only one, so do all who have come to know the truth, because of the truth that lives in us now and always will. The grace, mercy and peace of God the Father and of Jesus Christ, the son of the Father, shall be with us, with truthfulness and love all round.

I was extremely happy to find some of your children walking the path of truth, just as we have been given orders to do by the Father. And what I ask you now, noble mother—and I'm sending you not a new commandment but the same one you've had from the beginning—is that we should show love for each other. And what is love? It's going by His commands. And that is His command, the same you were told from the beginning to follow.

For the world has been invaded by a host of wrong-headed people who won't accept that Jesus has come as the Messiah in the flesh. There you have the deceiver and the Antichrist. Watch out for those people: you don't want to lose what we've built up, and you do want to collect your full reward.

Anyone who doesn't stick to the teachings of the Anointed, but goes beyond them, has nothing to do with God; the one who does keep to those teachings has both the Father and the son behind him. If someone comes to you and that isn't the teaching they bring, don't allow them in your house and don't say hello to them: if you even say hello to them you're a partner in their evil deeds.

There is much more that I could write to you, but I didn't want to do it on paper. I'm hoping to get to see you and speak face to face, so that our joy may be complete.

Greetings to you from the children of your sister community, whom God has also favored.

John

From the Elder,
To my dear friend Gaius, whom I truly love.

Dear friend, I pray that you may get along well and be healthy in every way. I know your soul is getting along well, because I had the great joy of receiving some brothers who testified about your honesty and how the truth guides your way. There is no greater joy I can have than to hear of my pupils' being guided by the truth.

Dear friend, you have given trusty service by what you did for those brothers—visitors whom you didn't even know. They reported your kindness to the assembled congregation. It would be good if you could also send them on their way provided for in a manner worthy of God, especially since, to maintain God's name, they set out without taking any contributions from the Gentile communities. We owe support to people like that if we want to be partners in spreading the truth.

I wrote a little note to the assembly, but that power-loving Diotrephes of theirs is completely unreceptive to us. So the next time I'm there I'll remind him of all the stuff he's done, vilifying us in the evilest terms—and as if that weren't enough, he not only won't put the brothers up himself, but he's saying if anybody else tries to, he'll throw them out of the assembly.

Dear friend, don't imitate the evil you see, imitate the goodness you see, because someone who does good comes from God. The evildoer has never seen God.

Demetrius is given a good reputation by everyone, as indeed the facts speak well of him. We report the same ourselves, and you know that our reports are reliable.

There's a lot I wanted to write you about, but I don't want to put it on paper. I hope to see you soon and speak face to face.

Peace to you. Greetings to you from your friends here. Please say hello personally to each of my friends there.

The Letter from
Jude

From Jude, slave of Jesus Anointed, brother of James;
To the chosen ones who live in God the Father's love and the safekeeping of Jesus Christ:
Mercy to you, and peace, and may love abound.

Dear friends, having every intention of writing to you about our shared salvation, I found myself obliged instead to write you a letter of warning to keep up the fight for the faith as transmitted to the holy ones once and for all. It seems that certain persons whose damnation is already on the books, with no respect for religion, have insinuated themselves in amongst you, twisting God's good will toward us into a license for debaucheries and defying our one and only overlord and master, Jesus Anointed.

I wish to remind you, though you know about all these things, that first the Lord rescued His people from the land of Egypt, and next he put to death those who broke faith with Him. And you know about the angels who didn't keep to their noble plane but left their proper station [in pursuit of mortal women,] how he keeps them chained forever in the darkness below hell to await their judgment on the Great Day. And how, no differently from them, Sodom and Gomorrah and the surrounding towns, where they unleashed their lust and went in pursuit of alien flesh,* were made an example of, shouldering the sentence of everlasting fire.

And these people in their dreamworld are just the same: they pollute the body, disregard authority, and even blaspheme the powers of the universe. By contrast, Michael the archangel, when he was arguing with the devil in a dispute over the fallen body of Moses, was too discreet to indict his adversary in blasphemous terms but simply said, "You will be punished by the Lord." But these ones heap blasphemy on things they know nothing about and take a corrupt approach to things they understand only on the physical level of an unthinking animal. Too bad for

---

* Angel flesh, as the angels (or "sons of God") in Genesis 6:1 had lusted after mortal flesh.

them! They traveled down the same road as Cain; the same offer that tempted Balaam melted their resistance; and in the same rebellion as the sons of Korah they perished. And these are the people who calmly sit beside you being a blotch upon our love-feasts, grazing off you like cattle: rainless clouds that float past on the winds; trees that, come the fall, are fruitless, deader than dead, and finally uprooted; wild waves of the sea, spewing the froth of their cheapness; stars gone off course, whose eternal destiny is the darkness of the pit.

Prophecy spoke of these people already in the seventh generation after Adam when Enoch said, "Here comes the Lord, surrounded by His holy myriads, to bring everyone to judgment and make every soul answer for the godless deeds it did in its ungodliness, for all the harsh words they spoke against Him in their criminal irreverence." These people are always whimpering and blaming fate while going wherever their greedy desires may lead them; and their mouths are full of grandiose words with which they kiss people's behinds to gain their own ends.

But you, dear friends, remember what was said to you before by the emissaries of our Lord Jesus Christ, how they told you: "Towards the end of Time people will come along playing games to suit their own godless desires." They are divisive people, purely emotional, with nothing spiritual about them.

But you, dear friends, building on your most holy faith, praying in a holy spirit, stay in the love of God as you wait for the mercy of our Lord Jesus Christ to bring life everlasting. Some people you pity for their divided hearts. Some people you pull out of the fire and save. And some people you pity, while still avoiding with revulsion so much as a piece of clothing polluted by contact with their bodies.

To the One who can keep you from stumbling and allows you to stand joyfully without blemish in the sight of His glory, to the one God, our Savior through Jesus Christ our Lord, to Him be glory, grandeur, might and authority, before the dawn of time, and now, and for all ages to come, let it be so.

Revelation of John

1

A Revelation of Jesus Anointed, which was given him by God in order to show his slaves that which must happen very soon: he in turn gestured to one of his messengers to bring it to his slave John, who reported the words of God and the testimony of Jesus Anointed with everything he saw. Lucky for him who reads and lucky for those who hear the words of prophecy and don't forget what is written there, because the time is near.

From John,

To the seven assemblies in Asia:

Grace to you and peace from the Is, the Was and the Will Be and from the seven spirits before His throne, and from Jesus Anointed, the bearer of witness, the trusted one, first of the dead to be born again and ruler of the kings of the earth. To him who loves us and absolves us of our wrongdoing with his blood, and who made us into a kingdom of priests serving God his Father, to him be the glory and the ruling power forever and ever, let it be so.

> *There he comes, amid the clouds,*
> *And every eye shall see him,*
> *Him whom they riddled with wounds before,*
> *They shall wail over him, all the tribes of the earth.* Yes, in truth.

I am Alpha and Omega, says the Lord God, the Is, the Was and the Will Be, the ruler of all.

I, John, your brother and fellow-shareholder in the present suffering and the coming kingdom and the endurance Jesus brings, landed on the island known as Patmos on account of the word of God and my bearing witness to Jesus. One day, it was the Lord's Day, I was taken up into the spirit and heard behind me a great voice like a trumpet saying: "What you see, write down in a book and send it to the seven assemblies—to Ephesus, to Smyrna, to Pergamon, to Thyatira, to Sardis, to Philadelphia and to Laodicia."

And I turned around to see who the voice was, talking there with me, and as I turned I saw seven golden candlesticks, and in the midst of all the candlesticks, what looked like the son of humanity dressed in a long robe and encircled round the chest with a band of gold. His head and hair were white as snow-white wool, his eyes like blazing fire, his feet like Lebanese brass smelted in the furnace, and his voice like the sound of a massive rush of water, holding seven stars in his right hand and with a sharp double-edged sword coming out of his mouth, and his face shone like the sun from having so much power within it.

And when I saw him, I fell at his feet half-dead, and he put his right hand on me, saying: "Don't be afraid. I am the first and the last and the most alive. And I was dead, but here I am, living forever and ever and holding the keys of Death and Hades. So write down what you see, both the things that are and the things that will be later on. As for the secret of the seven stars you see in my right hand and the seven golden candlesticks, the seven stars are the angels of the seven assemblies, and the seven candlesticks are the seven assemblies themselves."

2

"To the angel of the Ephesus assembly, write this:

Thus speaks the one who holds the seven stars in his right hand, who walks amidst the seven candlesticks of gold: I know your actions and your labor and your endurance, and that you do not put up with the wicked, and that you examined those who called themselves apostles and weren't, and exposed them as liars; and you possess endurance, and have put up with a lot for the sake of my name without growing weary. But I have one thing against you: you've lost the love you used to have. Think again of the heights you've fallen from, and go back to doing what you did before! Or else I'm coming by to remove your candlestick from its place, if you show no change of heart. This I must say for you: you hate the behavior of the Nicholasites as much as I do.

"Let everyone with ears hear what the spirit says to the assemblies: to the victor I will give the prize of eating from the Tree of Life, which is in the paradise of God.

"And to the angel of the Smyrna assembly, write this:

Thus speaks the First and Last, who was dead, and came alive. I know of your sufferings and poverty (actually, you possess great riches) and of the mudslinging you've taken from people who call themselves "Jews"—but they aren't Jews, they belong to the synagogue of Satan. Don't be afraid of what they may do to you. Get ready, the devil is about to throw some of you into jail to test you, and you will have sufferings ten days long. Be faithful unto death, and I will give you the crown of life. "Everyone with ears, hear what the spirit says to the assemblies. The victor will never suffer the injury of any other death.

"And to the angel of the Pergamon assembly, write this:

Thus speaks the bearer of the sword, double-edged and sharp: I know where you're living, it's where Satan's very throne is. And still you hold on to my name and did not repudiate my faith even in the days of Antipas, my faithful one who bore witness to me and who was killed in your area, where Satan has his home.

"But it puts me somewhat against you that you have people down there holding to the teachings of Balaam, who showed Balak how to trap the children of Israel in the pitfalls of eating pagan sacrifice-meat and acting like whores. And now you have these adherents of the Nicholasite teaching acting the same way. So turn your hearts around, or else I'm coming by soon and making war on them with the sword that comes from my mouth.

"Everyone with ears, hear what the spirit says to the assemblies: To the victor I will give manna never seen before, and I will put in his hand a white pebble, and written on the pebble will be a new name which no one knows but the person receiving it.

"And to the angel of the Thyatira assembly, write this:

Thus speaks the son of God, the one with eyes like gleaming fire, and whose feet are like smelted Lebanese brass. I know your actions: your love, your trust, your service, your endurance, and that your later deeds have outdone your earlier ones. But I hold it against you that you allow that Jezebel woman to go on calling herself a prophet and spreading her teachings and misleading my slaves into acting like whores and eating pagan sacrifice-meat. And I gave her time to repent, but she doesn't want to repent of her pandering. Watch me throw her down upon her sickbed and cast those who defiled themselves with her into tremendous sufferings, unless their hearts turn back from what she stands for; and as for her children, I will kill them dead. And all the assemblies will know that I am the scrutinizer of guts and hearts, and I will give each one of you what is indicated by your deeds. And I say to the rest of you in Thyatira, who have nothing to do with such teachings and were never acquainted with these 'profundities' of Satan as they call them: I will not heap upon you any further burdens; just hold on to what you have until I get there.

"And the one who wins out and keeps to my kind of actions right up to the end, I will give that one authority over the nations, and he will 'shepherd them with an iron staff, like so many clay pots that shatter at his touch'—the same authority I received from my Father—and I will give him the star of morning as his own.

"Whoever has ears, listen to what the spirit says to the assemblies."

3

"And to the angel of the Sardis assembly, write this:

Thus speaks the possessor of the seven spirits of God and the seven stars: I know your actions, the fact that you have the reputation of being alive, and you're dead. Look lively and straighten up your moribund remains, because I find your work to be incomplete in the sight of my God. Remember what it was like receiving the word, what it was like to hear it, and turn back to that and be sorry you let it go. If you don't keep awake, I will suddenly be there like a thief, and you won't know what time I will be coming to get you. But there are some names in Sardis that have not gotten the dirt on their clothes, and they shall walk with me dressed in white, because they deserve to.

"So shall the victor be draped in clothes of white, and I will never rub out his name from the Book of Life, and I will acknowledge him by name in the sight of my Father and His messengers.

"Whoever has ears, hear what the spirit says to the assemblies.

"And to the angel of the Philadelphia assembly, write this:

Thus speaks the holy, the truthful one, possessor of the key of David, who opens and none shall close again, who closes and none shall open again. I know your actions. Look, I have given you a door standing open in front of you which no one can close again, because you didn't have much strength and you still kept my word and didn't disavow my name. Watch, I am going to get some of the members of Satan's synagogue, who call themselves Jews—but they aren't, they're lying. And watch how I will make them come and bow down at your feet and realize that I have

come to love you. Because you preserved my words about endurance in
your heart, I in turn will preserve you from the time of trials that is going
to come over all of civilization to put all who live upon the earth to the
test. I'm coming quickly. Hold on to what you have and don't let anyone
take your crown away.

"The victor, I will make him a pillar in the temple of my God and from
it he shall never depart again; and I will write on him the name of my God
and the name of the city of my God, the new Jerusalem coming down out
of the sky from my God, and also my own name. Whoever has ears, hear
what the spirit says to the assemblies.

"And to the angel of the Laodician assembly write this:
Thus speaks the Let It Be, the witness trusted and truthful, the
sovereign of God's creation. I know what you do, that you're neither hot
nor cold. You should be either hot or cold! As it is, since you are
lukewarm and neither hot nor cold, I am about to spit you out of my
mouth. Because you say, 'I'm rich, I've made my fortune, I've got
everything I need,' and do not know that you are as wretched and pitiful
and poor and blind and naked as anyone, I advise you to buy from me
gold that is flame-tested in the fire, and then you'll be rich, and to put
white clothes on so as not to expose the shame of your nakedness, and
to smear a salve in your eyes so you can see. If any are my friends, I call
them to account and discipline them. So get eager and turn your hearts
around. See how I am standing at the door and knocking? If someone
hears my voice and opens the door, I will come in and have dinner with
them and they with me.

"To the victor, I will give him the prize of sitting with me on my
throne, just as I was the victor and sat down with my Father on His
throne. Whoever has ears, hear what the spirit says to the assemblies!"

4

Next I looked, and there was a door standing open in the sky, and the
voice I heard the first time, the one like a sounding trumpet, was
speaking to me: "Come up here and I'll show you what is destined to
happen later on." Straightway the spirit came over me, and suddenly
there was a throne set up in the sky. On the throne, a person sitting, and
the person sitting being like in appearance to jeweled jaspers and
carnelians. Roundabout the throne, a rainbow similar in appearance to

emeralds. And around that throne, thrones twenty-four; and upon the
thrones, twenty-four elders seated, draped in robes of shining white; and
upon their heads, crowns of gold. And radiating from the great throne
come lightning-bolts and sounds of thunder, with seven fiery lamps
burning before the throne, which are the seven spirits of God. And in
front of the throne, something like a sea of glass as clear as crystal. And
in the middle of the throne and around the throne, four creatures loaded
with eyes in front and back: the first creature, like a lion; the second
creature, like a calf; a third creature with a human face; and a fourth
creature like an eagle in flight. And the four creatures, each of them
having six wings apiece, are full of eyes inside and out, and day and night
they never rest from saying,

> Holy, holy, holy, the Lord God, ruler of all,
> The Was and the Is and the Shall Be.

And when the creatures give glory and honor and thanks to the occupant
of the throne, the one who lives for ages and ages, down fall the twenty-
four elders before the occupant of the throne, bowing before the one
who lives for ages and ages, and they throw their crowns at the foot of
the throne, saying

> It is only fitting, our Lord and our God,
> That You should have the glory and the honor and the powers,
> Since You created all
> And through Your will all came to be and was created.

5

And I saw, at the right of the occupant of the throne, a book with writing
on the inside and outside, sealed with seven seals. And I saw a mighty
angel heralding in a loud voice: "Who is worthy to open the book and
break the seals upon it?" And there was no one, no one in the sky or on
the earth or under the earth, who could open the book or look at it. And
I burst into tears because no one was found worthy to open the book or
look at it.

And one of the elders says to me: "Don't cry: to the lion of the tribe of Judah, the roots of David, went the triumph of opening the book and the seven seals upon it."

And I saw, in among the throne and the four creatures and the elders, a Lamb standing there as if its throat were slit, with seven horns and seven eyes which are the seven spirits of God, emissaries to all the earth. And he came forward and took it from the right hand of the occupant of the throne.

And when he took the book, the four creatures and the twenty-four elders fell down before the Lamb, holding each a harp and golden dish heaped with incense, which are the prayers of the faithful, and they sing a new song, saying:

> It is fitting that you should take the book and open the seals
> upon it,
> Since you were slaughtered and with your blood bought some
> of every tribe and tongue and people and nation for God,
> And made them over to God to be a ruling-class, His priests,
> And they shall rule over all the earth.

And I looked again and heard a voice of many angels in a ring around the throne, the creatures and the elders, and the number of them was millions of millions and thousands of thousands, saying with a loud voice:

> It is fitting that the Lamb that was slaughtered should be given
> the power and wealth and wisdom and strength and honor
> and glory and blessing.

And I heard every creature in the sky and on the earth and under the earth and on the waters and everywhere in between saying:

> To the occupant of the throne and to the Lamb
> Be blessings and honor and glory and ruling power
> For an age of ages.

And the four creatures said Let It Be. And the elders fell down in adoration.

6

And I looked on as the Lamb opened one of the seven seals, and I heard one of the four creatures saying with a voice like thunder, "Come!" And I looked again, and there was a white horse, with the rider of the horse holding a bow and arrows, and he was given a crown and rode out triumphant to triumph again.

And when he opened seal the second, I heard the second creature saying "Come!" And out came another horse, a red one, and the rider of the horse was given permission to remove peace from the face of the earth and make the people slaughter each other; and he was given a mighty sword.

And when he opened seal the third, I heard the third creature saying, "Come!" And when I looked there was a black horse, and the rider of the horse had a set of scales in his hand. And I heard what seemed a voice from the midst of the four creatures saying, "Fifty dollars for a pound of wheat, fifty dollars for three pounds barley; and careful the oil and wine aren't damaged."

And when he opened seal the fourth, I heard a voice of the fourth creature saying "Come!" And there was this horse of a sickly green, and the rider atop him had the name of Death, and Hades was following right behind him, and they were given power over a quarter of the earth, the power to kill them with sword and famine and plague and beasts that roam the earth.

And when he opened the fifth seal, I saw beneath the altar the souls of those who were slaughtered for the word of God and for the witness that they bore. And they wailed with a great voice, saying: "How long, O overlord holy and truthful, until you render judgment and avenge our blood on the inhabitants of the earth?" And they were each given a robe of white, and they were told to relax, it would take a little longer to round out the full number of their fellow-slaves, their brothers and sisters who were destined to be killed just like them.

And I saw when he opened seal the sixth, and a giant earthquake began, and the sun turned black as if dressed for a funeral, and the whole moon seemed to turn to blood. And the stars of the sky fell on the earth, like the fig-tree dropping its fruit when a strong wind shakes it, and the sky rolled up and disappeared like a scroll, and all the mountains and islands were moved out of position. And the kings of the earth and the biggest names, and the military brass and the wealthy and the strong, and everyone, slave or free, all hid in caves and inside the crevices of mountains, and they say to the peaks and crags, "Fall on us and hide us from the face of the occupant of the throne and from the fury of the Lamb! For we have come to the great day of their fury, and who can stay standing?"

7

Next I saw four angels standing at the four corners of the earth, holding down the four winds of the earth so no wind would blow on the earth or on the ocean or on any of the trees. And I saw another angel rising from the east holding a seal of the living God, and he shouted with a great voice to the four angels who had been authorized to devastate the earth and the ocean, saying, "Don't devastate the earth or the ocean or the trees until we give the slaves of our God a stamp upon their foreheads."

And I heard the number who received the stamp: one hundred forty-four thousand from every tribe of the children of Israel.

From the tribe of Judah, twelve thousand stamped with the stamp;
from the tribe of Ruben, twelve thousand;
from the tribe of Gad, twelve thousand;
from the tribe of Asher, twelve thousand;
from the tribe of Naphthali, twelve thousand;
from the tribe of Manasses, twelve thousand;
from the tribe of Simeon, twelve thousand;
from the tribe of Levi, twelve thousand;
from the tribe of Issachar, twelve thousand;
from the tribe of Zabulon, twelve thousand;
from the tribe of Joseph, twelve thousand;
from the tribe of Benjamin, twelve thousand stamped with the stamp.

Next I looked and saw a great crowd, beyond anyone's power to count, from every nation and all tribes and peoples and tongues standing before the throne and before the Lamb draped in robes of white and with palm-branches in their hands, and they shout with a great voice, saying, "Salvation to our God who sits on the throne and to the Lamb."

And all the angels were standing in a ring around the throne and the

elders and the four creatures, and they fell down in front of the throne
upon their faces and adored God saying,

"So let it be! To our God be the praise and glory and wisdom and blessing
and honor and power and strength for an age of ages, let it be so."

And one of the elders spoke up, talking to me: "These people draped
in robes of white, who are they and where did they come from?"

And I said to him, "Good sir, you yourself must know."

And he said to me:

> These are the ones just come from the Great Suffering.
> They washed their garments clean
> And bleached them white in the blood of the Lamb.
> That's why they're here before the throne of God
> And worshiping Him day and night in His temple.
> The One who sits on the throne shall settle down upon them.
> They shall not hunger ever again, nor thirst again,
> The sun shall not bear down too hard upon them, nor anything
>   burn them,
> Because the Lamb, close by the throne, will be their shepherd
> And lead them to the springs of the water of life,
> And God will wipe each teardrop from their eyes.

8

And when he opened seal the seventh, there was silence in heaven for
about half an hour. And I saw the seven angels who stood before God,
and they were given seven trumpets. And another angel came and stood
at the altar holding a censer of gold, and he was given incense aplenty to
put with the prayers of all the faithful upon the golden altar before the
throne. And the smoke of the incense offered by the prayers of the
faithful rose from the angel's hand before God. Then the angel took the
censer and filled it with fire from the altar and threw it down upon the
earth, making thunders and howling and lightning and earthquakes.

And the seven angels with the seven trumpets got ready to give their
blasts.

And the first one trumpeted, and it started hailing with fire and blood
mixed in, and it pelted the earth, and a third of the world burned up and a
third of all trees burned down and every blade of green grass was singed.

And the second angel trumpeted, and a mass of flaming fire as big as a mountain was thrown into the sea, and a third of the sea turned to blood, and it killed a third of the creatures in the sea that have souls, and a third of all boats were destroyed.

And the third angel trumpeted, and down from the sky fell a great flaming star like a torch and fell upon a third of all rivers and springs of water, and the star is known by the name of "the Wormwood," and a third of all waters changed to bitter wormwood, and many people died from the waters' being so acrid.

And the fourth angel trumpeted, and it struck a third of the sun and a third of the moon and a third of the stars, darkening a third of them and making the daylight shine a third less bright and the night likewise.

And I saw and heard an eagle flying in mid-sky saying with a loud voice: "Woe, woe, woe to the inhabitants of the earth for the remaining trumpet-blasts of the three angels who still have not trumpeted."

9

And the fifth angel trumpeted, and I saw a star from the sky falling to the earth, and it was given the key to the opening of the Pit, and smoke poured up out of the shaft like smoke from a giant chimney, and the sun and the atmosphere were blackened with smoke from the shaft. And locusts came up out of the smoke and poured over the earth, and they were given a power like the power possessed by the scorpions of the earth. And they were told not to harm any of the grass on the earth, or the vegetation, or the trees: only the people without the stamp of God on their foreheads. And they were granted the right not to kill them, but to torture them for five months, and the torture would be like the torture of a scorpion when it stings someone. And during that time the people will look for death but never find it; they will yearn to die, but Death will elude them.

And the appearance of the locusts was like horses readied for battle, and on their heads appeared to be crowns like gold, and their faces were like the faces of humans, and their hair like the hair of women, and their teeth were like those of lions, and they had breastplates like breastplates of iron, and the sound of their wings was like the sound of a mass of chariots rolling into battle, and they have tails like scorpions, with stingers, and in their tails is the power given them to brutalize humanity five months long. They have a king over them, the angel of the Pit, whose name in Hebrew is Abaddon, and in Greek he has the name Exterminator.

That was the first horror. Here come the two horrors still to go.

And the sixth angel trumpeted. And I heard a single voice coming from the four corners of the golden altar that stood before God, saying to the sixth angel, the one holding the trumpet: "Unleash the four angels who are tied up on the shores of the great Euphrates River." And they unleashed the four angels who were all ready for the very hour, day, month and year when they could exterminate a third of humanity. And the number of warriors in the cavalry was twenty thousand tens of thousands; I heard what the number of them was.

And this is what the horses looked like in my vision, with their riders astride them wearing breastplates of fiery red, smoky blue and sulphurous yellow, and the horses have heads like lions, and out of their mouths come smoke and fire and sulphur. And from those three disasters came the death of a third of humankind, from the fire and the smoke and the sulphur coming out of their mouths, since the power the horses have is in their mouths and in their tails, their tails being like snakes with heads that can do damage.

And the rest of humankind that wasn't killed by those disasters would not turn back from their evil handiwork and stop bowing before demons and idols of gold and silver and brass and stone and wood that cannot see or hear or move; nor would they turn back from being murderers, witches, whores and thieves.

10

And I saw another angel of might dropping down from the sky, draped in a cloud, with the rainbow on his head and a face like the sun and feet like pillars of fire, holding a booklet open in his hand; and he set his right foot down upon the water and his left foot down upon the land. And he yelled with a great voice the way a lion roars. And when he yelled, the seven thunders sounded their own voices. And when the seven thunders spoke, I was going to write it down and I heard a voice from out the sky saying, "What the seven thunders spoke, keep sealed, and don't write it down."

And the angel I saw standing on the sea and on the land raised his right hand skywards and swore by Him who lives for an age of ages, who created the sky and what's in it and the earth and what's in it, and the sea and what's in it: "No more delay shall there be! On the day of the sounding of the seventh angel, when he blows his trumpet, then the secret of God will also come to fruition, as He said when He brought the good news to His underlings the prophets."

And the voice I heard from the heavens was speaking again with me and saying, "Go take the open booklet from the hand of the angel standing on the sea and the land." And I walked over to the angel and told him to give me the booklet, and he says to me, "Take it and eat it up, and it will sour your stomach, but in your mouth it will be sweet as honey."

And I took the booklet from the angel's hand and ate it up, and in my mouth it was honey-sweet, and when I had eaten it, it soured my stomach. And they say to me: "You must prophesy further about the fate of many peoples, nations, tongues and kings."

11

And I was given a rod like a measuring-rod, with a voice saying, "Get up and go measure the temple of God and the altar and the number of worshipers inside, except the outside courtyard. Leave that outside your calculations and don't measure it, because it was given over to the pagans, who will be pounding the holy city hard for forty-two months.

"And I will give to my two holy witnesses, and they will prophesy for a thousand two hundred sixty days in their sackcloth vestments.

These are the twin olive trees and the twin candlesticks
That stand before the Lord of the Earth.

And if anyone is about to hurt them, fire comes out of their mouth and devours their enemies. So if anyone tries to hurt them, that's how he will die. These two have the power given to them to seal the sky so that no rain will fall during the days when they prophesy, and they have the power over the waters to turn them into blood and to batter the earth with all kinds of disasters as often as they wish.

"And when they have finished their testimony, the beast will come up from the Pit and make war against them, vanquish them and kill them. And their bodies will lie in the main square of the city which is known for spiritual purposes as 'Sodom' or 'Egypt,' the place where their Lord was crucified. And some of the peoples and tribes and tongues and nations look at their fallen bodies for three days and a half and won't let the bodies be put in a grave. And the inhabitants of the earth rejoice over them and feel wonderful and are about to exchange gifts to mark the occasion, because these two prophets were a torment to the inhabitants of the earth."

And after the three days and a half were done the breath of life from God entered into them and they stood up on their feet, and a tremendous panic overtook the observers. And they heard a great voice from the heavens, telling them "Come up here." And they passed up into the sky inside a cloud while their enemies looked on. And at that point there was a giant earthquake and a tenth of the city fell down, and seven thousand human identities were killed in the quake, and the rest were seized by fear and gave glory to the God of the sky.

That was the second horror. Here comes the third horror, close on its heels.

And the seventh angel trumpeted, and there were loud voices in the sky saying:

> Now the sovereignty of the world belongs to our Lord and the
> one He has anointed,
> And He shall reign for an age of ages.

And the twenty-four elders seated before God upon their thrones fell on their faces and adored God, saying:

> We thank you, Lord our God, ruler of all, the Is and the Was,
> For you have assumed Your power in all its greatness and
> become the king.
> And the nations were roused to anger,
> And then came Your anger,
> And the time for the dead to be judged,
> And the time to reward the prophets who were Your underlings
> And the holy ones and those who held Your name in awe,
> Both small and great,
> And the time to lay waste the wasters of the earth.

And the temple of God swung open in the sky revealing the Ark of the Covenant there in His temple, and there was lightning and voices and thunder and earthquakes and great storms of hail.

12

And a momentous sign appeared in the sky: a woman with the sun draped over her and the moon beneath her feet, and on her head a crown of twelve stars, with a child in her belly, and she's screaming with pain and in the agonies of childbirth. And another sign appeared in the sky: whoa! a giant reddish dragon with seven heads and ten horns, and on the heads seven jeweled tiaras, and its tail is sweeping a third of the stars from the sky and dashing them to earth. And the dragon is standing in front of the woman about to give birth, so that when she bears the child he can eat it up. And she bore a child, male, one "who would shepherd all nations with a staff of iron," and her child was snatched up to God and to His throne. And the woman fled to the wilderness, where she has a place that God keeps ready there so that they can take care of her there for days numbering one thousand two hundred sixty.

And a war started in the sky, Michael and his angels at war with the dragon. And the dragon fought back with his own angels beside him, but he wasn't strong enough, and there was no place for them in the sky any longer. Down came the dragon, the giant, the serpent, the ancient one, the one called "Slanderer" and "Satan," deceiver of all the world, hurtling down to earth, and his angels came hurtling down beside him. And I heard a great voice in the sky saying:

> From this moment on, salvation and power and sovereignty
> belongs to God,
> And authority to the Anointed of God.
> Overthrown is the accuser of our brothers,
> Who brought accusations to God against them day and night,
> But they conquered him instead because of the blood of the
> Lamb
> And because they bore witness to God's word
> And showed no concern for their lives right up to the point of
> death.

Be joyful about that, heavens above,
And all who lodge within them.
But woe to the land and the sea,
For the devil is down there with you now,
Full of tremendous anger,
Knowing that he has only a little time.

And when the dragon found himself cast down to earth, he ran after the woman who had borne the male child. But the woman was given the two wings of the eagle to fly off to her place in the wilderness and be nurtured there for a time, times, and half a time,* far from the face of the serpent. And the serpent opened its mouth and spewed out a river of water after her so she would be swept off her feet by the river. But the earth came to the woman's aid and opened its mouth and gulped down the river that the dragon had spewed out of his mouth. And the dragon was furious at the woman and went off to make war against the rest of her seed, people who keep the commands of God and hold to the testimony of Jesus.

And he took up a position on the sands of the sea.

13

And I saw a beast coming out of the sea, with ten horns and seven heads, and on the horns ten jeweled crowns, and its heads bore lordly titles of blasphemous arrogance. And the beast I saw was something like a leopard, with feet like a bear and a mouth like the mouth of a lion, and into his keeping the dragon gave his strength, his throne and his tremendous power. And one of the heads seemed to have been mortally wounded, but the mortal wound had been healed.

And the whole world followed the beast around in amazement and adored the dragon for giving its power to the beast, and they adored the beast, saying, "Who is the equal of the beast? Is anyone strong enough to take it on?"

And it was given a mouth with which to exalt itself to the point of sacrilege, and it was given free reign for its actions forty-two months

---

* If a "time" is a year and "times" is two years, then this is the same period of three-and-a-half years, or forty-two months, or 1260 days that the author keeps returning to.

long. And it opened its mouth to hurl insults at God, insulting His name and the lodgings of those who are encamped in the sky, and it was granted the right to make war against the holy ones and conquer them. And it was given power over every tribe and people and tongue and nation. And it was adored by all the inhabitants of the earth except those whose names, since the world's foundation, stand written in the Book of Life of the slaughtered Lamb.

If any have ears, let them hear:
If imprisonment is your lot, to imprisonment you will go.
If being killed by the sword is your lot, by the sword you will be killed.
That's where endurance comes in, and the faith of the holy ones.

And I saw another beast coming out of the ground, and it had two horns like a lamb and spoke like a dragon. And it has the full authority of the first beast to act in its place. And it makes the earth and its inhabitants bow down before the first beast who had been healed of his mortal wound. And it works great wonders, making fire from the sky come down upon the earth while the people look on, and it fools the inhabitants of the earth because of the wonders it is allowed to perform in the first beast's place; and it tells the inhabitants of the earth to put up a statue of the first beast, the one with the mortal wound who came back to life again.

And it was empowered to breathe life into the statue of the first beast, so the statue of the beast can speak and can cause those who don't bow down before the statue of the beast to be killed. And it forces everyone, the small and the great, the rich and the poor, the slaves and the free, to put a stamp on their right hand or their forehead, and makes it so that no one can buy or sell except those who are stamped with the name of the beast or with the number corresponding to his name. (Here is where intelligence comes in. Let whoever has a mind compute the number of the beast for himself, since the number corresponds to a person's name, and its number is six hundred sixty-six.)*

14

And I looked, and there was the Lamb standing atop Mount Zion, and

---

* "Nero the Emperor," in Hebrew letters, adds up to 666 (in both Hebrew and Greek, letters are also used as numerals). Many other solutions have been proposed.

with him one hundred forty-four thousand having his name and his Father's name written on their foreheads. And I heard a voice from the sky, a voice like a massive rush of water, and like a giant thunderclap; also, the voice I heard was like harpists, harping upon their harps. And they sing a new song, there in front of the throne and in front of the four creatures and the elders, and no one could learn the song but the one hundred forty-four thousand ransomed from the earth. These are the ones who did not pollute themselves with women: they are virgins who follow the Lamb wherever he goes. They were ransomed as a sampling of humanity for God and for the Lamb, and from their mouths no lie was ever heard, they are spotless.

And I saw an angel flying in mid-sky, bringing the good news which is good news forever to those based on earth, to every nation and tribe and tongue and people, saying with a great voice:

> Stand in awe of God and give Him glory,
> Because we have come to the hour of His judgment;
> And bow down before the Maker of the sky and land and sea and
>   springs of water.

And he was followed by a second angel saying: "Fallen! Fallen! Great Babylon is fallen, who made all nations drink the wine of her willful lewdness."

And those angels were followed by a third angel, saying with a great voice:

"If anyone adores the beast and its statue and accepts its stamp on the forehead or upon the hand, that person will also drink the wine of God's anger, thick and strong and undiluted, from the cup of His wrath; and he shall be tortured with fire and sulphur in front of the holy angels and in front of the Lamb, with the smoke rising from his torture for an age of ages. And all day long and all night long there is no relief for those who adored the beast and its statue, or for anyone who lets himself be stamped with its name. This is what requires steadfastness from the faithful who keep the commands of God and keep to their belief in Jesus."

And I heard a voice from the sky saying, "Write this down: How happy the dead who die in the Lord from now on. Yes, says the spirit, let them rest from their labors, since their good deeds have preceded them."

And I looked, and suddenly there was a white cloud, and seated on the cloud, the figure of a son of humanity, with a golden crown upon his head and a sharpened sickle in his hand. And another angel came out of the temple shouting in a loud voice to the one seated on the cloud:

"Put your sickle to work and harvest, because the harvest time has come, the crops of the earth are withered and dry." And the one seated on the cloud threw his sickle down upon the earth, and the earth was harvested.

And another angel came out of the temple in the sky, also holding a sharpened sickle. And another angel came from the altar who was in charge of the fire, and he called in a loud voice to the one with the sharpened sickle, saying: "Put your sharp sickle to work and pick the grapes of the vineyard of the earth, because its grapes have reached their prime." And the angel threw his sickle down upon the earth and picked the fruit of the vineyard of the earth and put it into the great winepress of God's anger. And they took the winepress outside the city and trampled the grapes, and so much blood flooded out of the winepress, the horses were up to their muzzles in blood for sixteen hundred miles around.

15

And I saw another sign in the sky, huge and wondrous, seven angels bearing seven final plagues, because they were to be the culmination of God's fury.

And I saw like a sea of glass mixed with fire, and those who won out over the beast and its image and the number of its name stood facing the glassy sea with harps of God. And they sing the song of Moses, the slave of God, and the song of the Lamb, saying:

> Great and wondrous are your works,
> Lord God, ruler of all.
> Just and truthful are your paths,
> O King of nations.
> Who would not stand in awe of you, Lord,
> And glorify your name?
> Because you alone are holy;
> Because all nations shall come and bow before you;
> Because you have made your rulings known to all.

And after that I looked again, and the temple of the Tent of Witness opened in the sky, and the seven angels bearing the seven plagues came out of the temple dressed in spotless gleaming linen and with bands of gold encircling their chests. And one of the four creatures gave the seven angels seven golden bowls full of the wrath of the God who lives forever and ever. And the temple filled up with the smoke of God's glory and His power, and no one could get into the temple until the seven angels were finished with their seven plagues.

16

And I heard a great voice from the temple saying to the seven angels, "Go pour the seven bowls of God's wrath upon the earth."

And the first one went and poured his bowl upon the earth, and a sore developed, nasty and miserable, on all the people who bore the stamp of the beast and adored his statue.

And the second one poured his bowl into the sea, and the water turned like dead men's blood, and every breath of life died off that was in the sea.

And the third poured his bowl into the rivers and springs of water, and it all turned to blood. And I heard the angel in charge of the waters saying:

> Justice is done, O Is and Was, O Holy One,
> By these judgments you made:
> Because they shed the blood of holy ones and prophets,
> You now have given them blood to drink,
> As they deserve.

And I heard the altar saying:

> Yes, Lord God, Ruler of all,
> True and just are your judgments.

And the fourth poured his bowl into the sun, and it received the power to scorch the people with its fire. And the people were scorched with serious burns and cursed the name of God, who had control of the plagues, and they didn't change their ways to give Him glory.

And the fifth poured his bowl upon the throne of the beast, and darkness covered the face of its empire, and they were biting their tongues in pain and cursing the God of heaven, what with their pain and their sores, and they still didn't turn back from their deeds.

And the sixth poured his bowl into the great Euphrates River, and its waters dried up to prepare the way for the Kings from the East. And I saw, coming from the dragon's mouth and the beast's mouth and the pseudoprophet's mouth, three unclean spirits like frogs. Actually, they're spirits of wonder-working demons, who go around to all the kings of civilization summoning them to war on the great day of God the Almighty. (Watch out, I will sneak up like a thief; lucky for you if you stay awake and keep your clothes on, so you don't have to walk around naked and be seen in that indecent state.) And they collected them all at a place called, in Hebrew, Armageddon.

And the seventh poured his bowl into the air, and a great voice came out of the temple from the throne, saying: "NOW!" And lightning and noises and thunder broke out, and an earthquake began, such a giant one that never since humanity was born had the earth seen an earthquake so huge.

And the great city broke in three pieces and the cities of the pagans fell, and great Babylon was not forgotten in God's sight, nor His promise to fill her cup with the wine of His vengeful fury. And the islands all fled, and the mountains were never found again. And a great storm of hail like cannonballs comes out of the sky and down upon the people, and the people cursed and swore at God for this plague, saying, "This is a terrible plague indeed."

17

And one of the seven angels with the seven bowls came over and spoke with me, saying: "Come here, and I'll show you the damnation of the great whore who sits on many waters, who has been a whore for the kings of the earth and has drugged the inhabitants of the earth with the wine of her whoredom." And he took me in spirit-form to a deserted spot.

And there I saw a woman seated on a scarlet beast blazoned with sacrilegious titles, with seven heads and ten horns. And the woman was draped in purple and scarlet and gilded with gold and precious stones and pearls, with a cup of gold in her hand, brimming with the nauseating scum and filth of her venery, and on her forehead an inscription of secret meaning: "Babylon the great, mother of whoredom and the nauseating filth of the earth." And I saw the woman getting drunk on the blood of the holy ones and the blood of the witnesses who stood by Jesus. And I was amazed to see her, utter amazement.

And the angel said to me, "Why are you so amazed? I will tell you the secret of the woman and the beast she rides on, the one with the seven heads and the ten horns.

"The beast you see once was, and is no more, and is coming back up out of the Pit and going to its destruction. And amazement will overcome the inhabitants of the earth whose names are not written in the Book of Life since the world's foundation, when they see how the beast was, and is no more, and is about to re-appear. Now this takes a mind with intelligence:

"The seven heads are seven hills on which the woman reclines, and are also seven kings. Five of them fell, one is still there, and the other didn't come along yet, and when he comes he hasn't long to stay. And the beast himself that was and is no more counts as an eighth along with the other seven, and is going to his destruction.

"And the ten horns you saw are ten kings, who have not mounted their thrones, but at some point they will have power as kings along with the beast. They all think as one and contribute all their force and authority to the beast. They will go to war with the Lamb, and the Lamb will conquer them, because he is the Lord of Lords and King of Kings, and those with him are those he called, hand-picked and trustworthy."

And he says to me, "The waters you saw where the whore is seated are countries and masses of people and nations and languages. And the ten horns you saw, and the beast himself, will come to hate the whore and will drive her into exile naked, and they will eat her flesh and burn her in the fire. God, you see, put this intention in their hearts and made them act with unity, giving their sovereignty to the beast until God's word has been fulfilled. And the woman you saw is the great city that holds kingly power over the kings of the earth."

18

After that I saw another angel coming down from the sky, possessed of tremendous power; and the earth lit up with his glory. And he shouted in a strong voice, saying:

"Fallen, fallen, Great Babylon is fallen: it's a nesting-place now for demons, and a fortress for every unclean spirit and for birds of every unclean and hateful kind; that's because the wine of her willful lewdness drugged all nations, and the kings of the earth came to her whorehouse, and the businessmen of the earth got rich off her driving lust for pleasure."

And I heard another voice from the sky saying:

"Get away, my people, get away from her and don't be a party to her crimes and don't let any of her plagues be visited on you, because her crimes are piled right up against the dome of heaven, and God has not forgotten her iniquity. What she gave you, give back to her twice over, doubling the measure of her own deeds; and the drink that she served up to you, mix it for her twice as strong. However much she glorified and indulged herself, give her that much more torment and grief, because in her heart she says: 'Here I am enthroned as queen! I'm not a widow and there'll be no grief for me.' For just that reason her plagues will break over her in a single day, with sickness, misfortune and hunger, and she shall be burned up in the fire: such is the might of the Lord God who has condemned her."

And how they shall wail and beat their breasts for her, those kings of the earth who visited her whorehouse and indulged themselves, when they see the smoke of her cremation, keeping a terrified distance from her agonies and saying:

> Horror, horror, the mighty city,
> Babylon, the city of strength!
> Alas that a single hour should bring your doom!

And the businessmen of the earth are weeping and wailing for her, because now there's no one to buy their wares any more—wares of gold and silver and precious stones and pearls, fine linens and silks, cloth of purple and scarlet, lemonwood and other such woods, all their ivory objects, all their objects of rich wood and brass and iron and marble, cinnamon, spices, incense-offerings, frankincense and myrrh, and wine and olive oil and flour and wheat, and cattle and sheep and horses and wagons, and the bodies and souls of human beings.

And your luscious fruit, the fancy of your heart, has gotten away from you,

And everything buttered and bright is dead and gone from you,
And none of those things will ever be seen again.
The vendors of these things who once got rich on her will keep their
terrified distance from her agonies, weeping and wailing and saying,

> Horror, horror! The magnificent city
> Draped in fine linen and purple and scarlet,
> Gilded with gold and precious stones and pearls!
> Alas that a single hour should wipe out all this wealth!

And every ship's captain and everyone sailing to one port or another
and all the sailors and people who ply the sea stood back and shouted as
they saw the smoke of her cremation: "Was there ever a city so great?"
And they poured dust over their heads and wailed, weeping and mourning:

> Alas, alas for the tremendous city
> Where all who had boats in the sea made their fortunes from her
>   luxurious ways!
> Rejoice over her, O heaven,
> You holy ones and missionaries and prophets,
> Since God has condemned her for her crimes against you.

And one mighty angel took a stone big as a millstone and hurled it into
the sea, saying:

> With just such a shuddering crash shall Babylon be dashed
>   down, the mighty city,
> And never be seen again.
> The sound of harpists and singers and flutists and trumpeters
> Will be heard in your streets no more.
> And all the craftsmen of every craft
> Will no more be found in you.
> The grinding of the mill
> Will be heard no more;
> The light of the lantern
> Will illumine you no more.
> The happy sounds of bride and bridegroom

Will be heard no more,
Because your merchants were the power-brokers of the earth,
Because your witchcraft led all nations astray,
And in your streets flowed the blood of prophets and holy ones
And all the slaughtered victims of the earth.

19

After that I seemed to hear the sound of a great multitude of people in the sky saying:

Alleluia!
The salvation and glory and power of our God!
Truthful and just are His judgments.
He condemned the great whore
Who corrupted the earth with her whoring,
And avenged the blood of His slaves who died at her hand.

And again they said:

Alleluia!
And the smoke rises from her into the endless ages.

And the twenty-four elders and four creatures fell down and adored God seated on His throne saying:

Amen, alleluia!

And a voice came forth from the throne saying:

Give praise to our God,
All you slaves of His,
All you who fear Him,
The small and the great.

And I heard a sound like a great multitude and like a massive rush of water and like mighty thunderclaps saying:

Alleluia!
The Lord God, Ruler of all, has mounted His throne.
Let us rejoice and be delighted and give Him the glory.
The wedding-day of the Lamb has come,
And his bride has made herself ready
And been given clean bright linen to be clothed in:
Her linen being the upright deeds of the faithful.

And someone says to me: "Write this down: How fortunate are those who are invited to the wedding-feast of the Lamb!" And he says to me: "These words are true and come from God." And I fell at his feet to adore him. And he says to me, "Careful, don't do that. I am a fellow-slave of yours and of your brothers who have been confirmed by Jesus. So give your adoration to God." (Being confirmed by Jesus means having the breath of prophecy.)

And I saw the sky opening up, and look, there was a white horse, with a rider trusty and truthful, who judges justly and battles for justice. His eyes are like the flames of a fire, and his head wears many crowns, inscribed with a name that no one knows but him. And the cloak that covers him is drenched in blood, and he is known by the name "Word of God."

And the warriors of the sky rode behind him upon their white steeds, all dressed in clean white linen. And he has a sharp-edged sword coming out of his mouth, with which to strike the nations down, and he will rule them "with a staff of iron," and he stamps on the winepress holding the wine of the vengeful fury of God, the Ruler of all. And written on his cloak and on his leg is the name "King of Kings and Lord of Lords."

And I saw an angel standing in the sun, and he shouted in a loud voice, saying to all the birds flying in midair:

"Come gather here for the great feast of God! You'll be eating king meat, general meat, strongman meat, horse meat, rider meat, and the meat of everyone free or slave, small or great."

And I saw the beast and the kings of the earth and their warriors massed to do battle with the rider on the horse and with his army. And the beast was trapped, and with him the pseudoprophet who did the signs and wonders for him with which he fooled the people into accepting the stamp of the beast and bowing down before his statue. They were both thrown alive into the lake of fire and burning sulphur. And the rest were killed by the sword of the rider on the horse, the sword coming out of his mouth; and all the birds had a banquet, eating their flesh.

20

And I saw an angel coming down out of the sky who had the key to the Pit, and also a huge chain in his hand. And he seized the dragon, the serpent of old, the Devil and the Satan, and put him in chains for a thousand years and threw him in the Pit and put the lid back on and sealed it shut. Now he can't lead the nations astray any more until the thousand years are done. After that he is destined to be let loose for a little while.

And I saw thrones, and those who mounted them were given the power to pass judgment. And I saw the souls of those who were executed because they stood by Jesus and the word of God and didn't bow before the beast or its statue, nor let themselves be stamped on their foreheads and hands: they came to life again and were crowned kings along with Christ for the next thousand years. (The rest of the dead didn't come to life till the thousand years were done.)

That was the first resurrection. How fortunate and holy those who take part in the first resurrection! No second death has any power over them; they shall be priests of God and the Anointed and shall reign with him for a thousand years.

And when the thousand years are done, Satan will be let out of his jail, and will set out to lead the nations in the four corners of the earth, Gog and Magog, astray and summon them to battle in numbers like the sands of the sea. And they came up to the broad plains of the Earth and surrounded the camps of the holy ones and their beloved city, when "fire came down from the sky and consumed them whole." And the devil, who had led them into it, was thrown into the lake of fire and sulphur, where he and the beast and the pseudoprophet shall be tortured all day and all night for all eternity.

And I saw a great white throne and the One seated upon it, and from His face the earth and sky fled away and never turned up anywhere again. And I saw the dead, the great and the small, arranged facing the throne. And books were opened, and one particular book was opened: the Book of Life. And the dead were judged according to their deeds, using what was written in the books about them. And the sea gave up the bodies of those who were in her, and Death and Hades gave up the bodies that they had, and they were judged, each by their deeds. Then Death and Hades were hurled into the lake of fire. This lake of fire is the death that comes after death. And if anyone's name wasn't found written in the Book of Life, they were thrown into the lake of fire.

21

And I saw a new sky and a new earth, since the original sky and the original earth went away, and the sea is no more. And the city of Holy Jerusalem I also saw, all new and coming down out of the sky from God, outfitted like a bride all dressed up for her husband. And I heard a great voice from the throne saying:

Here is God's lodging among humanity;

And indeed He will lodge among them, and they shall be His peoples, and God shall personally be there with them. And He shall wipe every tear from their eyes, and there will be no more death, nor grief, nor uproar, nor pain anymore, because what used to be is gone.

And the occupant of the throne said, "Watch Me make everything all over again." And He says, "Write this down; these words are reliable and truthful." And He said to me: "They've already come true: I am Alpha and Omega, the Beginning and the End. I will let the thirsty drink from the springs of the Water of Life for free. The winners will be given this fortune as their prize, and 'I will be a God to him, and he will be a son to Me.' But as for the spineless and the faithless and the despicable and the murderers and the whoremongers and witches and idol-worshipers and liars of every kind, their lot is the lake of burning fire and sulphur, the death after death."

And one of the seven angels who had the seven bowls containing the terminal plagues came over and talked with me, saying, "Come here, I'll show you the bride, the wife of the Lamb." And he took me in spirit-form to the peak of a great and lofty mountain and showed me the city of Holy Jerusalem coming down out of the sky from God endowed with God's glory, with a gleam like the costliest of jewels, like a jasper clear as glass. Great, high city walls; twelve gates, and atop the gates twelve angels; inscribed on the gates, the twelve names of the twelve tribes of the sons and daughters of Israel. Three gates to the east, three gates to the north, three gates to the south, three gates to the west. And the city wall, with twelve foundations bearing twelve names of the twelve apostles of the Lamb.

And the one who spoke with me had a measuring-rod of gold with which to measure the city, her gates and her walls. And the city was built square, with the length the same as the breadth. And with his rod he measured the city at twelve thousand miles for the length and the breadth, and her height is the same. And he measured the thickness of the wall at one hundred forty-four times the length of a man's, or rather angel's forearm. And the material of the city's wall: jasper, with the city itself of pure gold, as clear as glass. The foundations of the city wall: adorned with all kinds of precious stones. The first foundation: jasper; the second, sapphire; the third, chalcedony; the fourth, emerald; the fifth, sardonyx; the sixth, carnelian; the seventh, chrysolite; the eighth, beryl; the ninth, topaz; the tenth, chrysoprase; the eleventh, aquamarine; the twelfth, amethyst. The twelve gates: twelve pearls, each of the gates being made from a single pearl. And the city square: pure gold, transparent as glass.

And no temple did I see there: the Lord God, Ruler of all, is her temple, and so is the Lamb. And the city has no need of sun nor moon to shine for her: the glory of God already illumined her, and her lantern is the Lamb. And all nations shall walk in her light, and the kings of the earth will come and bring their glory to her. And her gates are never shut the whole day through (and the night won't exist there), and they shall come bringing the honor and glory of all nations to her. But nothing shall enter her that is polluted, nor anyone who commits abominations and lies: only those who are written in the Book of Life of the Lamb.

22

And he showed me a river of the Water of Life, gleaming like crystal, streaming out from the throne of God and the Lamb. And as it flows through the town square, on this side and that of the river stands the Tree of Life, whose crops are twelve, with each month yielding a crop of its own; and the leaves of the tree serve to heal people of all nations. And all the accursed things will not be around anymore. And the throne of God and the Lamb will be there, and His slaves will worship Him and see His face and have His name upon their foreheads. And there will be no more night, and they have no need of lamplight or sunlight, because the Lord God will shine upon them, and they will be kings forever and ever.

And he [Jesus] said to me: "These words are trustworthy and true, and the Lord God, breath of prophets, sent this messenger to show His slaves that which must happen very soon. So be on the lookout, I'm coming soon. The person is in luck who holds on to the words of prophecy in this book."

And I, John, the hearer and eyewitness of these things, when I heard and saw, I fell in adoration at the feet of the messenger showing me these things. And he says to me, "Careful, don't do that! I am your fellow-slave, along with your brother prophets and those who hold on to the words of this book. Give your adoration to God."

And he [Jesus] said to me: "Don't suppress the words of prophecy in this book, because the time is near. Let the criminal keep on with his crimes and the degenerate keep degenerating; and let the just keep acting with justice and the holy keep getting holier.

"Watch, I am coming soon, and I will have my rewards with me so as to give to each person what his deeds amount to. I am the Alpha and Omega, the first and the last, the beginning and the end.

"Fortunate are those who wash their garments so they will have the right to the Tree of Life and go through the gates into the city. Out with the low dogs and the practicers of magic and the promiscuous and the murderers and the idol-worshipers and everyone who approves or practices lying.

"I, Jesus, sent my messenger to report these things to your assembled communities. I am the root and stock of David, the bright star of morning."

And the Spirit and the Bride say, "Come!" And may the listener also say "Come!" And may the thirsty come, and may everyone who wants it get to drink of the Water of Life for free.

I stand as witness to all who hear for the words of prophecy in this book. If anyone puts anything into it, God will put the plagues described in this book into him. And if anyone takes anything away from the words of this book of prophecy, God will take away his rights to the Tree of Life and the holy city as described in this book.

Says the witness to these things: "Yes, I'm coming soon." Come, Lord Jesus!

The grace of Lord Jesus be with you all.

Glossary

The following is a discussion of a few crucial words from the New Testament. With the reader's convenience in mind, the Greek words are alphabetized under the English words most traditionally used to translate them—not necessarily the words used in this version at all. Under "baptism," for instance, you will find reasons why the Greek word *baptisma* should be translated as "washing" or "bathing."

Abba (ἀββά, *abba*). This is an intimate Aramaic word for "father," for use inside the family rather than when talking with other people, and it sounds like one of a baby's first few words. In short, it's "Papa" rather than "Father." For centuries this word has been considered one of the most important and perhaps *the* most important word in the Gospels, the keystone of a religious message which is theological and mystical as well as ethical. Jesus, in short, is not just the nice person who helps people and tells us to be gentle. He is also—in fact, he is *rather*—the person who calls God "Papa."

Adultery (μοιχεία, *moicheia*). The word appears to be fairly specific: marriage-breaking, not just illicit sexual activity, which would be πορνεία (*porneia*, "whoring"). Though the general drift of Jesus' teaching is toward temperance and modesty in all things, his explicit commandments seem focused more on the sanctity of the marriage-bond than on the illicitness of sexual activity. It is Paul who introduces us to the inherent evils of the "sinful flesh."

Amen (ἀμήν, *amen*). This Hebrew exclamation means literally "let it be," but is usually used with the force of "truly" or "believe me." Since "Amen" as an English word means "here ends my prayer," phrases like "Amen I say to you" have been rendered as something like "believe me" or "truly I tell you" so as not to leave the impression that Jesus ends his prayers before he begins them.

Angel (ἄγγελος, *angelos*); **devil** (διάβολος, *diabolos*). *Angelos* is the regular word for a "messenger" of any type. Most of the messengers in the

New Testament are of the heavenly kind, but the same word is also used for human messengers, including John the Baptist, and the heavenly messengers are frequently though not always described in the Gospels as "messengers of the Lord" or "messengers of God." In the Epistles and Acts, the word is increasingly used alone, though still in the sense of heavenly messengers. In Revelation, the word not only is used alone, but denotes beings with a ceremonial or symbolic function who may not have any messages to bear. In short, the word evolves from "messenger" to "angel" over the course of the New Testament, with the Gospels apparently showing an older usage than the Epistles (though conventional scholarly wisdom dates the Gospels later than most of the Epistles).

Diabolos means "slanderer" or "accuser," but in the Gospels is always used alone and never to describe humans (although human "accusers" are found in the Epistles).

Apostle (ἀπόστολος, *apostolos*). The word means "emissary" or "those sent out." Paul describes himself as an "apostle," and is generally conceded the title, but mostly it applies to the Twelve.

Baptism (βάπτισμα, *baptisma*); **baptize** (βαπτίζειν, *baptizein*). The most literal meaning is "dunking," but by extension it means "cleaning," "washing" or "bathing" and is so translated in this version. In the New Testament it means "baptism" too, but it is scarcely as abstract a word as "baptism" is in English; another form of the word (βαπτισμός, *baptismos*) is used in Mark 7:4 to mean "washing the dishes."

Behold (ἰδού, *idu*). To modern readers, "behold" suggests "stand there goggle-eyed while the miraculous occurs," as in "behold, the Red Sea parted." But *idu* occurs much too often and too trivially for that. Instead, it is used as a storytelling device, to mark the point where a story's principal plot element is introduced ("I was walking down the street when idu, . . .") or the outcome is given ("so you know what he did? idu, . . ."). In this version, *idu* is rendered variously as "all of a sudden," "next thing you know," "just then" and "look"—whatever will serve the purpose.

Blessed (μακάριος, *makarios*). This word denotes the blessings of good fortune and even financial prosperity, not just the blessings of grace, which would be expressed more specifically by some form of χάρις, (*charis*, "grace"). For that reason, the word is usually rendered here as "lucky" or "fortunate." In the Beatitudes, in particular, the word "blessed" is a trap: those who mourn, for example, are not "holier" in the present because they will be comforted, but destined to be "better off" in the future because they will be comforted.

Christ (Χριστός); **Messiah** (Μεσσίας). These are essentially the same word: "Christ" is Greek for "anointed," "Messiah" is Hebrew for "anointed," as John explains in 1:41. The Old Testament, of course, contains many references to Israel's hope that a savior will arise in its midst. However, the introspectively spiritual nature of Jesus' mission must have been a puzzlement and a disappointment to those who had expected a more militaristic Messiah—someone who would save the people not just "from their own wrongs," as in Matthew 1:21, but also from the Romans.

(Some commentators propose that Judas became disaffected for these reasons, and the explanation certainly looks plausible in the absence of any other satisfactory motive for the betrayal: if the money Judas gets is so little that he can throw it back in the high priests' faces, it's too little to be the sole reason.)

                                    *   *   *

The presence or absence of the article "the" as used with this word forms perhaps the most noticeable stylistic difference between the Gospels and the Epistles. In the Gospels it's "ho Christos" with the article, which makes it a title, "the Anointed." In the Epistles it's simply "Christos," which makes it a name, "Christ." The name Jesus is also used with the article in the Gospels and without it in the Epistles. As with the development of the word "angel" (see that entry), this suggests that the Gospels or their source-documents might be older and not later than most of the Epistles.

Church (ἐκκλησία, *ecclesia*). The word means "assembly" or "meeting," or even more literally, "calling everybody out to meeting." It will later mean "church," but it could scarcely mean that in the New Testament already. (Here essentially is the great struggle in reading the New Testament: not to view earlier events in light of later developments.) Certainly in Matthew 18:17, an injured party should if necessary "speak up at meeting," not "notify the authorities of the yet-to-be-established institutional church."

Even in the Epistles, Acts and Revelation, where we see the Christian religion being established, it would be misleading to speak of the "assembly" or "community" or "congregation" as a "church." For one thing, there are no church buildings yet.

More importantly, the worshipers in Galatia belong to the Galatian assembly while those in Laodicea belong to the Laodician assembly: they don't all belong to the same assembly or to one overarching "assembly of assemblies." They *do* all belong to the same "faith" ("membership in the faith" is a recurring phrase of Paul's), so that "faith" (*pistis*) is closer to meaning "church" in the modern sense than "church" is. But *no* New Testament word means "Christian Church" in the modern sense because there isn't yet a Christian Church in the modern sense. To be sure, some centralized structure is seen in the authority of Jerusalem to decide moral questions and police the other communities (see the fifteenth chapter of Acts). But the crucial difference remains: that the Christians of the various early communities are bound to each other by shared belief and not by shared organizational membership.

Conscience (συνείδησις, *syneidesis*). The English word "conscience" typically describes judgments of right and wrong regarding actions already completed: "guilty conscience," "clear conscience," "having something on your conscience." The Greek word isn't limited to judgments of right and wrong: the conception that we are children of God is also part of our "conscience," because it's more like our whole "religious consciousness" or "sensibility." Even more importantly, the Greek word doesn't just mean "ethical hindsight" about actions in the past: it's the "attitude" or "outlook" that produces action in the first place. With this in mind, Paul's urging to "wash your conscience" turns from a vague exhortation to "feel better" or "think nice" into something closer to home, like "giving your filthy attitude a bath."

Disciple (μαθητής, *mathetes*); **master** (διδάσκαλος, *didaskalos*). *Mathetes* is the regular word for "student," the same that would be used of any other student, and *didaskalos* is likewise the regular word for any teacher. Furthermore, "students" and "teachers" is just what the initiates and adepts of various spiritual traditions call themselves to this day. Therefore, this translation calls the "students" and their "teacher" just that, at least in the Gospels. The words ring a little strange, to be sure: in our day we don't normally think that wisdom qualifies as education.

Drachma (δραχμή); **denarius** (δηνάριον); **didrachma** (δίδραχμον); **stater** (στατήρ); **mina** (μνᾶ). This translation takes the lighthearted view that "it's only money" and doesn't try very hard to reproduce the exact details of ancient currencies, least of all as they figure in the Gospel parables.

It wouldn't work anyway. You can compare ancient sales of grain to modern sales of grain and conclude that "a drachma is so many dollars," but that's only true by the grain standard: you can't be assured that the other items in the ancient marketbasket kept all the same relations to each other that they would keep in modern times; in fact you can be sure they didn't. Real estate was cheaper and imported spices more expensive, and if you used either of them as a standard instead of grain, there would be more or fewer putative dollars in your reconstructed drachma; so how much can your estimate ever really mean?

As a rough guide, you might think of either a drachma or a denarius as like a dollar, a didrachma as two dollars and a stater as four dollars; a mina would then be a hundred dollars, and a talent would be much larger, more like a thousand dollars.

Engaged (ἐμνηστευμένη, *emnesteumènë*). In his commentary on the first chapter of Matthew in the *Abingdon Bible Commentary* (New York: Doubleday, 1929), J. Newton Davies explains that the engagements of Christ's time were more formal and unbreakable than those of our own day and carried with them both some of the rights and some of the responsibilities associated with marriage, possibly including cohabitation. Several words in Matthew and Luke seem to point in that direction: when Joseph considers if he should "break his engagement" to Mary in Matthew 1:19, the word is the same used elsewhere to mean divorce (as when Jesus condemns divorce). When Mary is found to be pregnant before she and Joseph have "gotten together" (Matthew 1:18), there seems to be the implication that they were about to set up housekeeping in anticipation of their coming marriage. Finally, in Luke 2:5 we see Joseph going to Bethlehem with his "fiancee," who is pregnant, with no suggestion of scandal on that account.

Faith (πίστις, *pistis*); **believe** (πιστεύειν, *pisteuein*). Does Jesus ask us to "believe" in him or just "trust" him? The words could be taken either way. In the public ministry as reported in Matthew, Mark and Luke, it doesn't seem plausible for Jesus to require a personal religious "faith" in his own person while trying to suppress premature reports that he's the Messiah. On the other hand, more than "trusting" is implied in John 1:7 when John the Baptist comes "to testify about the light, so that all might believe through him."

In fact, *pistis* seems to be a different word in John than in Matthew, Mark and Luke. It is only in John that the blessing is pronounced on those "who have not seen and have still believed." In the other three Gospels, Jesus wishes that the inhabitants of towns like Chorazin would trust him on the basis of what they *had* seen (Matthew 11:21). When Jesus passes from the earthly scene, the word's meaning changes again. The question of whether you trust Jesus and trust God may still be the ultimate question, but now the initial question must be whether you believe the messenger who comes with the good news.

With the passing of the apostolic age, there is still another shift. Now the need is to codify a message brought some time ago. Therefore the question isn't just whether you trust Jesus or believe Paul, but whether you subscribe to the truth of certain "articles of faith," such as the "basics" that Paul lists in First Corinthians 15:3–8: that Jesus was crucified for us and rose on the third day, that he appeared to Peter and the twelve, etc. This definition of "faith" as subscribing to the truth of certain things is the one that has mostly settled in, but note how far it is from the beginning.

Gospel (εὐαγγέλιον, *euangelion*). This translation leans toward the formula "good word" rather than "good news" as being more inclusive: if you tell me I'm going to hell unless I repent, you're certainly giving me the good word, but are you really giving me the good news, precisely?

In the Epistles, however, the question is not how to translate the word, but what it means: does it only refer to the orally proclaimed "good word," or does it already mean, at least sometimes, "the written Gospel"? It sounds like a reference to a written Gospel when Paul (First Timothy 5:18) quotes "Scripture" as saying that "the worker is worth his wages," a reference which is easily traced to Matthew 10:10 or Luke 10:7 (and is untraceable otherwise).

Heaven (οὐρανός, *uranos*). As in French, German and Italian, the regular word for "sky" is also used to mean "heaven."

Hell (γεέννα, *Gehenna*). The word *Gehenna* derives from the Valley of Hinnom, south of Jerusalem. The place had been used in previous times as an incinerator, and at other times had been a center of Moloch worship, one of the darkest and most horrific forms of paganism, in which children were sacrificed by fire to the bull-god. The trashfire and the Moloch worshipers were gone by the time of Jesus, and the name of Gehenna, ceasing to be purely local, had taken on an identity fused with that of the Hebrew Sheol. Sheol was originally conceived of as simply a dark and dismal place like Hades, but not a place of fiery punishment. For more information, see Leslie E. Fuller's article "Religious Development of the Intertestamental Period" in the *Abingdon Bible Commentary* (New York: Doubleday, 1929). Both heaven and hell are precisely "religious developments of the intertestamental period." As the Hebrew canon of the Old Testament ends, neither idea has been introduced. As the New Testament begins, both ideas are in place.

It is also worth noting that it is principally Jesus who threatens us with hellfire. Paul has nothing to say on the subject.

Honor (τιμάειν, *timaein*). The word that underlies *timaein* is τιμή (*timé*, "honor"), but also—in fact, primarily—the "price", "worth" or "value" of anything. "Honor your father and mother," then, means "value them and be willing to pay the price of them." Jewish tradition has long interpreted this commandment specifically: not to be respectful toward parents during one's adolescent years, but to help aging parents.

Jew, Samaritan (Ἰουδαῖος, *Judaeos*; Σαμαρίτης, *Samarites*). Does *Judaeos* mean "Jew" or "Judean"? Sometimes one, sometimes the other, sometimes either without distinction. The New Testament usage of the term is as imprecise as our own use of the terms "America" and "Russia." "Jew" is the only possible translation when Paul accuses Peter of being a hypocritical Jew (Galatians 2:14), since Peter isn't a Judean, but a Galilean. But only "Judean" is possible when Jesus stays in Galilee, fearing that the Judeans are looking to kill him (John 7:1). In general, this translation speaks of "Jewish" customs and religion and "Judean" politics, but the distinction is one that we make for our own benefit: in the Israel of the first century A.D., an American-style separation of church and state was the last thing anybody had in mind.

As for the Samaritans, you might think of them as the Protestants of Judaism, fellow Israelites who subscribe to the Law of Moses but don't recognize the authority of Jerusalem. As befits a related and neighboring tribe belonging to a rival sect of the same religion, the Samaritans are always spoken of as the most foreign and pagan people in the world.

Life (ζωή, *zoë*). Besides βίος (*bios*), the span of life (as in "biography"), and ψυχή (*psyche*), the breath of life, there is also *zoë*, being alive. All three words could be translated "life," but they could not be interchanged in Greek. In the New Testament, *zoë* is used only to mean the eternal life of those who are saved, and so in this version it is capitalized, "Life."

Love (ἀγάπη, *agápë*; φιλία, *philía*). Everyone has heard of the three Greek words for love: *eros*, *philía* and *agápë*—wanting, liking and loving. *Eros* is not much heard from in the Gospels, which speak often of adultery and whoremongering but seldom of lust in itself. *Philía* and *agápë* are both used quite a lot, particularly as verbs, *philô* and *agapô*. In this version, *philia* is sometimes rendered as "being a friend," whereas *agápë* is the love that could only be called love.

It is *philía* in John 11:36 ("see how much he meant to him"); and in John 16:27 ("and God Himself is your friend"). It is *agápë* in Mark 10:21, when Jesus feels love for the worldly young man; in Luke 7:47, when the fallen woman with the flask of ointment shows much love; in John 13:23, when the student Jesus loves, the teenaged John Evangelist, is resting his head on Jesus' chest; and in John 13:35, when Jesus says that love will be the mark of his followers. The difference, to be sure, does not always seem hard and fast.

In the last chapter of John the words are used strikingly together. Twice Jesus asks Peter if he feels *agápë* for him; twice Peter answers with *philía*; and finally Jesus says, "Well, so you feel *philía*, then?" Perhaps Peter is ashamed of expressing *agápë* for another man—though Jesus isn't and it appears to be a normal way of speaking—or perhaps in some subtler way he shies away from opening his heart full to the heart of Jesus. It's also possible that the difference means little or nothing and represents only an interchange of synonyms, as "sheep" and "lambs" and "feed" and "pasture" are interchanged in the same passage.

Agápë is a watchword of the early Christian communities as well. Their festive occasions are called *agápës*—"love-ins"—and their fundraising efforts on behalf of needy fellow Christians are also called *agápë*—"charity."

Magi (μάγοι, *magoi*). These would have been Persian priests versed in astrology and interpretation of dreams. Nothing in the Gospels says they were "three kings."

Men (ἄνθρωποι, *anthropoi*). *Anthropoi*, a constant word in the New Testament, means either men or women, and this translation generally avoids expressions like "good will toward men" if they would leave women out of account in a way that the Greek words don't, especially since Jesus himself consistently includes women in his associations, his teachings, and the subjects of his parables.

At the same time, it is not always strictly true that *anthropoi* are "people" and ἄνδρες (*andres*) are "men." In fact, sometimes both words are used of men, but with a distinction in social status, *anthropoi* being "fellows" and *andres* being "gentlemen." In any event, the Gospels contain more people and fellows than men or gentlemen—*anthropoi* is much commoner than *andres*.

Nations (ἔθνη, *ethne*). Like the Hebrew *goyim*, *ethne* has the basic meaning of "nations," but also, by extension, "foreign countries." And since Israel is a religious state, the word is further extended to mean "pagan lands." Similarly, *ethnikoi*, which means the "nationals" of a certain country, is extended to mean "foreigners" and "pagans." An example of the original meaning is "Go out and teach all nations" (Matthew 28:19). An example of the extended meaning is "Don't babble on like pagans" (Matthew 13:17).

O Ye of Little Faith (ὀλιγόπιστοι, *oligopistoi*). In Greek this is one word, "little-faithed-ones." In this translation it is rendered as "unbelievers."

Parable (παραβολή, *parabole*). The plainest translation would be "comparison," the most literal would be "putting things side by side." In short, the crucial thing about a parable is not the story element (there was a man who went sowing), but the comparison made and the way the comparison stands perhaps for something quite specific (the sower is the son of humanity, his seed is the word), though possibly also for something more general (each of us can be the Good Samaritan, everyone who needs our help is the man beset by thieves). In any case, a parable isn't just a story with a moral, it's a story with a key—which explains, for instance, why the high priests and Pharisees are so enraged to hear the story of the vineyard owner's son and the rebellious tenant-farmers: it doesn't just apply to them, it's about them.

Paraclete (παράκλητος, *parakletos*). The meaning of this word is hard to translate because it's hard to settle on in Greek. "Comforter," "adviser" and "advocate" all have some accuracy. The closest thing to a literal rendering would be "someone who puts in a word for you."

Pharisee (Φαρισαῖος); **Sadducee** (Σαδδουκαῖος). Many people vaguely assume that the Pharisees were members of the priestly class and the biggest religious dinosaurs of their time. In fact, both descriptions fit the Sadducees instead. The Pharisees were a lay group, and considered more liberal and up-to-date than the Sadducees. They were flexible enough, for instance, to see a distinction between unthinking and deliberate swearing (Matthew 23:16)—though Jesus blasts the distinction as irrelevant—and they were "modern" enough to be open to the idea of bodily resurrection, which the Sadducees considered a newfangled romantic notion.

Publican (τελώνης, *telónes*). Tax-collector. In Matthew, Mark and Luke tax-collectors are invariably named as the lowest form of male life, as whores are considered the lowest form of female life. Apart from the obvious drawback that they came demanding money, tax-collectors in Judea and Galilee were hated as traitors because they were collecting from their own kind in the service of Rome; as unclean because they were in constant contact with Gentiles; and as extortionary because they were working on commission.

Repent (μετανοεῖν, *metanoein*); **repentance** (μετάνοια, *metanoia*). The literal significance of the words is "changing your mind," but the usage of the words always implies "changing your mind and being sorry," not just "revising your opinion." The expression "a change of heart" suggests something of both the etymology and the meaning, and is sometimes used in this version.

Righteousness (δικαιοσύνη, *dikaiosyne*). What in heaven's name is "righteousness"? Paul never stops talking of it; it's evidently the most important thing to have. But it keeps slipping out of your grasp, especially when you try to make one passage harmonize with another as to its meaning. You might say it's the religious equivalent of being law-abiding citizens; etymologically it means "being just." The basic confusion is one of active and passive. Sometimes "being just" is active and means "justice in action" or "acting like upright people." Just as often, though, and particularly in some of the knotty passages in Romans, "being just" is passive and means "being classed among the just," "being acquitted," or "being cleared of guilt."

But what I called the "basic confusion" above is really only a confusion to us as modern readers: both active and passive meanings are consistent with Paul's thought and the New Testament's thought generally. Good standing with God, as both Jesus and Paul say, is originally passive in origin, because you can't earn it, it can only be conferred by God's free gift. But it then presumably continues in active mode as you start to live like the saved children of God that you are.

American readers must clear aside an additional obstacle here: the underlying notion of *conferred merit* does not square well with the American national philosophy that you stand or fall by your own actions and nothing else. But by Paul's classification, that philosophy would not be righteousness, but self-righteousness.

Sanhedrin (συνέδριον, *synedrion*). The Romans of this period were still relatively tactful about allowing their subject peoples to govern themselves in small matters and worship in their own way. (The emperor hadn't declared himself to be god yet.) The Sanhedrin, the chief instrument of Jewish home rule, was both the "high court," as in this translation, and the "supreme council" of the Jews. It could try crimes, including religious crimes; but only the Romans could inflict the death penalty, and the Romans wouldn't do so for reasons involving an alien religion. That is why Jesus was arrested as a blasphemer and heretic but had to be executed as some kind of revolutionary.

Scandal (σκάνδαλον, *scandalon*); **scandalize** (σκανδαλίζειν, *skandalizein*). Literally, a "scandal" is not a public embarrassment but a "stumbling-block," something—or someone—that trips you up, puts you off, leads you astray, or blocks your path. In this version the words are translated quite variously according to context: "let someone down," "lead someone astray," "offend someone," "be in someone's way."

Scribe (γραμματεύς, *grammateus*). Jesus spends quite a large part of his preaching time attacking the legalistic approach to religion and warning his followers not to get lost in the letter of the law. The best indication of what he is up against is the existence of a whole class of religious lawyers whose business it is to know whether Moses allows planting potatoes in months with an "r" in them. In this translation these people are called "canon-lawyers."

Servant (δοῦλος, *doulos*; διάκονος, *diakonos*; ὑπηρέτης, *hyperetes*). *Doulos*, the word behind "servant" in most of the parables, means "slave" and not "servant" and is rendered as "slave" in this version. It may shock our liberal sensibilities to see how Jesus nowhere in the Gospels preaches against slavery *and* repeatedly makes slavery a prototype for humanity's total submission to God, but there it is.

Three considerations may make this seem less gross:

1) The startling omissions in the teaching of Jesus are two: one, just mentioned, is that slavery is an unsuitable social fabric. The other is that Rome is an unsuitable landlord. Espousing either theme would have cut short his mission: he would have been killed at once, not after a while. Also, speaking to either theme of outward social reform would have totally eclipsed his central theme of innermost reform: he would then have been Spartacus, or Joan or Arc, but not Jesus.

2) The description Jesus gives of humanity's submission to God uses the practice of slavery as a metaphor or starting-point but transcends realistic slavery both for good and for evil: if we're bad slaves of God, we'll be punished worse than any slave on earth; if we're faithful slaves of God, we'll be given such freedom and such rewards that our slavery will not seem in any way restrictive. If the conception of Jesus transcends his social framework, so should our judgment of his conception.

3) Calling yourself "God's servant" and not "God's slave" is open to some gross implications of its own: that you don't belong to God, He's just trying to run you, and if you don't like the way He runs you, you're always free to serve another god!

At least Jesus never expressly condones slavery. Peter and Paul, though, condone it all too clearly by saying repeatedly that slaves should be obedient to their masters, when they ought to say that slaves should escape from their masters. At the beginning of the sixth chapter of First Timothy, Paul goes even farther and says that Christian slaves should not criticize their Christian masters for being slaveholders.

As for *diakonos* (the source of "deacon"), that word really does mean "servant," including waiters and waitresses. *Hyperetes* means something like "assistant"; notably, the high priests have such "assistants."

Sin (ἁμαρτία, *hamartia*); **sinners** (ἁμαρτωλοί, *hamartoloi*). As is in the cases of "baptism" and "heaven," the Greek word rendered as "sin" is less exclusively sacred and more of an everyday word than its traditional English translation; also, it may not have had quite so cursed and polluted a sound as "sin." Literally, *hamartia* is "missing the mark," as if we were aiming at something perceived as good, but picking the wrong targets and then also not shooting straight. For the reasons just given, and not to minimize the importance of human action for good or evil, this translation usually speaks of "errors" or "doing wrong" in place of "sin."

As for the "sinners," the term would apply not just to the authors of real crimes but to anyone not a good practicing Jew—which is why the expression "godless people" is sometimes used in this translation. The question of who qualifies as a "sinner" has some bearing on the biography of Jesus. Certainly the actual criminals were admitted to his society, but we do not have to imagine Jesus surrounded by nothing but society's dregs, if some of the "sinners" were perhaps quite moral people who had turned away—or just fallen away—from the legalistic Judaism of that age. In fact, the Gospels show Jesus as "too free with his associations" in both directions, up as well as down. In Luke's narrative, for instance, the common people are just as aghast (Luke 19:7) that Jesus has dinner with the powerful chief tax-collector, Zaccheus, as the Pharisees are to see Jesus talking with women of *that* kind.

This word, like "faith," seems to take on a different cast in Paul's Epistles from what it had in the Gospels. In the Gospels, both John the Baptist and Jesus are concerned with exterior actions, the "wrongs" that people do and should stop doing. In Paul's Epistles, notably in Romans 7:14–25, he develops the notion of "wrongfulness" as a corrupted interior state that produces bad actions, the "sin within."

Son of Man (υἱὸς τοῦ ἀνθρώπου, *huyos tu anthropu*); **Son of God** (υἱὸς τοῦ θεοῦ, *huyos tu theú*). These crucial expressions probably do not mean exactly the same thing every time they appear. When the Devil says "If you're the Son of God. . ." the words clearly imply the unique status of Jesus as God's son. In other passages, such as the Beatitudes, Jesus invites us all to be God's sons and daughters. Furthermore, the expression "son of," as borrowed from Hebrew, can be used to mean something like "the soul of" or "the living embodiment of." A clear example of this last usage is in John 17:12, where Jesus says he has not lost any of the disciples God gave him "except for the son of perdition," meaning "except for Mister Perdition himself." Likewise, the Roman captain who exclaims in Luke 23:47, "Truly he was an innocent man," and in Matthew 27:54, "Truly he was the son of God," may have meant the same thing by either account: "Truly he was the soul of godliness."

As for "Son of Man" (rendered here as "Son of Humanity"), that is one of the titles by which the coming Messiah is described in Old

Testament writings, and has also been found as an expression current in those times meaning something more like "this mother's son." The explanation that it is a Messianic title is the most natural reason why Jesus persistently describes himself in those words. The more general expression, however, seems to occur in Mark 3:28, "the sons of humanity will be forgiven."

Soul (ψυχή, *psyche*). This word is decidedly shifty in meaning and cannot mean just the same thing every time; it also can't be translated consistently and still correctly. Basically, the belief in a person's immortal soul was beginning to displace an older belief in a *mortal* soul, a spirit in a person that lives with the person but dies with the person's death. In this older usage, "life" is a better translation than "soul": "those who wished the life of the child are dead" (Matthew 2:20). "Soul" is the right translation, on the other hand, in "Don't fear those who kill the body but cannot kill the soul" (Matthew 10:28). It's no wonder that the language should be ambiguous on the point of the soul's immortality when the religious question itself was in hot dispute, as between the Pharisees (immortal) and the Sadducees (mortal).

Spirit (πνεῦμα, *pneuma*). This word, which contains an audible puff of air, is the regular word for "breath," and can even mean "wind," as in John 3:8. The notion of spirit as breath and breath as spirit links Christianity to such other major world religions as Hinduism and Buddhism, and is reflected in modern English by expressions like "breathing life into an enterprise." In this translation, "breath" and "spirit" are both used freely as the context of each passage may suggest, but in Greek the two are always one.

Talent (τάλαντον). A silver talent is not a silver coin; in size and format it's more like a silver cannonball and weighs 50 or 60 pounds. It is sometimes translated here as "bar of silver" (although "bar" is a lie) so as not to sacrifice the point of a parable to a learned discussion of ancient Middle Eastern currency.

Tempt (πειράζειν, *peirazein*); **temptation** (πειρασμός, *peirasmos*). The most regularly mistranslated words in the New Testament. The Greek words do not have the seductive tone and certainly not the sexual tone of the English words "tempt" and "temptation," nor the same implication that what "tempts" a person must be something alluring. Instead, the words signify "testing," "examining" or "making trial of" a person's character; and while a flash of pretty leg could be a test of a man's character, so could a most unlovely disaster, such as the "temptation" of Job—how "tempting" is being covered with boils? **Virgin** (παρθένos, *parthenos*). Though the virgin birth of Jesus is described in Matthew and Luke, the word "virgin" is not as crucial or as frequent a word in the New Testament as one might suppose. The passage from Isaiah (Isaiah 7:14) quoted as "a virgin shall conceive" in Matthew 1:23 could mean simply "a young woman will conceive." Also, the tradition of Mary's lifelong virginity is mentioned nowhere in the New Testament and doesn't seem to square well with passages like "he had no relations with her till she bore a son" (Matthew 1:25), "she bore her first-born son" (Luke 2:17), and "isn't he the son of Mary and brother of James, Joseth, Jude and Simon?" (Mark 6:3).

Roman Catholics consider that Joseph had no relations with Mary till she bore a son, nor thereafter; that she bore her first-, last- and only-born son, and that cousins could count as "brothers" in the countrified Aramaic sense of the term.

Catholic tradition has named Mary, wife of Cleopas, as the mother of the "brothers of Jesus." If that were true, it would still leave more than one passage in need of explanation.

On the other hand, the Mary-wife-of-Cleopas explanation squares well with Matthew 27:56 and Mark 15:40. In both cases, one of the faithful women watching as they bury Jesus is "Mary the mother of James and Joseph," according to Matthew, the Gospel that names James and Joseph as brothers of Jesus; and "Mary the mother of James and Joseth," according to Mark, the Gospel that names James and Joseth as brothers of Jesus. So is this "faithful woman" Mary, the mother of Jesus? If so, why the roundabout identification? Because Jesus has assumed such a special identity that his family isn't considered his family any more? A simpler explanation, at least of this case by itself, is that a different Mary is the mother of James and Joseth.

Mary, wife of Cleopas, is then mentioned by that name as standing at the cross in John 19:25, in words that may or may not describe her as the sister of Mary the mother of Jesus: "Among those standing by the cross of Jesus were his mother, his mother's sister, Mary wife of Cleopas, and Mary Magdalen." Probably those words do not describe the two women in question as sisters, for two reasons: 1) "Mary his mother's sister" would be the usual word order, not "his mother's sister Mary"; and 2) two sisters named Mary seems unlikely; most parents give each child a separate name.

The "brothers of Jesus" don't pass out of the record after the Ascension: they are mentioned as part of the faithful who gather between the Ascension and Pentecost. James in particular later becomes the head of the church at Jerusalem and is spoken of in the Acts of the Apostles, where he is still called "the brother of the Lord." The explanation that cousins count as "Aramaic brothers" seems supported by the faithful-women passages just mentioned in Matthew, Mark, and John. On the other hand, that explanation seems strained by the fact that only Jesus has such "Aramaic brothers," and that this supposedly lax usage is the only such lax usage in a genealogical vocabulary exact enough to include "brothers-in-law," "mothers-in-law," and generic "relatives."

In the end, neither a "virginal" nor a "non-virginal" reading of all passages comes out quite as simple and conflict-free as one might wish. However, the most important point is the one that *does* emerge most clearly from the Gospels as we have them: the Evangelists left no clear word on the subject of Mary's lifelong virginity *because they did not care*: as Jews, they believed in sexual modesty and temperance but did not have the kind of cult of virginity the Greeks and Romans maintained around Artemis and Diana. (Certainly we don't hear a cult of virginity in Elizabeth's cry of joy [Luke 1:25] that God gave her a child "on the day when he saw fit to lift my shame from before the world.") If Mary had been a lifelong virgin and the Evangelists had considered that important, they would have included a more explicit mention of the fact *and* excluded some of the ambiguous remarks they left in. "These things are written so that you may believe and have life in his name" (John 20:31) is an example of how explicit the Evangelists are when an important religious statement is to be made; and "he asked him this as a test, he himself knew what he would do" (John 6:6) is an example of how careful the Evangelists are not to leave a false impression. Certainly no such explicitness and no such care are expended on Mary's lifelong virginity. It doesn't even rate being mentioned.